INSIDE CONGRESS

INSIDE CONGRESS

A CQ READER

107th Congress

Scott Montgomery, Editor

CQ PRESS

A Division of Congressional Quarterly Inc.

Washington, D.C.

CQ Press
A Division of Congressional Quarterly Inc.
1255 22nd St. N.W., Suite 400
Washington, D.C. 20037

(202) 822-1475; (800) 638-1710

www.cqpress.com

Printed and bound in the United States of America

05 04 03 02 01   5 4 3 2 1

♾ The paper used in this publication meets the minimum requirements of the American National Standard for Information Sciences—Permanence of Paper for Printed Library Materials, ANSI Z39.48-1992.

Cover design: Brian Barth

Library of Congress Cataloging-in-Publication Data

[in process]

ISBN 1-56802-717-6

Contents

Contents

Preface

It is said by those who have worked both inside and outside of the Washington Beltway that the U.S. Congress is, in its most basic sense, just an oversized city council. It is best understood if you view its operations, behaviors and actions from the most provincial and parochial point of view. From this perspective, the House and Senate take on their truest — and most human — colors and hues.

This is not meant to belittle or trivialize the world's greatest democratic institution. Indeed, the Founders would probably be proud of the comparison and sorely disappointed if it were no longer true. They conceived and forged into being a deliberative body of men and women who span the gamut of human intelligence, emotion and political bias. Both geniuses and scoundrels have walked the halls of Congress, all equally secure in the knowledge that they have been chosen by the folks back home to speak on their behalf on matters of state and national policy. And until such time as those voters choose someone else to represent them, that heady presumption is a true reflection of our system of government.

Understanding Congress and this maelstrom of human thinking and interaction requires something more, however. It requires an attention to detail and nuance. The making of laws is a complex dance of words, votes and "intentions," which the other two branches of government — the executive and judicial — must interpret and put into effect. As such, one of the most important roles on Capitol Hill is played by the corps of men and women who belong to the journalistic press. It is our job to chronicle and analyze the actions of Congress as they are being made and to report the facts and findings back to American voters. Many newspapers, magazines and political journals help fill this important role in varied and select ways. For 56 years now, Congressional Quarterly has been the only private, independent, nonpartisan company to cover the actions and activities of Congress in their entirety. CQ's founders, Nelson and Henrietta Poynter, believed that readers would be served best by a journal that had no vested interest in legislation other than to describe and explain its contents — and how it came to be.

The *CQ Weekly*, which the Poynters launched in 1945, is *the* news magazine on Congress. The reporters, editors and researchers here at CQ cover the institution from the ground up. We attend every committee and subcommittee "markup" (where bills are made), and every legislative action on the House and Senate floors, as well as leadership maneuverings and backroom negotiations. The stories that go into the magazine each week are both factual and analytical. They endeavor to give readers a clear, unbiased and penetrating account of what Congress is doing and why.

This volume is a compilation of stories that have appeared in the *CQ Weekly* over the past year. They have been chosen and introduced by one of the magazine's senior editors, Scott Montgomery, with an eye toward giving students of Congress a palpable, "you are there" insight into the institution and its members. The final collection reflects the work of a great many people, including the reporters whose names appear in the text, the research department at *CQ Weekly*, which contributed its usual vigilance for accuracy in both word and nuance, and photographer Scott J. Ferrell. In particular, it is important to note the work of the news editors of the magazine who, under the guidance of managing editor Susan Benkelman, sharpened these stories into their final form. In addition, Ross Baker of Rutgers University and Michael Bailey of Georgetown University provided great insight in reviewing an early draft of this compilation.

But in the end, this is about those 535 men and women who occupy elected positions in the House and Senate and determine the shape of our society as well as the ambitions of the nation. And they do so, in much the same way as a local town council member, county supervisor or state legislator: one vote at a time.

David Rapp
Executive Editor, *CQ Weekly*

Introduction

This is a fascinating time to study the U.S. Congress. It is almost impossible to overestimate the significance of having Republicans and Democrats at near-equal standing in the House and the Senate. Neither party is willing to settle into the traditional minority role of objecting to the majority's agenda but ultimately conceding to its power. On nearly any issue today, the minority party holds out hope of winning because it requires only the wooing away of just a handful of members from the majority side. Why concede when the election that could turn it all around and put you in control is never more than two years away? This state of equilibrium amplifies the political consequence of every issue, making almost every vote a pitched battle for control.

The net result is that passing bills and getting the president to sign them into law is much more difficult than in the past. It remains relatively straightforward in the House for the majority to push through most of what it wants since it still controls the calendar and the rules for floor debate. But that fragile control often holds only as long as the victory is expected to be merely symbolic. In recent years, majority coalitions have prevailed on topics ranging from abortion, campaign finance overhaul and legislation to guarantee that a portion of any surplus be used to pay off long-term debt. None of those bills came close to enactment, however. The minute a bill has a chance of passing in the Senate and winning the president's signature to become law, the road gets much tougher. For example, Congress has come close but failed to reach final agreement on a wide range of issues including gun control, increasing the minimum wage, providing money for land conservation and updating juvenile crime laws. Even the appropriations bills that fund government operations and must be passed every year have become tangled in disputes that have made omnibus, or bundled, appropriations bills more common. Congress often resorts to omnibus packages because the opposition to a particular controversial spending bill can be tempered by tying it to another, more popular, bill.

But there have been achievements. A closely divided Congress revamped welfare in 1996, and in the first months of the 107th Congress, in 2001, Congress agreed to the deepest tax cuts in more than 20 years. The key in both of these examples was that passage of the bills was seen to be politically valuable to both Republicans and Democrats. In this era when no one has the power to force a policy on an unwilling minority, such compromise is likely to remain the only way to succeed. It just won't happen very often.

The book that follows is designed to serve as a guide to the real-world application of these principles of the contemporary Congress. Throughout this book, Congressional Quarterly has tried to provide a view of Congress that is at every turn authentic. Each article is intended to exemplify the pivotal components in a closely divided Congress, whether those components are people or devices of power.

The opening section, "The Modern Congress," demonstrates how the make-up of Congress is more important than ever because of the heightened potential for influence by individual members. The following section, "Congressional Elections," illuminates the underlying factors that in large measure determine who comes to Washington to be in Congress. "Political Parties and Leaders" delves deeply into the political management of Congress in these rebellious times, and

"Congressional Committees" focuses the same sharp eye but takes it another layer down. The tumultuous opening of the 107th Congress has moved the next part, "Rules and Procedures," out of the arcane and into the limelight, illustrating the big-picture impact that even the smallest of details can have on what Congress does. The next part, "Congress and the Making of Public Policy," provides a host of examples of how matters of genuine public need intersect with the machinery of Congress, for good and bad. "Congress and the President" is an exploration of a relationship between two branches of government, offering snapshots of this ever-evolving alliance. Congress' relationship with other critically important outside groups is carefully considered in the final parts, which cover the courts, the bureaucracy and interest groups.

The action is imprecise and the influences collide as often as they blend, but this is indeed the authentic Congress.

The Modern Congress

A decade-long shift from single-party dominance into near-equilibrium was capped on Jan. 7, 2001 with the convening of the 107th Congress. It was the most closely divided Congress since 1953. Republicans in the House retained the majority for the third straight election, after 40 years of firm Democratic Party control. In the Senate, Democrats gained seats and brought the chamber to a 50-50 tie, controlled nominally by the tie-breaking vote of Republican Vice President Dick Cheney. Republicans have retained House control since the 'Republican Revolution' of 1994. That year, the GOP claimed 35 formerly Democratic seats, propelled by Newt Gingrich's Contract With America and public dissatisfaction with President Bill Clinton's tax increase and failed health care proposal. But in every election since 1994, Republicans have seen their margin of control slip. As Speaker in 1995, Gingrich ruled the House with a 26-member voting majority. In 2001, Speaker J. Dennis Hastert has only five more votes than the 218 needed for a majority.

The culture of Congress evolves like any other. And the new culture is defined more sharply by the mathematics of power than by any other force. When a party controls a chamber by dozens of votes, as the Democrats did for so many years, the minority party can do little more than offer token resistance to the will of the majority. Most votes are routine because their outcome is structured by the mechanisms of power. But when the difference between majority and minority is down to a handful, the stakes heighten on almost every vote.

Today's culture represents a move away from the stability of absolute authority into an era where the power structure teeters. The modern Congress, as exemplified by the 107th, is always on the verge of chaotic stalemate. Small voting blocs spontaneously erupt on just about every issue, fully charged with the power to determine policy — or stall it. Free agency in this environment can be its own reward. Leaders have fewer tools to enforce the party discipline that traditionally has provided smooth management in Congress. The methods party leaders long relied upon to discipline members who defied them can carry dangerous consequences. For example, Sen. Jim Jeffords was a Republican from Vermont until a dispute with leaders in his party over education funding grew into a prolonged and increasingly tense disagreement. Party leaders put another Republican senator in charge of the education bill on the Senate floor to demonstrate their displeasure with Jeffords' public stand against his party, and for that and other reasons Jeffords left the GOP, became an Independent and flipped the 50-50 Senate into Democratic control.

In the end, the modern Congress constantly has its eye on the next election. Each election year, the majority is up for grabs, which makes every issue potentially decisive in the political calculation.

A Congress of Newcomers

Each Congress has, to some extent, its own character and characteristics. The most pivotal of these tends to be legislative experience, which has dropped in the last decade as turnover among members has increased.

Quick Contents

Two-thirds of the House has never legislated in a recession or worked with a president other than Bill Clinton. More senators have a term or less under their belts than at any time in two decades. This shrinking tenure — and the record number of Senate women — are the distinguishing characteristics of the 107th Congress.

A Less Experienced House
Tenure in the House has declined sharply in the past decade. As the 107th Congress begins, 65 percent of the members, or 281 of those represented in the dark, right-hand bars in this graph, have been in office 8 years or less. By contrast, at the start of the 102nd Congress in 1991, the comparable figure was 53 percent, or 229 of the members represented in the light, left-hand bars.

Only one in three members of the House of Representatives this year was on Capitol Hill during the Cold War. Just 35 percent were in the House when somebody other than Bill Clinton was president, and only a bare majority have known congressional life under Democratic control.

Although seniority in the Senate remains somewhat constant — the average length of senatorial service at the start of 2001 is a little longer than 11 years, as it has been for the past decade — House tenure is continuing a steep decline that began in the early 1990s. That makes the 107th Congress as remarkable for what its members have not experienced as for what they have.

Almost two-thirds of the members of the House, 65 percent, were first elected in 1992 or since. That means they have never served during a recession, were never called on to debate policies affecting the Soviet Union, did not have a say in authorizing the Persian Gulf War, have known federal surpluses in some cases longer than they have known deficits — and are preparing to do business with a Republican president for the first time. For the 48 percent elected in or since the GOP takeover of Congress in 1994, this year will be their first experience in something other than a divided government.

This is a marked change from a decade ago, before an anti-incumbent sentiment, the last round of redistricting and the GOP sweep ushered in a new generation of lawmakers. Two out of five of the House's members, 38 percent, had been in office for more than 10 years when the 102nd Congress convened in 1991, while only 53 percent had been in office for eight years or less.

In the Senate, while the average length of service has not fluctuated much — and while four of the six longest-serving senators in American history are now in office — there is a parallel wave of relative newcomers. As the 107th Congress began, 45 senators had been in the chamber for six years or less, a figure

By Julie R. Hirschfeld / Jan. 20, 2001

not matched since 1981.

This comparative lack of experience among the rank and file — both on a range of issues, and in dealing with different power relationships in Washington — is yet another complicating factor for those in the congressional leadership and the new Bush administration.

All are promising to push for achievements in a Capitol more closely divided along party lines than at any time since the 83rd Congress convened in 1953, the onset of the Eisenhower administration. The House has 221 Republicans, 211 Democrats, two independents and a vacancy almost certain to be filled this spring by another Democrat. The Senate is evenly divided, 50 Republicans and 50 Democrats, so the nominal GOP control of Congress resides in the executive branch — in the tie-breaking vote of Dick Cheney, the new Republican vice president.

History of Division

One result of this razor's edge partisan split is that the House, especially, is an institution in which fewer and fewer members have experience in a Capitol where comity was more regularly apparent. Many say this comity was partly because it was so clear then who was in control and who was not. Only 130 House members are left from the 101st Congress, which adjourned in 1990 and in which the Democrats had an 85-seat advantage.

Of those who have arrived since then, says Norman Ornstein, a political scholar at the American Enterprise Institute, "their entire experience in Congress has been a period of enormous tumult and sharp partisan acrimony, and sharp partisan division, so they don't have much to fall back on in terms of an example of how the institution can function as a cooperative place."

Congress has been slowly but steadily getting older — the average age was 53 years old a decade ago, 54 two years ago and is 55 this year (with 54.4 the average House member's age and 5 9.8 the average senator's age) —

49-50 Years in the House	47-48	45-46	43-44	41-42	39-40	37-38	35-36	33-34	31-32	29-30	27-28	2
1	1	1	1	1	1	2	2 / 1	2	2 / 2	1 / 3	7 / 7	

but that trend nonetheless reflects this demographic truth: A growing percentage of the membership of the 107th Congress came of age, entered the work force and perhaps got involved in politics in the 1970s and 1980s — during the so-called "me" generation, in which national trends pointed to a resurgence of individual-based, rather than community-oriented, thinking.

Lawmakers now "are less institution-minded," Ornstein said in a Jan. 10 interview. "It just means that you have a challenge for the leaders to get them to think about not just their own ideas or their own party, but the larger institution."

Some "Old Bull" veterans of the Congresses before the 1990s, especially Democrats, see as the turning point in this regard the Republican takeover of six years ago — a victory engineered by Rep. Newt Gingrich of Georgia (1979-99), who rose from the back benches to the Speaker's chair by waging a charismatic campaign against the House as an institution.

"In the Gingrich era, there were no feathers, it was just arrows . . . Everybody became an independent contractor," said former Rep. Dan Rostenkowski, D-Ill. (1959-95), perhaps the best known electoral casualty of the 1994 election.

In a Jan. 16 interview, Rostenkowski said the tone in Congress has changed since his 14-year tenure as chairman of the House Ways and Means Committee, largely because more junior members have never witnessed the atmosphere of cooperation in Washington in which he believes he functioned most effectively. All but two of his years as chairman were during

Republican presidencies. "We cooperated because they wanted to write history, and I wanted to write law," he said. "Everything is one-upsmanship these days."

Beyond the partisan tone that has characterized the past decade, diminished levels of prior political experience also may have diminished Congress' ability and inclination to form bipartisan alliances and issue-based coalitions. A seasoned legislator experienced at cutting deals and reaching out to the other party to grease institutional gears — whether at a local or state level — may be better equipped to do so in Washington than an inexperienced lawmaker.

While the levels of prior service in elective office have stayed relatively constant since the 106th Congress for both House members and senators, the percentage of this year's freshmen in both chambers who can claim prior elective office has shrunk. In the 107th, 73 percent of new House members have held prior

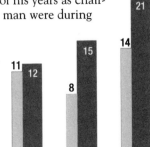
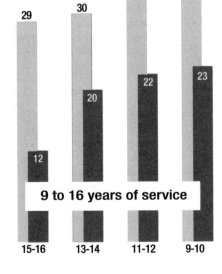
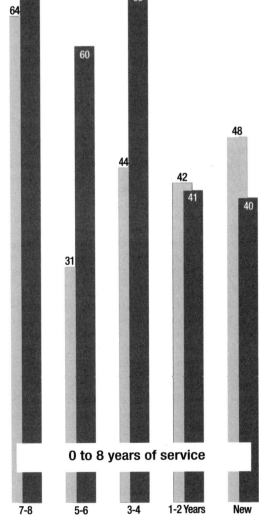

9 to 16 years of service

0 to 8 years of service

-24   21-22   19-20   17-18   15-16   13-14   11-12   9-10   7-8   5-6   3-4   1-2 Years in the House   New Members

Women and Minorities in the 107th Congress

This is a roster of the women and ethnic minority group members who are representatives and senators in the 107th Congress. It does not include the non-voting delegates from the District of Columbia and the Virgin Islands, both of whom are black women; the delegates from American Samoa and Guam, both of whom are Asian and Pacific Islanders; or the resident commissioner for Puerto Rico, who is Hispanic. All are Democrats.

Blacks
House (36 — 1 R, 35 D)
Alabama: Earl F. Hilliard, D
California: Barbara Lee, D; Juanita Millender-McDonald, D; Maxine Waters, D
Florida: Corrine Brown, D; Alcee L. Hastings, D; Carrie P. Meek, D
Georgia: Sanford D. Bishop Jr., D; John Lewis, D; Cynthia A. McKinney, D
Illinois: Danny K. Davis, D; Jesse L. Jackson Jr., D; Bobby L. Rush, D
Indiana: Julia Carson, D
Louisiana: William J. Jefferson, D
Maryland: Elijah E. Cummings, D; Albert R. Wynn, D
Michigan: Carolyn Cheeks Kilpatrick, D; John Conyers Jr. D
Mississippi: Bennie Thompson, D
Missouri: William Lacy Clay Jr., D
New Jersey: Donald M. Payne, D
New York: Gregory W. Meeks, D; Major R. Owens, D; Charles B. Rangel, D; Edolphus Towns, D
North Carolina: Eva Clayton, D; Melvin Watt, D
Ohio: Stephanie Tubbs Jones, D
Oklahoma: J.C. Watts Jr., R
Pennsylvania: Chaka Fattah, D
South Carolina: James E. Clyburn, D
Tennessee: Harold E. Ford Jr., D
Texas: Sheila Jackson-Lee, D; Eddie Bernice Johnson, D
Virginia: Robert C. Scott, D

Hispanics
House (19 — 3 R, 16 D)
Arizona: Ed Pastor, D
California: Joe Baca, D; Xavier Becerra, D; Grace F. Napolitano, D; Lucille Roybal-Allard, D; Loretta Sanchez, D; Hilda Solis, D
Florida: Lincoln Diaz-Balart, R; Ileana Ros-Lehtinen, R
Illinois: Luis V. Gutierrez, D
New Jersey: Robert Menendez, D
New York: Jose E. Serrano, D; Nydia M. Velázquez, D
Texas: Henry Bonilla, R; Charlie Gonzalez, D; Rubén Hinojosa, D; Solomon P. Ortiz, D; Silvestre Reyes, D; Ciro D. Rodriguez, D

Asians and Pacific Islanders
House (4 — 4 D)
California: Mike Honda, D; Robert T. Matsui, D
Hawaii: Patsy T. Mink, D
Oregon: David Wu, D

Senate (2 — 2 D)
Hawaii: Daniel K. Akaka, D; Daniel K. Inouye, D

American Indians
House (1 — 1 D)
Oklahoma: Brad Carson, D
Senate (1 — 1 R)
Colorado: Ben Nighthorse Campbell, R

Women
House (59 — 18 R, 41 D)
California: Mary Bono, R; Lois Capps, D; Susan A. Davis, D; Anna G. Eshoo, D; Jane Harman, D; Barbara Lee, D; Zoe Lofgren, D; Juanita Millender-McDonald, D; Grace F. Napolitano, D; Nancy Pelosi, D; Lucille Roybal-Allard, D; Loretta Sanchez, D; Hilda Solis, D; Ellen O. Tauscher, D; Maxine Waters, D; Lynn Woolsey, D
Colorado: Diana DeGette, D
Connecticut: Rosa DeLauro, D; Nancy L. Johnson, R
Florida: Corrine Brown, D; Carrie P. Meek, D; Ileana Ros-Lehtinen, R; Karen L. Thurman, D
Georgia: Cynthia A. McKinney, D
Hawaii: Patsy T. Mink, D
Illinois: Judy Biggert, R; Jan Schakowsky, D
Indiana: Julia Carson, D
Kentucky: Anne M. Northup, R
Maryland: Constance A. Morella, R
Michigan: Carolyn Cheeks Kilpatrick, D; Lynn Rivers, D
Minnesota: Betty McCollum, D
Missouri: Jo Ann Emerson, R; Karen McCarthy, D
Nevada: Shelley Berkley, D
New Jersey: Marge Roukema, R
New Mexico: Heather A. Wilson, R
New York: Sue W. Kelly, R; Nita M. Lowey, D; Carolyn B. Maloney, D; Carolyn McCarthy, D; Louise M. Slaughter, D; Nydia M. Velázquez, D
North Carolina: Eva Clayton, D; Sue Myrick, R
Ohio: Marcy Kaptur, D; Deborah Pryce, R; Stephanie Tubbs Jones, D
Oregon: Darlene Hooley, D
Pennsylvania: Melissa Hart, R
Texas: Kay Granger, R; Eddie Bernice Johnson, D; Sheila Jackson-Lee, D
Virginia: Jo Ann Davis, R
Washington: Jennifer Dunn, R
West Virginia : Shelley Moore Capito, R
Wisconsin: Tammy Baldwin, D
Wyoming: Barbara Cubin, R

Senate (13 — 3 R, 10 D)
Arkansas: Blanche Lincoln, D
California: Barbara Boxer, D; Dianne Feinstein, D
Louisiana: Mary L. Landrieu, D
Maine: Susan Collins, R; Olympia J. Snowe, R
Maryland: Barbara A. Mikulski, D
Michigan: Debbie Stabenow, D
Missouri: Jean Carnahan, D
New York: Hillary Rodham Clinton, D
Texas: Kay Bailey Hutchison, R
Washington: Maria Cantwell, D; Patty Murray, D

Members' Occupations
107th Congress

	HOUSE			SENATE			CONGRESS
	DEMOCRAT	REPUBLICAN	TOTAL	DEMOCRAT	REPUBLICAN	TOTAL	TOTAL
Actor/Entertainer		1	1		1	1	2
Aeronautics		1	1	1		1	2
Agriculture	8	17	25	1	5	6	31
Artistic/Creative		1	2*				2*
Business/Banking	56	103	159	8	16	24	183
Clergy	1	1	2		1	1	3
Education	53	38	92*	8	8	16	108*
Engineering	1	8	9				9
Health Care	3	1	4				4
Homemaker/ Domestic	1	1	2	1		1	3
Journalism	1	7	9*	1	6	7	16*
Labor	1	1	2		1	1	3
Law	84	71	156†	28	25	53	210†
Law Enforcement	7	3	10				10
Medicine	6	8	14		3	3	17
Military		2	2		1	1	3
Professional Sports		3	3		1	1	4
Public Service/ Politics	70	56	126	18	10	28	154
Real Estate	2	22	24	2	2	4	28
Secretarial/Clerical		2	2				2
Technical/Trade	1	2	3				3
Miscellaneous	1	5	6				6

* Total includes Independent Bernard Sanders of Vermont; † Total includes Independent Virgil H. Goode Jr. of Virginia.
Note: Some members say they have more than one occupation.

Members' Religious Affiliations
107th Congress

	HOUSE			SENATE			CONGRESS
	DEMOCRAT	REPUBLICAN	TOTAL	DEMOCRAT	REPUBLICAN	TOTAL	TOTAL
African Methodist Episcopal	2		2				2
Baptist	33	30	64†	2	7	9	73†
Christian Church	3		3				3
Christian Reformed Church		2	2				2
Christian Scientist		5	5				5
Disciples of Christ	1		1				1
Eastern Orthodox	1	3	4	1	1	2	6
Episcopalian	7	23	30	3	7	10	40
Jewish	24	2	27*	9	1	10	37*
Lutheran	8	8	16	3	1	4	20
Methodist	16	34	50	10	6	16	66
Mormon	3	8	11	1	4	5	16
Pentecostal		3	3				3
Presbyterian	15	23	38	3	7	10	48
Roman Catholic	76	49	125	14	10	24	149
Seventh-day Adventist	1	2	3				3
Unitarian	1	1	2	1		1	3
United Church of Christ / Congregationalist		3	3	3	2	5	8
Unspecified Protestant	13	25	38		3	3	41
Unspecified, other	7		7		1	1	8

* Total includes Independent Bernard Sanders of Vermont; † Total includes Independent Virgil H. Goode Jr. of Virginia.

office, down from 83 percent two years ago. Only 64 percent of the new senators have held elected office before, down from 78 percent two years ago.

"It may be that the junior members have had less opportunity to learn that their opponents don't have horns, so to speak," said John R. Hibbing, a political science professor at the University of Nebraska at Lincoln. Still, he said, "I think it's going to be a really tough time to foster cooperation. . . . I think it will be tough even for senior members" of the Senate.

'New Blood'

Hibbing and others are more concerned about the effects of an increasingly junior Congress on the institution's legislative agenda. A less senior House and Senate might not be as savvy about the intricacies of the legislative process, they say, and might be less likely to produce substantive bills that can navigate the labyrinth of the legislative process and emerge intact in a Congress with such a tiny working majority.

"There are some fairly dire consequences of having a legislative body that is too junior," Hibbing said. His 1991 book, "Congressional Careers: Contours of Life in the U.S. House of Representatives," maintained that while junior members introduced more legislation and made more speeches, their bills were typically referred to several different committees and ultimately died — clear signals that their policy work was less focused — while senior members' bills more often became law.

"A more selective, successful and focused legislative agenda is something that should be encouraged," he said. "I think we're actually pushing things down to where we get people who are throwing all kinds of things in the legislative hopper and not as many doing focused work."

But the injection of youth and inexperience into Congress has its advocates. While their learning curve may be steep and long, new members can reinvigorate long-stalled debates, some say, and the approaches of political neophytes can change the legislative dynamic.

"It is, in the long term, like hitting the 'refresh' button on your computer — it keeps us in touch," Jack Horner, director of member services for the House Republican Conference, said in a Jan. 11 interview. "It's not that [GOP members are] any less conservative — they're representing the same districts — it's that the way we're approaching the issues as conservatives has matured."

Advocates of term limits for Congress also argue that "career politicians" risk becoming politically entrenched, arrogant and out of touch with their constituents as they gather seniority and power. Since losing a pivotal 1995 Supreme Court case, they have been fighting for their cause on individual cases with sporadic success. On Jan. 17, for example, Sen. Paul Wellstone, D-Minn., abrogated a pledge to serve two terms by announcing his candidacy for reelection in 2002.

For House Democrats, the trend means the number who have experienced life in the majority is dwindling — to 119, or 56 percent of the caucus this year. (By contrast, 114 Republicans in the 107th, 52 percent of the GOP Conference, have never served in the minority.) And only three chairmen from the 103rd Congress, the most recent one run by the Democrats, remain as the ranking minority members of those committees: Michigan's John D. Dingell of Energy and Commerce, Wisconsin's David R. Obey of Appropriations and Massachusetts' Joe Moakley of Rules.

Operating from the minority, albeit a sizable one, has prompted House Democratic leaders to invite their centrist members to help develop legislative strategy and policy. Likewise, Democrats who have never been in the majority have learned to forge alliances with moderate Republicans in order to have greater influence over what goes on in the House.

"It's a very different caucus for those reasons," Tom Eisenhauer, a spokesperson for Democratic Caucus Chairman Martin Frost of Texas, said Jan. 11. "It's a more diverse caucus, it's a more moderate caucus, it's a more pragmatic caucus."

Another Year of the Woman?

The 107th Congress also is notable for the boost in the number of female senators. In 1992, the much-heralded "Year of the Woman," only five of 11 female nominees won Senate seats. In 2000, all six women nominees were elected and a seventh woman — Democrat Jean Carnahan of Missouri — was appointed to the seat to which her late husband was elected. As a result, a record 13 women are in the Senate now, up from nine in the 106th Congress. By contrast, the House gained a net of three women this year, to 59, or 14 percent of the membership, less than a single percentage point gain from the 106th Congress.

Political experts say the Senate gains and the backgrounds of the new female representatives foretell a bright future for women on Capitol Hill. The vast majority of women in the 107th Congress are professional politicians who have increasingly been able to position themselves to take on and win competitive races. Fifty-three of the 72 women (74 percent) have prior experience in elected office. Nine of the senators (69 percent) and 43 of the representatives (73 percent) used a local or state office to catapult to Congress.

"There are more and more women who are holding positions that have served as springboards in the House, and so more are primed to run," said Irwin Gertzog, an adjunct professor of political science at Rutgers University who is an expert on women in politics.

Recognizing that it is less difficult and less costly to run in an open-seat election contest than to try toppling an incumbent, female politicians have also gotten more savvy. "They were careful, calculating politicians . . . who were able to elbow their way into winning primaries," said Gertzog, who also attributes women's electoral gains to a more progressive political culture in which "more Americans are prepared to not be influenced by gender as they vote."

Few are willing to speculate yet about what effect the arrival of more women on Capitol Hill — most notably in the historically male Senate — might have on the way Congress functions. But few rebut the premise that the increasing number of women will alter an institution that has lagged behind most other venues in reflecting shifts in cultural and workplace norms.

"Very simply, women will always be in the room," Ornstein said. "What we've seen in the past in terms of how the Senate functions, the 'old boy' club . . . they just can't operate in the same way."

Nor will women's influence necessarily be confined to the everyday workings of the Capitol, scholars said. While their gains in the Senate may not be enough to switch the outcome of votes, they may constitute a critical mass of female voices which — if the three Republicans and 10 Democrats band together on an issue — could put a great deal of symbolic pressure on their male counterparts.

"If you have one after another of the women getting up and taking the same position on one of these issues, it cannot help but penetrate the consciousness of many of these men," Gertzog said. "It's not likely that it will change their minds, but it will have subtle effects."

By the Numbers

Ethnic minorities made no significant electoral gains in 2000, and will again make up about 12 percent of Congress. Racial diversity increased in the 103rd Congress, after House boundaries were redrawn for the 1992 elections because of redistricting, but has since flattened.

The Senate again has only three minority members, none of them black or Hispanic: Hawaii Democrats Daniel K. Akaka, a native Hawaiian, and Daniel K. Inouye, a Japanese-American, and Ben Nighthorse Campbell, R-Colo., an American Indian.

In the House, no parts of the country are newly represented by ethnic minorities this year. Of the 36 black House members (8 percent), only one is a freshman: William Lacy Clay Jr., D-Mo., who succeeded his father. The one freshman among the 19 Hispanics (4 percent) is Hilda Solis, D-Calif., who replaced a Hispanic she defeated in the primary.

The range of backgrounds also has not shifted much since the 106th Congress. The number of members who have served in the military — 133 in the House, 38 in the Senate — continues its decade-long decline. The majority of the 107th Congress has experience in the legal profession, the business world or the public sector. Nearly 40 percent list "law" as an occupation, 34 percent "business" and 29 percent have been public servants. Roman Catholic continues to be the most common religious affiliation, with 149 members claiming it.

The youngest senators, at 40, are Peter G. Fitzgerald, R-Ill., and Blanche Lincoln, D-Ark. The oldest, at 98, is Strom Thurmond, R-S.C., who also holds the record for the longest senatorial service ever, 46 years. Robert C. Byrd, D-W.Va., is second on that list, at 42 years; Edward M. Kennedy, D-Mass., is fifth, at 38 years and two months; Inouye is sixth, at 38 years.

In the House, freshman Adam Putnam, R-Fla., is the youngest member, at 26, while Benjamin A. Gilman, R-N.Y., is the oldest, at 78. ◆

Moderates and Mavericks

Narrow margins in both chambers of Congress have given centrists the opportunity to supply the margin of victory for their causes almost at will. But as we have seen in years past, the coalition of moderates is not a monolithic voting bloc that throws its weight in a single direction. The 107th Congress provides moderates the opportunity to help determine policy, but that doesn't guarantee they will.

The days of ramming bills through Congress on party-line votes may not be over, but the task is becoming harder.

When the voters elected a 107th Congress with an evenly divided Senate and a House that has a six-vote Republican majority, it became clear that both parties would have to throw their old playbooks out the window.

President Clinton pushed his 1993 budget reconciliation package (PL 103-66) through a Democratic Congress without a single Republican vote, and since they took control of Congress in 1995, Republicans have shown a tendency to rely on party-line votes. In 1995, they pushed parts of the "Contract With America" through without Democratic support. More recently, they passed their Medicare prescription drug plan and the fiscal 2001 House Labor, Health and Human Services, and Education appropriations bill in June with support from only a handful of Democrats.

This time, "Republican leaders will have to rule from the center, not from the right, or risk losing those of us in the middle," said Christopher Shays, R-Conn., a leading House moderate. "If our side chooses to be more partisan, they're going to lose key votes."

With the margins of control so tight, the future will be written largely by two groups: moderates who cast the swing votes in both parties, and the mavericks who generally stick with their leaders but periodically break free to pursue their own agendas, usually tied to one or two issues. These are the lawmakers who will be crucial if the 107th Congress is to be a turning point in the partisan wars rather than a waste of two years.

Congressional Quarterly's annual studies of presidential support and party unity, based on roll call votes in 2000, are a good indication of who the swing voters are likely to be. Based on their voting records, the lawmakers to watch when major legislation moves through the 107th Congress will include Republican Sens. Lincoln Chafee of Rhode Island and James M. Jeffords of Vermont; Democratic Sens. Robert C. Byrd of West Virginia and John B. Breaux of Louisiana; Republican Reps. Constance A. Morella of Maryland and Sherwood Boehlert of New York; and Democratic Reps. Ralph M. Hall of Texas and James A. Traficant Jr. of Ohio.

While some of these are lawmakers who simply like to go

Norwood, left, and Dingell worked together to get a managed-care overhaul through the House in 1999.

their own way — such as the cantankerous Traficant in the House and Byrd in the Senate — most cling to the middle of the road because they are convinced that is what their constituents want.

"The center is where the action is going to be," Democratic Sen. Evan Bayh of Indiana, who cosponsored an education overhaul proposal by centrist Senate Democrats in the 106th, said in a Dec. 11 interview.

Congressional leaders "need to realize that lawmakers do a lot of damage when they're simply out to score debating points or bash the other party," said John R. Hibbing, professor at the University of Nebraska at Lincoln. "The people in the middle are very important. [Senate Republican Leader Trent] Lott, [House Speaker J. Dennis] Hastert and [Senate Democratic Leader Tom] Daschle need to reach out to them and do what's right, not just what's right for their parties."

The Moderates and the Mavericks

Centrists have commanded considerable attention since the Nov. 7 elections, and President-elect George W. Bush has made much of his willingness to work with Democratic centrists such as Breaux who can help him build coalitions in Congress. The focus is certainly justified. If Bush hopes, for example, to restructure federal education programs to give states more leeway to achieve general goals, he cannot count on Senate Republicans alone.

Instead, Bush will have to work out a deal with like-minded Democrats from the center, and that could mean turning to one Senate Democrat who did everything he could to keep Bush out of the White House: Joseph I. Lieberman of Connecticut, who ran for vice president. Lieberman sponsored an education overhaul plan in the 106th that bore striking similarities to the Bush plan.

The centrists, however, are not the only ones who can make the difference when a bill faces a close count. Some of the most effective bipartisan dealmakers are not moderates; they are simply mavericks who cross party lines when they have enough interest in a particular issue to do so.

Neither Republican Rep. Charlie Norwood of Georgia nor Democratic Rep. John D. Dingell of Michigan will ever be accused of being a centrist, yet they formed an alliance that pushed a far-reaching managed-care overhaul through the House in 1999 — and may be able to get through the Senate in the 107th.

By David Nather and Adriel Bettelheim / Jan. 6, 2001

Similarly, Republican Sen. Orrin G. Hatch of Utah, a reliable conservative on most issues, joined forces with Democratic Sen. Edward M. Kennedy of Massachusetts in 1997 to fight for the legislation that created the State Children's Health Insurance Program (PL 105-33). Hatch often found himself battling his Republican colleagues on that issue. He prodded them to add more money and specific benefits, and he had to sell fiscal conservatives on the idea that they could help uninsured children without creating a new runaway entitlement program.

Sens. John McCain, R-Ariz., and Russell D. Feingold, D-Wis., similarly cling to their respective parties' orthodoxy on many issues, but joined forces to push a much-discussed campaign finance overhaul that is likely to re-emerge this year.

At the same time, simply being a swing voter in Congress does not necessarily mean a lawmaker has influence. Morella and Hall this year were once again at the top of CQ's lists of lawmakers who break party ranks — but they have not shown an ability to translate their centrist voting habits into legislative deals. Morella, who voted with her party exactly half of the time in 2000, is tolerated by GOP leaders because she keeps a Democratic-leaning district in the GOP column. Yet she sits on the relatively low-profile Science and Government Reform committees, and rarely takes a lead on high-profile issues.

Centers of Gravity

The 106th Congress showed that a few strong-willed lawmakers can make a difference. In the 107th, it may be impossible to get anything done without them.

Already, they are manuevering to capitalize on their position of strength. For example, a coalition of approximately 30 conservative Democrats known as the Blue Dog Coalition has asked Hastert and other House GOP leaders to be included in the drafting of legislation dealing with health care and budget policy. The Blue Dogs consistently vote with the Republican majority on tax, budget and some social issues, and they know the Bush administration needs their support to pass its legislative agenda.

"We want to be involved on the front end, not just be counted on for votes after the legislation is written," said Rep. Chris John, D-La., a leader of the Blue Dogs. "We see our role as being a kind of referee between Democratic concerns and the folks on the Republican side who want to work with us. If it's done right, we can put things on the table that pass."

Middle-of-the-road Republicans have also formed groups similar to the Blue Dogs, though their membership tends to be more diverse and includes conservatives with a reputation for reaching across party lines. The 62-member Republican Main Street Partnership, for example, includes lawmakers from the House and Senate, as well as several governors, and is dedicated to forging bipartisan solutions on education, the environment, budget policy and Social Security.

Lawmakers also have formed informal alliances. Reps. Amo Houghton, R-N.Y., and Tim Roemer, D-Ind., in December pulled together an as-yet-unnamed bipartisan caucus of eight House members. The lawmakers pledged to help draft common-sense legislation that could pass muster with majorities of both parties.

For all the talk about bipartisan cooperation since the election, some skeptical observers fear that continued political posturing in advance of the 2002 elections will keep meaningful legislation from passing.

The University of Nebraska's Hibbing believes the majority of Democrats and Republicans actually are not far apart on some highly debated issues such as raising the minimum wage or repealing the inheritance tax. However, he says, party leaders tend to frame the issues in divisive ways to embarrass the opposition and score debating points.

David T. Canon, a political science professor at the University of Wisconsin-Madison, said the tone of the next Congress will be set early. For instance, if Bush quickly decides to stick with his campaign pledge and push for legislation to cut taxes by $1.3 trillion over the next decades, the two parties could quickly "circle the wagons" and begin pitched partisan battles.

A more pragmatic approach, Canon suggested, would involve seeking more limited tax cuts — perhaps by inviting centrist Democrats to help craft a bipartisan bill to greatly reduce the estate tax. President Clinton vetoed Republican legislation to entirely eliminate the estate tax during the 106th Congress.

Beyond the Votes

There are a number of players who could facilitate bipartisan agreements. Among House Republicans, Nancy L. Johnson of Connecticut showed an ability to work with Democrats in the 106th Congress, teaming up with Rep. Charles B. Rangel of New York on a bill that would have used tax credits to help build new schools and Rep. Benjamin L. Cardin of Maryland on a child support bill that would have let low-income mothers keep more of the support payments collected by the states.

Both bills were killed by opposition from GOP conservatives, but it will be harder for them to ignore Johnson with the narrower margins of the 107th. Democrats say she pays attention to the right social policy issues and makes an honest and open-minded effort to broker bipartisan deals.

Michael N. Castle of Delaware, a soft-spoken former governor, could play a critical role in shaping Republican education policy. A member of the Main Street Partnership, Castle co-chairs the group's education policy task force and has spoken out in defense of a federal role in improving education. He prefers to stress research funding over other, more active forms of federal intervention, and he generally goes along with the party's view that states and school districts should have more autonomy — but he could be an important ally of the Democrats if conservatives try to push that view too far.

Other Republicans likely to work with Democrats to resolve one or two issues while generally sticking to the party line on everything else include Norwood and Greg Ganske of Iowa. These two health care mavericks — Norwood is a dentist, Ganske a plastic surgeon — put together the 1999 managed-care overhaul bill that passed the House with the support of 68 Republicans and nearly all Democrats. The two, who wrote the bill with Dingell, failed to get their bill through a conference committee dominated by Republican opponents, but they are already preparing for another try in the 107th.

Both work with Democrats on the issue because their interests happen to coincide. Democrats are the strongest allies for the kinds of rules Norwood and Ganske want, including a broad right to sue health plans in state court. But they were able to draw enough House Republicans over to their side to pass the managed-care bill over the leadership's objections — and are starting to peel away enough Senate Republicans that a victory in the 107th is a possibility.

Another issue specialist is Rep. Jim Kolbe, R-Ariz. Unlike Norwood and Ganske, Kolbe is considered a moderate, but his work across the aisle focuses on one crucial issue: Social Security. Kolbe worked with Democratic Rep. Charles W. Stenholm of Texas on an overhaul bill that would have created private savings accounts, similar to the proposal Bush advocated during the campaign.

Among House Democrats, Dingell, the dean of the House, tried negotiating with the GOP on managed-care when many in his caucus were wary of compromising with Republicans on such issues. He worked out a compromise with Norwood and Ganske that, in the end, was little different from the bill Democrats had been proposing all along.

Still, Dingell agreed to a few basic limits on the right to sue managed care plans that most Democrats never would have considered; for example, he accepted a Ganske proposal to exempt health plans from punitive damages if they had clearly followed the advice of independent reviewers.

That was not enough of an exception for many Republicans, but it showed Dingell was willing to listen, and Democrats trusted him to work with Republicans without selling them out. That quality will be critical if the 107th Congress is to succeed in passing the managed-care overhaul that failed in the two previous Congresses.

Living Up to Their Potential

In the Senate, James M. Jeffords, R-Vt., is a centrist who has the potential to reach across party lines. Jeffords teamed up with Kennedy in 1999 to win passage of legislation (PL 106-170) to help individuals with disabilities go to work without losing their health insurance; he pushed a reauthorization of the Individuals with Disabilities Education Act (PL 105-17) through Congress in 1997, and cosponsored a Kennedy bill to allow the federal government to prosecute "hate crimes" related to sexual orientation or gender.

However, Jeffords is under a lot of pressure from Republican leaders not to stray too far from the party line. In the 106th, for example, he let Republican conservatives load up a proposed reauthorization of the 1965 Elementary and Secondary Education Act (ESEA) with divisive riders, including a voucher-like proposal, that eventually doomed the package when it reached the floor.

And on managed care, when some House Republicans were taking their first steps to allow patients to sue their health plans, Jeffords stuck with a narrower GOP plan designed mainly to undermine similar efforts in the Senate. The 50-50 split could liberate him in the 107th, but only if he is willing to challenge his party.

On the Democratic side, Breaux was known as a centrist, bipartisan dealmaker with his fingerprints on all kinds of issues long before he showed up in Bush photo ops. He has been best known lately for his efforts to restructure Medicare, which have drawn more interest from Republicans than Democrats, but he also has tried to break stalemates on Social Security, education and health care for the uninsured.

Breaux helped broker the deal to pass the 1996 legislation allowing people to change jobs without losing health insurance (PL 104-191), but most of his recent efforts have been ill-timed or simply unsuccessful. Still, he has built up a strong reputation in his years of leading bipartisan centrist coalitions in the Senate, and few other Democrats can match his ability to use his good relationships with Republicans to find common ground.

Breaux sees himself as a bridge to independent voters who are more interested in pragmatic solutions than party politics. If their time truly has arrived, then Breaux should be in heavy demand over the next two years.

Lieberman, whose stature has grown immensely with his vice presidential candidacy, could easily be drawn into a partisan, fighting stance as an emerging leader of the Democratic Party. But that would be out of character for him. One potential development to watch for might be a Bush-Lieberman alliance on overhauling education.

Despite the fact that they ran on opposite tickets, Bush and Lieberman have strikingly similar views on the issue that tops most voters' priority lists. Both have proposed collapsing the 50-odd federal programs under the ESEA into five grants aimed at achieving general goals — in whatever way the recipients want to achieve them. The biggest difference is that they picked different goals.

Most Democrats are skittish about such a hands-off approach to federal education spending, but Lieberman was able to win over 12 other Democrats when his plan came up for a Senate vote in May. Whenever Bush decides it is time to push for such an overhaul, striking a deal with Lieberman could give him the kind of public-relations coup he needs to make it happen.

Another Bush-Lieberman alliance could come on an equally controversial subject: social services delivered by religious groups. Bush campaigned heavily on his belief that faith-based organizations can do a better job of delivering some services, such as drug treatment, than conventional programs. The view has angered Democrats and civil liberties groups, who are wary of chipping away at the wall between church and state and believe that helping such groups could lead to federally subsidized employment discrimination.

Lieberman, however, showed no such qualms during the presidential campaign; he also cosponsored a Senate version of last year's community renewal bill with Sen. Rick Santorum, R-Pa., that included federal aid to faith-based social services programs. If Bush wants to expand the government's partnership with religious groups, he could go much further by having Lieberman in his corner. ◆

> *The 106th Congress showed that a few strong-willed lawmakers can make a difference. In the 107th, it may be impossible to get anything done without them.*

Congressional Elections

Congressional elections are governed as much by arithmetic science as political art. The candidate on the stump is, of course, influential in the fate of his or her campaign, but long before the business group luncheons and the parade route handshakes, the race in many districts has been reliably stacked. Either an entrenched incumbent has a stranglehold on the local electorate and its available campaign contributors, or the demographics of the district as it was drawn favor one party or the other. In a given election year, the vast majority of seats are not in play.

But that does not mean there is no drama in congressional elections. The money being spent in politics has never been greater. In the last few years, the once-extraordinary $1 million per candidate House race has become commonplace. The elections of 1996, 1998 and 2000 each set records for money raised or spent. And all of this would not be true if it were impossible to influence the outcomes. While there is little doubt about the outcome in many districts, dozens of congressional races are packed with competitive excitement. In one Ohio district in the 1990s, for instance, incumbents were defeated three elections in a row. Most of these districts are located in suburban areas between the urban centers that are typically Democratic and the rural areas that have become strongly Republican. These swing districts are at the heart of every congressional election, particularly in this era when the two major political parties are so evenly matched. It has become a truism that the party that wins most of the suburban swing districts takes a majority in the House of Representatives.

In addition, populations grow and shift, evolving the social and political character of communities. It is not at all uncommon for districts to become more Republican or Democratic over time. Every 10 years, states redraw their congressional districts using fresh demographic data from the U.S. Census. This process is complex and highly charged, since it easily can determine the future of veteran lawmakers, especially in states that have lost population and therefore congressional seats. The 107th Congress already has seen a few longtime House members announce their retirements once it became clear that the new district being drawn for them in the 2002 elections would be less hospitable to their political background. At the same time, shrewd state lawmakers can take advantage of their role in drawing congressional boundaries to design districts ideally suited to run in themselves.

A Tied Election

A few months after the polls closed, a county-by-county analysis of the 2000 presidential election revealed a pronounced split in the American electorate. To an even greater degree than was previously understood, suburban voters determine the balance of power in Washington. Democrats and Republicans have comparably sized bases, but neither has figured out how to satisfy that base while attracting middle-ground voters.

Behind the bare statistics of the virtual dead heat in last year's presidential and congressional elections is a more complex reality: a nation riven into three distinct parts by ideology, geography and demographics.

One side of this political triangle is rural, white, located in the Rocky Mountain and Great Plains states and the conservative South — and is overwhelmingly Republican.

The opposite side is intensely urban and has a large contingent of minorities. It dominates much of the mid-Atlantic and Northeastern states and the Pacific Coast — and is just as overwhelmingly Democratic.

Making up the third leg is a geographically and demographically diverse group that has a common trait: residence in the suburbs. Shifting away from its historically Republican roots, it split pretty much down the middle in 2000 — helping ensure that the election would end in a virtual tie.

These three starkly different segments of the nation have emerged from the smoke and fog of the 2000 race for the presidency. And as each national party now tries to chart a course for the milestone battles coming up in 2002 and 2004, Republican and Democratic strategists are groping for a battle plan that might break the deadlock.

The problem is, each party is so firmly attached to its base constituencies that it is difficult for either to reach far enough into the political center to gain a clear majority — despite each party's declaration that it embodies the moderate view and that the other side really represents the extreme.

A county-by-county analysis of the 2000 election results, based on Congressional Quarterly's compilation of official returns, shows that the nation's current partisan balance is the sum of regional and demographic divisions that the parties will be hard-pressed to overcome.

With many suburbs that once were GOP strongholds now trending Democratic, both parties will be focusing on gaining the initiative in these areas. But it is not clear how either one would be able to grab a decisive advantage.

Many suburban voters, according to political analysts, feel the pull of Republicans' calls for tax cuts, increased parental choice in educational options and private investment of Social Security funds. But just as many seem to favor Democratic liberalism over Republican social conservatism on issues such as abortion, gay rights and gun control.

So as they bid to establish "majority party" status, both Democratic and Republican strategists face the double bind of attracting new voters without alienating their core supporters: social liberals, minorities and organized labor for the

By Gregory L. Giroux / Feb. 17, 2001

Democrats; social and business-oriented fiscal conservatives for the Republicans.

Rep. Adam Smith, D-Wash., a prominent member of the centrist New Democrat Coalition, summed up the problem for party strategists. "The key in any of these elections is the swing voters, those folks who will vote for one party or the other in a given election...," Smith said. "The question is, who are they and how do you get them?"

As Clear as Gray and White

Each party's strengths and weaknesses are as clear as the colors used on CQ's map to denote the counties carried by Republican George W. Bush (white) and those carried by Democrat Al Gore (gray). *(Map, pp. 12–13)*

The most reliable Republican areas still form an "L" — a pattern first described by Congressional Quarterly after three consecutive GOP presidential victories in the 1980s. It takes in the Rocky Mountain and Plains states and sweeps south and east to envelop the Old South.

Some of these states are longtime GOP strongholds; others have swung Republican over recent years in response to the perceived liberalism of the national Democratic Party.

Even more than usual, the rural regions that define many of these states rejected the Democratic nominee in 2000. In many counties, Gore finished 20 percentage points or more behind the 1996 rate of his predecessor on the Democratic ticket, Bill Clinton, whose Southern charm won over some white working-class voters who had wandered away from the party.

Bush's rural gains put him over the top in several states that Clinton had carried, including Clinton's home state of Arkansas, Gore's home of Tennessee, and the usual Democratic dominion of West Virginia. *(Chart, p. 18)*

But the once-dominant GOP showing in the suburbs has slipped. While Bush improved slightly on 1996 GOP nominee Bob Dole's performance in suburban counties, he still finished well below the percentages that Republican presidential candidates were accustomed to receiving before Clinton's first win in 1992. *(Chart, p. 17)*

The Democrats' power base, meanwhile, lies along the Pacific Coast, where many residents are more culturally liberal than the Republican Party as a whole, and in states in the Northeast and Midwest, where social liberalism and labor unions tend to be strong.

California, which gave the nation GOP Presidents Richard M. Nixon and Ronald Reagan, has swung especially hard to the Democrats. The nation's most populous state — it will have 53 of the 435 House seats after the 2002 election and 55 of the 535 electoral votes in 2004 — is now a basic building block for the Democrats' election strategy.

In each of these regions, the Democrats' advantages are built on a foundation of complete and unshakable

2000 Presidential Vote, by County

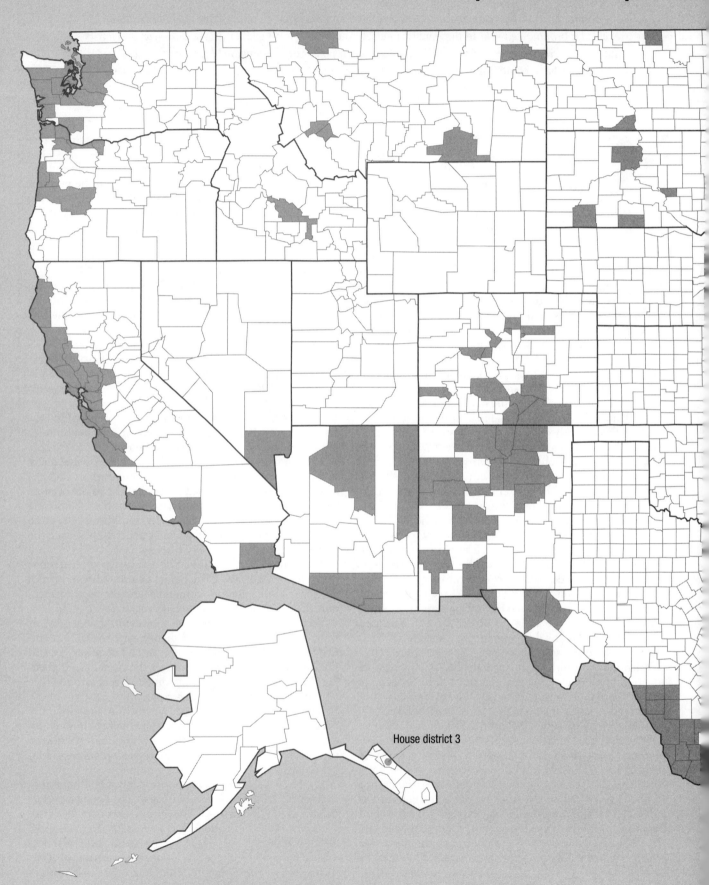

House district 3

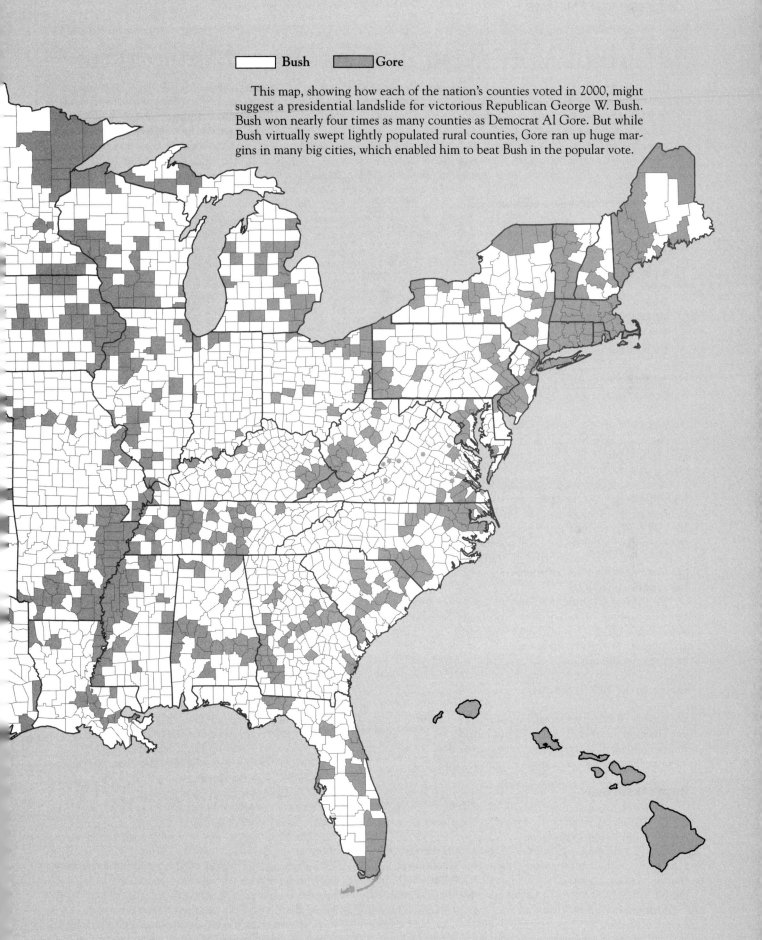

Bush **Gore**

This map, showing how each of the nation's counties voted in 2000, might suggest a presidential landslide for victorious Republican George W. Bush. Bush won nearly four times as many counties as Democrat Al Gore. But while Bush virtually swept lightly populated rural counties, Gore ran up huge margins in many big cities, which enabled him to beat Bush in the popular vote.

Urban Vote Remains Strongly Democratic

The Democratic Party has politically dominated most of the nation's major cities since the 19th century, when the party's appeal to immigrants fueled the growth of urban Democratic "machines." This strength was supplemented by the alliance between the Democrats and organized labor in industrial cities. And over the past few decades, increasing populations of loyally Democratic minority voters have stretched the party's advantage to overwhelming levels. In the sample of cities below, Democrat Al Gore outran Republican George W. Bush in 2000 by ratios ranging from 2-to-1 (in Denver) to nearly 19-to-1 (in Detroit). But even the urban vote is subject to regional variation, with Bush doing much better in some cities of the conservative South. For example, Bush's edge in Jacksonville — a city that has a large military-related population and incorporates much of its own suburbia — was crucial to his narrow and controversial election-clinching victory in the state of Florida.

CITY	2000 Total Vote	2000 Winner	1996 Winner	1984 Winner
San Francisco	319,771	Gore, 76%-16%	Clinton, 72%-16%	Mondale, 67%-31%
Denver	198,347	Gore, 62-31	Clinton, 62-30	Mondale, 50-48
Jacksonville [1]	265,181	Bush, 57-41	Dole, 50-44	Reagan, 62-38
Chicago	961,059	Gore, 80-17	Clinton, 80-15	Mondale, 65-34
Baltimore	192,404	Gore, 83-14	Clinton, 79-16	Mondale, 71-28
Boston	184,603	Gore, 72-20	Clinton, 74-20	Mondale, 63-36
Detroit	300,478	Gore, 94-5	Clinton, 92-5	Mondale, 80-19
St. Louis	124,752	Gore, 77-20	Clinton, 75-18	Mondale, 65-35
New York	2,186,436	Gore, 78-18	Clinton, 77-17	Mondale, 61-39
Philadelphia	561,180	Gore, 80-18	Clinton, 77-16	Mondale, 65-35

[1] Totals shown are for Duval County, Fla. Jacksonville encompasses all of Duval County except the communities of Atlantic Beach, Jacksonville Beach, Neptune Beach and Baldwin.

Sources: State election offices; CQ's America Votes books.

dominance in the big cities. (*Chart, above*)

The political power behind that grip is the party's long-lasting hold on the loyalties of minority group voters, especially African-Americans.

Despite an effort at outreach to black voters — including high-profile speakers and performers at last summer's Republican National Convention in Philadelphia — exit polls showed Bush received just 9 percent of that group's votes, less even than other recent GOP presidential candidates.

Republican leaders say, though, that they have not given up on a breakthrough that could help get them back in the hunt for the urban vote.

"By and large, I think that Bush has an opportunity with a large megaphone to talk to some constituencies that agree with us on a lot of issues but aren't voting with us — Hispanics, some African-Americans, techies — people who ought to be voting more with us," said Rep. Thomas M. Davis III, R-Va., chairman of the National Republican Congressional Committee (NRCC), the party's House campaign arm.

For the purposes of this story, "urban" is defined as within the borders of a city; "suburban" applies to areas within a standard metropolitan statistical area but outside the core city's limits; and "rural" is equivalent to areas defined as "non-metropolitan" by the Office of Management and Budget.

Bush's Rural Rule

Although Gore ran more than 500,000 votes ahead of Bush nationally, Bush carried nearly four times as many counties: 2,472 to 675 for Gore.

This fact underscores Bush's dominance in the nation's rural areas. Bush swept sprawling Plains and Mountain states that have many counties but few people. Gore's strength, by contrast, was concentrated in a few heavily urbanized states.

Bush's showing in Montana was typical. He defeated Gore in the state by 25 percentage points, the largest victory margin for any Republican presidential candidate in Montana since Warren G. Harding in 1920. Bush's performance

in Montana was all the more impressive in that Clinton carried the state for the Democrats by 3 percentage points in 1992 and only lost it by 3 percentage points in 1996.

Bush did not lose a single county in Nebraska, Utah and Wyoming. He lost just one county each in Idaho and Nevada; two each in Kansas and North Dakota; and five each in Montana and South Dakota.

Strong rural support also enabled Bush to come close in Minnesota, Iowa and Wisconsin, which Gore had viewed as locked into his electoral vote base: These states voted for Democrat Michael S. Dukakis in 1988 and for Clinton twice.

Why did Bush thrive and Gore fail in rural America?

For one thing, analysts say that cultural issues helped Bush and hurt Gore. Rural residents are more likely than their suburban and urban counterparts to be opposed to abortion rights and gay rights and supportive of gun owners' rights. Analysts say rural residents are more likely to attend church services, and issues of character and trust resonate more strongly with these voters.

Marty Wiseman, a political scientist at Mississippi State University, said the "lines are being more clearly drawn than ever before between rural, traditional values and those that would be more commonly found in urban settings."

"The further you got from the city, the more Republican it got," said NRCC head Davis.

"That's because this election, despite all of the talk about tax cuts and reforming Social Security, was largely a cultural election," Davis contended.

There are Democratic observers who concur that the atmosphere of scandal that shadowed Clinton — especially in the years after his 1996 re-election — was a burden to Gore, especially in more socially conservative areas.

Surveys conducted by Democratic pollster Stan Greenberg found that Democrats had their largest advantages on issues such as protecting the environment and passing a health care "patients' bill of rights." But Republicans polled strongly on tackling moral problems facing the country.

Virginia, New Jersey Races May Serve As Referendums on GOP Rule

While most major election contests are a year away, there are a handful of states in which there is no vacation from politics.

Most prominent this year are Virginia and New Jersey, which will hold contests for governor. These races will be watched as early tests of public opinion about the direction of the new Bush administration and Republican-controlled Congress.

In both Virginia and New Jersey, Republicans will be defending their hold on the governorship, while Democrats plan to mount vigorous takeover efforts.

But there is a big difference between the states: Virginia Republicans are seeking to stay on a roll that has brought them to political dominance in the state, while the New Jersey GOP will be trying to break a losing trend in major statewide races.

Needing a 'V' in Virginia

The election for governor of Virginia is important for Republicans, who are trying to extend their winning streak for that office to three consecutive elections.

But for Virginia Democrats, the contest has an even higher level of urgency: They need a win this year to rescue them from the partisan oblivion to which they have been exiled in statewide politics.

Like most Southern states, Virginia had a longstanding tradition of Democratic dominance. Just a decade ago, Democrats held all three statewide constitutional offices — governor, lieutenant governor and attorney general — and held majorities by wide margins in both chambers of the state legislature. Democrats also made up a majority of the state's congressional delegation.

But they have suffered a string of losses since then. Republican Gov. George F. Allen was elected in a landslide in 1993, and the GOP swept the statewide offices four years later, led by Republican gubernatorial victor James S. Gilmore III. Republicans won control of both legislative chambers in 1999.

And in 2000, the GOP scored a crowning victory, when Allen ousted two-term Democratic Sen. Charles S. Robb and gave Virginia two Republican senators. Four-term GOP incumbent John W. Warner is the state's senior senator.

Despite their setbacks, Democrats have two things going for them.

One is that Virginia politics allows frequent opportunities for comebacks. It is the only state in which governors cannot succeed themselves after serving a single four-year term.

As a result, Gilmore — who in January was elected by the Republican National Committee as its chairman — is ineligible to seek re-election as governor, as was Allen in 1997.

Democrats also have their strongest possible candidate this year in high-tech tycoon Mark Warner.

Warner, who made a fortune in the cellular telephone business, made a splash in his first bid for political office. In 1996, Warner — then a political unknown — took a surprising 47 percent of the vote in a two-man race with Republican incumbent Sen. Warner (no relation).

Mark Warner is expected to spend heavily on his 2001 campaign from his own pockets, as he did in his Senate bid. But this time, he already has brought in substantial campaign donations from other sources.

His strong ties to the technology sector, a major factor in the politics of the populous Northern Virginia suburbs of Washington, are viewed as a big asset.

And while Warner is running unopposed for the Democratic nomination, the Republicans face the prospect of a two-candidate brawl for their nod.

Vying to succeed Gilmore are the other two Republican state elected officials: Lt. Gov. John Hager, a retired tobacco company executive, and Attorney General Mark Earley.

Earley is a prodigious vote-getter. He outperformed Gilmore and Hager in 1997 when he beat Democrat Bill Dolan for attorney general with 57 percent of the vote. Earley has also sought to reach out to black

(Box continues on page 16)

Greenberg wrote that the "conservative cultural rebellion against Clintonism" contributed to Gore's defeat. He said Gore "ran behind expectations, not among upscale voters, but among the downscale — the non-college white electorate where values concerns were most pronounced."

Greenberg found a "pattern of anti-Clinton feeling in Midwest states with significant rural and small-town populations." He said that anti-Clintonism was "particularly pronounced" in Missouri, Wisconsin, Iowa, Kentucky and Ohio. Clinton carried all five states in 1992 and 1996; Bush won three of the five — Missouri, Kentucky and Ohio — and only narrowly lost Wisconsin and Iowa, which had not voted Republican for president since 1984.

"Bill Clinton's personal ratings were particularly low and the trust issue particularly pronounced in the battleground states central to an Electoral College majority," Greenberg wrote.

Democratic Rep. Ted Strickland, who represents a number of poor rural counties in southern Ohio's 6th Congressional District, saw another problem for Gore: rural voters who were dissatisfied with the economy.

The Clinton presidency was associated with strong national economic growth, but, Strickland noted, the upswing was not felt in many rural areas.

"Unless the economy turns around in some of these areas, Mr. Bush could be feeling some of the same dissatisfaction four years from now that Mr. Gore experienced this year," Strickland said.

Historically, when the farm economy goes sour, the party occupying the

(Continued)
voters, a sizable constituency in Virginia that generally votes strongly Democratic.

But Hager's 1997 defeat of former Democratic Rep. L.F. Payne Jr. — who began the campaign a heavy favorite — was as impressive as Earley's victory.

The GOP nominee will be picked at the party's state convention in Richmond on June 2. The state Republican Party last year chose this nominating method over a primary.

A convention made up of party activists is seen by many Virginia political analysts as benefiting Earley over Hager. Though both men have close ties to social conservatives, Earley is regarded as having stronger rapport with this key Republican constituency.

Gilmore, never shy about wading into party nomination fights, asked Hager late last month to run for re-election as lieutenant governor in the interest of party unity.

But Hager refused, saying that he would "keep on trucking."

The general election outcome appears too close to call at this early stage of the race. Warner is expected to run well in Northern Virginia, his home base and the state's most reliably Democratic territory.

Either of the Republicans would likely have an advantage elsewhere in the state. Hager is from the Richmond region, and Earley is from the Chesapeake area in southeast Virginia.

Mainly rural western Virginia may be up for grabs. Though the region is conservative-leaning, Warner performed respectably there in his 1996 Senate race. But he may have to mute or calibrate his position in favor of some gun control measures when campaigning in this area. Opposition to Democratic presidential nominee Al Gore's support for gun control was one reason this region swung so strongly to Republican George W. Bush last November.

New Jersey: An Early Exit

State law barred two-term Republican Gov. Christine Todd Whitman from running this year for a third term. So both major parties have long been gearing up for the race to succeed her.

The post-Whitman era began nearly a year earlier than scheduled, though. The governor was confirmed by the Senate Jan. 30 as President Bush's choice to head the federal Environmental Protection Agency.

While there may be state pride in Whitman's appointment to the high-profile post, her ties to Bush may not be an unalloyed blessing for Republicans seeking to regain footing in a state that has been trending Democratic in big races. Bush lost New Jersey to Democratic presidential nominee Al Gore by 56-40 percent.

"Democrats want to figure out how to translate Gore's win in the state to the gubernatorial race," said Rider University political scientist David P. Rebovich.

Rebovich said Democrats will try to tie the GOP nominee for governor to parts of Bush's conservative agenda that are unpopular in the state. "The trick here for New Jersey Republicans is to maintain their independence."

But Somerset County Republican Chairman Dale Florio contended, on one hand, that Bush will be more popular in New Jersey as president than he was as a candidate, and on the other hand, that national issues will have limited relevance in the state-level race. "There are a lot of issues that will interest the people of New Jersey . . . but people will really be looking at the [governor's] race based on the candidates," Florio said.

Yet Bush's poor New Jersey showing was symptomatic of the GOP's recent problems. Also in 2000, Democrat Jon Corzine held off Republican Rep. Bob Franks (1993-2001) for the seat left open by retired Democratic Sen. Frank R. Lautenberg (1983-2001). And Whitman won re-election in 1997 by just 1 percentage point over Democrat Jim McGreevey.

McGreevey, now the mayor of the New York City suburb of Woodbridge, is likely to again be the Democratic nominee for governor this year. Citing his strong 1997 performance, Democratic officials are trying to clear the field for McGreevey in the June 5 primary.

Republicans, on the other hand, appear headed for a primary fight.

Holding the inside track is Donald DiFrancesco, the state Senate president who became acting governor when Whitman left for the EPA job. DiFrancesco, like Whitman, is regarded as a moderate on social issues.

But he could face a stiff challenge from Jersey City Mayor Bret Schundler, a darling of conservative activists who is a strong advocate of school choice and opponent of abortion rights.

—*Gregory L. Giroux and Sandra Basu*

White House often takes the lion's share of the blame.

The situation in 2000 had a parallel in 1986, during the Republican administration of Ronald Reagan. The national economy had been booming, but the farm economy was not doing well.

The result then was a voter backlash in several farm states. The defeats of two one-term GOP senators from usually Republican states — James Abdnor of South Dakota (by Democrat Tom Daschle) and Mark Andrews of North Dakota (by Democrat Kent Conrad) — helped the Democrats reclaim the control of the Senate they had lost in the 1980 elections.

Gore's positioning on other issues, such as his strong connection to environmental groups, vexed some rural voters.

Republican Rep. Jo Ann Emerson said this was the case in her district, southeastern Missouri's 8th.

The 8th, which abuts Arkansas, voted for Clinton in 1992 and 1996, yet backed Bush by a 20 percentage-point margin last November.

Clinton "was never perceived as a liberal or as an environmental extremist," said Emerson. "He never had to speak about environmental issues as clearly and as loudly as Vice President Gore."

Emerson said that her district, along with being "very pro-life" and "very pro-gun," is "very conservative when it comes to over-regulation."

Straw in Their Hair

Presidential candidates often cite their rural upbringings to help cultivate

GOP's Suburban Slippage Aided Gore

The suburbs of most U.S. cities, with their overwhelmingly white and wealthy populations, once were Republican strongholds. But over the past few decades, many suburbs became more racially, ethnically, economically — and politically — diverse, even as the Republicans' affiliation with religious conservatives raised qualms among some suburban voters. The results are illustrated in the chart below. Democratic presidential nominee Al Gore carried each of the states listed — California, Illinois,

Michigan, New Jersey, New York and Pennsylvania — in 2000, aided by greater suburban support than was typical for Democratic candidates through the 1980s. The last column shows how much better George Bush ran in these suburban counties in his 1988 victory than did George W. Bush in 2000. Figures in that column are rounded based on exact percentages and may vary slightly from the difference between Republican votes in the 1988 column and Republican votes in the 2000 column.

STATE	COUNTY	LOCATION	2000	1996	1992	1988	Bush 1988-Bush 2000 (%)
CALIFORNIA	Orange	southeast of L.A.	Bush, 56-40	Dole, 52-38	Bush, 44-32	Bush, 68-31	12
	Riverside	southeast of L.A.	Bush, 51-45	Dole, 46-43	Clinton, 39-37	Bush, 60-40	8
	Santa Barbara	northwest of L.A.	Gore, 47-46	Clinton, 47-42	Clinton, 43-35	Bush, 54-45	8
	Ventura	west of L.A.	Bush, 48-47	Clinton, 44-43	Clinton, 37-36	Bush, 62-37	14
	STATEWIDE		**Gore, 53-42**	**Clinton, 51-38**	**Clinton, 46-33**	**Bush, 51-48**	**9**
ILLINOIS	Cook	parts outside Chicago	Gore, 57-41	Clinton, 54-38	Clinton, 44-39	Bush, 58-41	18
	Lake	north of Chicago	Bush, 50-48	Clinton, 45.6-45.5	Bush, 44-37	Bush, 64-36	14
	DuPage	west of Chicago	Bush, 55-42	Dole, 51-40	Bush, 48-31	Bush, 69-30	14
	STATEWIDE		**Gore, 55-43**	**Clinton, 54-37**	**Clinton, 49-34**	**Bush, 51-49**	**8**
MICHIGAN	Macomb	northeast of Detroit	Gore, 50-48	Clinton, 49-39	Bush, 42-37	Bush, 60-39	12
	Oakland	north of Detroit	Gore, 49-48	Clinton, 48-44	Bush, 44-39	Bush, 61-38	13
	Wayne	parts outside Detroit	Gore, 53-44	Clinton, 53-37	Clinton, 42-40	Bush, 56-43	12
	STATEWIDE		**Gore, 51-46**	**Clinton, 52-39**	**Clinton, 44-36**	**Bush, 54-46**	**7**
NEW JERSEY	Bergen	NYC suburbs	Gore, 55-42	Clinton, 53-39	Bush, 44-42	Bush, 58-41	16
	Monmouth	NYC suburbs	Gore, 50-46	Clinton, 48-40	Bush, 44-38	Bush, 61-38	15
	Morris	NYC suburbs	Bush, 54-43	Dole, 49-41	Bush, 52-32	Bush, 68-31	14
	STATEWIDE		**Gore, 56-40**	**Clinton, 54-36**	**Clinton, 43-41**	**Bush, 56-43**	**16**
NEW YORK	Nassau	Long Island	Gore, 58-38	Clinton, 56-36	Clinton, 46-41	Bush, 57-42	19
	Rockland	NYC suburbs	Gore, 57-40	Clinton, 56-36	Clinton, 47-41	Bush, 57-42	17
	Suffolk	Long Island	Gore, 53-42	Clinton, 52-36	Bush, 40-39	Bush, 61-39	19
	Westchester	NYC suburbs	Gore, 59-37	Clinton, 57-36	Clinton, 49-40	Bush, 53-46	16
	STATEWIDE		**Gore, 60-35**	**Clinton, 60-31**	**Clinton, 50-34**	**Dukakis, 52-48**	**12**
PENNSYLVANIA	Bucks	north of Philadelphia	Gore, 50-46	Clinton, 45-42	Clinton, 39-38	Bush, 60-39	14
	Chester	west of Philadelphia	Bush, 53-44	Dole, 49-41	Bush, 44-35	Bush, 67-32	14
	Delaware	southwest of Philadelphia	Gore, 54-43	Clinton, 49-40	Clinton, 42-41	Bush, 60-39	17
	Montgomery	northwest of Philadelphia	Gore, 54-44	Clinton, 49-41	Clinton, 43-40	Bush, 60-39	16
	STATEWIDE		**Gore, 51-46**	**Clinton, 49-40**	**Clinton, 45-36**	**Bush, 51-48**	**4**

Sources: State election offices; CQ's America Votes books

a common-man image. Clinton emphasized his childhood in Hope, Ark., and Dole mentioned growing up in Russell, Kan.

Though it is well known that Bush and Gore are children of privilege, each tried to strike a homespun pose in their outreach to rural voters.

Gore often spoke of working summers on his family's farm in Carthage, Tenn. When Gore moved his campaign headquarters from Washington, D.C., to Nashville in September 1999, it was viewed as a symbolic effort to get more in touch with the everyday lives of ordinary Americans.

Bush made frequent visits to his ranch in Crawford, Texas, two hours away from the state capital of Austin where he presided as governor. He was often seen during the campaign wearing jeans and cowboy boots.

But Bush also frequently spoke of "restoring honor and dignity" to the White House, a not-so-subtle reference to Clinton's personal scandals. It was a message that resonated with socially conservative rural voters.

Some Democrats complained that the Gore campaign compounded its problems by making little or no effort to attract rural voters. Strickland said Clinton came to his district four times during his presidency, but Gore did not

come to the district once during the 2000 campaign.

"It was as if my part of Ohio did not exist in this campaign," Strickland said.

It can hardly be said that there was a great "coattails" effect in Bush's victory for House Republicans. The GOP lost a net of two House seats nationally.

Yet the GOP's issue advantage in rural areas helped the party capture four contests for seats formerly held by Democrats that were crucial to the Republicans' continued, if narrow, control of the House:

• Republican Sam Graves won the seat in northwestern Missouri's 6th

Big Rural Gains Helped Bush Clinch White House Win

A huge advantage in rural areas enabled Republican George W. Bush to win his razor-thin Electoral College victory in 2000. The eight states in this chart — Arkansas, Kentucky, Louisiana, Missouri, Nevada, Ohio, Tennessee and West Virginia — have large rural populations, and all backed Bush after giving their electoral votes in 1996 to the Democratic ticket of President Bill Clinton and Vice President Al Gore. The rural jurisdictions listed within each state were those in which Bush showed the most improvement over 1996 GOP nominee Bob Dole. Figures in the far-right column are rounded based on exact percentages and may vary slightly from the difference between GOP votes in the 1996 column and in 2000.

STATE	COUNTY/PARISH	LOCATION	Congressional District	2000 Winner and Percentage	1996 Winner and Percentage	Bush Improvement over Dole 1996 (%)
ARKANSAS	Scott	far west; Oklahoma border	3	Bush, 60-36	Clinton, 53-33	27
	Pike	southwest	4	Bush, 57-40	Clinton, 55-33	24
	Prairie	east-central	1	Bush, 53-45	Clinton, 62-29	24
	Arkansas	east	1	Bush, 53-45	Clinton, 63-29	24
	Montgomery	west	4	Bush, 57-38	Clinton, 53-33	24
	STATEWIDE			**Bush, 51-46**	**Clinton, 54-37**	**14**
KENTUCKY	Owsley	east	5	Bush, 80-19	Dole, 53-37	27
	Hickman	far west; Missouri border	1	Bush, 54-44	Clinton, 56-32	22
	Trimble	north; Indiana border	4	Bush, 60-38	Clinton, 49-39	21
	Union	far west; Illinois/Indiana border	1	Bush, 51-47	Clinton, 57-31	21
	Carlisle	far west; Missouri border	1	Bush, 54-44	Clinton, 56-34	21
	STATEWIDE			**Bush, 57-41**	**Clinton, 46-45**	**12**
LOUISIANA	La Salle	central	5	Bush, 75-23	Dole, 45-39	30
	Cameron	southwest; Texas border	7	Bush, 62-34	Clinton, 51-33	29
	Catahoula	central	5	Bush, 61-36	Clinton, 52-34	27
	Winn	north-central	5	Bush, 63-34	Clinton, 51-38	26
	Sabine	west; Texas border	4	Bush, 65-32	Clinton, 47-39	26
	STATEWIDE			**Bush, 53-45**	**Clinton, 52-40**	**13**
MISSOURI	Mercer	far north; Iowa border	6	Bush, 68-30	Clinton, 44-42	26
	Reynolds	southeast	8	Bush, 56-42	Clinton, 55-31	26
	Scotland	far northeast; Iowa border	9	Bush, 61-36	Clinton, 47-37	25
	Shannon	southeast	8	Bush, 59-38	Clinton, 50-35	24
	Grundy	northwest	6	Bush, 63-33	Clinton, 44-40	23
	STATEWIDE			**Bush, 50-47**	**Clinton, 48-41**	**9**
NEVADA	Lander	central	2	Bush, 77-19	Dole, 50-30	27
	White Pine	east; Utah border	2	Bush, 64-31	Dole, 40.03-39.97	24
	Elko	northeast; Idaho/Utah borders	2	Bush, 78-18	Dole, 55-27	23
	Humboldt	north; Oregon border	2	Bush, 73-23	Dole, 51-32	22
	Pershing	northwest	2	Bush, 69-27	Dole, 47-36	21
	STATEWIDE			**Bush, 50-46**	**Clinton, 44-43**	**7**
OHIO	Meigs	southeast; West Virginia border	6	Bush, 59-38	Clinton, 45-38	20
	Vinton	southeast	6	Bush, 55-41	Clinton, 49-35	20
	Mercer	west; Indiana border	8	Bush, 68-28	Dole, 50-36	18
	Noble	east	18	Bush, 57-38	Clinton, 43-40	18
	Gallia	southeast; West Virginia border	6	Bush, 59-38	Clinton, 43-41	18
	STATEWIDE			**Bush, 50-46**	**Clinton, 47-41**	**9**
TENNESSEE	Sequatchie	southeast	3	Bush, 56-42	Clinton, 49-42	14
	Obion	northwest; Kentucky border	8	Bush, 50-49	Clinton, 54-37	13
	Morgan	east-central	3	Bush, 51-47	Clinton, 52-39	12
	Polk	southeast	3	Bush, 52-46	Clinton, 51-40	12
	Rhea	east-central	4	Bush, 60-38	Dole, 49-43	12
	STATEWIDE			**Bush, 51-47**	**Clinton, 48-46**	**5**
WEST VIRGINIA	Tyler	northwest; Ohio border	1	Bush, 66-31	Clinton, 53-26	39
	Webster	central	3	Gore, 53-45	Clinton, 69-20	25
	Preston	north	1	Bush, 63-34	Dole, 41.3-41.1	22
	Randolph	east-central	2	Bush, 55-42	Clinton, 54-33	22
	Lewis	central	2	Bush, 59-38	Clinton, 47-37	22
	STATEWIDE			**Bush, 52-46**	**Clinton, 52-37**	**15**

Sources: State election offices; CQ's America Votes books

District left open by retired Democratic Rep. Pat Danner (1993-2001).

• Melissa Hart won western Pennsylvania's 4th District, which Democratic Rep. Ron Klink (1993-2001) had left open to run for the Senate.

• Shelley Moore Capito won in West Virginia's 2nd District to succeed nine-term Democrat Bob Wise (1983-2001), who was making a successful bid for governor.

• Mark Kennedy won narrowly in southwestern Minnesota's 2nd District, ousting Democratic Rep. David Minge (1993-2001).

All four districts voted for Clinton in 1992 and 1996 and Bush in 2000.

"Rural America believes in freedom," Kennedy said. "Bush did a good job of enunciating how in many, many ways he was for freedom, and I think that people had a sense of Gore . . . that he was more for having the government having more control over your life."

Capito is regarded as a moderate on some social issues, including abortion. But her campaign's emphasis on conservative values was evident in an Oct. 25 news release attacking House Democratic leader Richard A. Gephardt of Missouri, who campaigned for her Democratic opponent, Jim Humphreys.

The release said Gephardt was "anti-West Virginia" for voting against parental notification for a minor's abortion and against a constitutional amendment that would bar desecration of the U.S. flag.

Davis of the NRCC referred to Hart's district, a blue-collar area in the Pittsburgh region, as "culturally conservative," adding that Hart "won it on guns and abortion."

Sticking to Their Guns

A political reversal on the issue of firearms regulation was one of the biggest setbacks endured by the Democrats in Campaign 2000.

After two students used high-powered weapons in a massacre at Columbine High School in Littleton, Colo., in April 1999, Democrats sought to gain the initiative on the gun control issue by demonstrating that gun violence is not confined to urban centers.

But a 1999 House vote aimed at requiring background checks on purchases at gun shows — what Clinton and most Democrats called "closing the gun show loophole" and described as common-sense regulation — was highly unpopular in rural areas. So was Gore's call for licensing of all handguns.

According to Greenberg, 48 percent of people who voted in last November's presidential election owned guns, up from 37 percent in 1996. He attributed that to a strong groundswell of political activism among supporters of gun owners' rights.

"That 11-point rise in the gun-owning electorate was not produced by massive gun sales; it was produced by the increased engagement and mobilization of pro-gun voters," Greenberg said.

Strickland recalled campaigning at an event last year and speaking to several older men who were selling guns.

"One of them said, 'You know, I don't want Al Gore taking my guns, but I don't want George Bush taking my Social Security either,' " Strickland said. "I suspect the gun issue won out over Social Security."

William Galston, a professor at the University of Maryland and centrist Democrat who was a domestic policy adviser to President Clinton, said Gore's strong support for gun control did more to fire up the other side than his own.

"I say that with some chagrin, as someone who believes strongly in reasonable gun safety legislation, as I think most Democrats do, but it's clear that there is a lot of intensity on the other side of that issue that we have to think through," Galston said.

The issue also played out to the Democrats' detriment in several congressional races.

For example, the Democrats had high hopes of recapturing the House seat in east-central Kentucky's 6th District: Democratic former Rep. Scotty Baesler (1993-99), who had left the seat open for a 1998 Senate bid that failed, was challenging his freshman Republican successor, Ernie Fletcher.

But the 6th District's constituency is mainly conservative and pro-gun, and Baesler's past support for gun control measures drew him the vocal opposition of the National Rifle Association (NRA). This was a major factor in his unexpectedly lopsided loss: Fletcher defeated Baesler by 18 percentage points.

Yet even as this issue helped Bush swamp Gore in many rural areas, it aided Gore's ability to hold his own in many of the nation's suburban regions. This — combined with his dominance in the core cities — put Gore over the top in a number of key battleground states of the Northeast, Midwest and Far West.

A New Age

During their long histories as exclusive provinces of wealthy white Protestants, suburbs were identified with Republican politics. As late as 1988, when the elder George Bush ran successfully for president, the GOP still dominated in many traditionally Republican bedroom communities.

But the Republicans' continued edge then masked evolutionary changes that would alter the suburbs' political dynamic.

Many suburbanites — even a large number of affluent professionals who might have been sympathetic to Republican economic stances — hold moderate or liberal views on social issues such as abortion rights and gun control. Thus developed a suburban wariness of the national Republican Party's conservatism on social issues and its alliance with religious conservative activists.

According to centrist Democratic groups such as the Democratic Leadership Council (DLC) and New Democrat Network, suburban gains for their party were ensured by its tendency — since Clinton's overtly centrist first presidential campaign in 1992 — to speak the suburbanites' language of the technology-driven "new economy."

"This is the bottom line: The New Economy is creating a new electorate that demands a new politics," DLC president Al From wrote in a special "Why Gore Lost" issue of Blueprint, the organization's policy magazine.

"The sharp class differences of the Industrial Age are becoming less distinct as more and more Americans move into the middle and upper-middle classes. . . ," From wrote. "The new electorate is affluent, educated, diverse, suburban, 'wired' and moderate. And it responds more favorably to the New Democrat political philosophy than to any other."

Also, increased economic opportunity and laws barring housing discrimination have made the suburbs dramatically more diverse in ethnicity and race, drawing in large numbers of traditionally Democratic-voting urbanites.

NRCC head Davis argues that these changes have played a definitive role in the Democrats' suburban gains.

He even suggests that the definition of suburbs needs to be adapted to include the outer counties of metropolitan areas — now typically described as "exurban" — which are increasingly being enveloped in suburban sprawl and which also tend to vote more conservatively and Republican than the older inner suburbs.

Davis said counties that lie immediately outside central cities, which political analysts refer to as suburbs, have

In 1984, Reagan received 62 percent of Virginia's presidential vote and 48 percent of the Arlington County vote — a 14 percentage-point difference. By 2000, the gap had increased to 18 percentage points, as Bush received 52 percent of the statewide vote but just 34 percent of the vote in Arlington County .

There are exceptions to the GOP suburban slide. Republican candidates continue to do quite well in suburban areas of states regarded as conservative bastions, especially in the South. For example, most counties outside Char-

state had he achieved a stronger showing in the suburbs of Philadelphia — the city that held the Republican National Convention that nominated Bush for president.

Bush lost Montgomery County, located northwest of Philadelphia, by 10 percentage points — the largest margin of defeat for a Republican presidential candidate in the county since conservative Barry M. Goldwater lost it by 14 percentage points in his landslide defeat by Democrat Lyndon B. Johnson in 1964. Mainly affluent Montgomery is home to Philadelphia's famed "Main Line" suburbs.

Bush also lost Bucks County, north of Philadelphia, and Delaware County, southwest of the city, by the largest vote margins for a Republican candidate since Goldwater.

Back in Virginia, Davis' home district gave Gore a 2 percentage-point edge last November, about the same as Clinton's 1996 victory margin. Four-term Republican Davis has been able to politically dominate the district, which cuts across the Northern Virginia suburbs of Washington, D.C., largely because he is widely viewed as a centrist Republican.

Elsewhere, Democrats have been consolidating gains in suburban House districts long known as Republican strongholds.

Democratic Rep. Rush D. Holt — who captured New Jersey's 12th District in a major 1998 upset over Republican incumbent Mike Pappas — again surprised a number of observers in 2000, as he fended off a fierce challenge by Republican former Rep. Dick Zimmer (1991-97) in one of the year's closest races.

Democratic Reps. Joseph M. Hoeffel of Pennsylvania's 13th District and Dennis Moore of Kansas' 3rd District fended off determined Republican opposition to win second terms in suburban seats.

Democrats also added another trophy last year in New York's 2nd District. Their nominee, Steve Israel, easily beat Republican Joan B. Johnson for the seat left open by Republican Rep. Rick A. Lazio for his ultimately failed Senate bid against Democrat Hillary Rodham Clinton.

Republican registrants outnumber Democrats in the 2nd, located in Long Island's Suffolk County suburbs. Though Democrat Thomas J. Downey previously had a long tenure in the seat

Adam Schiff was one of four California Democrats to win GOP-held seats in 2000. Schiff beat incumbent James E. Rogan in suburban Los Angeles' 27th District, once a GOP bastion.

"actually turned into cities."

Davis cited Arlington County, Va., which is located across the Potomac River from Washington, D.C., as an example of a county that was once largely suburban but which has adopted urban qualities.

Arlington has large Latino and Asian-American populations and numerous ethnic restaurants and shops.

"Arlington was a suburban county when I grew up," said Davis, whose own district, Virginia's 11th, abuts Arlington. "The people who move into Arlington today aren't moving to be away from the city, they're moving to be in the city, near the action."

In the 1950s, when Davis was a boy, Arlington County gave Republican presidential candidates about the same vote percentages as they received statewide. But the gap has significantly widened since then.

lotte, N.C., Columbia, S.C., and Atlanta voted strongly Republican.

Sport-Utility Voting

Gore's relative success in key suburban areas was essential to his victories in crucial states.

In Michigan, which Gore won narrowly, the Democrat carried Oakland and Macomb counties outside of Detroit. Both voted Republican for president as recently as 1992.

In Illinois, which Gore carried decisively, Bush lost by 56-41 percent in the Cook County suburbs of Chicago — where his father won by 58-41 percent in 1988.

Bush narrowly carried Lake County, north of Chicago — which in 1984 gave 68 percent to the Republican ticket headed by Reagan.

Pennsylvania went narrowly for Gore. But Bush would have won the

(1975-93), Republican Lazio subsequently dominated it for eight years.

Political Power Crisis

One of the most troubling developments for GOP election strategists is the party's backslide in suburban areas in California, which has contributed to a series of Democratic gains in the nation's mega-state.

In the presidential contest, the Bush campaign spent heavily in California. But Bush lost the state by 12 percentage points, only a marginal gain over Dole in 1996.

Three Southern California Republican incumbents were ousted in the same election.

Two of them had represented areas of suburban Los Angeles: James E. Rogan (1997-2001), who lost a historically expensive contest to Democrat Adam Schiff in the 27th District that broke campaign spending records; and Steven T. Kuykendall (1999-2001), who was overtaken by the comeback victory of Democratic former Rep. Jane Harman (1993-99) in the 36th District.

The other, Brian P. Bilbray (1995-2001), lost to Democrat Susan Davis in the 49th District, which reaches from downtown San Diego to the city's affluent northern suburbs.

Democrats also made a pickup in California's 15th District, which Republican Rep. Tom Campbell left open in 2000 for a Senate bid that failed.

Republicans recruited state Rep. Jim Cunneen, a fiscally conservative, socially moderate candidate in the mold of the popular incumbent, for whom he once worked as a top district aide. Republican strategists touted Cunneen as the perfect fit for the Silicon Valley district. Yet he lost to Democratic state Rep. Mike Honda by a whopping 13 percentage points.

Democrats now hold a 32-20 advantage in the House delegation, assuming their expected victory in this spring's 32nd District special election to replace the late Democratic Rep. Julian Dixon (1979-2000), who died Dec. 8.

With Democratic Gov. Gray Davis and a Democratic-dominated state Legislature in place, California alone accounts for more than a third of the districts in which Democrats have complete control over the redistricting process.

One big problem for Republicans in California is that the suburbs tend to lean toward moderation on social issues — while the state party organization is dominated, as it has been for many years, by activists who hold strongly conservative views on those issues.

GOP Rep. Davis, who as NRCC head encouraged Republican candidates in 2000 to run as moderates if that would help them get elected, acknowledged his party's California quandary.

"Until the state party comes to grips and looks in the mirror and decides it wants to start winning elections again, instead of being right, we're just not going to be competitive out there," Davis said.

Democrats' Urban Renewal

As in most of the nation's populous states, the Democrats' greatest numbers are found in California's metropolitan cities. For example, Gore defeated Bush in San Francisco 76 percent to 16 percent, a 60 point edge that bettered Clinton's 1996 vote performance by 4 points.

Strength in the cities has been a foundation of the Democratic base going back to the 19th century, when the party attracted the nation's burgeoning population of immigrants who felt excluded by a Republican Party then dominated by nativist sentiment.

The Democrats' urban dominance was enhanced and cemented during the administration of President Franklin D. Roosevelt, whose New Deal policies appealed directly to industrial workers, liberal city-dwellers (including many Jewish voters) and blacks (many of whom had stayed loyal to the GOP, the "Party of Lincoln").

The Democratic percentages have only become larger as the cities have become increasingly populated by African-Americans — now the party's most loyal voters — and Hispanics. Many city-dwelling whites also are Democrats, including "limousine liberals" who reside in more upscale areas, or working-class laborers who belong to unions.

As a result, Democrats represent an overwhelming percentage of urban congressional districts. The small handful of Republicans who represent urban districts tend to agree with the positions of labor unions on issues such as increasing the minimum wage and opposing trade measures.

If Republican candidates have nowhere to go but up in the cities, they have shown no signs of significant im-provement.

As recently as 1988, the elder Bush won 30 percent of the presidential vote in the city of Chicago; George W. Bush took just 17 percent of the Chicago vote last year as the Republican nominee. Reagan took 46 percent in the New York City borough of Queens in his 1984 landslide; Bush took just 22 percent of the Queens vote last year.

The cities provide Democrats with a valuable cache of votes to offset their deficits in some suburbs and most rural areas. Democratic presidential candidates rely on strong showings in cities such as Detroit and Philadelphia to carry critical "swing" states.

In last year's Senate race in New York, Democrat Hillary Rodham Clinton won New York City by more than 1.1 million votes, while she lost the rest of the state by about 275,000 votes. In Michigan, then-Rep. Debbie Stabenow's wide Democratic victory margin in Wayne County, which includes Detroit, enabled her to unseat Republican Sen. Spencer Abraham (1995-2001).

The problem for Democrats is that the urban vote does not have the clout that it used to. The populations of many cities have been static or even declined over the past few decades, while suburban and exurban populations have boomed. As a result, cities now make up a much smaller percentage of the total vote than in the past.

In 1952, New York City cast 48 percent of the statewide presidential vote. In the 2000 race, New York City voters accounted for just 32 percent of the statewide electorate. In 1952, Chicago voters cast 41 percent of the statewide vote in the presidential election, compared to 20 percent in 2000.

And Republicans, looking for a silver lining, point to local victories in Democratic strongholds such as New York City, where Republican Rudolph W. Giuliani is mayor, and Los Angeles, which is headed by Republican Richard Riordan.

But most GOP successes in cities have come despite — and not because of — their candidates' partisan label.

Giuliani backed New York Democratic Gov. Mario M. Cuomo in his unsuccessful 1994 re-election bid and opposes national GOP platform positions on most social issues. Riordan endorsed California Democratic Sen. Dianne Feinstein for re-election last year. ◆

The Lines of Battle

Long before statehouses begin redrawing congressional districts using the latest census data, members of Congress mobilize their lobbying efforts. Money is raised, lawyers are hired and alternative maps are prepared. It is assumed that Republicans can make significant long-term gains in Congress because they have control of many state capitals, but Democrats thought the same thing in 1990 and four years later they lost control of the House in a GOP landslide.

In 1991, as the Georgia legislature redrew its congressional districts in accordance with new census numbers that gave the state an additional House seat, the national Democratic Party stayed out of the way.

State Democrats seemed to have the matter well in hand with wide majorities in both houses of the state legislature and Zell Miller in the governor's office. But state House Speaker Thomas B. Murphy had his own agenda: to get Republican Newt Gingrich, Murphy's representative in Congress, out of his back yard.

The map Murphy helped draw succeeded in moving Gingrich into another district, but it splintered surrounding Democratic strongholds and left several Democratic incumbents in less-secure seats.

Democrats went from holding nine of the state's 10 congressional seats before redistricting, to holding just four of 11 by 1995 — the year Gingrich became Speaker of the House.

"I don't think the General Assembly fully understood what was at risk with Congress," said former Rep. George "Buddy" Darden, a Georgia Democrat who had been in Congress 10 years before losing his redrawn seat in 1994. "They [national Democrats] should study the Georgia example as the perfect way not to do it."

Today, as states prepare to go through the decennial redistricting process again, national Democrats say they will not make the same mistake. Both parties in Washington are bracing for a battle over drawing the lines that will determine who holds control of Congress for the next 10 years.

The Democratic National Committee and the Republican National Committee have launched redistricting programs in which they are busily studying state voting laws, giving members of Congress advice on how to protect their voting bases and raising money for what probably will be a slew of lawsuits filed against the final state lines.

DNC chairman Terry McAuliffe already has pledged to raise $10 million for the Democratic effort.

"This is a top priority for the chairman," said DNC spokesperson Jenny Backus. "This is critical for winning back the House."

Among the main goals of the Democratic Party is to persuade its members to put party unity above personal agendas in order to avoid a fiasco similar to the one that occurred in Georgia.

Martin Frost, D-Texas, who is leading the House Democrats' redistricting strategy this year, has met with the Democratic congressional delegations of every state in recent months to pass along his message of unity.

"We're urging that they work together as a delegation," said Frost.

As head of IMPAC 2000 — a political committee formed to provide resources and raise money for the Democrat's re-districting strategy — Frost also is helping the delegations hire lawyers to study state and national election law that will come into play during the redistricting process.

Following the 1991 map drawing, more than 40 states ended up in court battling over their congressional lines.

Democrats believe the courts again will have the final say in determining the fate of many state lines. They want lawyers prepared with their own maps and legal arguments to push for scenarios that will best help their cause.

National Republicans are less forthcoming about their budget and strategy. They say Washington can have only a small impact on the redistricting process.

"The governors and the state legislatures do this," said Rep. John Linder, R-Ga., who is head of the task force on redistricting at the National Republican Congressional Committee. "It would be overreaching for us to tell them how to do it."

Changing Times

With so much at stake, national Republicans are making their views felt in state capitols. No place better exemplifies that than Texas, where Rep. Joe L. Barton has revived the Texans Against Gerrymandering political action committee (TAGPAC) to raise money to cover the cost of hiring lawyers and lobbyists to influence how the lines in Texas will be drawn.

Barton formed the PAC in 1990 for that year's redistricting and now has the combined muscle of fellow Texans Majority Leader Dick Armey and Majority Whip Tom DeLay behind the effort.

"We think Texas is very critical in redistricting," Armey said. "Everybody expects California to be a disaster, and Texas historically has been a badly gerrymandered state."

If national Republicans do play the smaller role Linder

Jigsaw Politics

This is the first installment in a yearlong series in the CQ Weekly on how the decennial redistricting process will play out in key states. Reapportionment of the 435 seats in the House, as required every 10 years by the Constitution, must be accomplished by the complex process of redrawing congressional districts in the 43 states that have more than one member in the House. That process, which began the week of March 5 with the release of census data, must be completed before the primary election season next year, and has the potential to determine the balance of power in Congress for the next decade.

By Karen Foerstel / March 10, 2001

says he envisions, it would be a shift from what the party did 10 years ago. Back then, because Republicans were considered an entrenched minority in the House and controlled only a handful of state legislatures, the national party formulated one broad strategy to help their party in every state.

At the same time, state Republicans, because of their paltry numbers, were much more dependent on national money and therefore were much more easily influenced by the national organization.

Times have changed.

"Republicans today have many more seats at the table in different states, and the individual Republicans in individual states are much more in control this time," said Benjamin Ginsberg, a lawyer with the firm Patton Boggs, who has worked with Republicans on redistricting for more than a decade and joined President Bush's legal team in last year's Florida recount battle.

Going into the last round, Democrats had complete control (the legislatures and governorships) over redistricting in states encompassing 172 districts. Republicans had complete control of just five, with the remaining districts drawn under split party control or by independent redistricting commissions.

This year, the Democrats' control has shrunk to 144 districts, while the Republicans' control has soared to 98 districts.

Parties Differ in Defining Roles

Ginsberg said the Republican Party will be able to serve an important role as a clearinghouse of information and advice for state lawmakers, but the ultimate decisions on remapping will be in the hands of the states.

Linder agreed. "Democrats are overreaching their role," he said of his rival party's redistricting plan. "I can't imagine state legislators in Georgia turning around [to Congress] and saying, 'How do you want us to draw the maps?'"

But just as Republican gains over the past decade have led the national party to change its game plan, Democratic losses have forced that party to rethink its strategy.

Ten years ago, Democrats were convinced they would always hold the House majority — having been in control without interruption since 1955 — and did little to work as a team for the broader good of the party. Most House Democrats at that time had never experienced the bitter taste of being in the minority.

But Republicans gained a majority in the House in 1995 and have held it since. Today, nearly half the Democratic caucus has never served in the majority.

Democrats admit they fell victim to their own arrogance.

"It's much better now than 10 years ago," Frost said. "We had senior members who wanted to strike side deals and work on their own. Now we have younger members willing to work together."

Learning From the Last Time

One of the first things Democrats are doing as a team is hiring lawyers to represent their state delegations during the upcoming redistricting battles.

So far, about half a dozen Democratic congressional delegations have hired lawyers, and many more are making plans to do so.

"The [Michigan] delegation is preparing to address the challenges of redistricting and will be fully prepared with legal counsel for the battles that loom before the state legislature and the courts," said Rep. John D. Dingell, D-Mich., who is heading up his delegation's redistricting program.

Michigan is slated to lose one seat in 2002. Republicans, who control the state House, state Senate, governorship and state Supreme Court, are expected to target a Democratic seat for elimination.

Delegations' lawyers are studying the history of voting rights laws in various states, developing map outlines, analyzing demographic shifts, and preparing legal arguments to defend Democratic maps before the courts.

"A lot of the law has not been totally settled in the courts," said Sam Hirsch, with the law firm Jenner & Block, which has been hired by several Democratic delegations, including Texas and Ohio. "We're getting a good and thorough understanding of the relevant law. We want to make sure whatever we propose is, in fact, legal."

The lawyers are being paid by a combination of money raised by the state delegations and money from Frost's IMPAC 2000 committee. Aides say IMPAC 2000 will be a "multimillion-dollar" operation to assist with redistricting over the next two years.

A number of lawsuits already have been filed by various state party activists in preparation for the upcoming battles. In Ohio last December, state Democrats filed two suits — one state, one federal — to force the courts to set strict deadlines for finalizing new district lines. The party hopes to ensure that disputes are settled before primary elections begin.

Two similar suits were filed in Texas, and others have been filed on various grounds in Minnesota, Utah, Virginia and Wisconsin, according to the National Conference of State Legislatures.

Members Hire Lobbyists

While Frost and other national Democrats are working to keep House members unified and working as a team, several lawmakers are taking matters into their own hands.

Along with lawyers hired to represent state delegations, several House members have independently hired lobbyists to track the redistricting activity surrounding their home bases.

Often, state lawmakers will look beyond party loyalty or even legal precedent, and instead place personal relationships and political ambition above all else in drawing congressional lines.

Because members of Congress cannot always spend quality time with their state-level colleagues, lobbyists can help forge positive relationships.

In New York, a state that will lose two seats, Democratic Reps. Gary L. Ackerman and Maurice D. Hinchey have hired lobbyists.

Because the state legislature is split — Democrats hold the House and Republicans control the Senate — it is likely that one Republican seat in upstate New York and one Democratic seat in the New York City area will be eliminated.

"I hired her to ensure that the people of the 26th congressional district are represented in the reapportionment discussions," Hinchey said of his $3,000-a-month lobbyist. "I'm here [in Washington], and that person is in New York."

Hinchey predicted other members may soon get into the act. He said the lobbyist he hired has been contacted by several other members expressing an interest in her services.

Tim Storey, redistricting coordinator with the National Conference of State Legislatures, said he has not heard of any other members hiring lobbyists during the reapportionment process.

"I think that is relatively unique," Storey said. "Now, that's paid lobbying. There will be all other manners of lobbying going on in all its varieties."

Storey said state legislators become exceptionally popular at the start of each decade. Or, as one Republican close to the redistricting effort said: "It's the one time when state legislators can get their calls returned immediately."

Storey said he began to see representatives of the national parties dropping in at redistricting meetings of the National Conference of State Legislatures about a year and a half ago.

As much as politics and the law play into remapping, Storey said it also comes down to personal relationships. Congressmen "better pay attention or you'll be at a greater disadvantage in 2002," he warned. "It's very personal. You don't want to anger the guy who can draw you into oblivion."

Along with personal connections, the parties are hoping money will make a difference in the way state lines are drawn.

Individual members of Congress and the national parties actively raised and contributed money for state lawmakers across the country to help them win election last year.

In Texas, the national parties poured millions of dollars into a state Senate race that was key in determining who would control the chamber. Republicans won the race and held onto their 16-15 seat majority. The state House is controlled by Democrats. Texas will pick up two congressional seats in redistricting.

The National Republican Congressional Committee contributed $50,000 to GOP state lawmaker Todd Staples in his bid for the seat. The NRCC gave an additional $468,000 to the Texas State GOP.

The Democratic Congressional Campaign Committee gave Staples' opponent, lawyer David Fisher, $1,000 and sent nearly $2.4 million to the state Democratic party.

In the end, total spending in that state Senate contest set a record for a state legislative race.

Many members of Congress today are still hosting fundraisers for their local officials in hopes of currying favor with them.

Personal Politics

There is no preventing self-interest from working its way into the map-drawing process. Frequently, state lawmakers draw redistricting lines with the intent of creating new congressional seats in which they themselves could run.

Darden, the Georgia Democrat who was an inadvertent victim of his own party's control of redistricting, pointed out that of the seven Georgians who first won seats in Congress during the 1992 elections that followed the last redistricting cycle, all but one came directly out of the state legislature.

"The way it works in reapportionment is, you look out for yourself," Darden said. "The [state] House and Senate members were looking out for themselves."

That may be even more true this time around.

Since 1990, term limits have been enacted for state lawmakers in 13 states, according to the advocacy group U.S. Term Limits. Hundreds of state representatives and senators, including 75 in Florida, 42 in Ohio and almost 100 in Michigan, will be forced to leave their jobs at the end of the year. Many political observers believe that will prompt more state lines to be drawn out of political self-promotion.

"That's the wild card," Storey said. "Some of these state lawmakers are thinking about that."

National Republicans say there is little they can do to prevent such personal agendas from leading the redistricting process. Linder admitted House members and congressional candidates with the closest ties to the state legislatures will "have the inside track."

"There will be an awful lot of internal politicking going on," Linder admitted, "and I'm not the least bit interested in getting involved."

But ex-congressman Darden said the confluence of personal and political agendas should push national Democrats to take as large a role as possible over the next two years.

"The DNC didn't pay much attention to Georgia last time because they thought there was no way Georgia could blow it," Darden said.

"Don't assume because you have control of the state legislature that it will necessarily translate into a favorable plan. . . . In my view, Democrats in 2001 will pay a lot more attention to drawing congressional lines because they know, having experienced what took place in 1991, that disaster can occur." ◆

Voting on Campaign Spending

Rewriting campaign finance laws for congressional races took a dramatic turn in the 107th Congress. The Senate reversed years of opposition by passing a broad overhaul of the campaign finance system in April, but then prospects in the House, which had twice passed similar legislation, became uncertain. Congress is always wary of tinkering with the laws that affect its livelihood. Moreover, bills that have no realistic chance of becoming law attract more votes because they allow members to show support for an issue without having to worry about the consequences of changing law.

In just days, the campaign finance bill that would end the era of unlimited "soft money" spending will be considered by a House that looks much like the ones that passed nearly identical legislation twice before.

Of the 252 members who voted for campaign finance overhaul in 1999, the last time it came to the floor, 226 are still in Congress.

The debate that begins when Congress returns on July 10 could be the triumphant endgame for sponsors Christopher Shays, R-Conn., and Martin T. Meehan, D-Mass. The first overhaul of the nation's campaign finance laws in 30 years is tantalizingly close after years of setbacks and delays.

Yet although the landscape is familiar to Shays and Meehan, victory is far from assured. In significant ways, the terrain has shifted since the House last considered campaign finance legislation, and the differences present obstacles that the Shays-Meehan coalition has yet to prove it can surmount.

The Senate, where their bill formerly went to die, finally said yes April 2 to a similar piece of legislation (S 27), sponsored by Arizona Republican John McCain and Wisconsin Democrat Russell D. Feingold. But in doing so, the Senate added a provision that would double the amount of "hard money" that candidates could accept directly from contributors. That gave some Democrats more reason to doubt the wisdom of supporting the bill at all. At the same time, the mere fact of Senate passage, coupled with President Bush's statement that he may sign campaign finance legislation that reaches his desk, seems to have prompted longtime supporters of a soft-money ban to reconsider the consequences of such a ban now that it could well become law.

House Republican leaders, whom Shays and Meehan have outmaneuvered before, have again acquiesced to demands for a vote. But in preparing to oppose Shays-Meehan (HR 2356), they have chosen not to simply defend the current system; they have offered an alternative designed to drive a wedge through the diverse coalition Shays and Meehan have counted on in the past. What is more, the GOP leadership's bill also could

frustrate the efforts of Shays and Meehan to win over an important bloc of new members: Republican freshmen.

Supporters of the Shays-Meehan bill have been courting GOP freshmen, at least in part to compensate for votes they may lose within the black and Hispanic caucuses, whose members have been expressing new doubts about banning the now unlimited soft-money contributions to national political parties.

One prominent member of the Congressional Black Caucus — Maryland Democrat Albert R. Wynn, chairman of the group's campaign finance task force — already has bolted. Wynn has put his name on the alternative bill drafted by Ohio Republican Bob Ney, chairman of the House Administration Committee.

The Ney-Wynn bill (HR 2360), which has the support of Speaker J. Dennis Hastert, R-Ill., and other GOP leaders, would restrict soft money rather than ban it.

It also would maintain the current limits on regulated hard-money contributions — another play for the votes of black and Hispanic members, as well as other Democrats who criticized the Senate bill's higher hard-money limits.

With the blessing of McCain and Feingold, Shays and Meehan have altered their

Quick Contents

On the eve of a House debate of campaign finance legislation that could well become law, a few pivotal groups are being showered with attention by supporters of the two main bills to be considered.

Shays, left, and Meehan, right, successfully guided their bill through the House in 1998 and 1999, only to see it die in the Senate. But in 2001, the hurdle has been in the House.

By John Cochran / July 7, 2001

Counting Votes

In September 1999, when a nearly identical version of the Shays-Meehan bill came to a vote, it passed 252-177. Supporting the bill were 197 Democrats, 54 Republicans and one Independent. Today, 182 of those Democrats are still in the House, as are 43 of the Republicans. The lone Independent is back.

Theoretically, that means the Shays-Meehan measure starts with 226 votes. Add the 13 freshman — 11 Democrats and two Republicans — who in January became cosponsors of a version of the bill, and the number goes to 239, a majority.

But that's just on paper. The view on the House floor is considerably more complex, and for the bill's supporters, discomfiting. Below is a look at the blocs likely to be critical when the bill goes to the floor for debate the week of July 9.

Congressional Black Caucus

Members: 38 Democrats, including two non-voting delegates.

How they last voted: All but three members who were in the House in 1999 voted for Shays-Meehan. One of the dissenters did not vote at all. The caucus has two new members since that vote.

Prospects today: The caucus has taken no position, but many have expressed new doubts about banning "soft money," which they say is critical to get-out-the-vote and voter registration efforts in minority communities. The decision by Albert R. Wynn of Maryland, left, to back the Ney bill over Shays-Meehan highlights the uncertainty in this group.

Congressional Hispanic Caucus

Members: 18 Democrats, including two non-voting delegates.

How they last voted: All but two of the current members were present in 1999, and voted for Shays-Meehan.

Prospects today: The Hispanic caucus, chaired by Silvestre Reyes of Texas, left, has taken no position, but members are concerned about banning soft money and raising the limits on "hard money." They have talked of joining forces with the Black Caucus, and also have discussed linking campaign finance to an overhaul of election systems, but so far neither idea has been formalized.

Republican Freshmen

Members: 30.

How they last voted: All have been elected since the 1999 vote.

Prospects today: Most say they are undecided. Slightly more than half (16), including Shelley Moore Capito of West Virginia, left, were aided in their races by campaign finance leader Sen. John McCain, R-Ariz., who has written to remind them of his support. Two in the group cosponsored a version of Shays-Meehan introduced in January. A few others have declared their opposition.

Progressive Caucus

Members: 54 Democrats and one Independent, including 19 members of the Black Caucus and six members of the Hispanic Caucus. Two members are non-voting delegates.

How they last voted: All but two were present in 1999. Only one voted against Shays-Meehan.

Prospects today: The caucus, chaired by Dennis J. Kucinich, D-Ohio, left, has taken no formal position, and some have criticized the Senate bill's doubling of the limit on individual hard-money contributions. Still, many are likely to vote for Shays-Meehan.

— John Cochran

bill to hold the line on hard money for House races, while doubling the limits for Senate candidates. But it is a fragile compromise that even Shays does not like, and it might come undone.

The Shays-Meehan bill also retains a provision in the Senate bill — in part to ease the concerns of black and Hispanic members — that would allow state and local parties to solicit soft-money contributions of up to $10,000 for get-out-the-vote efforts in federal races, as long as they did not mention a candidate's name. But that may not be enough to keep those minority groups behind the bill, and it exposes the bill to criticism that it no longer provides the total ban on soft money that has been the heart of the "reform" movement. Shays and Meehan, who spent the recess week lobbying for their bill, said that is among the elements they may try to alter before a vote.

Soft money is the cash that party committees collect without regulation. Although soft money is supposed to be used for party-building activities such as get-out-the-vote drives, critics say it has been improperly funneled directly into races as a way to circumvent the limits imposed on hard-money contributions. A study released July 3 by the Brennan Center for Justice at the New York University School of Law found that in the 2000 elections, state and national parties together spent only about 8 percent of their soft money on voter mobilization and other traditional "party-building" activities.

The course of the debate may not be clear until mid-week, but Shays and Meehan expect the Ney-Wynn bill to hit the floor first, with their bill offered as a substitute. Still, both sides have been positioning themselves for the debate since the Senate voted.

The 30 Republican freshmen are being lobbied aggressively by both sides, putting those newcomers between their party's leadership and supporters of the Shays-Meehan bill. Few, so far, have declared a public position.

Tough Spot for GOP Freshmen

Shelley Moore Capito, R-W.Va., is typical: She said July 3 that she is studying both bills and plans to watch the debate unfold. She wants to be sure the bill she votes for will reduce the amount of money flowing through political campaigns while providing a level playing field for everyone.

"I'm just going to stay close and monitor the situation," she said.

But Capito and 15 other Republican freshmen face another complication: Crusader McCain campaigned for them last year, and now he expects them to support his cause. He has sent pointed letters to the freshmen, as well as others for whom he campaigned, reminding them of their time together on the stump.

Two of those members, Ed Schrock of Virginia and Melissa A. Hart of Pennsylvania, also signed a Common Cause "contract for reform," promising to support a "complete" soft-money ban and to oppose legislation that falls short of that. Fellow freshman Republican Todd R. Platts of Pennsylvania signed the pledge as well, though McCain did not make appearances for him.

Spokesmen for Schrock and Hart said their bosses are studying the two main bills. A spokeswoman for Platts, who was unavailable to discuss the coming debate because of a death in the family, said she did not know where he stands.

Schrock, who also was unavailable during the recess because of a family emergency, never promised to support McCain's overhaul bill, said his spokesman Tom Gordy. Capito and others said the same.

Schrock supports banning soft money in federal elections, but wants to be sure the bill protects free-speech rights and does not "federalize" state and local political parties, Gordy said.

Hart said it would be irresponsible to "rubber-stamp" any bill, although she said she wants to end the soft-money system, according to her spokesman, Brendan Benner. Hart also will look closely at the provision in Shays-Meehan that would allow state and local parties to raise some soft money for get-out-the-vote efforts, Benner said.

"The congresswoman supports an outright ban on soft money," he said. "Neither of the bills explicitly does that, so that makes it even more complicated."

Matt Keller, legislative director for Common Cause, said he and his group are not happy with the limited soft-money provision now in Shays-Meehan, something Shays himself wishes was not in the bill. But Keller said it is written tightly enough that the group can still support the bill. Federal candidates and national parties, for example, would be forbidden from playing any part in raising or spending that money.

"If we can break the direct nexus that exists between large donors to parties and access to federal policy-makers, we'll have taken a step forward," Keller said.

Listening Sessions With Freshmen

On the other side, Majority Leader Dick Armey, R-Texas, has held "listening sessions" with freshmen and others. Just before the recess, Hastert spokesman John Feehery met with other Republican press secretaries to discuss the Ney-Wynn bill and to urge them to wait before committing to either bill.

"I was trying to advise them to keep their powder dry, that the Ney-Wynn bill is going to be a good, strong, bipartisan alternative and that their bosses ought to take a look at it," Feehery said.

At the same time, Ney, Hastert and other Republicans have accused McCain and his supporters of trying to intimidate freshmen. McCain denies that.

"I thought in many cases there was an understanding that they would support reform," McCain said of the House members he campaigned with and has

now written to. "But it wasn't a demand on my part. I didn't think that would be appropriate."

Among Democrats, who have provided the lion's share of the votes for Shays-Meehan in the past, some say the talk of defections is overblown. Minority Leader Richard A. Gephardt, D-Mo., has pledged to put his muscle behind the bill, and one of his aides predicted that "when the lights go on," Democrats will be lined up en masse behind the bill again.

"I think all this talk about Democrats flaking off this bill is just that," the aide said. "We haven't seen any significant erosion."

Meehan and Shays say they are confident the coalition that backed their bill before will support them again. "The House has twice passed this bill," Meehan said when it was unveiled June 28, "and our bill enjoys support from members across the political spectrum."

Most members of the left-leaning Progressive Caucus, some of whom had objected to increasing hard-money limits, now seem prepared to back Shays-Meehan again.

But support within the black and Hispanic caucuses is shaky at best. In addition to losing Wynn, Bennie Thompson, D-Miss., says he will vote for neither Shays-Meehan nor the Ney-Wynn bill. He supports public financing for campaigns.

Black Caucus members say a poor showing at the polls in November, as well as allegations that blacks in Florida and elsewhere were wrongly prevented from voting, have heightened their sensitivity to the need for energetic get-out-the-vote and voter education programs. Banning soft money might hinder such efforts, they say.

Hispanic members share those concerns, and members of both groups have discussed making their support for a campaign finance bill contingent on seeing action on "election reform," legislation that would overhaul voting procedures.

Some say they are agonizing over the decision, but others, like Thompson, say the issue is not of concern to most voters. "When I go home to my district," he said, "I have yet to hear a constituent ask me about campaign finance reform." ◆

Ballot Questions

The spectacle of the unresolved presidential election triggered many calls for changing the election system and led to the introduction of many bills in Congress. But months later, the push to change the way we conduct elections bumped against traditional partisan splits over how big a role the federal government should play.

It was an embarrassing revelation for the world's most prosperous and enduring democracy: lost ballots, candidates in court, election workers haggling over the meaning of a dimple on a punch card.

The 2000 presidential election had devolved into a protracted court fight and exposed the nation's election system as an unreliable hodgepodge of local standards, inconsistent procedures and old equipment, running in many cases on meager budgets and the kindness of volunteers.

Congress responded to the Florida debacle, and the street protests it spawned, with a rush to devise remedies. Members of both parties called news conferences, introduced bills and declared that the nation needed sweeping changes in the way it elected its leaders.

"The experience of the last election must never, ever be repeated," Sen. Robert G. Torricelli, D-N.J., said in a January news conference with Mitch McConnell, R-Ky.

But six months after the November election drew to a controversial conclusion in the Supreme Court, lawmakers are confronting fundamental questions about federal involvement in what has long been the province of states. Congress still faces pressure to fix the system, but the pressures to preserve the status quo may be even greater.

The Constitution grants Congress wide authority to regulate the election of federal candidates; the question is whether Congress will choose to use it.

The groups most affected and most angered by the problems that came to light in 2000 were blacks and other minorities, who have historically been at the margins of political power. They say their treatment was reminiscent of the systematic abuses minorities suffered before the federal government stepped in to secure the franchise with the 1965 Voting Rights Act.

"The outcome of election 2000 was to dissipate, deteriorate and undermine the fundamental right to vote," said Rep. Sheila Jackson-Lee, D-Texas.

Still, lawmakers in both parties remain leery of mandating national standards for state-run systems. State and local officials are united in their opposition to edicts out of Washington. And companies that manufacture voting machines also favor the wide-open competition of locally run systems.

Unless the mood on Capitol Hill shifts, the business of running elections is likely to remain in the hands of local governments, where it has been since the nation's founding.

"We want to ensure that the elections in America continue to be run at the state and local level," said Bob Ney, R-Ohio, chairman of the House Administration Committee, which is drafting a bill on election system changes. "I think it's important to make clear that we don't want to federalize or nationalize the election process. Our decentralized system of government has served us well."

Some say Congress should forcefully mandate changes, and that position gained new influence in the debate when the Senate flipped to Democratic control. The primary bill promoting national standards for voting machines, access to polling places and the upkeep of voter rolls (S 565) is sponsored by the incoming chairman of the Senate Rules and Administration Committee, Christopher J. Dodd, D-Conn.

The Senate's incoming majority leader, Democrat Tom Daschle of South Dakota, supports the bill, which would order states to adopt "uniform and non-discriminatory" statewide standards for voting machines and election procedures by 2004. Daschle also is backing a competing measure from McConnell, Torricelli and others that would create standards and offer federal money to encourage states to comply, but would not require states to follow the standards.

Congress almost surely will act, even if it stops short of mandates. Members of both parties agree that Congress should provide, perhaps for the first time ever, federal money to pay for improving elections. It remains to be seen how much money will be provided — one bill proposes $2.5 billion over five years — and whether it would be in the form of an annual appropriation or a one-time infusion of cash.

"It's going to cost some money if you're going to get confidence back in our system," Ney said.

Many members also support attaching strings to those dollars, requiring that states provide guarantees of accuracy and establish safeguards against accidentally tossing qualified voters off the rolls or turning them away from the polls.

State officials want the cash to buy new machines, educate voters and train election workers, but they do not want federal mandates. They say they are working on the problems exposed by the 2000 election. According to the National Conference of State Legislatures, more than 1,600 election "reform" bills have been introduced in state legislatures and 167 have passed. More than 20 bills are awaiting signatures from governors. Florida, notably, has already put the finishing touches on its own revamp.

Bush v. Gore

But federal aid will not satisfy those calling for national standards for elections, and they promise a fight.

Some see new leverage for their cause in the Supreme Court ruling in *Bush v. Gore,* which stopped recounts of Florida's presidential ballots and effectively handed the presidency to Republican George W. Bush over Democrat Al Gore. In a 5-4 decision, the majority said the recount should be halted because standards for determining voter intent on partially punched ballots varied by county and therefore violated constitutional rights to equal protection. Proponents of national standards say the logic for a uniform system is inescapable in that decision.

By John Cochran / June 2, 2001

In May of 2001, the House Administration Committee, which is considering legislation to overhaul election systems, conducted an expo for companies that sell high-tech voting machines. Committee staff member Robert Bean, left, gets a demonstration from Dennis Vadura, middle, and Frank Weibe, right, of Web Tools International.

He said the widespread concern stirred by the five-week post-election standoff in Florida seems to have cooled. The public's attention has wandered to other things.

"I give lots of presentations about the November elections, and I almost never get questions about this," Sabato said. "It was so 'yesterday.' "

Emotional Stakes

Members of Congress have a personal stake in the nitty-gritty of election administration, especially at a time when the balance of power between the two major parties is so close. Their political future, not to mention their legitimacy as lawmakers, hangs on how elections are run and how votes are counted back home.

Some proponents of federal "election reform" talk of even higher stakes. Members of the black caucus and other advocates of mandates, including Dodd, say it is a civil rights issue, and they draw emotional parallels to the struggles of the 1960s to end segregation and secure equal rights for African-Americans. Many of the problems with voting machines and confusion over voter rolls, which caused poll workers to keep some properly registered voters from casting ballots, occurred in precincts dominated by minorities, immigrants and the elderly. The U.S. Commission on Civil Rights is investigating and is expected to issue a report this month.

In the ensuing debate about the fairness of the system, the black caucus and others have talked about the importance of federal intervention to protect minority voting rights.

When they talk about upgrading voting machines and securing voter rolls, they refer to past marches and slain activists. They pointedly cite a high-water mark of federal involvement in assuring the franchise for minorities: the Voting Rights Act that ended literacy tests and other discriminatory tactics aimed at keeping blacks from voting.

"So many people have fought and died for the right to vote," said Rep. Barbara Lee, D-Calif., at a press conference May 16. "Medgar Evers. Martin Luther King . . . "

Lee and other members of the black caucus have rallied behind the legislation sponsored by Dodd and Rep. John Conyers Jr., D-Mich., (HR 1170) that would order states to change the way they run elections. They have even discussed making their votes on campaign finance legislation now pending in the House contingent upon action on election overhaul.

Under the Dodd-Conyers measure, voting systems, for example, would have to be designed to notify voters when they had made a mistake on their ballots, such as voting twice for a single office, and give them a chance to fix their errors. States would have to mail sample ballots and voting instructions 10 days before Election Day and offer provisional ballots, which permit people whose names do not appear on registration rolls to cast a vote on Election Day while election officials verify that the person was omitted from registration lists improperly. After the 2000 election, officials in Florida and elsewhere faced accusations that they had improperly turned people

"I think *Bush v. Gore* opens the door," said Jackson-Lee, vice chairwoman of the Congressional Black Caucus. "And the reason is that the Supreme Court said there must be uniform standards. Now, obviously you would like to think that the 50 states could collaborate together and uniform standards all of a sudden would be there at the end of the day. Frankly, I don't think that will occur."

What voters want Congress to do — and how much they care about the issue — is anyone's guess. Polls taken immediately after the 2000 election showed an appetite for change, although pollsters have not asked the question since.

However, fears that 2002 will bring a repeat of last fall's mess may prompt Congress to help states upgrade their voting machines. In pressing for broad action, Jackson-Lee and other members of the black caucus predict widespread outrage if the problems seen in the 2000 elections crop up again in 2002. Time to act is running short, they say.

Charles Stewart, a political scientist at the Massachusetts Institute of Technology, said the public and the press will be watching next year for a repeat of election problems found in such places as Florida's Palm Beach County.

And unless the system improves, problems should be easy to find, he said. "Then the Jell-O will really hit the fan," Stewart said. "Even if things go just as they usually go, there will be Palm Beach counties all over this country."

Larry Sabato, a University of Virginia political scientist, said the public expects some response from Washington, but probably not sweeping changes.

"Congress will have to do something," Sabato said. "What is that something? Probably it will be enough, as far as the public is concerned, to give money to states."

away from the polls because of sloppy voter registration records.

"In federal elections, national elections, there must be basic, minimum standards," Dodd said. "In the 1960s, we said there was no compromising on access to public accommodations — restrooms and restaurants. We think a voting booth deserves no less a status than a restroom or a restaurant."

'All Votes Compromised'

A Democratic "special committee on election reform," created in the House after efforts to establish a bipartisan panel collapsed, says Congress should consider uniform national standards for maintaining registration lists, identifying voters at the polls and handling other aspects of elections.

Conyers, who is on the election committee and a member of the Congressional Black Caucus, sees a clear national interest at play. When ballot recounts and lawsuits in Florida held up the presidential election last year, the nation learned that America's election system is a patchwork affair, spread across 50 states and more than 3,000 counties. It also learned that problems in one state can affect voters everywhere, he said.

"All our votes were compromised by the election procedures and problems in Florida," Conyers said. "You really have to have tunnel vision not to see that voting is a national problem. It's not a state-by-state problem."

Some in Congress have questioned whether they have the authority to dictate election rules to states. But Conyers dismisses any questions about congressional power. On that point, he says, the Constitution is clear.

Article 1, Section 4, leaves it to each state to set the "time, place and manner" of House and Senate elections, but it says Congress may "by law make or alter such regulations" at any time. (*Legal provisions, p. 31*)

"What we want to do is set basic minimum federal standards," Conyers said. "For those who are worried about questions of authority and jurisdiction, rest your little hearts and minds. It's written into the Constitution."

Conyers points out that as a practical matter, if Congress sets regulations for federal elections, all others would fall into line because no state is likely to bear the expense of maintaining one voting system for federal elections and another for state and local races.

Many legal scholars agree with Conyers' interpretation of the Constitution.

"When it comes to federal elections, Congress has considerable power if it chooses to exercise it," said Richard Pildes of New York University Law School.

Congress also can force changes in state laws by attaching conditions to federal money, much as it has used highway dollars to force states to set speed limits on interstates, Pildes and others said. That authority, which the courts have upheld, is rooted in Article 1, Section 8, of the Constitution.

In addition, there is the Constitution's 14th Amendment, guaranteeing all citizens equal protection under the law, and the 15th Amendment, forbidding states from denying anyone the right to vote on the basis of race. If there is evidence that minority voters or others are being treated unfairly, Congress has the power to step in.

It was the 14th Amendment's guarantee of "equal protection" that formed the basis for the Supreme Court ruling in *Bush v. Gore.* The court's majority concluded that Florida's recounts violated the Equal Protection Clause because different counties used different standards to determine which votes to count.

But the court also took pains to limit its ruling to the standoff in Florida, writing that "the problem of equal protection in election processes generally presents many complexities."

That qualifier has muddied the waters for analysts and scholars. The wider implications of *Bush v. Gore,* if any, are still unclear, said Nate Persily, a professor at the University of Pennsylvania Law School.

"The reach of the ruling could be anything from insignificant to transformative," Persily told a study panel from the National Conference of State Legislatures on May 9. "We're only at the beginning of analyzing it."

Pildes says *Bush v. Gore* seems at least to provide an opening for requiring some internal uniformity in the way states and counties run elections. Congress would have the power to pass laws enforcing such uniformity in both state and federal races, Pildes said.

But Pam Karlan, a Stanford University law professor, said she doubts *Bush v. Gore* gives Congress any more power than it already has.

"A lot of it depends on whether lower courts take it and run with it," Karlan said. "But I don't read *Bush v.*

Gore and say, 'Whoa, there's a new equal-protection argument here.'

"This case I look at and say, 'There's going to be a lot of litigation here, but I don't know that it's going anywhere.'"

Bruce Cain, director of the Institute of Governmental Studies at the University of California Berkeley thinks state and local control of elections is secure, unless Congress wants to "underwrite this whole enterprise."

Elections are like education, he said: The tradition of local control is so long, the costs so varied and the bureaucracies so entrenched that Congress would have trouble meddling with the status quo even if it wanted to.

The real power of the *Bush v. Gore* decision may lie in the fear of lawsuits, which could prod states to act. The American Civil Liberties Union already has filed four lawsuits based on the ruling, demanding that California, Georgia, Florida and Illinois get rid of voting systems it says are flawed and discriminatory.

Partnerships, Not Mandates

In the House Administration Committee, now the center of the House debate on the issue, Ney and top Democrat Steny H. Hoyer of Maryland have crossed party lines to strike an agreement in principle on "election reform." They will work to define the federal role in overhauling the nation's election system, but they have agreed to avoid mandates on states.

In the Senate, McConnell and Torricelli have been joined by Sam Brownback, R-Kan., and Charles E. Schumer, D-N.Y., to produce a bill that steers clear of mandates.

Their bill (S 953) is a synthesis of two competing pieces of legislation that would make the grant money it offers contingent on states adopting provisional balloting and meeting standards for accuracy, accessibility and accountability. A new Election Administration Commission would set the standards.

Schumer said that approach would help encourage changes while respecting the long tradition of local control.

"A carrot is much better than a stick," he said. "I've talked with many secretaries of state. They'd be on the warpath if we mandated something."

Local control works, Brownback said. Some counties in his home state of Kansas, for example, are content with hand-counted paper ballots.

The Power of Congress

States and counties have operated — and paid for — the elections of federal officeholders since the nation's founding. But legal scholars say Congress has several sources of authority within the Constitution to determine how federal elections are run.

■ **Article 1, Section 4:** "THE TIMES, PLACES AND MANNER OF HOLDING ELECTIONS FOR SENATORS AND REPRESENTATIVES, SHALL BE PRESCRIBED IN EACH STATE BY THE LEGISLATURE THEREOF; BUT THE CONGRESS MAY AT ANY TIME BY LAW MAKE OR ALTER SUCH REGULATIONS, EXCEPT AS TO THE PLACES OF CHOOSING SENATORS."

Analysis: This section gives Congress power to regulate congressional elections. In practice, that means Congress can affect how all elections are run, since states are unlikely to maintain separate voting systems for federal candidates.

In 1842, Congress used its authority under this section to require states to elect their congressional delegations from single-member districts. At the time, some states elected more than one House member from a single district.

In February, the Supreme Court reaffirmed Congress' power over congressional elections in a case called *Cook v. Gralike*, striking down a Missouri law that required a ballot label for candidates opposing term limits. The court stressed that any authority states have over congressional elections is delegated from Congress.

■ **Article 1, Section 8:** "THE CONGRESS SHALL HAVE POWER TO LAY AND COLLECT TAXES, DUTIES, IMPOSTS AND EXCISES, TO PAY THE DEBTS AND PROVIDE FOR THE COMMON DEFENSE AND GENERAL WELFARE OF THE UNITED STATES . . ."

Analysis: Using the taxing and spending authority granted by this section, Congress has attached strings to federal money to compel states to change or adopt laws. It could do the same with money sent to states for modernizing voting equipment and training election workers.

In the 1980s, South Dakota officials challenged the power of Congress to withhold federal highway money to force them to raise the legal drinking age. In 1987, the Supreme Court upheld Congress' authority in *South Dakota v. Dole*.

■ **The 14th Amendment, Section 1:** "ALL PERSONS BORN OR NATURALIZED IN THE UNITED STATES, AND SUBJECT TO THE JURISDICTION THEREOF, ARE CITIZENS OF THE UNITED STATES AND OF THE STATE WHEREIN THEY RESIDE. NO STATE SHALL MAKE OR ENFORCE ANY LAW WHICH SHALL ABRIDGE THE PRIVILEGES OR IMMUNITIES OF CITIZENS OF THE UNITED STATES; NOR SHALL ANY STATE DEPRIVE ANY PERSON OF LIFE, LIBERTY, OR PROPERTY, WITHOUT DUE PROCESS OF LAW; NOR DENY TO ANY PERSON WITHIN ITS JURISDICTION THE EQUAL PROTECTION OF THE LAWS."

Analysis: This amendment forbids states from applying their laws in a discriminatory or arbitrary way; it could be construed to apply to election procedures that treat ballots differently. Section 5 of the amendment expressly gives Congress the power to pass legislation to enforce its provisions.

■ **The 15th Amendment, Section 1:** "THE RIGHT OF CITIZENS OF THE UNITED STATES TO VOTE SHALL NOT BE DENIED OR ABRIDGED BY THE UNITED STATES OR BY ANY STATE ON ACCOUNT OF RACE, COLOR, OR PREVIOUS CONDITION OF SERVITUDE."

Analysis: This amendment protects the voting rights of minorities. Section 2 of the amendment expressly gives Congress the power to pass legislation to enforce its provisions.

■ *Bush v. Gore:* Legal scholars and public officials are still debating the broader implications of the Supreme Court's ruling in *Bush v. Gore*, which stopped ballot recounts in Florida last December and allowed Republican George W. Bush to claim that state's 25 electoral votes and thus the presidency. Much attention has focused on two paragraphs.

In the first, the court relies on the Equal Protection Clause of the 14th Amendment to stop the recounts because counties used different standards to determine the intent of voters: "THE RIGHT TO VOTE IS PROTECTED IN MORE THAN THE INITIAL ALLOCATION OF THE FRANCHISE. EQUAL PROTECTION APPLIES AS WELL TO THE MANNER OF ITS EXERCISE. HAVING ONCE GRANTED THE RIGHT TO VOTE ON EQUAL TERMS, THE STATE MAY NOT, BY LATER ARBITRARY AND DISPARATE TREATMENT, VALUE ONE PERSON'S VOTE OVER THAT OF ANOTHER."

But the court also sought to confine the ruling's impact: "OUR CONSIDERATION IS LIMITED TO THE PRESENT CIRCUMSTANCES, FOR THE PROBLEM OF EQUAL PROTECTION IN ELECTION PROCESSES GENERALLY PRESENTS MANY COMPLEXITIES."

—*John Cochran*

Their populations are so small that anything more sophisticated — and expensive — makes no sense, he said. (*Technology, p. 32*)

At recent hearings on Capitol Hill, state and county officials have been quite clear: They want the federal government to be a partner in the effort to improve elections, not a dictator.

"I want something that debunks the myth that we have federal elections," Ohio Secretary of State J. Kenneth Blackwell told the House Administration Committee on April 25. "We don't. We have 50 state elections where the president and other federal officeholders are elected. I want to make sure we don't go down the slippery slope of federalizing elections."

Blackwell and others want federal guidance in setting standards and identifying the best practices in election administration. They also want federal money to help pay for new equipment and the training of election workers.

But ultimately, state and local officials say they know best what kinds of equipment and procedures work for their constituents.

"We're not asking you to solve the problems," Arkansas Secretary of State Sharon Priest told the House Administration Committee. "We need some help. But states and localities are working to address the problems. "

Companies that make the equipment argue that innovation in voting technology will be stifled if a single voting system is imposed upon states and counties.

"That's not good for us," said Travis Harrell of Austin-based Hart Inter-

Civic Inc., which makes the eSlate Electronic Voting System, "that's not good for the government, that's not good for the country."

Florida has acted decisively. On May 9, Republican Gov. Jeb Bush signed the most sweeping election overhaul passed by any state so far.

The bill bans error-prone punch-card voting machines and orders counties to replace them by 2002 with electronic or "optical-scan" machines. It sets aside state money for the new equipment, a computerized statewide voter-registration database and education for both voters and poll workers.

Other states also have acted:

• Georgia has passed a law requiring a uniform statewide system by 2004. The state will conduct a pilot project to test electronic "touch-screen" voting in municipal elections this year.

• Maryland's Democratic Gov. Parris N. Glendening has signed a bill requiring the state to work with counties to adopt a uniform voting system. The state will cover half the costs of modernizing voting machines statewide.

• Indiana's governor has signed a bill that could eliminate punch-card and lever voting machines by 2005. The state will establish a fund to help counties pay for updating machines.

Some states, including Kansas, Virginia and South Dakota, have passed measures aimed at improving the maintenance of voter rolls, according to the National Conference of State Legislatures. Others, including Montana and Pennsylvania, have launched studies of their election procedures.

"Some critics have recently suggested that states are dragging their feet on enacting necessary reforms, that we are waiting for federal money to address this problem," said Democrat John A. Hurson, majority leader of the Maryland House of Delegates. "Nothing could be further from the truth." ◆

Varied Needs, Varied Systems

The 1,900 registered voters of Chase County, Kan., still vote with pencil and paper. And odd as it may seem in this computerized age, County Clerk Sharon Pittman says the system works just fine.

"Check a box," Pittman says. "No hanging chads."

Now consider Los Angeles County, home to 4.1 million registered voters. Ballots are printed in seven languages, including Korean and Tagalog. Last November, the county's voters cast nearly 2.8 million ballots — more than statewide totals in 41 of the 50 states.

"Can you imagine us with paper ballots on election night?" said County Clerk Conny B. McCormack. "It's only funny in the most macabre sense."

McCormack wants to get her county into the computer age by replacing the 1968-vintage punch-card machines with electronic "touch-screen" voting. But when that will happen, no one can say. The estimated cost is $100 million.

As Congress and state lawmakers look to improve the fairness and accuracy of the nation's election system, few disagree that part of the answer is new technology. But the needs are so diverse that a national solution is likely to remain elusive.

What is more, early results from one ongoing study suggest new technology is not always an improvement over the old standbys.

Researchers at the Massachusetts Institute of Technology and the California Institute of Technology found that polling places using electronic voting machines saw a higher percentage of spoiled or unmarked ballots than those using "lever machines," technology introduced in the 19th century.

After the spectacle of Florida's recounts, some in Congress have focused on eliminating punch cards. Those machines, used widely in Florida, taught the nation about "hanging" chads, the little bits of paper left when voters do not punch completely through a punch-card ballot.

But in Utah, 23 of the state's 29 counties use punch cards, and Republican state House Speaker Martin R. Stephens told a House committee recently that the system works fine. Meanwhile, Florida, Georgia and other states are scrambling to get rid of punch cards. Florida plans to lease optical scanners, like the machines used to grade standardized student tests, for the 2002 elections. Georgia plans to test touch-screen machines in this year's municipal elections.

Which system is best?

The MIT/Caltech study looked at data from more than 2,700 counties and municipalities, and found that overall, 2 percent of presidential ballots cast in the past four elections were spoiled or unmarked. Problems were fewest in counties using lever machines, paper ballots and optical scanners.

Counties using punch cards and electronic machines saw the most problems.

The results from new electronic machines indicate that makers may still be struggling to make the ballot designs user-friendly, said one of the researchers, Stephen Ansolabehere of MIT. Or, he says, voters are still getting used to the new technology. Or both.

Everyone seems to agree that whatever system a county uses, the ballots should be tallied as they are cast in each precinct, not later at a central location. That is the surest way to catch ballot errors before voters leave the polling place, officials and researchers say.

Most agree that technology is not the only answer. Voter education is important. So is training for poll workers.

Larry Sabato, a University of Virginia political scientist, worries that all the talk about voting machines might distract from the need for education and training.

"This is so American," Sabato said. "We have a tendency to blame inanimate objections for our shortcomings."

—John Cochran

Political Parties and Leaders

In the United States Congress, political power can be derived from two places: a large constituency, or the force of personality (or stubbornness) of an individual. America's two-party, majority-rule system is designed to favor the political power of large constituencies. Buildings in Congress are made to accommodate the collective authority of parties with expansive offices that sprout off opposite corners of grand committee rooms; one for the majority, one for the minority. On the floor of the House and Senate there are gathering spaces for party members called cloak rooms.

Yet, in the quintessentially American way, the ability of one person to impose one idea on the machinery of our government can be, for him or her, richly rewarding. The maverick is nothing new to American politics. It was nothing new in the days of Teddy Roosevelt. But today, the delicate balance of power in Washington provides an inducement for political rebellion by making nearly every act of defiance instantly and dramatically influential. Party leaders continue to appeal to their members for loyalty because without it there is no way to govern. And for the most part, party leaders get the discipline they seek. Party identification provides many advantages to politicians, from access to the financial resources of an extensive machine to a more structured and direct connection to higher levels of power. Generally speaking, it is worth it for members of a party to heed the call of their leaders, and to follow.

But sometimes, with some politicians, party loyalty becomes secondary to devotion to a cause. In the 107th Congress, the most obvious examples are those Republicans who support legislative issues in direct opposition to party leaders, such as on campaign finance overhaul and on the so-called patients' bill of rights. In both cases, the stubbornness of a single advocate was decisive in getting the issues on the legislative agenda. Sen. John McCain, R-Ariz., threatened to block all other issues from consideration — no idle threat in the Senate, where rules give individual senators great power to stall legislation — unless a debate on campaign finance legislation was scheduled. Rep. Charlie Norwood, R-Ga., had demonstrated his willingness in years past to cut deals with Democrats to advance legislation that would give patients in health maintenance organizations (HMOs) greater leverage in disputing treatment decisions. In the end, Norwood's rebel stand made him the focus of a White House courtship that ended with an agreement on a bill between him and President Bush. The final resolution of that legislation remained in dispute into the fall of 2001, but it was Norwood's willingness to buck the will of his own party that brought the issue to the fore.

The Temptation to Rebel

The 107th Congress opened with a Senate split 50-50 between Republicans and Democrats. The GOP's control of the chamber hung on the tie-breaking vote of Vice President Dick Cheney and the ability of the party to maintain internal discipline. But the Senate is designed to give individuals disproportionate power and the 50-50 split only exaggerated that reality.

It did not take long — day one of week one — for the 50-50 Senate to be reminded of the power a single senator may wield, and to presage a freewheeling political dynamic in which the temptation for maverick solo missions will compete with pressure to fall into line.

Congressional Republicans and President Bush began together the week of Jan. 22, but by the end of the first day, it was clear that not everyone was following the script. Bush campaign rival Sen. John McCain, R-Ariz., fulfilled his oft-reiterated promise and wedged campaign finance overhaul onto the early Senate agenda by threatening to force a vote — never mind that neither Bush nor GOP leaders want to pass the bill, let alone pass it as one of the first acts of this new presidency.

At nearly the same moment as McCain's latest declaration, Bush's home state GOP ally, Sen. Phil Gramm, announced that he had put Bush's campaign tax cut proposal into bill form, choosing not to wait until the White House had finished writing its own, and briefly eclipsing the president's effort to talk about education.

Any resentment Gramm may have engendered for grabbing the limelight was short-lived, and he more than made up for it by bringing along another maverick soul, Georgia Democrat Zell Miller, as an original cosponsor of Bush's sweeping tax plan. Miller's unexpected presence on the bill allowed Republicans to instantly dub the plan "bipartisan," and served as a quick reminder that it will be both Republican and Democratic renegades giving their respective leaders splitting headaches in the 107th Congress.

"The temptation and the opportunities are great because there is a vacuum to be filled — bipartisanship, common-sense solutions," said Sen. Gordon H. Smith, R-Ore. "It does roil your base, but about a third of the electorate is very taken with that kind of politics, and you get to 51 percent by including people in the center."

For Democrats, who purported to welcome Bush's calls for bipartisanship, Miller's Jan. 22 announcement set off a shock wave. Miller blindsided Minority Leader Tom Daschle, D-S.D. — who needs to keep his troops unified to have a powerful voice now that the White House and Congress are both in GOP hands — as well as home state colleague Max Cleland, a Democrat who faces a potentially difficult re-election bid in 2002.

Unity is critical for Democrats if a coalition with moderate Republicans is to be formed, but Daschle declined to criticize Miller in public, taking only the slightest dig for having learned of Miller's decision through media reports.

"It's my hope that I'll have an opportunity to make my case prior to the time people make their decisions on issues," he said.

In his inaugural work week, Bush got far better treatment from freshman Miller than he got from Senate Finance Committee Chairman Charles E. Grassley, R-Iowa., who told The Washington Post that the ultimate size of Bush's signature tax cut is likely to be "$1 trillion or a little more." Grassley promptly got back on message.

All in all, the week provided clear evidence that lawmakers of all stripes are going to need some time to get used to the dramatic reshaping of government — a Congress and the White House controlled by Republicans for the first time since President Dwight D. Eisenhower's first term.

"We're still testing the waters to figure out who the hell is in charge," said a top Senate GOP aide. "And we're learning quickly that it isn't us."

The conflicting impulses to stand out or stand in line caught liberal Republican Lincoln Chafee of Rhode Island, for one, who said he felt torn between the "pressure to be a good, loyal Republican" and his own campaign platform that favored reducing the national debt over Bush's tax cut agenda.

Ohio Republican George V. Voinovich, who in the cause of debt reduction unflinchingly opposed GOP bills last year that would have eliminated the so-called marriage tax penalty and the estate tax, ducked reporters' efforts to determine whether his attitude has changed now that any single senator can tip the scales against his party.

Democrats also are adjusting to their new roles. Liberal lion Edward M. Kennedy, D-Mass., alternated between booming blasts at Bush over his choice of controversial conservative John Ashcroft for attorney general, and pussycat-like praise for the new president's education plan.

For his part, cagey moderate John B. Breaux, D-La. — touted as a critical swing player — was being careful not to stray from the Democratic fold early on. Breaux appeared at a Jan. 23 news conference to endorse a "New Democrats" education alternative, and he signaled in an interview afterward that he was in no hurry to join Miller in accepting the full range of Bush's tax cuts.

"I don't think [Miller's announcement] gives it a majority," Breaux said of the Bush tax plan.

Bush's focus during his first week was on a major overhaul of federal aid to public schools, which he hopes will swiftly and smoothly advance as his first big legislative win.

But both parties are girding for a showdown over the size and shape of that upcoming tax bill. Bush's position in that argument was dramatically enhanced by Federal Reserve Board Chairman Alan Greenspan, who embraced tax cuts in testimony before the Senate Budget Committee on Jan. 25. Greenspan earlier had said paying down the national debt

By Andrew Taylor / Jan. 27, 2001

Lott, shown meeting with Olympia J. Snowe, R-Maine, and John B. Breaux, D-La., faces a maverick factor as he tries to run the Senate. But the maverick factor can help, too. Phil Gramm, R-Texas (at right), was able to draw Sen. Zell Miller, D-Ga., into supporting Bush's tax cut proposal.

was his preferred use of the budget surplus but even larger surplus projections have swayed his thinking. Few needed reminding of how critical Greenspan's support was to the success of President Bill Clinton's deficit reduction package eight years ago.

The week also brought speedy confirmation of the majority of Bush's Cabinet nominees. The Senate confirmed seven Cabinet members by voice vote shortly after Bush was sworn in Jan. 20, including the secretaries of State, Defense and the Treasury. Four more were confirmed Jan. 23 and 24, and votes on three other high-level appointees are expected the week of Jan. 29. The controversial Ashcroft nomination would then be the single unconfirmed Cabinet choice, but a vote could come by the end of the week of Jan. 29.

What's Next?

Beyond education and the confirmations, other elements of the early Republican agenda on Capitol Hill are anything but clear. It appears that floor consideration of Bush budget and tax proposals are months away. Other than a bill to implement a Clinton-brokered proposal to pay off U.S. debts to the United Nations, the early congressional agenda is fuzzy at best.

Other possibilities, say lawmakers and staff aides, include reviving bankruptcy legislation pocket-vetoed by Clinton last month; bills to create Social Security and Medicare "lockboxes;" and a multibillion-dollar, fiscal 2001 supplemental appropriations bill. The latter in particular promises to test the relationships of GOP members of the Appropriations committees, their conservative rivals and Bush.

Poised to step into the legislative vacuum is McCain, Bush's rival from the GOP presidential primaries. He has worked for years with Democratic Sen. Russell D. Feingold of Wisconsin on legislation to overhaul campaign finance laws, and insisted on early action for his signature issue to battle what McCain calls an "iron triangle here of lobbyists, big money, special interests and legislation."

Monday, Jan. 22, was both the first day for senators to introduce legislation and the first workday of the new administration. The simple fact that McCain introduced his bill was

greeted with great fanfare by the national media, who depicted it as the opening shot in an early battle royale over the ability of Bush to control the national agenda.

"I also have a mandate," McCain declared when he introduced the latest version of his bill.

The battle will indeed come, though Bush's veto pen promises to dramatically reshape the debate. For one thing, opponents such as Sen. Mitch McConnell, R-Ky., no longer need to resort to scorched-earth filibuster tactics.

McCain originally demanded a debate as one of the first orders of Senate business, and Majority Leader Trent Lott, R-Miss., countered with an offer of floor time late in the year. McCain won assurances Jan. 26 that the issue will hit the floor by mid to late March.

As expected, Bush issued a directive Jan. 22 to put back in place Reagan-era restrictions on international family planning aid that Clinton had reversed in 1993 and that have bedeviled Congress' annual ability to pass the foreign aid budget.

Bush's first week in office undeniably went more smoothly than the early days of Clinton's presidency, which were roiled by an immediate flap over the nomination of Zoe Baird to be attorney general and by an unwelcome focus on his controversial promise to overturn a ban on homosexuals serving in the military.

Bush sought, successfully for the most part, to keep the focus on education and on his promise to establish a spirit of bipartisanship. Perhaps recognizing that despite the numerical situation of the Senate, issues seldom divide the parties evenly, Bush set out to build his own majorities by mixing the Texas charm that gained some repute in Austin with well-placed invitations to influential Democrats as well as Republicans.

The wooing immediately bore fruit, as his education initiative — streamlining federal aid to public schools — earned widespread praise and appears likely to pass fairly quickly. The still-undrafted measure would reauthorize the Elementary and Secondary Education Act (ESEA); it builds upon a bill that stalled amid a partisan — and little noticed — Senate debate last year. The arrival of Bush im-

Miller: Why So Surprised?

Sen. Zell Miller, D-Ga., said he was shocked that so many people were shocked by his decision Jan. 22 to cosponsor a bill based on President Bush's tax cut plan.

For Miller, who just days before his tax bill announcement was the first Democrat to declare support for controversial attorney general nominee John Ashcroft, this endorsement was not remarkable.

After all, he had campaigned last year on the evils of high taxes — winning with 58 percent of the vote — and had cut taxes when he was Georgia's governor, too.

"Washington is quite different from Georgia," Miller said after leaving a meeting with Senate Minority Leader Tom Daschle, D-S.D., a few hours after Miller and Phil Gramm, R-Texas, held a news conference on the tax bill.

Georgians might not bat an eye at such boldly conservative stands by their Democrats, but Miller said Capitol Hill instantly was consumed with curiosity about the depth of his party loyalty.

"In this weird atmosphere," he said people ask, " 'Does this mean you're going to change parties?' "

Miller said the answer is no.

He said he just sees the combination of high tax rates, record surpluses and a possible economic downturn as "an opportunity to reach across party lines and really practice bipartisanship, not just talk about it."

— *Matthew Tully and Emily Pierce*

mediately changed the terms of the debate, lifting it onto the front pages of major newspapers and making it a top story on television network news programs. Democrats such as Kennedy, who led the charge against the GOP plan months ago with election-year alternatives such as school construction, have switched to singing Bush's praises.

"I just commend the president for putting education first on the national agenda. He did so in the course of the campaign, and now he's doing so in Congress," Kennedy said after a Jan. 23 meeting with Bush. "I think he'll get a very positive response. . . . There are some areas of difference, but the overwhelming areas of agreement and support are very, very powerful."

Bush is borrowing from Clinton by choosing a leftover item from the prior Congress as his first major legislative initiative. When Clinton took office, the first order of legislative business was to enact a long-stalled bill (PL 103-3) to require businesses to permit employees to take leave for the birth of a child or illness in the family. That bill had been vetoed twice by President George Bush in 1990 and 1992.

Another early "chip shot" for Clin-

ton was enactment of "motor voter" legislation (PL 103-31) to require states to register voters when they obtain or renew their driver's license. That bill had been vetoed in 1992.

"The Bush administration, wisely, is picking some issues where there's a greater likelihood they're going to get a substantial number of Democrats to support them," said Sen. Christopher J. Dodd, D-Conn. "They've learned the lesson of the Clinton administration: start with some successes where you can."

Mandates and Parallels

Both Bush and Clinton began their presidencies with their party controlling Congress and hungering for the chance to pursue languishing agendas.

Both also entered office with shaky mandates from the public. Bush lost the popular vote to former Vice President Al Gore; Clinton took office in 1993 having taken only 43 percent in a three-way contest with President George Bush and Reform Party nominee Ross Perot.

Clinton came into office supported by comfortable majorities in both the House and Senate. But he also had to confront a deficit far worse than he had

anticipated during a campaign in which he promised the middle class a tax cut.

Bush has a far less cushioned majority, and his battle-scarred congressional leaders must manage a sometimes fractious party that often papered over its internal divisions to oppose Clinton.

"President Bush has a very narrow majority in the House, and a one-vote margin in the Senate, and an economy that's very fragile," said Senate Majority Whip Don Nickles, R-Okla. "I think he'll be successful in getting his budget and tax package through, but I don't think it's going to be strictly partisan as President Clinton's was."

And it will require coordination within the GOP.

"These [GOP leadership] guys haven't demonstrated over the last couple of years any particular legislative skill or any particular tactical brilliance," said a Republican who served lengthy stints in both the GOP-controlled Congress and Republican administrations. "If anybody was looking to be led, it's this crowd."

Bush's smooth start was greatly helped by the early deal reached between Lott and Daschle on organizing the evenly divided Senate. Lott had caught tons of flak from his GOP colleagues in forging an agreement that gives Democrats equal representation on committees and greater influence over setting the Senate agenda.

One of the selling points of the 50-50 agreement reached Jan. 5 was that it cleared the way for speedy confirmation of Bush's Cabinet and avoided an early inside-the-Beltway fight over arcane Senate organizational issues that might have drawn attention away from Bush and his agenda.

Lott said he found satisfaction that the reverse was true. "A couple of others have said quietly, 'You did the right thing,' " Lott said. "Bush thinks so. He feels very strongly that I was helpful."

However, the 50-50 situation on committees promises to bedevil Bush when his tax bill hits the Senate.

"There are several Republicans who aren't that happy with the president's initial [tax] proposal," said Max Baucus of Montana, the top Democrat on the Finance Committee. "Don't forget the 50-50 dynamic on committees. It's unclear how all that is going to work out, but it's potent." ◆

A Tough Leader in a Delicate Position

House Majority Whip Tom DeLay is a hard-nosed conservative who relishes the nickname "The Hammer," which he earned for pressing party members to vote the party line. But with the GOP majority historically thin, how does a never-compromise leader fit in?

Late last year, as Congress inched toward a budget deal with President Bill Clinton, House Republican Whip Tom DeLay of Texas interrupted the gentle give-and-take of final negotiations and declared that he would rather shut down the government than give in to higher spending demands.

Many GOP lawmakers cringed. But while DeLay absorbed barbs for his remarks, Speaker J. Dennis Hastert, R-Ill., quietly explained to White House negotiators that he was hamstrung by his dependence on DeLay and the hard-line conservative votes for whom he speaks.

Ultimately, Clinton relented, inking a deal conservatives could swallow, and at the same time rewarding a good-cop-bad-cop routine that may also figure prominently in the legislative strategy of the new White House occupant, President Bush.

The compassionate conservatism and centrist coalitions that have been the talk of Capitol Hill might seem to leave the firebrand DeLay at the margins, but Republicans say his inflammatory style and unyielding positions will continue to help the GOP broker favorable deals with Democrats.

"He defines where the conservative viewpoint is on issues," said GOP consultant and former Bush campaign strategist Ed Gillespie. "You can't split the difference until you define what the differences are. Until you define those issues, we run the risk of having our agenda hijacked."

Since his December outburst, DeLay has been nearly silent, fueling speculation by some observers that he has been muzzled. There remains a school of thought among some Republicans that Hastert, now in his second term as Speaker, is growing in the role at the expense of his close ally DeLay.

They point out that in the recent selection of new committee chairmen, several of the candidates backed by DeLay — including Philip M. Crane, R-Ill., who was vying for the Ways and Means Committee, and Saxby Chamb-

DeLay admits he has stayed out of the spotlight lately to give President Bush plenty of room to outline his agenda. But DeLay says he will always speak up for conservative views.

liss, R-Ga., who wanted the Budget panel — were defeated.

DeLay acknowledges that he has deliberately avoided drawing attention to himself, but he said he has been doing so to give Bush the opportunity to present his agenda unfettered.

"Obviously, I haven't been out in front of the cameras for weeks," DeLay said Jan. 30. "That was a concerted effort of staying away from the press for a while, let the president have his agenda, don't confuse what is going on here. So I took a step back."

He said, however, that he has no plans to curb his conservative zeal or combative reputation.

"I don't know that I can change," he said. "I've always been very passionate about what I believe in."

In fact, his reputation for tough tactics is as strong as ever. House supporters of overhauling the campaign finance system say DeLay, a leading opponent of such legislation, recently was twisting arms against the proposal.

"He has told individual members, and particularly freshmen, that if they cosponsor the campaign finance reform bill in the House . . . that they can expect to get no money from downtown,"

a GOP staff aide said.

DeLay's spokesman Jonathan Barron called that "utter nonsense."

"Mr. DeLay has urged members to oppose campaign finance legislation," Barron said. "[But] he has always done everthing possible to retain and expand the Republican majority."

In a New Landscape

Far from receding into the background, colleagues and friends say DeLay will easily find a spot in the new political era.

"He's conservative and aggressive, but he's also the most pragmatic whip there's ever been," said former Rep. Bill Paxon, R-N.Y. (1989-99) "He has the incredible ability to adapt himself to the changing terrain."

Paxon pointed to DeLay's work as the chief lieutenant of former Illinois Rep. Edward Madigan's (1973-91) 1989 campaign for whip against then-Georgia Rep. Newt Gingrich (1979-99). The race was hard-fought, but Madigan's narrow defeat did not harm DeLay's future. By the time Gingrich ascended to Speaker, DeLay was well-established in the leader's inner circle.

Paxon predicted DeLay will have an

By Karen Foerstel / Feb. 3, 2001

essential part in enacting Bush's agenda over the next two years.

"He'll be at the center of every legislative victory," Paxon said. "The Bush agenda couldn't happen without the conservative base. If you don't have a base, you're dead."

Indeed, with the narrow, five-seat voting margin in the House, there will be many instances when Bush will have to rely solely on a unified Republican conference to pass proposals when Democrats cannot be persuaded to join. Republicans say DeLay will be the man charged with keeping conservatives happy and on Bush's side.

House Republicans say DeLay is well aware of possible splits between GOP conservatives and moderates. And despite what DeLay himself says about not changing, those close to him say he will work to prevent splits from becoming public and causing political damage to the GOP — even if that means sometimes holding his tongue.

"He's going to have to be more careful," said one GOP insider. "The fact is the press will be looking for internal Republican fighting. DeLay likes the idea of having the heart and soul of conservatives, but he'll have to do that without undermining Bush's agenda."

Close friends of the whip say Bush's calls for bipartisanship and compassionate conservatism are not inconsistent with DeLay's aggressive style.

"In Washington, too often people think bipartisanship means moderating everything and coming up in the middle," said DeLay's chief deputy whip, Roy Blunt, R-Mo. "But we can have bipartisanship by sticking to our goals and then reaching out to people."

He added: "I don't hear that talk about a centrist agenda from the administration. I hear about the administration reaching out in a bipartisan way to achieve the goals we want."

While DeLay may appear less combative in the new Congress, Republicans say that largely will be the result of having a GOP administration with which DeLay can work, in contrast to the Clinton administration that DeLay constantly opposed.

"Bush is clearly conservative," said Dan Mattoon, vice president of congressional affairs at BellSouth and a former staffer at the National Republican Congressional Committee who worked closely with DeLay.

"DeLay's operation will not change at all. The only difference is he's now

got a president who believes in many of the same things he does and he's not going to have to be fighting all the way."

Even some moderate Republicans say DeLay's brand of conservatism will be needed to keep the GOP unified.

"The majority of the Republican conference is more conservative in its leanings," said Sherwood Boehlert, R-N.Y., a member of the moderate Tuesday Group. "[DeLay] will continue to speak out for the conservative element. And that ain't all bad. . . .We must make certain that no faction is ignored."

Moderate Democrats, however, are not so sure. They argue that the evenly divided Senate will require that conservatives such as DeLay move toward the center. If not, the Democrats predict little will be accomplished.

"They can ramrod anything through the House, but they have to show me where they can get votes in the Senate," said Rep. Charles W. Stenholm, D-Texas, a member of the moderate Blue Dog Coalition.

Stenholm criticized DeLay and other House leaders for not working more closely with Democrats over the last six years. If that does not change, Stenholm said, "I can hardly wait until the next elections."

Texas Ties

Bush and DeLay have not always walked in lockstep on policy or politics.

In 1999, when Bush was vying for the GOP presidential nomination, the then-Texas governor attacked a plan pushed by DeLay to revamp the earned-income tax credit — a program designed to help the working poor — in order to make up for a budget shortfall.

At the time, Bush slapped Congress for trying to "balance the budget on the backs of the poor." DeLay shot back that Bush needed "a little education on how Congress works. I don't think he knew what he was talking about."

Some GOP insiders say tensions between Bush and DeLay go back to 1990, during the administration of Bush's father, when DeLay joined the fight against the senior Bush's budget plan.

Despite their home-state connections, Bush and DeLay are not close personally. One Republican close to the whip described Bush and DeLay's relationship as "professional."

DeLay admits they have not had the opportunity to form a close friendship over the years, but he says "we get along really well."

"As far as I have seen, there's no tension at all," he said.

While DeLay may not yet have a close bond with Bush, he has a solid history with Vice President Dick Cheney, who served in the House as the Republican whip from 1988 to 1989.

During the 1988 GOP presidential convention, DeLay approached Cheney, asking to be part of his whip organization. Cheney gave DeLay the apparently insurmountable task of persuading the convention's rules committee to grant floor privileges to members of Congress. House Republicans had tried for years to obtain such accommodations.

In the end, DeLay not only pushed the proposal through the rules committee, he accurately predicted the final vote. Afterward, Cheney made him a top member of the whip team.

While DeLay has a reputation for precision as the GOP's chief vote counter, he has not been without defeats, most recently in the races for committee chairmen. He threw his weight behind Crane, an anti-tax conservative who once led the American Conservative Union, to chair the Ways and Means Committee, but Crane's loss nearly was unanimous. Moderate Bill Thomas, R-Calif., won the post.

Some say the defeat shows a waning of DeLay's power, but others insist DeLay knew Crane did not have the broad support necessary to win the race. They argue that DeLay backed Crane's candidacy out of deference to the conservative wing.

While DeLay was not successful in securing chairmanship positions for Crane or Chambliss, he did block an attempt to grant some chairmen waivers from their term limits. By ensuring that no chairmen stayed beyond six years, DeLay won kudos from conservatives and moderates alike.

Boehlert said DeLay supported his successful bid to take over as head of the Science Committee, a position that opened only because waivers were not granted for anyone.

"He clearly recognized in the contests for chairs that moderates had to be considered," Boehlert.

And though he swears he will remain resolute on his principles, DeLay is trying to adopt the new lexicon. When he called Bush's agenda conservative, he instantly doubled back to add "compassionate."

"See," he said, "I've already changed." ◆

The Party Without the President

For the eight years of the Clinton presidency, the Democratic Party had a reliable, high profile and articulate messenger. But without a unifying voice coming from the White House during the 107th Congress, Democrats had to build a new strategy for conveying their message.

In 1992, when Republicans lost their White House leader and faced life in the congressional minority on their own, Senate Republican Leader Bob Dole of Kansas staked dramatic claim to the helm of the GOP.

Dole stood before the press just a day after President George Bush was defeated at the polls and announced that he would represent the 57 percent of Americans who voted against Bill Clinton — including the 19 percent who sided with Ross Perot.

"If Bill Clinton has a mandate," he said, "then so do I."

Today, Democrats face the same situation, but they have not responded with a Bob Dole moment. Instead, they have set about executing a strategy of combine and conquer. They have knitted their ranks together as a single front line rather than as troops behind one bully-pulpit leader.

Congressional Democrats have used the team concept to overcome their circumstance, seizing control of the party and steering it to several legislative victories in the opening months of the Bush presidency. They won a compromise on President Bush's tax plan by making a home for moderate Republicans, and held together to push a broad campaign finance bill past Republican leaders in the Senate.

With the high-wattage names of Clinton and Gore off the stage, Senate Democratic Leader Tom Daschle of South

By Karen Foerstel / April 14, 2001

Dakota and House Democratic Leader Richard A. Gephardt of Missouri have now joined in a strategy to give the party as many spokesmen as it has members.

"There are a lot of people who speak for the party," Daschle said recently when asked who is the new face of the Democrats. "We don't lack for good messengers."

Indeed, Daschle and Gephardt shared the spotlight for the party's first major public event of the year when they sat in matching chairs to respond to Bush's address to Congress in February.

Since then, Democrats in the two chambers have created "rapid response" teams composed of rank-and-file members from across the party's ideological spectrum who help devise policy stands on issues and react quickly to GOP proposals. (Box, p. 40)

Their tactic of deputizing everybody to speak for the party is helping Democrats stay together — a top priority now that Clinton no longer serves as a guiding beacon.

In the Senate, Democrats take credit for cutting Bush's $1.6 trillion tax cut by $400 billion after a Democratic amendment to pare back the Bush plan drew enough crossover Republicans to win approval. In the House, they have been bowled over by Republicans' superior numbers, but throughout the tax debate Democratic leaders have allowed varying factions of the party to play key roles. The conservative "Blue Dog" Caucus took the lead in attacking GOP plans to vote on a tax cut before a final budget was enacted. Then the Progressive Caucus was allowed to offer their plan for a $300 tax rebate to every American as the party's alternative to Bush's plan to eliminate the so-called marriage penalty.

And the lack of a central Democratic figure has an added bonus: It has left some Republicans wondering how to fight back.

"It's gotten more difficult," said GOP consultant Eddie Mahe. "Daschle should be [our target], but he doesn't come across as radical, duplicitous or strident. When you watch him on television, he's not screaming, yelling or red-faced."

Gephardt is no help to Republicans, either.

"Gephardt's not big enough [to attack]," Mahe said. "I don't think the American people would focus on him at all. He's not unique. There's no persona you can work with."

Democrats on Capitol Hill met with former Clinton officials on an alternative to Bush's tax plan. Daschle, left, and Gephardt, middle, unveiled the plan with Rangel.

AP PHOTO / DENNIS COOK

Rapid Response

Democrats in the House and Senate have begun organizing teams to speak on particular issues. The groups do not have centrally developed scripts, but the goal is to provide immediate reactions to Republican proposals, particularly those from the White House. Democratic leaders in the House say more than 50 members are assigned to the assorted teams, while Senate Democrats have not finalized all their categories.

HOUSE

BUDGET
- John M. Spratt Jr. of South Carolina
- Robert T. Matsui of California
- Benjamin L. Cardin of Maryland

TAXES
- Charles B. Rangel of New York
- The Blue Dogs

EDUCATION
- Bob Etheridge of North Carolina
- Max Sandlin of Texas
- George Miller of California

CHOICE (ABORTION RIGHTS)
- Jan Schakowsky of Illinois
- Nancy Pelosi of California
- Nita M. Lowey of New York

DEFENSE
- Ike Skelton of Missouri
- Gene Taylor of Mississippi
- John P. Murtha of Pennsylvania

ENVIRONMENT
- Frank Pallone Jr. of New Jersey
- Edward J. Markey of Massachusetts
- Ellen O. Tauscher of California

PRESCRIPTION DRUGS
- Joseph Crowley of New York
- Bernard Sanders, Ind., of Vermont
- Pete Stark of California

MEDICARE
- Henry A. Waxman of California
- Jim McDermott of Washington

SOCIAL SECURITY
- Robert T. Matsui of California
- Earl Pomeroy of North Dakota

AGRICULTURE
- Charles W. Stenholm of Texas
- Marcy Kaptur of Ohio

SENATE

BUDGET/TAXES
- Max Baucus of Montana
- Kent Conrad of North Dakota
- Charles E. Schumer of New York

HEALTH/EDUCATION/LABOR
- Edward M. Kennedy of Massachusetts

ENVIRONMENT
- Harry Reid of Nevada
- Barbara Boxer of California

FOREIGN POLICY
- Joseph R. Biden Jr. of Delaware

For better or worse, Mahe said, Clinton's departure has left the Democratic party without a shining star.

"I can't think of a Democrat on the national scene that's big enough [to attack]," he said. "None are big enough. None we can make big enough."

New Tactics, Same Ideology

This strategy is not without risks, some Democrats acknowledge. The unity that has come in these early weeks by letting everyone have his say could lead to splintering later on.

The lack of one defined leader also makes it more difficult to set a comprehensive agenda, so Democrats are focusing their energies by following the centrist course Clinton set.

In late January, Rep. Charles B. Rangel, D-N.Y., the ranking member on the tax-writing Ways and Means Committee, organized a two-hour meeting with committee Democrats and former Clinton Treasury Secretaries Lawrence Summers and Robert E. Rubin.

Rangel said he speaks "at least every other week" with Summers and Rubin, as well as with other former Clinton officials, on economic and tax issues. At the start of the year, Rangel hired former Clinton congressional liaison Chuck Brain to work as a special assistant for the committee.

"When we had the White House, we had experts there to discuss these things with and get advice," Rangel said in an interview April 10. "We don't have that now. So after we have prepared our positions among ourselves, we need to continue that advice."

The January meeting with Summers, Rubin and Rangel was just the beginning of Democratic outreach to Clinton's old guard.

Democratic leaders in the House and Senate speak monthly — if not weekly — with the likes of Gene Sperling, Laura Tyson and Jack Lew, who made up Clinton's econom-

ics team.

Sen. Kent Conrad of North Dakota, ranking Democrat on the Budget Committee, said he has spoken to Rubin half a dozen times in the past three months, and to Sperling at least two or three times.

"There is no White House. There is no Treasury Department. We lost a tremendous amount of resources," Conrad said. "There is a recognition that we're going to have to pull up our socks and get our work done."

Part of that effort also includes a new reliance by Democrats on outside organizations to provide information that previously came from Clinton's Cabinet.

Leadership aides say Democrats are turning more frequently to such groups as Citizens for Tax Justice and the Center on Budget and Policy Priorities, two nonpartisan economic think tanks, to do their number crunching.

"We get lots of people calling us and asking us for information," said Bob McIntyre, director of Citizens for Tax Justice. "We get 50 calls a week from Democratic leaders and rank and file."

With the start of the Bush administration, Democratic leaders on Capitol Hill said their No. 1 priority was not to develop an attack plan against the Republicans, but rather to ensure that their own troops were united.

In the House, Gephardt and Democratic Caucus Chairman Martin Frost of Texas reviewed the most basic aspects of the party's structure.

They decided that the Cannon Caucus Room — where the party holds its weekly meetings — was too cold and expansive, so they rearranged the chairs to create a closer, more intimate setting.

Gephardt began meeting more regularly with all the ranking Democratic members of the House committees. Coordination between House and Senate Democrats has increased greatly this year, aides say. Gephardt's and Daschle's staffs meet weekly, while the leaders themselves talk every few days.

In February, Gephardt asked Conrad to address the House leadership to discuss his budget agenda. Conrad's proposal to preserve one-third of the surplus for debt reduction, one-third for tax cuts and one-third for additional spending has since become the Democratic mantra in the budget debate.

Conrad said he talks frequently with his counterpart on the House Budget Committee, John M. Spratt Jr. of South Carolina, and that the two committee staffs talk at least once a week.

Rangel said he has also been working with Senate leaders during the tax debate. "I'm in love with Conrad," Rangel said. "I steal all his charts."

Rangel is coordinating with factions within his own caucus, meeting about a dozen times this year with conservative Blue Dogs and more liberal members of the Progressive Caucus to hear ideas on budget and tax issues.

"They have to be involved. We can't afford to leave someone behind," Rangel said. "We're not just selling [our tax proposal] to each other, we're also selling it to the constituents. . . . They are our salesmen. They have to believe in the product."

Rep. Dennis J. Kucinich of Ohio, chairman of the Progressive Caucus, said Rangel "bent over backwards" to allow Democratic progressives to put their $300 rebate proposal on the floor.

Democratic leaders also are working with the moderate Democratic Leadership Council, which is chaired by Sen. Even Bayhe, D-Ind. On April 5, Daschle and Gephardt participated in a press conference with the Progressive Policy Institute — an arm of the DLC — in which they unveiled a proposal for boosting the high-tech economy.

The "rapid response" plan is another avenue for fostering involvement from all corners of the party.

"We're trying to get people engaged, particularly because we don't have the White House," said Rep. Rosa DeLauro of Connecticut, who overseas the teams in the House. "We want to encourage people to speak out. We cannot rely on the president any more, so we have to look to ourselves."

Those who have been put in charge of the rapid response teams range from Blue Dog members Gene Taylor of Mississippi and Charles W. Stenholm of Texas, who are heading the defense and agriculture teams, respectively, to Progressive Caucus members Henry A. Waxman of California and Jan Schakowsky of Illinois, who lead the Medicare and reproductive rights teams, respectively.

"It's a step in the right direction," Taylor said about the leadership's inclusion of him and other Blue Dogs in the plan. In January, Taylor refused to vote for Gephardt for Speaker, saying the leadership had not tried hard enough to solicit all views.

"They're hopefully listening," Taylor said. "Hopefully, they'll broaden the base and let people with differing backgrounds come forward."

One of the first things Taylor did as head of the defense team was distribute a paper he wrote titled "Simple Truths About Democrats and Defense." The paper is meant to provide talking points for the upcoming defense debate and for members running for re-election in strongly pro-defense districts. The paper lists defense programs supported by Democrats in recent years.

It also points out that while Republicans are often seen as the party of the military, none of the current House GOP leaders served in the armed forces, while the top three House Democrats, as well as Daschle, have past military service.

"Although no party has a corner on patriotism or valor, Democrats who support our military are neither unique nor alone," Taylor's paper reads. "The House includes 53 Democratic members who served in the nation's armed forces."

The DNC and Congress

Further evidence that the party is trying to embrace its lack of a White House leader can be seen in the Democratic National Committee (DNC).

On April 4, Terry McAuliffe, the new chairman of the DNC, spoke to the House Democratic Caucus, a meeting aides say they have not seen in years. Two weeks earlier, he attended a luncheon with Senate Democrats, another rare event. During both meetings, McAuliffe outlined a long list of changes he is making within the committee and pledged to devote more time and resources to congressional and local races than ever before.

"It's a different environment today," McAuliffe said in an interview April 11. "For eight years we had the bully pulpit of the White House. We don't have that any more. It's harder to get our message out now. It's only effective if we all say the same thing."

In order to do that, McAuliffe has revamped the DNC, cosmetically and structurally. He trimmed the staff and then treated those who remained to a minor refurbishment of the building that includes new paint, new carpeting and in-house Starbucks coffee.

Where once the DNC did its polling to meet the needs of the White House — to the extent that Hill Democrats seldom saw the results — the updated DNC will pay for all polling for the Democratic Congressional Campaign Committee (DCCC) and the Democratic Senatorial Campaign Committee (DSCC). Democrats at all levels will see the results.

"Now, the whole Democratic party will be speaking off the same page," McAuliffe said.

McAuliffe said his efforts appear to be paying off. The DNC said it took in more than $7 million in direct-mail fundraising during the first quarter of 2001, breaking the 1996 record of $5 million.

Rep. Nita M. Lowey of New York, who took over as chairman of the DCCC this year, said she, too, has met with many Democrats in recent months and was told to be more inclusive and to listen more to local, rather than national, concerns.

"I heard that over and over again from my colleagues," she said. "In some districts, the right to choose or guns may be key issues, but that may not be the case in other districts."

The multifaceted approach has its dangers. "There simply isn't a single flag-bearer," said Democratic strategist Alan Secrest. "There will be multiple faces that make it hard to agree on a single issue."

But Democrats recall that while Clinton was a master communicator for the party, he also provided endless ammunition for the opposition. They hope Bush will do the same.

"There are pros and cons to the Bush White House. They have an identifiable person that people will listen to, but it's a double-edged sword," said Rep. Adam Smith of Washington, campaign chair for the centrist New Democrat Network. "Republicans will live or die by Bush. In six months to a year, when things get tougher for Bush, we'll have to be ready to pivot off of that." ◆

41

Speaking in Burlington, Vt., Jeffords said the Republican Party's direction under Bush has not been what he had expected and he could not support it.

The Senate Switch

Tensions have long been apparent between the conservatives in leadership positions in the Senate Republican Party, and moderates among the rank-and-file. But the extent to which moderates felt marginalized within their own party was not fully understood by anyone — including GOP leaders — until James M. Jeffords of Vermont left to become an Independent.

All along, the 50-50 Senate was understood to be fragile and unforgiving. And a change in control because of a single, untimely departure might set off a shock wave of extraordinary consequences.

Yet no one expected this. One Republican, feeling increasingly uncomfortable with his party and his president, decided to change his political identity and in doing so changed the world around him, too.

When Vermont Sen. James M. Jeffords announced May 24 that he would leave the Republican Party and turn control of the Senate over to the Democrats, he did precisely that. Not only will Majority Leader-to-be Tom Daschle, D-S.D., assume power in this new Senate, but so too will old hands like Edward M. Kennedy, D-Mass., Robert C. Byrd, D-W.Va., and Patrick J. Leahy, D-Vt.

Jeffords' stunning decision has remarkable consequences for George W. Bush's agenda and his presidency. Jeffords' impact on the Senate as an institution in the tripartite U.S. democracy promises to be even more profound.

Republicans had hoped to spend much of the rest of the year passing piecemeal tax bills to complement Bush's landmark cuts in tax rates. Now, the summer will feature liberal icon Kennedy leading the charge, first to pass a patients' bill of rights, later to raise the minimum wage.

By Andrew Taylor / May 26, 2001

It now will be up to the crafty Byrd, who returns to the post of Appropriations Committee chairman, to shepherd the fiscal 2002 spending bills through a Senate composed of 50 Democrats, 49 Republicans and an Independent Jeffords, who will caucus with the Democrats.

All-important nominations of federal judges will have to pass through a Judiciary Committee likely chaired by the liberal Leahy. Bush's designs for a multibillion-dollar missile defense system will face renewed skepticism, as will his plans to permit drilling for oil in the Arctic National Wildlife Refuge in Alaska.

Democratic chairmen will have the power to hold hearings on legislation, schedule bills for committee votes and launch investigations into administration policies — as well as to delve into possible future scandals.

A Senate controlled by Democrats offers the party a national megaphone and gives them power to proactively offer an agenda to counter Bush's, rather than having to use the guerrilla tactics available to the minority.

But it also carries responsibilities for Democrats. Now that they will control the Senate, they will have a far greater ability to counter Bush's agenda with their own. In short, Democrats will share the accountability for making democracy work — and share the blame for gridlock.

"When you're in the minority you can sit back and watch government self-destruct," said Paul C. Light, director of governmental studies at the Brookings Institution. "Now Democrats will have a stake in governing."

An Old-Fashioned Senate?

The Senate traditionally runs on unanimous agreements, and the potential for filibusters makes 60 votes the practical threshold for most bills. Split evenly between the parties, it was always seen as the ultimate test for Bush's legislative agenda. Now the dynamics of this crucible will change dramatically.

Now, it will be Democrats bringing legislation to the floor and Republicans lobbing the hand grenades, perhaps in the form of popular amendments to cut taxes.

Daschle has for years chafed at the way Trent Lott, R-Miss., ran the Senate, using parliamentary tactics to deny Democrats for weeks at a time the opportunity to offer popular amendments on issues such as a patients' bill of rights, campaign fi-

nance overhaul or an increase in the minimum wage.

Daschle promises to run the Senate the old-fashioned way: throw a bill on the floor, let all sides take a whack at it for a week or two — hopefully not three — and wrap it up late on a Thursday. This strategy requires the majority, particularly one with a 51-49 edge, to take tough votes and to stick together. But being able to establish the terms of the debate is a key advantage.

"We may lose some of the things we put on the table, but we set the table," said Sen. Charles E. Schumer, D-N.Y.

For Republicans, who had nominal control under the 50-50 Senate but often lost votes, the return to the minority does not mean they will lose opportunities to push Bush's agenda.

"Under Senate rules, as we've learned from the Democrats when they were in the minority, you can offer amendments and issues that are important to you as an individual senator or as a party," said Lott, who will step aside for Daschle as soon as Congress returns from the Memorial Day recess.

Republicans and Democrats were quick to point out that although majority control of the Senate will change, the composition of the membership will not. And that the key to winning a majority is to win the center.

Can Daschle hold Democratic moderates such as Zell Miller of Georgia, Ben Nelson of Nebraska, and John B. Breaux of Louisiana? Or can they be lured away by Bush, who holds the power to sign their legislative priorities into law?

For Republican moderates, such as Olympia J. Snowe and Susan Collins of Maine, the most important question may well be whether to cast their lot with a center-left coalition comprised mostly of Democrats or to try pulling their party and their president toward the center.

Snowe said Jeffords' defection "should be a wake-up call for our party's leaders that the voices of moderate Republicans must be welcomed and respected. It demonstrates that,

---

Lott, left, did not realize the rumors of Jeffords' departure from the GOP were true and did not begin lobbying to keep him until it was too late. Daschle, center, quietly courted the Vermont Republican after learning he might be receptive. Daschle and Reid, right, will become the Senate's top two leaders.

CQ PHOTOS / SCOTT J. FERRELL

quite literally, the Republican Party can be the majority party only as long as it is big enough to accommodate the divergent views of the broad spectrum of Republicans throughout the country."

The week of May 21 was among the most surreal in recent memory inside the capitol. It opened with a scattering of rumors that Jeffords might defect, mentioned during the Sunday morning talk shows.

But the talk failed to stir the White House or Senate Republican leaders, who had been unhappy with Jeffords' stand against Bush's budget. They did not know, it became clear, that this was no idle threat by a grumpy party loyalist. They did not know Jeffords had been mulling the idea for weeks.

By Tuesday, the talk-show gossip had become menacingly real. Jeffords met with Vice President Dick Cheney at the Capitol around noon that day, and the news spread at the weekly GOP policy luncheon shortly thereafter. Jeffords was ferried to the White House for a mid-afternoon one-on-one with Bush in the Oval Office.

By most accounts, the meeting did not go well. Bush asked Jeffords if his administration had treated him poorly, and Jeffords responded that the problems were over policy.

But, Jeffords made clear, they also were intractable. He would later tell Vermont reporters that he used his time alone with Bush to say "very frankly that I think he'll be a one-term president if he doesn't listen to his moderates."

There was little Bush could do but ask Jeffords to hold off until the tax bill was finished so Democrats would not suddenly control the conference committee on a piece of legislation that had traveled so far. "It was clear the senator's mind had already been made up," White House spokesman Ari Fleischer said May 24.

A Brief Delay, a GOP Offer

By late Tuesday, the Senate was in a frenzy, and Jeffords began informing his colleagues. He pulled Lincoln Chafee, R-R.I., off the Senate floor to speak privately on the top of the steps to the Capitol. He told Larry E. Craig of Idaho, a fellow member of the now-defunct "singing senators" quartet. He promised an announcement the next day.

On Wednesday, however, Jeffords said he would delay his decision and make an announcement in Vermont 24 hours later, prompting a last-ditch efforts by Republicans to keep him. Speculation bloomed about a leadership post for the Vermont iconoclast. Just before he got on the plane to Burlington, Jeffords met with about 10 of his colleagues in a heartfelt meeting just off the Senate floor.

"It was the most emotional time that I have ever had in my life, with my closest friends urging me not to do what I

The Transfer Of Leadership

Sen. James M. Jeffords of Vermont has announced that he will leave the Republican Party and become an Independent. He will do so no sooner than June 5, but when he changes his party affiliation, Tom Daschle, D-S.D., will automatically become the Senate Majority Leader.

Trent Lott, R-Miss., will become the minority leader, and all the chairmen of the Senate's 20 committees will switch from Republicans to Democrats. The special 50-50 power-sharing agreement that Lott and Daschle previously struck will dissolve.

A new organizational resolution will have to be approved by the Senate, finalizing committee rosters and giving freshmen, who without the 50-50 plan will have no assignments, seats on committees. The resolution, which must be negotiated and is subject to a filibuster, will give Democrats one-seat majorities. It is expected to leave unchanged the even split of staff and resources that had been agreed to under the 50-50 deal.

—*Andrew Taylor*

was going to do because it affected their lives very substantially," Jeffords recalled in his announcement.

By leaving the GOP, Jeffords will strip his colleagues — including some close friends — of their chairmanships. Charles E. Grassley of Iowa, who along with Jeffords was among the handful of GOP freshmen in the 1974 post-Watergate class, saw his long-sought dream of running the Finance Committee dissipate after a maddeningly short few months in control.

As for Democrats, most were careful not to say anything impolitic before the announcement was final. Daschle, who along with Democratic Whip Harry Reid of Nevada quietly worked to cement Jeffords' decision to join their caucus, secluded himself with colleagues and aides.

Reid, who promises to be a major player in helping Daschle run the Senate, would be in line to head the Environment and Public Works Committee. But he opted to step aside, several senators confirmed, to focus on the whip post and to offer Jeffords the chairmanship of the committee.

"He's a team player par excellence," said Joseph I. Lieberman, D-Conn.

Adding to the tumult was renewed speculation that Georgia Democrat Miller might leave his party and preserve a 50-50 Senate run by Republicans. "This might be a short-lived [Democratic] majority," said a Democratic lobbyist roaming the halls of the Senate on Wednesday.

But Miller, who later acknowledged in a televised interview that he had toyed with the idea of making some sort of switch, quickly settled the rumors: "I will not switch to the Republican Party and have no need to proclaim myself an independent," Miller said in a statement. "But a word of warning to my fellow Democrats at this time," Miller added ominously: "What is sorely needed around here is much more getting along and much less getting even."

Jeffords gave his speech at a hotel in Burlington. Around Washington, he is known as an uninspiring orator, and in hallway conversations he can be halting. But in Vermont, Jeffords was forceful and direct.

He said today's national Republican Party had lurched too far to the right to accommodate the moderate-to-progressive traditions of the party in Vermont.

"It is only natural to expect that people like myself, who have been honored with positions of leadership, will largely support the president's agenda. And yet, more and more, I find I cannot," Jeffords said. "Looking ahead, I can see more and more instances where I'll disagree with the president on very fundamental issues — the issues of choice, the direction of the judiciary, tax and spending decisions, missile defense, energy and the environment."

The switch in control comes as the Senate agenda was

sure to turn to issues Democrats would have forced onto the agenda anyway. They were poised to take advantage of Senate rules that permit any senator to offer unrelated legislation to most bills that come to the floor.

The looming shift in power will focus much attention on Daschle, a soft-spoken but steely protégé of former Majority Leader George J. Mitchell, D-Maine (1980-95). Mitchell skillfully ran the Senate from 1989 to 1995, and many insiders believe he inflicted extraordinary damage to the presidency of the elder Bush.

It also gives such legends as Byrd and Kennedy their gavels back. In fact, the re-emergence of Byrd, whose penchant for home-state projects is legendary, gives Republicans a bogeyman to help paper over their own internal divisions on federal spending.

House and Senate Republicans faced the prospect of an internal holy war this summer on appropriations, as conservatives insisted on meeting Bush's demand for a 4 percent spending increase while more moderate appropriators argued that was not realistic.

Byrd could become a convenient scapegoat for higher spending, but he signaled May 24 that he would endeavor to live within the spending limits set by the fiscal 2002 budget resolution (H Con Res 83). "The change in the Senate majority does not change the fundamental dynamics of the . . . appropriations process," he said.

House Republicans are free to continue passing Bush's agenda untrammeled. In fact, some lawmakers and aides suggested a renewed emphasis on Republican purity in the House because many concessions to the Senate would no longer be made in advance. "It lets us be a little more conservative than we would have been," said a GOP leadership aide.

Republicans had always worried the Senate might switch hands, but most people focused on the possibility that an elderly member such as 98-year-old Strom Thurmond, R-S.C., might die and be replaced by a Democrat.

It is to Democrats' advantage that they did not take over the Senate by any default or fluke. It is difficult to imagine the triumphant entrance of Daschle onto the national stage had he become majority leader through no effort of his own.

"We know that we have a divided government — Republicans in the White House and now Democrats leading the Senate," Daschle said in remarks carried live on cable networks. "The only way we can accomplish our agenda, the only way that the administration will be able to accomplish their agenda, is if we truly work together."

Aftermath

As Republicans met after Jeffords' announcement to discuss their next steps, Snowe urged them to give moderates a position in the leadership, which was awarded to Arlen Specter, R-Pa., the next day.

"This should never have happened," Snowe told reporters after what was said to be a difficult party meeting. "For the first time in history, we had all three branches of government, and now we've lost it. Hopefully, we're going to learn something from that."

Bush spoke in Cleveland after Jeffords' announcement, but he rejected suggestions that the party had failed him: "I respect Sen. Jeffords, but respectfully, I couldn't disagree more."

Democrats will have to work together, as well. One potential problem concerns the decision of Joseph R. Biden Jr., D-Del., to waffle on the question of whether he would take the chairmanship of the Foreign Relations Committee, where he is the top Democrat, or return to the helm of Judiciary, where he has seniority.

If Biden were to opt for Judiciary, which could offer a platform for his national political ambitions, it would create a domino effect that would shuffle the leadership of several committees. The loser in this scenario would be Tom Harkin, D-Iowa, who would lose the politically valuable chair of Agriculture just as a difficult re-election bid heats up.

"That's a legitimate concern," Biden said.

Harkin said he has no doubts he will get the Agriculture chair, and aides to other senators who would be affected by a Biden switch dismissed the notion that it might actually occur.

Meanwhile, Republicans used the waning days and hours of their ability to control the floor to win confirmation of several nominations, including the controversial pick of Theodore Olson to be solicitor general.

On May 23, for example, a total of 19 nominations were confirmed, and during the legislative "wrap-up," six bills were passed by unanimous consent.

"It feels like we're the Polish parliament passing bills and naming government officials as the German tanks come into view outside the walls of Warsaw," quipped a GOP leadership aide.

Nuts and Bolts

The looming transformation of a 50-50 Senate to 50-49-1 unravels the carefully negotiated power-sharing accord reached by Lott and Daschle in January. Under that plan, committee rosters were evenly divided, as were the allocations of staff resources and office space.

The all-important question of the makeup of Senate conference committees was left unresolved, and in a sign of how difficult managing the Senate had become, Lott and Daschle still had not settled that issue even though a bankruptcy bill had passed both chambers and was ready for final negotiations.

Now, Democrats will have an edge in conference talks.

Jeffords' decision to bolt the GOP will take effect once the tax bill conference report is sent to president Bush.

Once Jeffords becomes an independent, Daschle will automatically become majority leader, a post which gives him authority to set the floor schedule.

Among the first tasks will be to establish new committee rosters to give Democrats a one-seat edge in every committee save for the traditionally evenly split Ethics panel.

It takes agreement of both parties in the Senate to name committee rosters, but Republicans are not expected to offer a major struggle. There was an explicit understanding when Daschle and Lott negotiated the 50-50 agreement that if either party won outright control, that party would earn a single-seat edge on committees.

"I have changed my party label, but I have not changed by beliefs," Jeffords said to close his seismic announcement. "Indeed, my decision is about affirming the principles that have shaped my career. I hope that the people of Vermont will understand it. I hope in time that my colleagues will as well. I am confident that it is the right decision." ◆

A Majority Leader's Real Debut

Tom Daschle, D-S.D., became majority leader in early June, when James M. Jeffords of Vermont switched from Republican to Independent. But the broad implications of that switch only became clear when Daschle succeeded in getting a patients' bill of rights passed by the Senate, showing that he was capable of using his authority in setting the Senate agenda to impose Democratic priorities on the national agenda. At the time, no one anticipated that President Bush, who opposed that bill, could maneuver the House into protecting him from having to sign or veto it.

Quick Contents

Senate Majority Leader Tom Daschle used the common tactic of threatening to delay a holiday recess, and the uncommon tactic of holding his party in line, to produce a big legislative victory on a patients' bill of rights. But the Senate remains closely split and success on Daschle's next agenda item is by no means assured.

Tom Daschle's forceful debut as Senate majority leader was made with the help of every floor leader's greatest friend: the irresistible lure of the recess.

Aided significantly by the overpowering desire of senators to fly home for the July Fourth break — and by an unbroken string of floor vote victories — the South Dakota Democrat made good on a promise that the Democrats' signature patients' rights bill would be passed intact and on time.

The final 59-36 vote on the bill (S 1052) was obviously a big win for the rookie majority leader. But Senate insiders also were impressed that Daschle held to his pledge to bring the bill to a conclusion before releasing members for their break.

"We had a job to do," Daschle said, "and we did it."

To be sure, Daschle had plenty working in his favor. Republicans made it clear they did not want to be seen holding up the bill, which scores high in public opinion polls. And Democrats stood fast with Daschle, dutifully casting difficult floor votes and rearranging travel schedules to make sure the majority leader's threats of a weekend session were taken seriously. But it was by no means a flawless performance. Daschle seemed to overplay his leverage on a fiscal 2001 supplemental spending bill, in the process aggravating appropriators in both parties.

"Listen, Daschle said he was going to move this, this was his priority, and he's held his troops together and he's . . . made compromises that kept a firm coalition of support together," said Thomas E. Mann, a senior fellow at the Brookings Institution. "You've got to say, 'First test passed with flying colors.' "

As he did with campaign finance legislation, which passed the Senate in April when Democrats were in the minority, Daschle held his caucus together against GOP assaults. And as with campaign finance, and the education bill that followed, the hurly-burly method of letting bills live or die — or change shape entirely — on the Senate floor seems once again to be at the fore.

Whether Daschle's win on patients' rights translates into future success remains to be

Daschle's big win on patients' rights does not assure future victories.

seen. Senate rules offer the minority ample ways to derail even the strongest majority leader, much less one with only a 51-49 margin to back him up. Despite the promising start, Daschle will have plenty of chances to take his lumps with debates on increasing the minimum wage, energy policy, overhauling the electoral system and adding a prescription drug benefit to the Medicare system.

A Good Start

Still, so far so good for Daschle, who took over as Senate leader on June 4. For more than a week, he vowed to keep the Senate in for as long as it took to pass the patients' rights bill. A rare Saturday session was promised. Daschle threatened to keep the Senate in session every day of the recess, except on Sunday and the Fourth of July itself.

Threatening members' sacrosanct recesses is one of the few ways of getting the notoriously difficult-to-control Senate to bend to a majority leader's will. Sometimes it works;

By Andrew Taylor / June 30, 2001

Plenty of Sparks Generated By Senate's Power Transfer

After a month-long negotiation that became a case study in distrust, mixed signals and petty bickering, the Senate finally gave voice vote approval to a critical resolution (S Res 120) that completes the transfer of power to the Democrats.

The June 29 resolution means Democrats will claim a one-seat edge on Senate committees to reflect the Senate's switch to Democratic control.

What was remarkable about the talks was that on each of the three final sticking points — the treatment of Supreme Court nominees, making the individual objections of a senator to a judicial nomination public and preserving committee pacts on office space — Republicans and Democrats essentially agreed. And had since early June.

After weeks of waffling, the five Republican senators negotiating with Majority Leader Tom Daschle, D-S.D., dropped demands for a futile vote on a plan to guarantee floor debate on Supreme Court nominees even when the Judiciary Committee rejected them.

Democrats had initially offered only non-binding language noting that "most but not all" Supreme Court nominations have received floor votes in recent history. (An exception was Associate Justice Abe Fortas' 1968 nomination to become chief justice, which died by filibuster.) But exasperated Republicans held out for more, and Democrats ultimately said they "have every intention" of bringing high court nominees to the floor.

But Democrats immediately embraced a GOP bid to require that senators who kill home-state judicial nominees with "blue slips" reveal such moves to the public.

But it took weeks to massage the terms under which Judiciary Committee Chairman Patrick J. Leahy, D-Vt., and ranking Republican Orrin G. Hatch of Utah would accomplish the goal. Leahy repeatedly said his word should have been good enough. Instead, they issued a joint letter.

Space Wars

Among the most sensitive topics was the allocation of office space in the Capitol and in the Senate's three office buildings. The top Republicans and Democrats on most committees agreed earlier this year, when the Senate was 50-50, to freeze staff budgets and office allotments in the event one party claimed a clear majority in the middle of the session.

But Daschle, who said he would honor those agreements, insisted on reiterating that they remained subject to the authority of the Rules Committee. Anxiety peaked when the new Rules Committee Chairman, Christopher J. Dodd, D-Conn., installed Sen. Hillary Rodham Clinton, D-N.Y., into additional space.

Clinton already was granted the additional rooms under Senate rules that provide bigger offices to members representing more populous states, but another senator was slow to move out. Everyone agreed that Clinton deserved the space, but the fact that it was Dodd's first act as chairman unnerved Republicans. The whole episode — including a New York Post story headlined "Hill's Office Hijack" — demonstrated just how touchy office space questions have become. "The Democrats have had the gavel for two weeks, and the first thing they do is give Hillary more space," a Republican aide told the newspaper.

Said another GOP aide: "All politics is local, and space is the most local of all."

— *Andrew Taylor*

sometimes it doesn't.

"It's a lot easier to threaten to keep members around and have votes than it is to do it," said Daschle's predecessor, Minority Leader Trent Lott, R-Miss. "Members have a way of saying 'adios.' "

But Daschle kept restating his threat. "I think that [Republicans] still doubt whether we're going to stay here and finish," he said Thursday, June 28, as the pressure to complete the bill began to intensify. "But I will tell you that we will be . . . here and voting on Saturday and on Monday, and I've made that clear."

Said top bill sponsor Edward M. Kennedy, D-Mass.: "Every [Democrat] knew that Tom Daschle was serious about this at the beginning, and I don't think the Republicans did, because we've seen what's happened when it's been threatened by other leaders."

Beyond threatening the recess, Daschle also refused to turn to President Bush's $6.5 billion must-pass fiscal 2001 appropriations bill (S 1077) until he won assurances that the patients' rights bill could be completed before the recess. This, too, was a tactic straight from the majority leader's playbook: hold hostage a bill dearly sought by the president of the opposing party as leverage to win cooperation from the president's allies on the matter at hand.

Daschle's decision to hold off action on the supplemental — despite a direct appeal from Bush in a June 27 telephone call — bought him intense criticism from Republicans, who said Daschle was putting the nation's trial lawyers ahead of its fighting men and women. "That is poor leadership and that is misplaced priorities," said GOP Conference Chairman Rick Santorum of Pennsylvania.

But rather than deflect the supplemental question, Daschle embraced it; adding its passage to the list of things the Senate would do before its recess. The organizing resolution (S Res 120), establishing committee rosters to reflect the shift in Senate control from 50-50 to a 50-49-1 chamber led by Democrats, was on the list, too. (*Box, this page*)

Daschle went two for three: His efforts on the supplemental failed to bear fruit, and had no apparent impact on the Senate's communal decision to wrap up the patients' rights bill.

Instead, the supplemental was put off until the Senate returns July 9, leaving little time to pass the bill, get it conferenced with the House and on to Bush's desk before the Pentagon would have to curtail certain training and hiring activities.

In the process, Daschle disappointed top appropriators, including Chairman Robert C. Byrd, D-W.Va., by refusing to put aside the patients' rights bill to allow for consideration of the supplemental. Top Appropriations Committee Republican Ted Stevens of Alaska pleaded with Daschle to move to the supplemental so a quick conference with the House could get the bill to Bush's desk before the break. But Daschle held out for a deal on the patients' rights bill. He wanted Republicans to agree to a finite, manageable list of amendments, but with none forthcoming work on patients' rights slogged on.

For his part, Byrd scoffed at suggestions he was putting Daschle through his paces over the supplemental. "It's not an early test of Daschle. Forget it," he said in an interview. "It's an effort to get this bill done — keep it within its $6.5 billion allocation — and get it on the president's desk."

The situation with appropriators got downright ugly Thursday, June 28 when the notoriously cranky Stevens faced off with Daschle on the floor, and took umbrage when Daschle intimated that passing the supplemental was more important than Stevens' plans to go salmon fishing. (Box, this page)

Stevens said it was imperative to pass the supplemental immediately, that the House — also preparing to adjourn for the all-important recess — would be willing to stay in Washington to wrap up the supplemental. In fact, the House had made it clear they would take off no matter what, said House Appropriations Committee spokesman John Scofield.

Republicans objected that Daschle was, in Lott's words, "holding our nation's security and our armed forces hostage" to "legislation that will help trial lawyers." But Republicans acknowledged Daschle was only trying to gain whatever edge he could.

"Lott said at a meeting the other day he'd do the same thing," said lead bill sponsor John McCain, R-Ariz.

During his six-year tenure as minority leader, Daschle often chaffed at the way Republicans ran the Senate. Par-

Daschle's 'Cheap Shot'

In a week in which he tried to make all the right moves, Majority Leader Tom Daschle, D-S.D., made one high-profile stumble that left the Senate buzzing. He insulted one of the chamber's most senior Republicans.

During a June 28 exchange with Daschle on the floor, ranking Appropriations Committee Republican Ted Stevens pressed for action on a crucial supplemental appropriations bill (S 1077). With the possibility of a weekend session looming, Stevens vented frustration about a possible delay in his plans to check on a forest fire in his beloved Alaska, and to heed the "urgent call of the king salmon."

Daschle said the supplemental was "more important than fishing. . . . Vacations are secondary to work."

Oops.

Stevens jumped to his feet. "That is a little bit of a cheap shot. I am not talking about a vacation. I am willing to stay here as long as any other senator," he fumed. "I'm talking about the realities of the House. Leader, I am not going to forget that. That was a cheap shot."

Off the floor Stevens was livid, but a contrite Daschle instantly saw his blunder and called to apologize. "Tom called me, and we agreed that we all say things in the heat of battle," a calmer Stevens said later. "We've been friends for a long time, and we just agreed to forget that."

— Andrew Taylor

ticularly in the two years leading up to the 2000 elections, Republicans went to great lengths to minimize opportunities for Democrats to cast floor votes on agenda items such as the patients' rights bill, campaign finance overhaul and gun control. Republicans acknowledged privately that they were trying to protect vulnerable lawmakers from politically difficult votes.

The Old-Fashioned Way

Upon taking control, Daschle promised to run the Senate the old-fashioned way by bringing a bill to the floor, letting members fight for a week or two, then using whatever power was at his disposal to wrap it up. Often that means the opposition simply gets tired of fighting a losing battle, which is what happened on the patients' rights bill.

"Why stay here for three more days and end up with the same bill?" asked Bill Frist, R-Tenn., one of the GOP's floor leaders on the measure.

Observed a chuckling Christopher J. Dodd, D-Conn., of the Republicans' plight: "If you're in a hole, stop digging and get out."

Kennedy credited Daschle with successfully dissuading Democrats to offer amendments that might have extended the debate. Such amendments would have detracted from the impression Democrats hoped to convey to the public: Republicans were stalling.

For their part, Republicans fumed that Daschle was threatening to delay a holiday recess to ram through the patients' rights bill after he had "slow-walked" Senate action on Bush's landmark education bill (S 1). That measure took seven weeks of on-again, off-again Senate debate, and Daschle used delaying tactics to try to extract additional funding for pet programs.

Republicans also realized that caving in to Daschle's threat would make the majority leader look good. "It's become a little manhood test on both sides," said Chuck Hagel, R-Neb. "And that's not good. . . . We've got to stay above that."

Daschle's threats were not without risk, however. Lawmakers have only so much patience, and he might have faced revolt had members been forced to skip Fourth of July parades and quality time with their families back home.

Throughout the week, Daschle denied he was playing hardball by promising weekend sessions or by holding off on bringing up the supplemental until the patients' rights bill was passed. In fact, Daschle sought to dispel any notion that he was trying to use that bill as leverage to make Republicans knuckle under and allow a final vote on patients' rights.

"I'm just your humble little majority leader," Daschle said, "doing his job." ◆

Congressional Committees

Traditionally, committee chairmen wielded a tremendous amount of power as the gateways for legislation. The only bills that moved were bills the chairmen wanted, and over decades of Democratic Party control, some veteran chairmen in the House of Representatives grew the jurisdiction of their committees into impressive kingdoms of legislative authority. But the Republican takeover of the House in 1995 ushered in a new era for the role of chairmen. Then-Speaker Newt Gingrich kept much of the legislative power for himself, making his chairmen in many cases simply conduits for his policy ideas. In addition, the GOP changed the House rules, giving chairmen six-year term limits, an unheard of curtailing of power. This bold stroke shattered the fiefdoms of the old Democratic House, fulfilling a GOP promise to make the House less hidebound than it had been, but the change further weakened the institutional power of those who hold the gavels. The 107th Congress marked the end of the self-imposed terms for many chairmen, leading at least three senior GOP lawmakers to retire rather than carry on without the mantel of committee leadership. Prospective replacements, which in the past were chosen strictly by seniority and the preference of the Speaker, were put through an application process that included job interviews before the party's Steering Committee, yet another winnowing of the once-unquestioned authority for chairmen.

Still, with all that has changed, the committees remain a central component of the operations of Congress. Chairmen retain a level of autonomy that makes them important figures to be dealt with in the House and Senate, and their committees are the forum in which policy proposals are honed into legislation. At the same time, the emerging management style of President Bush seems to have elevated the importance of committees because the White House, in contrast to previous administrations, does not send Congress detailed legislative proposals. Instead, the administration offers policy guidelines and principles, and leaves the detail work of writing bills to the give-and-take of committees.

Seniority Is No Longer Enough

When the GOP won control of the House in 1994, it imposed a six-year term limit on its committee chairmen, triggering a wave of retirements from the House in 2000 and ushering in a new method of choosing chairmen.

Saxby Chambliss, the Republican from Georgia, sat quietly in an empty room in the basement of the Capitol on Dec. 5, shuffling through a file of notes balanced on his lap.

The man who served as the vice chairman of the House Budget Committee during the 106th Congress was waiting to be called into his first job interview in more than six years.

The position: Budget Committee chairman.

As he waited, another applicant, Rep. Jim Nussle, R-Iowa, was in the room next door using big charts and a Power Point computer presentation to make his pitch for the same job.

When Chambliss was finally called, he entered the room armed only with his notes and a bag of Georgia peanuts, which he handed out to the selection panel, better known as the Steering Committee.

Chambliss and Nussle were the first two members to take part in a historic new process for selecting committee chairmen. In the past, chairmen have been selected purely by seniority, or simply at the discretion of the Speaker, as was the case under the reign of Speaker Newt Gingrich, R-Ga. (1979-99).

This year, however, members vying for chairmanships — some with more than two decades of congressional experience, some just completing their second term in office — went through in-depth interviews during which they were questioned on legislative strategies, leadership abilities and communications skills.

To a remarkable extent, the new system implemented by Speaker J. Dennis Hastert of Illinois has opened the traditionally insulated decision of who runs committees, and therefore who sets the congressional agenda, to the wishes of rank-and-file members of the Republican Conference.

With the opening and closing of a door in the Capitol basement, through which 29 candidates for chairmanships paraded during two days of secluded interviews, it could be seen that some new traits will be prized in choosing chairmen. Along with the traditional influences of seniority, contacts and the will of the leadership, add these characteristics to the likely choices in the 107th Congress: communication skills and the watchword of 2001, bipartisanship.

"It was unlike anything I've ever been through," said Nussle as he emerged from his 30-minute interview. "It started off with an eery amount of silence. It was a nerve-racking event. I'm sure [the Steering Committee members] were thinking to themselves, 'Holy cow. I'd hate to go through that.'"

The interviews took place in a small room with white walls and tables set in a circle. The Steering members sat at the tables, and the candidates either sat with the others, or, as Nussle did, stood in the middle throughout their presentation and subsequent questioning.

Even those on the Steering Committee admitted discomfort at having to judge their colleagues and friends.

"I had some reservations about making people grovel for something that should have been sort of like an entitlement because of their seniority," said Rep. Sonny Callahan, R-Ala., one of the 23 men and two women who make up the Steering Committee. "But this [interview process] has given me a great appreciation for the depth of talent we have in the conference."

The entire GOP leadership, from Speaker to conference secretary, and select committee chairmen are automatically appointed to the Steering panel under conference rules. They take 11 of the 25 seats. The other 14 members are elected to the panel by their classmates or regional colleagues.

Those non-leadership members almost unanimously say they have an obligation to consult their rank-and-file colleagues before casting their votes for chairmen. In addition, each Steering Committee member has his own list of priorities that will influence the choices.

Although the new process allows expanded input from the rank and file, Hastert and Majority Leader Dick Armey of Texas retain greater say than any other committee member. The Speaker has five votes in the chairmanship balloting; the majority leader has two votes. Everyone else has one.

The committee is slated to name its nominations for chairmen on Jan. 4. Unlike in the past, when the Speaker sought conference approval of all his chairmanship choices with a single vote, each nomination will be presented on an individual ballot. If any nominee is rejected, the vacancy will be sent back to the Steering Committee to choose a new nominee.

Members of the Steering Committee say they are well aware of the burden that rests on their shoulders.

"I take it very seriously," said Rep. John M. McHugh of New York. "We're a product of the committee process. If we select chairs who are unwilling or incapable of creating a good product, it will have a profound effect on our conference, the Congress and the American people."

A New Era

The new interview process is a direct result of term limits on chairmanships that Republicans instituted when they first won control of the House in 1994. Those six-year limits are up at the end of this year, and there are 13 committees now in need of chairmen.

Throughout the past year, Hastert was lobbied hard to grant waivers for a number of the term-limited chairs, but he refused to do so.

Instead, anyone who wanted a waiver was told he could apply for one, and then get in line for the interview process

By Karen Foerstel / Dec. 9, 2000

like everyone else.

"The Speaker has tried to create a fair, equitable, more open process," said Hastert communications director Pete Jeffries.

The move has the overwhelming support of rank-and-file Republicans, who last month voted 27-141 to defeat a proposal that would have repealed the limits.

The new interview process is a far cry from previous years when seniority — and leadership connections — ruled supreme.

Longtime Hill-watchers say that during the Gingrich era

Crane, talking to aides before his interview with the Steering Committee, would have ascended to the chairmanship of Ways and Means under the old, seniority-based system.

it was easy to figure out who would become the next chairmen by watching which members were frequent visitors to the Speaker's office.

Under Gingrich, the Steering Committee was charged with officially voting on the slate of chairmen presented to them by the Speaker, but "it was pretty perfunctory," admits Rep. Dave Camp, R-Mich., who is now serving his second term on the panel.

Democrats used a similar system during their 40 years of House control.

Members of today's GOP Steering Committee praise Hastert for instituting the interview process and allowing greater input from the rank and file.

"In general, it has really been beneficial for us to understand where everybody's coming from," said panel member Iowa Rep. Tom Latham. "In the long term it will be beneficial because every new chair will have a plan in place. Everyone will have thought through their agenda and their strategies."

Other panel members say the new and open selection process will force members to stay on their toes and present their best legislative abilities. "It's giving those people who are hoping to be chairmen an indication that, 'Hey, if I do not meet the criteria . . . I might not be here next time,' "

said Callahan.

But some observers say the competition may prove divisive and result in ill will between the winners and losers, making productivity difficult next year.

"There's no question it will create hard feelings," said John J. Pitney Jr., associate professor of government at Claremont McKenna College in California. "It's a clash of ambitions, and when they clash, there's always blood on the floor."

Pitney predicted that there will ultimately be little deviation from the seniority system in choosing chairmen. "It's the easiest and least painful way to go," he said. "They could save themselves a lot of trouble by going with seniority. Republicans have enough heavy lifting as it is."

Seniority

Indeed, while the new process looks beyond seniority, the issue is still very much on the minds of the Steering Committee members.

"Seniority is an element, but we as a committee haven't settled on the notion of how it will impact our decisions," said Steering member Rep. John E. Sweeney of New York.

Others on the panel said they will use seniority only as the tie-breaking factor between candidates who prove equal in all other categories.

But one very influential member of the Steering panel said seniority will be his No. 1 priority.

"Seniority is really important," said House Whip Tom DeLay of Texas. "I start with seniority and then everything else follows."

Length of service has carried great weight in several of the chairmanship races now being waged.

On the Budget Committee, Nussle is touting himself as the most senior Republican vying for the top seat. Although Chambliss holds the title of vice chair, he has served on Budget for only two years, compared with Nussle's six years.

"I walk in as the most senior member of the committee," Nussle said. "Anyone else who goes in without the seniority has to overcome the issue of experience."

Chambliss counters that as vice chair he worked as the "right-hand man" of current Budget Chairman John R. Kasich of Ohio. Kasich is retiring from Congress at the end of the year.

Two other more-junior members, Reps. John E. Sununu of New Hampshire and Nick Smith of Michigan, are also vying for the top Budget post.

Seniority also is an issue in the race for the powerful Ways and Means chairmanship, which was left open by the retirement of Rep. Bill Archer of Texas, who was term-limited out of the spot.

Rep. Phil M. Crane of Illinois is next in line, but he faces an aggressive challenge from Rep. Bill Thomas of California, who is third on the totem pole.

Before entering his Steering Committee interview, Thomas said he would not talk much about seniority. He

The Steering Committee's Members and Mission

The Republican Steering Committee includes members of the House leadership as well as representatives elected from caucuses — primarily based on geographic region — within the party. This is the first time the committee, which typically handles only committee assignments, interviewed prospective candidates for chairmanships. The selection of chairmen has traditionally involved a mix of seniority and the discretion of the Speaker.

The chart below lists the members, their title or the group they represent, and a note on their philosophy for choosing chairmen or possible political influences.

— *Karen Foerstel*

	TITLE OR REGION	NOTES
J. Dennis Hastert, Ill.	Speaker	Has five votes on Steering Committee.
Dick Armey, Texas	Majority Leader	Has two votes on Steering Committee.
Tom DeLay, Texas	Majority Whip	Says seniority is paramount in selecting chairmen.
Roy Blunt, Mo.	Chief Deputy Whip	DeLay suggests they will vote together on chairmen.
J.C. Watts Jr., Okla.	Conference Chairman	Wants strong communicators who can make the GOP case directly to the public.
Christopher Cox, Calif.	Policy Committee Chairman	Has a strong reputation for working with Democrats.
Deborah Pryce, Ohio	Conference Vice Chairman	As Rules member, remains close to Hastert.
Barbara Cubin, Wyo.	Conference Secretary	Bipartisanship of chairmen "absolutely essential."
Thomas M. Davis III, Va.	NRCC Chairman	Says ideology is secondary to having a plan for the committee.
C.W. Bill Young, Fla.	Appropriations Committee Chairman	Ascended to chairmanship based on seniority in 1998.
David Dreier, Calif.	Rules Committee Chairman	Chosen by Hastert to chair Rules in 1998.
Vacant	Ways and Means Committee Chairman	Bill Archer of Texas retired.
Ken Calvert, Calif.	California	Will consider the wishes of California members.
Sonny Callahan, Ala.	Cotton South	Interview process has made him change his previous view that seniority was most important.
Dave Camp, Mich.	East North Central	Ability to work with party leaders is first consideration.
Tom Latham, Iowa	Great Plains	Says interviews helped chairmen develop plans.
Ralph Regula, Ohio	Mid-Atlantic	Feels responsibility to represent regional interests.
John. M. McHugh, N.Y.	Atlantic Coast	Believes this selection process will set a good tone for the 107th Congress.
John Linder, Ga.	Southeast	Wants chairmen who are "not too confrontational."
Cass Ballenger, N.C.	Tidewater South	Considers voting "very much an improvement" over old seniority system.
Joe L. Barton, Texas	West South Central	Believes Steering Committee will follow the lead of Hastert, Armey and DeLay.
Bob Stump, Ariz.	West	Was interviewed by his colleagues for chairmanship of Armed Services Committee.
Don Young, Alaska	Small states	Was interviewed by his colleagues for chairmanship of Transportation and Infrastructure Committee, though he faces no opposition.
Jerry Moran, Kansas	105th class	Feels "total obligation" to consider wishes of his class.
John E. Sweeney, N.Y.	106th class	Feels an "absolute" responsibility to consider wishes of his class.
John Culberson, Texas	107th class	Replaced Archer in Congress.

did, however, wear on his lapel a large red, white and blue button he dug out of his files from the 1980s that read, "Save America, Bentsen-Roth, Pickle-Thomas Super IRA."

The button was a not-so-subtle reminder to the panel that Thomas, who helped create a new individual retirement account, has been involved in key legislation for many years.

"Crane isn't the only senior member on the committee," Thomas said, pointing to the button.

During his presentation, Thomas presented Hastert with a letter that, according to Thomas, is signed by a majority of the Ways and Means members expressing their support for him as chair.

And just to be safe, Thomas took a cue from the Chambliss peanut gambit and brought bags of California pistachios for the Steering members.

Also running for the Ways and

Means chairmanship is E. Clay Shaw Jr. of Florida, who is currently fourth in line for the post.

Personal Ties

An advantage Crane may have over Thomas and Shaw is the home-state connection he shares with Hastert. Many predict that it will be exceedingly difficult for Hastert not to side with a fellow Illinoisan.

Many Steering members, in fact, say regional alliances will factor into their decision-making process.

Panel member Rep. Ralph Regula of Ohio said region is an issue for him in the race for the Commerce Committee, which pits W.J. "Billy" Tauzin of Louisiana against Michael G. Oxley of Ohio."I do have a responsibility to represent [my colleagues from Ohio]," Regula said. "Oxley is an Ohio person. It's in my mind."

Along with regional alliances, members serving on the Steering Committee as representatives of their classes say they will also consider the opinions of their colleagues.

"I have a total obligation to them," said Jerry Moran, R-Kan., who was elected by the GOP class of the 105th Congress to represent them on the panel. "I'm very interested in the opinions my classmates have about who they want as chairmen of their committees."

And the new interview process forces many members of the Steering panel to pick among close friends and colleagues with whom they have worked over the years.

Members admit it will be hard to ignore such personal ties. "I don't think you can separate any of those things in this business," said Steering member John Linder of Georgia.

It will be particularly difficult for panel members Bob Stump of Arizona and Don Young of Alaska to overlook their personal ties in two races. Both are running for chairmanships themselves. Stump is in a contested race for the Armed Services Committee. He is being challenged by Reps. Curt Weldon of Pennsylvania and Duncan Hunter of California.

Young is running unopposed for the Transportation and Infrastructure Committee.

Bipartisanship

One topic that repeatedly cropped up during the candidate interviews, ac-

House Leaders in the 107th Congress

— REPUBLICANS —

Speaker of the House
J. Dennis Hastert, Ill.

Majority Leader
Dick Armey, Texas

Majority Whip
Tom DeLay, Texas

Conference Chairman
J.C. Watts Jr., Okla.

Conference Vice Chairman
Deborah Pryce, Ohio

Conference Secretary
Barbara Cubin, Wyo.

Policy Committee Chairman
Christopher Cox, Calif.

National Republican Congressional Committee
Thomas M. Davis III, Va.

— DEMOCRATS —

Minority Leader
Richard A. Gephardt, Mo.

Minority Whip
David E. Bonior, Mich.

Caucus Chairman
Martin Frost, Texas

Caucus Vice Chairman
Robert Menendez, N.J.

Democratic Congressional Campaign Committee
Unnamed

Congressional Black Caucus
Eddie Bernice Johnson, Texas

cording to Steering members, was the ability to reach across the aisle and work in a bipartisan way next year.

With the new, narrower majority in the House, and what could be a 50-50 split in the Senate, members say next year's chairmen must be able to forge consensus between the parties in order to pass legislation.

"We have to achieve the doable, which is a little different from the past," said Steering member McHugh. "Most folks came into the interviews with a narrow rather than a broad agenda."

Steering member Barbara Cubin of Wyoming called bipartisan skills "absolutely essential" for chairmen next year.

Such sentiment could favor the only

two women running for chairmanships.

Reps. Marge Roukema of New Jersey, who is vying for the Banking Committee, and Sue W. Kelly of New York, who has applied for the Small Business chairmanship, are both members of the moderate GOP Tuesday Group.

Roukema, who is the senior member of the committee, is facing Rep. Richard H. Baker of Louisiana. Kelly is running against Rep. Donald Manzullo of Illinois.

Although many Steering members expressed desire for bipartisanship, several warned that they do not want chairmen to abandon GOP ideals simply because of the narrow House majority.

Instead, they said they want chairmen who will take advantage of the Republican-controlled Congress and the potentially Republican White House to push forward the party agenda.

"I don't want our chairs to think that bipartisanship means doing everything the Democrats want them to do," said GOP Conference Chairman and Steering member J.C. Watts Jr. of Oklahoma.

"We shouldn't reach out [to Democrats] at all costs and abandon everything we want to accomplish."

Watts said his top priority in picking chairmen will be communication skills. "Somebody who can generate as much press as possible for telling our side of the story," Watts said. "I would like to see them put as much emphasis on communications as they do on policy."

Leadership Sway

While each Steering member has a personal set of criteria, many agreed that leadership's opinion will weigh heavily on their decisions.

The new interview process has allowed for greater input in selecting chairmen, but ultimately the Speaker could still have the final say.

"I would think the members would have to be somewhat sensitive to the leadership," said Regula. "The chairmen are really their team. We want to know something about what the captains are thinking."

Panel member Rep. Joe L. Barton of Texas agreed that the desires of the Speaker, majority leader, and whip will be hard to ignore.

"If those three all spoke with a united voice," Barton said, "it would be very unlikely the rest of the group would go the other way." ◆

A Tense Opening for the 107th

The intraparty splits that will haunt Speaker J. Dennis Hastert, R-Ill., throughout the 107th Congress emerged on the very first day. The importance of committee seats caused a flare-up among a small group of Republicans who opposed Hastert's decision to split one committee into two.

Minutes before House Republicans unanimously re-elected J. Dennis Hastert of Illinois as Speaker of the House on Jan. 3, a small group of angry GOP members called a meeting with Hastert to condemn one of his first decisions of the new Congress.

About 15 Republicans on the Commerce Committee promised Hastert that they would fight the leadership decision to strip away part of the panel's jurisdiction and hand it over to a new Financial Services Committee.

During the hourlong meeting, the Republicans shuttled back and forth between the small meeting room on the second floor of the Capitol, where they complained bitterly to Hastert, and the House floor 20 feet away, where they cast their votes to retain him as Speaker.

The jurisdictional split that renamed the Commerce Committee the Energy and Commerce Committee and replaced Banking and Financial Services with Financial Services was included in a new House rules package that was adopt by a party-line vote, 215-206.

The fact that no Republican voted against the package on the opening day of the 107th Congress, despite several requests by members to postpone floor action until the jurisdiction dispute was settled, shows the loyalty Hastert has among his House troops.

But the tensions over the committee split — which in itself was designed in part to head off a nasty division that was opening between two lawmakers vying for control of Commerce — offers fresh evidence of how difficult Hastert's job will be in his second term as Speaker.

The grand, egalitarian process of selecting chairmen by rank-and-file vote instead of leadership dictum drew praise, but it simultaneously exposed the intraparty fissures between conservatives and moderates that began challenging Hastert at the outset of the new Congress.

The Senate, too, roiled beneath the surface of a placid vote on Jan. 5 that set new committee ratios reflecting the 50-50 partisan split of that chamber. Republican Leader Trent Lott of Mississippi managed to win approval of the organizational plan he negotiated with Democratic Leader Tom Daschle of South Dakota, but the cost to Lott of meeting Daschle's core demand on committees began accruing instantly.

The transition to a new Congress more evenly split between the parties than either chamber has been in decades began uneasily the week of Jan. 1, making clear that the peacekeeping job faced by Hastert and Lott — as well as Daschle and House Minority Leader Richard A. Gephardt, D-Mo. — will be extraordinarily difficult.

Hastert's work began even before his new reign, during the meeting at the time of the speakership vote.

Members at the meeting said no voices were raised or foul words exchanged despite the strong disagreement, but that was largely out of respect for the opening-day atmosphere.

"If this had happened six months from now, all hell would have broken loose. But nobody wants to be disruptive today," one member said, adding that tempers could flare soon. "There's 24 of us [Republicans on Commerce] and a lot of votes coming down the road."

Many moderate members of the GOP are fuming over the 14 new chairmen picked this year, saying their wing of the party is not well represented among the new leaders.

Tom Petri, R-Wis., a moderate who lost to John A. Boehner of Ohio in his bid for the Education and the Workforce Committee, sent out a press release calling the chairmanship selection process a "purge of moderate Republicans."

Many moderates also were angered at the rejection of Marge Roukema, R-N.J., who, if she had won her bid for the Banking chairmanship, would have been the first woman ever to head a major committee. President-elect George W. Bush offered to name her U.S. Treasurer, but Roukema declined the job. She would have had to resign from the House to take the position.

Democratic Trouble

In addition, Hastert will have to work on his relationship with a Democratic Party that, just as it was in the previous two years, is focused on winning control of Congress in the next election in 2002.

Democrats picked up two seats in last fall's elections, and they hope the Republican monopoly of the White House and both branches of Congress will prompt voters to call for a divided government in the next elections and give Democrats House control.

Despite the warm handshake between Hastert and Gephardt during the session's opening day — and Hastert's admonition to members of both parties to "get over" the divisive presidential election — Democrats were quick to launch partisan attacks.

Even before the House was graveled into session, Democrats blasted Republicans for refusing to give them more seats on the various House committees in order to more closely reflect the overall party ratio in the chamber.

"Republicans had the opportunity to offer an olive branch, and they broke it off," said Martin Frost of Texas, chairman of the House Democratic Caucus. "This doesn't exactly demonstrate fairness."

Maxine Waters, D-Calif., said she was personally "offended" by Hastert's opening day speech to the House. "This attempt to send a message that despite what happened [with the presidential elections] that everyone will lock arms and

By Karen Foerstel with Alan K. Ota / Jan. 6, 2001

have a love fest, it's not real," said Waters. "Some of us will not 'get over it.' "

Just as Republicans are dealing with internal divides, Democrats face similar intramural skirmishes.

Two conservative Democrats refused to support Gephardt for Speaker during the opening day procedural vote, prompting the caucus to expel one of them — James A. Traficant Jr. — and effectively widen their deficit in the House.

While Gephardt and other Democratic leaders say they hope to find common ground with Republicans and the

Hastert, right, introduced new chairmen, left to right, Thomas (Ways and Means), Boehner (Education), Tauzin (Energy and Commerce) and Sensenbrenner (Judiciary).

White House, more liberal members say they will fight efforts to move the party toward the center.

"We're not pretending that our troubles are coming only from Republicans," said Waters, a member of the liberal Democratic Progressive Caucus. "We're going to be more vocal, have more challenges inside our caucus."

Peter A. DeFazio of Oregon, another Progressive Democrat, agreed and admitted that Gephardt, like Hastert, will be busy over the next two years trying to keep his party unified.

"Dick [Gephardt] is in a very difficult position," he said. "He'll have to figure out a way to hold us together with these tensions."

New Chairmanships

Hastert's first task of the 107th Congress the week of Jan. 1 was overseeing a historic new way of selecting committee chairmen.

More than two dozen Republicans ran for 13 chairmanships that were left vacant mostly as a result of term limits imposed for the first time in history on committee chairmen. Incoming chairmen of the Committee on Standards of Official Conduct and the House Administration Committee are appointed by the Speaker rather than selected through the Steering Committee process. Joel Hefley of Colorado will lead the ethics panel, but Hastert had not chosen a chairman for Administration by Jan. 5.

Rather than following the traditional seniority system and granting the chairmanship to the next person in line on the committee, Hastert decided to open the top posts to

competition. A stream of senior and junior members interviewed with the GOP Steering Committee for the chairmanships throughout the week of Dec. 4.

Steering members made their final nominations after a six-hour meeting Jan. 4, and the entire Republican Conference confirmed those nominations several hours later.

Ultimately, seniority did not prevail under the new system, and Hastert must now heal many bruised egos of members who lost.

At the top of that list is Philip M. Crane of Illinois, who has served on the Ways and Means Committee for 25 years but lost the chairmanship to Bill Thomas, R-Calif., who has almost 10 years less tenure on the panel.

Although Hastert had been expected to back Crane, a home-state colleague, he instead voted for Thomas on the Steering Committee ballot, said Hastert spokesman John Feehery. Tallies were not released for individual races, but Hastert's office said the Thomas vote was unanimous.

Immediately following the Steering Committee's selection of Thomas the morning of Jan. 4, Hastert met with Crane to break the news. To soften the blow, Hastert offered to make Crane chairman of the Joint Taxation Committee, but Crane declined the job. He did, however, accept a waiver from the term limits rule so he could retain his chairmanship of the Ways and Means Subcommittee on Trade.

Hastert called or met with all of the members who lost chairmanship races, leadership aides said, and will continue to work on mending fences over the coming weeks, offering consolation prizes to several of the rejected candidates.

Divided Jurisdiction

Another senior member who was rejected for a chairmanship bid is Roukema, who was next in line for the Banking and Financial Services Committee, behind Jim Leach, R-Iowa, who was term limited out of the position.

The leadership's decision to split the Commerce Committee's jurisdiction with the Banking panel left Roukema with no place to go.

Many members argued that the split was done not so much for policy reasons, but in order to defuse the bloody battle that had erupted between W.J. "Billy" Tauzin of Louisiana and Michael G. Oxley of Ohio, who were both vying for the Commerce Committee chairmanship.

Tauzin was awarded the slimmed-down Energy and Commerce panel, while Oxley was given the newly constituted Financial Services Committee.

The Solomonic move by Hastert to "divide the baby," in Tauzin's words, underscored the dire straits faced by House leaders in trying to quell bitter battles among Republicans for the top positions on key committees.

However, the decision to divide and weaken the authority of Commerce seemed to make ample sense from a public policy standpoint. The jurisdictional change brought the authority of the new Financial Services Committee in line with the goal of the 1999 financial services overhaul (PL 106-102), which was aimed at shattering walls between the banking, securities and insurance industries.

The barriers had first been erected between banks and securities companies by the 1933 Glass-Steagall Act. Other barriers between banks and insurers were raised by the 1956 Bank Holding Company Act.

The broadened authority for the new Financial Services panel parallels that of the Senate Banking, Housing and Urban Affairs Committee. Unlike the House, the Senate historically has kept the oversight of the three industries under one panel.

Senate Banking, Housing and Urban Affairs Chairman Phil Gramm, R-Texas, gave the House's action his blessing. "It would certainly make my life easier," he said.

In an interview on Jan. 2, shortly after a late-night meeting during which the House Republicans approved by voice vote the proposal to create the new committee, Hastert said the decision was based on solid policy grounds.

"Policy should drive this. And that's what we're doing," he said. "I studied this all during the vacation. And I talked to a lot of people. I came to the logic this is the right thing to do."

While the decision may have made sense for policy reasons, it triggered a political storm on Capitol Hill, especially among Commerce Committee members of both parties.

Ranking Democrat John D. Dingell of Michigan immediately labeled the turf change "misguided and asinine." On the floor, he warned that the decision could lay the groundwork for a "splendid disaster" comparable to the savings and loan mess of the 1980s.

During the meeting between Hastert and Commerce Committee Republicans on Jan. 3, angry members charged that they had never been consulted about the change and that their years of experience working on insurance and securities issues would now go to waste.

Several members of Commerce have requested permission to serve on both panels in order to continue their work on the issues. It is unclear whether they will be allowed to do so.

Hastert told Commerce members that negotiations would continue in the upcoming weeks to "clarify" exactly what jurisdiction will be stripped away. One point of contention is who will have authority over Internet policy questions.

Several Commerce members also asked Hastert to review which issues previously handled by the Banking panel might be transferred to Commerce.

"We're not going to agree wholesale to taking away our jurisdiction," swore one member who attended the meeting with Hastert.

Roukema said that while she may agree with the jurisdictional change on policy grounds, she questioned its timing. "A lot of people don't want to see this mixed up with the chairmanship races," she said. "The sole reason they are doing this now" is because of the race between Oxley and Tauzin.

After the Steering Committee made its official recommendations on Jan. 4, Roukema said that she was "gravely disappointed" but that she would be "gracious and a good sport as a member of the Republican team."

Asked whether her rejection was a signal by the leadership that moderates would not play a major role in the GOP agenda this session, Roukema responded, "We will make ourselves have a strong voice this Congress."

Despite the anger of some, other moderates said they

Rules Approved

The House and Senate each approved new rules to govern their operations in the 107th Congress.

The Senate
• The Senate approved a plan by voice vote Jan. 5 to restructure the chamber's organization to reflect its new 50-50 party-line split.
• The heart of the plan splits every committee evenly between the parties, but leaves Republicans as chairmen to reflect the tie-breaking vote of Vice President-elect Dick Cheney. The full Senate will be allowed to vote on a motion to place legislation on the floor calendar that is stalled by a deadlocked committee vote.
• The plan provides Republicans and Democrats with equal staff and office space.
• The plan prohibits senators from filing cloture motions on bills as a way to block amendments from being considered.
• Also, leaders of each party pledged not to "fill the amendment tree" to block the other party from offering amendments.

The House
• The House voted, 215-206, along party lines Jan. 3 to adopt a revised set of organizational rules (H Res 5).
• One rule included in the original slate of proposed changes, which would have resurrected the practice of allowing proxy votes in committee when members cannot be present, was dropped.
• The new rules moved jurisdiction over issues involving securities and insurance from the Commerce Committee to a newly created Financial Services Committee, which replaced the Banking and Financial Services Committee. The Commerce Committee was renamed the Energy and Commerce Committee.
• The Select Committee on Intelligence was expanded from 16 to 18 members, giving each party one more seat.
• Reporting requirements for unauthorized appropriations were expanded. Under the new rules, appropriations bills that include unauthorized spending must also include details about when the program was last authorized and for how much.

Who's In, Who's Out

The week of Jan. 1, the House elected 13 new chairmen to run committees after self-imposed term limits ended the tenures of sitting chairmen.

Armed Services Committee
IN: Bob Stump **OUT:** Floyd D. Spence

Budget Committee
IN: Jim Nussle **OUT:** John R. Kasich (retired)

Energy and Commerce Committee
IN: W.J. "Billy" Tauzin **OUT:** Thomas J. Bliley Jr. (retired)

Financial Services Committee
IN: Michael G. Oxley **OUT:** Jim Leach (committee was called Banking and Financial Services)

Education and the Workforce
IN: John A. Boehner **OUT:** Bill Goodling (retired)

Judiciary Committee
IN: F. James Sensenbrenner Jr. **OUT:** Henry J. Hyde

International Relations Committee
IN: Henry J. Hyde **OUT:** Benjamin A. Gilman

Resources Committee
IN: James V. Hansen **OUT:** Don Young

Science Committee
IN: Sherwood Boehlert **OUT:** F. James Sensenbrenner Jr.

Small Business Committee
IN: Donald Manzullo **OUT:** James M. Talent

Transportation and Infrastructure Committee
IN: Don Young **OUT:** Bud Shuster (retiring Jan. 31)

Veterans' Affairs Committee
IN: Christopher H. Smith **OUT:** Bob Stump

Ways and Means Committee
IN: Bill Thomas **OUT:** Bill Archer

were generally pleased with the selection process and the ultimate roster of chairmen.

"The roster tonight is better than if we had just followed seniority," said moderate Tuesday Group member James C. Greenwood, R-Pa.

Greenwood said moderates won a major victory with the selection of Thomas as chairman of Ways and Means.

"That was the biggest one of all," Greenwood said. "Thomas is a Tuesday Group member. He's fundamentally pro-choice. Crane's supporters were the most conservative."

Members of the Steering panel also said they were satisfied with the new selection process, though it was painful.

"It wasn't something a guy would say was a day at the beach. It was like choosing among your children," said Steering panelist Ralph Regula, R-Ohio. "But it was done very fairly. Hastert didn't try to influence the vote. He didn't make a big deal out of [his personal opinions.]"

On Jan. 5, House Appropriations Committee Chairman C.W. "Bill" Young, who took over the committee in 1998 and therefore was not term-limited, announced the names of the 13 subcommittee chairmen known as cardinals. Many changed committees because of the term limit rule. The new appropriations subcommittee chairmen are:

- Labor-HHS — Ralph Regula of Ohio
- Agriculture — Henry Bonilla of Texas
- Commerce-Justice-State — Frank R. Wolf of Virginia
- District of Columbia — Joe Knollenberg of Michigan
- Energy and Water — Sonny Callahan of Alabama
- Foreign Operations — Jim Kolbe of Arizona
- Interior — Joe Skeen of New Mexico
- Legislative — Charles H. Taylor of North Carolina
- Military Construction — David L. Hobson of Ohio
- National Security — Jerry Lewis of California
- Transportation — Harold Rogers of Kentucky
- Treasury-Postal — Ernest Istook of Oklahoma
- VA-HUD — James T. Walsh of New York.

Democrats Angry About Rules

On opening day, Gephardt attacked the Republican rules package as an effort to "undermine the rights of Democratic members."

Democrats had hoped to win additional seats on House committees to reflect the new, narrower margin between the two parties. They said they also wanted the package of new rules to instruct the Judiciary Committee to take up legislation to overhaul the presidential election process and prevent future voting discrepancies similar to the ones that emerged during last year's presidential race.

Democrats have charged the Republican party with "disenfranchising" minority voters.

"Voices were stifled on election day," Gephardt said on the House floor. "This is completely unacceptable. We should not have unequal voting procedures in any part of the country or ever hear again about voter intimidation."

The one Democrat to support the GOP package also voted for Hastert for Speaker. Traficant's support for Hastert had been expected for months and he had built a history of voting with the GOP. After the vote for Speaker Democrats promptly yanked his committee assignments.

But Traficant was not alone in the Democratic caucus in opposing Gephardt. Gene Taylor of Mississippi took his colleagues by surprise when he rose on the House floor and yelled the name of John P. Murtha, D-Pa., during the roll call vote for Speaker.

Taylor said he decided to abandon Gephardt in November after Democrats re-elected their House leadership without debate. Taylor said Gephardt did not open the elections to nominations for other candidates.

"I was so [angry]," Taylor said. "I told Gephardt the next day, 'Don't count on my vote.' "

Taylor said Democrats should have considered other candidates in the wake of Gephardt's failure to win back the House majority. "Someone's got to point out that when the coach keeps losing, you don't give him a bonus," he said.

Liberals Promise Action

Gephardt also faces dissent from more liberal members of his party who say they are unhappy with the party's steady move toward the center in recent years.

"This coming Congress you can expect to see progressives being very active on issues," said Dennis Kucinich, D-Ohio, chairman of the House's Progressive Caucus.

Kucinich said his liberal colleagues will push for national health care and nuclear disarmament and against any efforts to privatize Social Security. He also questioned calls among Republicans and Democrats for tax cuts this year.

On Jan. 4, Gephardt said Democrats would likely support larger tax cuts than they had in the past while promising to work with GOP President-elect George W. Bush to find compromise tax language.

"Because of the large forecast in the surplus and the slowing economy . . . we've got to revise the amounts we were looking at before," Gephardt said.

Kucinich, however, said consumer confidence had dropped significantly in recent years. He said if Americans chose not to spend their tax savings, the cuts would do little to help the economy.

Although moderate Democrats, such as the Blue Dog Caucus, say a centrist agenda is needed to ultimately win back Congressional control, liberals argue just the opposite.

"You can't get to 218 without reasserting our base," said DeFazio, referring to the number of House members needed to hold a majority. "I just don't buy what the Blue Dogs and other moderates are trying to peddle."

He added: "We certainly are going to try to assert ourselves in the caucus and in the House itself so the world knows . . . there is a Democratic wing of the Democratic Party."

The first internal battle Democrats will face this year, however, will not be on policy. It will be over who heads the national party.

In early February, the Democratic National Committee will elect a new chairman. The leading candidate is Terry McAuliffe, a longtime Democratic fundraiser who has strong ties to Bill and Sen. Hillary Rodham Clinton.

It had appeared that McAuliffe would coast to an easy victory, but liberal Democrats, particularly African-Americans, are now launching an insurgent campaign to elect former Atlanta Mayor Maynard Jackson to the post.

On Jan. 4, Jackson met in the Capitol with the Congressional Black Caucus, which threw its weight behind his race.

Waters is serving as co-chair of the campaign.

"There are these back-room kind of centrist leaders who decided what they'll do with the DNC without any kind of consultation with liberals and African-Americans," Waters said of McAuliffe. "This will be the first fight to see where this party is going." ◆

Claiming Turf with A Gavel

Republican leaders in Congress were accustomed to setting their own agenda during the Clinton administration because they had no interest in coordinating with a Democratic White House. But the election of George W. Bush changed that dynamic, forcing GOP committee chairmen to rethink their roles.

The new House and Senate chairmen who will preside over business and regulatory issues in the 107th Congress find themselves in an unusual position: adjusting to the reality of their party controlling both Congress and the White House.

Tradition dictates that they defer to the new administration and promote its agenda. But the chairmen have their own priorities and constituencies, and they are carefully weighing how and when to take the lead in the elaborate dance of governing.

One lawmaker with no compunction about forging ahead is House Energy and Commerce Committee Chairman Billy Tauzin, R-La., a Democrat until 1995 whose wide-ranging agenda recalls the committee's days under John D. Dingell, D-Mich., in the 1980s and early '90s. *(Tauzin, p. 81)*

Other chairmen are being more circumspect, but a number are moving to stake out their turf, anticipating disputes concerning which panels will have primacy over the new economy and other high-profile business issues.

"Obviously, the Commerce Committee wants to take away this committee's jurisdiction over intellectual property, patents and copyrights," new House Judiciary Committee Chairman F. James Sensenbrenner Jr., R-Wis., said bluntly in a Jan. 31 interview. "These are clearly within our jurisdiction and will remain so if Judiciary members on either side of the aisle have anything to say about it."

In an obvious shot across Tauzin's bow, Sensenbrenner and Judiciary Committee members approved changing the name of the Subcommittee on Courts and Intellectual Property to the Subcommittee on Courts, the Internet and Intellectual Property during a Jan. 31 organizational meeting.

One of the first items on Sensenbrenner's agenda will be the reintroduction of a sweeping bill to overhaul the nation's bankruptcy laws. The bill, which President Bill Clinton pocket-vetoed before leaving office, would limit the use of Chapter 7 bankruptcy filings, which allow cancellation of all debts that cannot be repaid after non-essential assets are liquidated. The legislation is a top priority for the credit industry, and Sensenbrenner hopes to move it quickly by holding only a full committee markup.

By Adriel Bettelheim / Feb. 3, 2001

CQ PHOTO/SCOTT J. FERRELL

Thomas' first months as Ways and Means chairman are likely to be dominated by the Bush administration's desire for a $1.6 trillion package of tax cuts.

Protecting Computer Data

Sensenbrenner may also take up the complex issue of how to protect information collected from computer databases. Limiting the use of such personal data would have major implications for companies that repackage information such as real estate listings and stock quotes.

Also jockeying for position with Tauzin and Sensenbrenner is Michael G. Oxley, R-Ohio, who heads the Financial Services Committee. The panel was created by House Republican leaders to resolve a two-year battle between Tauzin and Oxley for chairmanship of the Energy and Commerce Committee.

Oxley's chairmanship gives him jurisdiction over banking, securities and insurance, but he and Tauzin are expected to clash over how their committees share oversight of business conducted over the Internet.

One concern is who gets to regulate the networks that automatically match stock buy and sell orders. A power-sharing arrangement brokered by Speaker J. Dennis Hastert, R-Ill., left Tauzin convinced he has control over the issue, but Oxley and allies such as Richard H. Baker, R-La., have other ideas.

On the increasingly potent issue of Internet financial privacy, Oxley and Senate Banking, Housing and Urban Affairs Committee Chairman Phil Gramm, R-Texas, have argued that Congress needs more time to evaluate a 1999 financial services law (PL 106-102). That law requires companies to give consumers a chance to opt out of giving personal information to financial service companies that share it with unaffiliated businesses.

Taxes are expected to dominate Bill Thomas' first months as chairman of the House Ways and Means Committee, driven by the Bush administration's desire for a $1.6 trillion tax cut package that includes reducing income tax rates and easing the "marriage penalty" for dual-income couples. But like past Ways and Means chairmen, Thomas, a California Republican, probably will insert a few longtime priorities of his own into whatever bills come before him.

The chairman's past business tax proposals — which include breaks for energy generation and alternative power sources — have taken on a prescient tone in light of the rolling blackouts that have plagued his home state. Thomas has suggested extending tax credits for wind-generated energy and allowing more generous depreciation schedules for equipment used to generate it.

Thomas also is expected to continue to assert control over his specialty, health care. Prescription drug coverage for seniors will resurface, both because President Bush has proposed a short-term program for low-income Medicare beneficiaries, and because Democrats want to keep the issue alive for the 2002 elections.

He will be called on to defend the GOP's approach, which relies on the private sector to provide drug coverage options for seniors. But he may prefer to work on the more politically difficult task of overhauling Medicare through comprehensive legislation. "Members of the House and Senate would like to go beyond the president's proposal," Thomas said after Bush unveiled his Medicare prescription drug plan Jan. 29.

In the Senate, the elevation of Charles E. Grassley, R-Iowa, to the chairmanship of the Finance Committee bodes well for agriculture interests. His farm-state roots, and those of ranking Democrat Max Baucus of Montana, have led some observers to joke that the two will find a way to make

farming tax-free.

One of Grassley's priorities is the creation of "Farm and Ranch Risk Management Accounts," which would provide tax benefits to farmers who set aside savings they can draw on in difficult financial times. Grassley also hopes to make a few smaller tax fixes that would benefit farmers, such as excluding certain rental income from self-employment taxes.

Replaying Old Fights

Some of the new committee chairmen expect to replay battles fought in the 106th Congress — this time with a GOP ally in the White House. For example, House Education and the Workforce Committee Chairman John A. Boehner, R-Ohio, will press for a managed-care overhaul bill that is business-friendly. That means a measure that would not greatly expand patients' right to sue their health plans.

Boehner's panel claims jurisdiction because it oversees the 1974 Employee Retirement Income Security Act (PL 93-406), which sets rules for pension and health care plans.

Another prospect for the Education panel, aides say, would be a bill to promote what Boehner calls "union democracy." The idea is to fill in gaps that Boehner maintains have emerged in the 1959 Landrum-Griffin Act, which is supposed to give rank-and-file workers "a full, equal and democratic voice in union affairs." Boehner says some labor leaders ignore the act and have excessive control over financial matters and union elections.

If Boehner forces the issue, he can expect a confrontation with organized labor, which has provided some of the Democrats' staunchest support in recent elections.

The fight over stewardship of public lands is another old battle that could be rekindled. New House Resources Committee Chairman James V. Hansen, R-Utah, has been pressing the Bush administration to overturn a number of Clinton administration environmental initiatives, including a ban on timber cutting in roadless areas, new hardrock mining regulations, and

the designation of national monuments in the West.

"We are looking closely at every single regulation and trying to see what should be done," Hansen said Jan. 31. While he likely will defer to the White House, Hansen might initiate legislation to change the 1906 Antiquities Act, which Clinton used to designate monuments.

Hansen's predecessor at Resources, Don Young, R-Alaska, moved to the Transportation and Infrastructure Committee, where he may get an early opportunity to outline his position on a controversy involving unions that could provoke the kind of fight Boehner will face if he presses a "union democracy" bill.

Conservatives want the government to revoke labor agreements requiring the use of organized labor on federally funded projects such as the new, $2.2 billion bridge linking Washington's Maryland and Virginia suburbs along the I-95 corridor.

Unions, which want the agreements in place, are anxious to see what Young — who has a mixed record on regulatory issues — will do. Last year, he backed the Conservation and Reinvestment Act (CARA) over the objections of Western conservatives, who said the lands initiative would interfere with local governmental decisions.

Donald Manzullo, R-Ill., new chairman of the House Small Business Committee, is expected to devote time to "bundling," the federal policy of consolidating several procurement contracts before seeking bids. Many Republicans and Democrats believe bundling makes it harder for small businesses to bid on federal contracts and may press for legislation to discourage the practice.

The International Relations Committee is not usually associated with business and regulation, but new Chairman Henry J. Hyde, R-Ill., has indicated he will explore trade and export policy. One of Hyde's early priorities is reforming the Export Administration Act, which deals with export controls and balancing national security with commercial concerns. ◆

One Working Relationship

Before President Bush accepted a compromise tax package that included $1.3 trillion in tax cuts, the top Republican and Democrat on the Senate Finance Committee worked together to try building support for a $1.62 trillion bill, showing the importance of personal relationships.

When they took control of the powerful Senate Finance Committee this year, Iowa Republican Charles E. Grassley and Montana Democrat Max Baucus spent much of their suddenly valuable time arguing about a seemingly mundane subject: office space.

The committee is chronically short of Capitol Hill real estate, and the senators' staffs felt strongly about their quarters, especially the Democrats who were housed in far-flung office cubicles in the Hart Building. Republicans were in a comparably comfortable suite in the Dirksen Building near the committee's hearing room.

But when it became clear that the issue might lead to a bitter impasse, Grassley simply ceded half the GOP's prime office suites to the Democrats. Baucus responded by agreeing to committee rules more favorable to Republicans than to Democrats, despite the 50-50 makeup in the Senate.

At least for now, such is the partnership at the top of the Finance Committee in the 107th Congress. The two leaders are ready compromisers who go back more than a decade as legislative cohorts on many issues. Both are energetic and not particularly smooth farm-state legislators willing to reach out to the other party to get a deal done.

The plain-spoken but tenacious Grassley's greatest pride is being the only working farmer in a Senate once populated with them. "I'm just a farmer from Butler County," he once said. "What you see is what you get." Baucus, since joining the Senate the week after his 37th birthday, has generally preferred behind-the-scenes activity to the spotlight.

Their relationship and their similar world view suggests that they may offer the best chance for writing a tax bill — the first and perhaps most significant bill they will face this year — that can win bipartisan support.

As the committee begins drafting its version of the tax bill, the question is whether their pragmatic, compromising style can work in an atmosphere of partisanship, where items at the top of the agenda are often the most divisive. Most challenging will be the Senate leadership's tendency to impose its own will on the committee. Three of the top four party leaders have seats on Finance, and they have their own ideas about what is best for their respective parties.

In the past, GOP leaders have not hesitated to overrule the panel chairman when his plans did not coincide with theirs. Already, Republican leaders appear to be testing Grassley and Baucus, by threatening to bypass Finance and put before the Senate their own bill to increase the minimum wage and give tax breaks to the businesses with the biggest minimum wage payrolls.

Those familiar with the panel say Grassley's biggest challenge will be reasserting the committee's jurisdiction. "To some effect, the Finance Committee was irrelevant in the last Congress," said former Finance member Richard H. Bryan, D-Nev. (1989-2001), now a lawyer in Las Vegas. A key question, Bryan said, is "whether or not Grassley will be allowed to run the committee."

Grassley is pushing hard to do so. "We can't let the jurisdiction of the committee be usurped," he said. Baucus is more than happy to help defend the panel's territory. "It certainly is the top priority of the chairman and myself," he said.

Compounding that challenge is President Bush's apparent lack of enthusiasm for negotiating the details of his $1.62 trillion tax cut proposal with Democrats. The House passed its tax measures largely without Democratic input, although Republican leaders have won votes from the minority party on some proposals. The Finance Committee is expected to mark up its version of Bush's bill the week of May 14.

By Lori Nitschke / April 21, 2001

Grassley, in suit, and Baucus, in shirtsleeves, have been on Finance together for 16 years, developing a rapport they hope works to their mutual benefit in the tax debate.

CQ PHOTOS / SCOTT J. FERRELL

61

Grassley concedes that he is uncertain whether he and Baucus will be able to steer the committee away from the precipice of partisanship. Asked if that would be possible, he said, "I think on almost everything except the tax bill."

Grassley's and Baucus' performance in managing the tax debate will not only set the tone for the bill's future, but also will speak volumes about their own prospects for successfully running one of the most influential committees at the Capitol. In addition to moving the deepest tax cut in two decades, the committee this year will likely consider the solvency and proposed expansion of Medicare, trade liberalization and the reauthorization of welfare-to-work programs.

If their handiwork on the tax bill is picked apart by the full Senate, or if it is rewritten beforehand by the leadership of the two parties, Grassley and Baucus likely will find it difficult to manage the rest of their committee's agenda. Baucus has the added pressure of running for re-election next year in a state that voted overwhelmingly for Bush.

Former Finance Committee member Bob Kerrey, D-Neb. (1989-2001), who as a farm state senator and party maverick often worked with both men, predicted that Grassley and Baucus will find it difficult.

He portrays the partisan tone as emanating from the White House, just as he said it did in 1993 when Bill Clinton relied entirely on Democratic votes — Kerrey's crucial among them — to enact the first tax bill of his presidency. This year, "it would be much easier to do if the president had gone to their leaders . . . and said, 'Okay. I want to cut taxes. I know it's different than what you want to do. Let's see if we can work an agreement out,' " said Kerrey, now president of the New School University in New York.

Bob Packwood, R-Ore. (1969-95), who as Finance Committee chairman moved, against long odds, a massive tax overhaul measure (PL 99-514) through the Senate in 1986, said he did not know if such a feat would be possible in the more partisan Congress of today.

"Something has changed. It has nothing to do with revenue estimates or if there is a surplus. It's a difference in the nature of partisanship, and I can't explain it," said Packwood, who now runs his own Washington lobbying firm, Sunrise Research.

A Defining Moment

When it became clear last November that the defeat of William V. Roth Jr., R-Del. (1971-2001), and the retirement of Daniel Patrick Moynihan, D-N.Y. (1977-2001), would de-

liver the top spots on the committee to Grassley and Baucus, they began to set up a system for working together.

Over a breakfast in the Senate dining room soon after the election, the two men set ground rules for their mutual dealing. They would meet weekly to try to resolve disagreements on the committee before impasses occurred. If confronted with a problem they could not solve on their own, they would encourage party leaders to join them. It was this agreement that led them to reach out to Majority Leader Trent Lott, R-Miss., and Minority Leader Tom Daschle, D-S.D., in an attempt to structure the tax debate. So far the four have not met, however.

Grassley and Baucus say their own meetings have been productive, and frank. There is "none of this senatorial positioning," Baucus said in describing their conversations. "He says, 'What do you think of this?' I tend to tell him." Grassley terms their relationship "extraordinarily good."

The committee staffs — run on the GOP side by a 15-year Grassley aide and on the Democratic side by a former Clinton administration official — do not always get along as well, and there have been some disagreements, particularly about the office space. Grassley's plan to divide the panel's space will not be carried out until next month. (*Committee aides, p. 63*)

Despite working well with Baucus on issues this far, Grassley acknowledges that in some situations the two sides may not be able to work together. "There may be times as the leader of the Democrats, he's going to have to go his way and me as the leader of the Republicans go our way. Whenever that happens, not much will get done," Grassley said.

Though the committee has a long tradition of working across party lines, its recent history is not replete with legislative accomplishment. Roth and Moynihan, who ran the committee for the previous five years, were close friends, but under their stewardship the panel often found itself overruled — or usurped in advance — by party leaders.

Many committee members long to return to the days when the chairman succeeded in being a vigorous guardian of the panel's prerogatives. Prominent among Finance Committee chairmen with such reputations were Democrats Russell B. Long of Louisiana (1948-87) and Lloyd Bentsen of Texas (1971-93) and Republicans Bob Dole of Kansas (1969-96) and Packwood.

In the 106th Congress, senators would often emerge from closed-door meetings of the committee talking about how Lott or Majority Whip Don Nickles, R-Okla., both of whom are members of the panel, had berated Roth or otherwise

Finance Committee's Top Tax Staff

KOLAN L. DAVIS
Majority Staff Director

Davis, 43, has spent his entire professional life working for Charles E. Grassley, R-Iowa. Soon after obtaining his law degree from Indiana University in 1984, he was hired as counsel to the Judiciary Subcommittee on Administrative Practice and Procedure, which Grassley then chaired. He joined Grassley's personal staff in 1987 as an adviser on tax and foreign policy issues and continued as Grassley's tax aide until becoming chief counsel on Judiciary's Administrative Oversight and the Courts panel in 1995. Grassley chaired that subcommittee from 1995 through 2000 and Davis focused on proposals to overhaul personal bankruptcy law. Davis also was the senator's legislative director from 1998 to 2001.

MARK A. PRATER
Republican Tax Counsel

Prater, 42, is one of the few holdovers on the staff from the days when its chairman was Bob Packwood, R-Ore. (1969-95). An Oregon native, he has worked at Finance since 1990 and has been involved in writing all the tax bills before Congress since becoming chief GOP tax counsel in 1993, the last year that a major tax increase was enacted. When Packwood resigned, Prater stayed to advise the next chairman, William V. Roth Jr., R-Del. (1971-2001). Before coming to the Hill, Prater practiced at Dunn, Carney, Allen, Higgins and Tongue in Portland and was a tax associate for the accounting firm Touche Ross and Co. He won a law degree in 1994 from Willamette University and a master's degree in tax law from the University of Florida.

JOHN C. ANGELL
Majority Staff Director

Angell, 47, is among the highest-ranking Clinton administration refugees back on Capitol Hill. He was the top congressional lobbyist for the Energy Department under Secretary Bill Richardson. Before that, he spent a decade by the side of fellow Californian Leon E. Panetta. Angell was the House Budget Committee chief of staff for seven years, including the four when Panetta (1977-93) was the panel's chairman. He followed Panetta to the Office of Management and Budget at the start of Clinton's presidency and was then a senior adviser to Panetta during his tenure as White House chief of staff. In that job, Angell handled budget, labor, energy and environmental policy. He is a 1980 graduate of Loyola University Law School.

RUSSELL W. SULLIVAN
Democratic Tax Counsel

Sullivan, 39, joined the staff in 1999 as top tax counsel to Daniel Patrick Moynihan of New York (1977-2001), then the ranking minority member. As a result, he has some experience in writing Democratic tax packages to be offered as alternatives to GOP plans. He was particularly involved in rallying Democrats around a substitute for the GOP's 1999 bill to cut taxes $792 billion over a decade. Sullivan was previously legislative director for Bob Graham of Florida, a Finance member. Before joining Graham's staff in 1995, he was a Peat Marwick auditor in his native Arkansas and in Texas, and he was an income tax planner for Vinson and Elkins in Washington, D.C. He is a 1988 graduate of the University of Texas Law School.

---

made it clear that the chairman had been overruled.

Even if efforts to open the lines of discussion with Lott and Nickles do not bear fruit, Grassley insists he won't allow himself to be similarly passed over.

The first challenge to that authority appears to be coming on the GOP leadership's proposal to combine the minimum wage hike with tax benefits for the retailers, restaurants and small businesses that employ most low-wage workers. Nickles is in charge of putting together the measure in time for a Senate debate next month. Leadership aides have re-

peatedly said they will not send the bill to Finance, despite the bill's tax implications.

Unless Grassley is given ample say on the tax provisions beforehand, he will use his parliamentary powers to block Nickles from putting the bill before the Senate, said Jill Kozeny, Finance's communications director.

Changing of the Guard

While Grassley may face some of the same challenges Roth did, it would surprise many in both parties if he responded in the same passive manner. In many

ways, he could not be more different from Roth, who rarely exchanged more than pleasantries with colleagues or reporters and disliked unscripted events.

Almost daily, Grassley goes out of his way to find reporters who are covering issues in which he is involved, and he is willing to endure their seemingly endless questions, no matter how far the discussion strays. He rarely holds back an answer, though confusion sometimes remains afterward about precisely what the chairman has said. Grassley has been known to mangle words, and his desire to provide up-to-the-minute information can lead to misunderstandings in a place where political tides and legislative strategies are constantly shifting.

Baucus, by contrast, tends to speak haltingly, leaving the impression that he is pondering the ramifications of what he is saying just as the words are passing his lips, but he is also more accessible than his predecessor.

While Grassley and Baucus may not be as polished as some of Finance's former leaders, neither are they as taciturn as Roth or as professorial in their approach as Moynihan. Instead, it is clear that they will bring more energy to the center of the committee dais than it has seen in several years — and that rural America is likely to benefit.

At age 67, Grassley still keeps farmers' hours. He often leaves his townhouse in Arlington, Va., before 5:30 a.m. to jog and then heads to his Hart Building office space by 7:30. He strives for punctuality and has been known to start meetings early, almost unheard of in the congressional culture of chronic tardiness. During weekends and recesses, Grassley religiously returns to Iowa to tend to constituents' needs or to help his son, Robin, work the family farm.

An accomplished runner who has completed the New York City Marathon several times, Baucus, 59, can be spotted jogging alongside the Potomac River or walking his dog near his Georgetown home, sometimes even when the Senate is in recess. Still, a placard on his desk in the Hart Building declares "Montana Comes First."

Both men are now reaping the benefits of the Senate's respect for seniority. Baucus has been on Finance since his arrival in 1978. Grassley has been on the panel for 16 years since his arrival in 1981.

Pet Projects

Past chairmen and others on the committee often found places for their pet proposals in the major tax bills of the last two decades, and this year is unlikely to be an exception.

Grassley says he will not write his own priorities into the tax package if doing so would leave insufficient room under the bill's cost ceiling to accomplish these tenets of Bush's plan: cutting personal income taxes, repealing the estate tax, alleviating the tax code's "marriage penalty" and creating tax credits for the purchase of medical insurance. He describes his own ideas as "relatively

minor as far as cost is concerned." Among them are allowing farmers and fishermen to set up tax-deferred savings accounts to be tapped in economically tough times (S 313), and enhancing tax credits for producing energy with wind turbines (S 530) or through the burning of plants, known as biomass.

Grassley says his desire to help develop alternative energy sources — which he shares with Ways and Means Committee Chairman Bill Thomas, R-Calif. — is born of the interest of many Iowa farmers. Many whose land can no longer sustain corn and soybean crops are growing grasses and other plants that harness energy. Along those lines, Grassley is perhaps the Senate's most ardent defender of tax breaks for ethanol, a gasoline additive made from corn, although he has made no move to include an ethanol provision in this year's bill.

Baucus' priorities include the farm accounts that Grassley wants and a bill (S 742) the two have written to alter pension law. It is similar to a House measure (HR 10) that would increase tax incentives for saving for retirement and would attempt to make pensions more portable.

Like many in his party, Baucus says any major tax cut should occur at the same time Congress moves to shore up Social Security and Medicare and to expand the federal health insurance program to include prescription drug coverage for its elderly beneficiaries. Baucus' legislative priorities are often focused on strengthening rural health care, a desire he shares with Grassley.

Facing a campaign for re-election in 2002 in a state that backed Bush by 25 percentage points over Al Gore in last year's presidential election, Baucus sounds more eager than many in his party for enactment of a major tax cut this year. "I'm very hopeful that we will get a tax bill that has a large majority," he said in a recent interview. "I believe it's so good for the country. If it's 51-50, it's just going to send partisan signals."

Reaching a Budget Compromise

Baucus was one of 15 Democrats who voted with all 50 Republicans for the Senate version of the fiscal 2002 budget resolution (H Con Res 83), which calls for no more than $1.27 trillion in tax cuts between 2001 and 2011 — a figure that is 78 percent the size of what Bush has proposed. The House has backed Bush's tax cut figure. Talks to find a compromise are expected to in-

tensify when members return the week of April 23 from their spring recess.

Shortly before the Senate voted to adopt its budget measure April 6, Daschle and Edward M. Kennedy, D-Mass., had a long discussion on the floor with Baucus and his top tax aide, Russell W. Sullivan. The talk was not about that measure, Baucus' spokesman said, but if Daschle expected Baucus to vote the leadership line, it was clear he was disappointed and likely will be again.

Though Baucus says he welcomes Daschle's reclaiming of a seat on Finance after a six-year absence, the minority leader's presence could increase the pressure on Baucus when the tax bill is considered.

In the interim, Baucus said his main task is to determine where the rest of the panel's Democrats stand on tax proposals. Three of them — John B. Breaux of Louisiana, Blanche Lincoln of Arkansas and Robert G. Torricelli of New Jersey — joined Baucus in voting for the budget resolution, and they are considered most amenable to backing GOP ideas when the measure comes up. Daschle, however, is expected to press them to vote instead for their party's plans.

Such proposals might also be designed to attract the votes of GOP moderates. Thus far, Vermont's James M. Jeffords appears to be the only GOP member of Finance likely to oppose the Republican line. He has said he would not support a tax bill that cost as much as $1.4 billion in lost revenue over the next 10 years.

Some members of the panel may still work to balloon the size of the bill. GOP conservatives such as Lott, Nickles and Phil Gramm of Texas all have suggested the country could benefit from a tax cut deeper than Bush has proposed. But Gramm is no longer expected to go against the grain. He is slated for a seat on the conference committee that will settle the final form of the budget resolution — including the total size of the tax cut that may move through the Senate under expedited reconciliation provisions.

With so many essential elements still unknown, it is difficult to predict how Finance's first bellwether markup will turn out. Grassley said his first hope is that — if he can cut a deal among the committee members — the leadership will not "meddle" with the result. Then, he added with a quick smile: "But, of course the leadership will meddle. They're members of the committee." ◆

Rules and Procedures

The United States Congress is a complex institution with a vast, layered web of rules and procedures that govern its operation. Some of those rules, particularly in the Senate, are no more than historical habit, the precedents set by the way things were done before. But others, especially in the House with its powerful Rules Committee, are ironclad regulations that leave little room for interpretation.

Even before a Congress begins considering legislation, it must formally organize its members by electing leaders and assigning others to committees. In the first months of the 107th Congress, this system played a remarkably high-profile role in both the House and Senate, demonstrating how procedure can sometimes eclipse substance. In the Senate, for example, a bill that would have rewritten the laws of bankruptcy spent months in limbo because of a hitch in procedure. The Senate implemented nearly all elements of the 50-50 power-sharing agreement, but it never resolved the question of how to choose members for House-Senate conference committees, which meet to reconcile the differences between versions of a bill passed in the House and Senate. Traditionally, the majority leader chooses conferees, but in the 50-50 Senate Democrats wanted a say in the matter. The bankruptcy bill had passed both chambers in slightly different form in February, but because the Senate had no procedure for naming members to the conference committee with the House, the bill stalled until Democrats took a clear majority in June and gained the authority to name conferees without question.

The Senate's 50-50 split for the first six months of 2001 drew much of the attention about rules and procedures, but the House, too, had procedural issues. Chief among them was the episode involving the campaign finance legislation that was considered in July. Before a bill can go to the House floor for consideration, the Rules Committee must review the bill and set the terms for debate, including the number of amendments to be allowed and the amount of time to be spent debating them. The rule specifying those issues must be approved on the House floor before the bill itself can be taken up. But in the case of the campaign finance bill, which had a host of enemies in the Republican House leadership, the rule that was approved in committee drew opposition on the floor from the bill's supporters. They said the terms of debate were unfairly designed to make the bill more difficult to pass by requiring individual votes on more than a dozen technical changes they sought to make in their bill. The result was the 203-228 defeat of the rule — including 19 Republican votes to reject — a rare case of Republicans defying Speaker J. Dennis Hastert. Without a rule the campaign finance bill could not be considered, leaving its future uncertain.

Equality in the Senate

The lengthy delay in determining who won the presidency in 2000 left the Senate in its own state of uncertainty. But those early days made clear one thing that would remain true deep into the 107th Congress: Democrats would use whatever leverage they have for all it's worth.

Senate leaders the week of Dec. 4 were coming to grips with the stark realities of organizing the chamber under an unprecented 50-50 ratio. Democrats were playing hardball, insisting on a "power sharing" arrangement that would give them equal say in everything the Senate does. Republicans were digging in their heels, insisting that George W. Bush's presumptive ascendancy to the White House would a give them the controlling, 51st vote of a Vice President Dick Cheney.

Imagine the senators' coming dilemma, then, when they meet again the week of Dec. 11 and also reconcile their starkly opposing views with the still incredible permutations that may flow from the ongoing legal contest for the presidency.

The Florida Supreme Court's decision on Dec. 8 to order a recount of key counties could effectively put talks of 50-50 on hold, since the Senate could conceivably go 51-49, Republican, but with Al Gore in the White House.

But even that scenario, which would have Gore's running mate, Joseph I. Lieberman of Connecticut, resigning his Senate seat to be replaced by an appointee of his state's Republican governor, would not have to occur until Inauguration Day on Jan. 20. That means the Senate will be at 50-50 for at least 17 days after convening on Jan. 3, with still-Vice President Al Gore casting tie-breaking votes.

That puts Democrats in the driver's seat, at least temporarily. Or does it? No one in the Senate seems to know.

Opening Gambit

Democratic Leader Tom Daschle put Republicans on clear notice the week of Dec. 4 that his definition of power sharing is more involved than his early requests for equal committee ratios and more staff and office space.

It turned out the opening bid by the South Dakota Democrat went well beyond anything expected by Republicans as the two parties started negotiations on how to organize an evenly divided Senate.

At a Dec. 7 meeting, Daschle presented Trent Lott, R-Miss., the GOP leader, a lengthy Christmas list of items that Daschle said are part and parcel of a true power-sharing arrangement for organizing the Senate in the 107th Congress.

His proposals included equal representation on all committees and equal staff budgets. But it went on to call for assurances that Democrats would get some of the prerogatives of setting committee hearing and markup agendas; scheduling floor time on their legislative agenda items; having evenly divided representation on the Senate side of House-Senate conference committees; and controlling parliamentary procedures to affect the flow of floor debate and introduction of amendments.

In other words, every procedural step of running the modern-day Senate would fall under the joint control of the two party leaders.

Republicans vow, and Democrats privately acknowledge, that Daschle will get nowhere near everything he's asking for. Still, Daschle said, "Everything ought to be on the table."

The Lott-Daschle talks are a unique moment in the modern Senate. Both men are under great pressure, not just to obtain the best arrangement for themselves and their respective caucuses, but also to set a precedent they can live with should one party or the other suddenly fall into the minority. They have both known that could happen any day or hour should only one senator switch parties or die in office. (There is no sign of the former, but nine senators are over the age of 70.)

The late-breaking news Dec. 8 that the presidential race was still riding a legal roller coaster only accentuated that point.

The negotiations are being played out against the backdrop of a bitterly contested presidential election and in the wake of a Senate session as partisan as any in recent memory. What is more, Democrats have signaled a willingness

By Andrew Taylor / Dec. 9, 2000

GOP leader Lott was taken aback by the Democrats' proposals for "power sharing." Talks will only get more complex if it appears the presidential contest could hang in the balance.

CQ PHOTO / SCOTT J. FERRELL

Senate Leadership In 107th Congress

——— REPUBLICANS ———

Majority Leader
Trent Lott, Miss.

Assistant Majority Leader
Don Nickles, Okla.

Conference Chairman
Rick Santorum, Pa.

Conference Secretary
Kay Bailey Hutchison, Texas

Policy Committee Chairman
Larry E. Craig, Idaho

National Republican Senatorial Committee
Bill Frist, Tenn.

——— DEMOCRATS ———

Minority Leader
Tom Daschle, S.D.

Minority Whip
Harry Reid, Nev.

Conference Chairman
Tom Daschle, S.D.

Conference Secretary
Barbara A. Mikulski, Md.

Policy Committee Chairman
Byron L. Dorgan, N.D.

Democratic Senatorial Campaign Committee
Patty Murray, Wash.

to take the fight to the floor when the Senate reconvenes on Jan. 3, raising the possibility that the first public event of the supposedly new, feel-good, bipartisan Senate would be a bitter fight over issues such as whether a committee should have 11 Republicans and 10 Democrats or be split 10-10. Fighting over what could be cast as petty issues of staff funds and office space could be a public relations nightmare for a party whose presidential candidate promised a new tone in Washington.

"I think [Daschle's] list was far more elaborate than Lott anticipated," said a GOP aide.

The possibility that the talks might drag on through next month is alarming to lawmakers of both parties still hopeful of healing past divisions.

"I think there will be a strong instinct to try and work it out," said John D. Rockefeller IV, D-W.Va. "The last thing in the world the Senate wants is to get into a fight over this. That would be a continuation of [the partisanship] we've seen. That's that.

"On the other hand," he added, "50 is 50."

Republicans remain confident that the public would not stand for an extended battle over organizational matters just as the new president — if it is Texas Gov. George W. Bush — takes office. They believe Daschle ultimately will prove unwilling to force a public floor fight — especially as the Senate must consider critical nominations for the secretaries of State, Defense and Treasury.

"The ultimate threat that you have at the end of all of this is a filibuster on organization, and we just don't believe that the Democrats can sustain a filibuster on organizational issues," said a top aide to a committee chairman. "It's something the public just wouldn't stand for."

The Dec. 7 session was the first of what promised to be many meetings required to sort out the delicate questions required to get the 50-50 Senate organized. It is clear the two sides have completely different notions of what sorts of concessions Republicans, who have held the majority since

Twists and Turns Of the Last 50-50 Senate

On only one previous occasion, in 1881, has the Senate organized with an equal number of Democrats and Republicans.

For senators seeking a precedent to guide them on such "power sharing" questions as evenly divided committee ratios, the side that ultimately organized the Senate that year — the Republicans — rewarded themselves with a one-vote edge on the major committees.

According to an account published in 1984 by the Senate Historian — and recirculated recently by Senate staffers —19th-century Senate leaders confronted the same dilemma that now clouds the chamber's ability to organize itself.

The elections of 1880 produced a Republican president, James Garfield, and a Senate of 37 Republicans, 37 Democrats and two Independents. One Independent announced he would vote with Democrats; the other, William Mahone, was a member of a breakaway faction of Virginia Democrats. Democratic leaders believed they had 39 votes, enough to retain committee chairs, but perhaps more importantly, to control of the extensive patronage jobs that came with the selection of the Secretary of the Senate and the Sergeant at Arms.

Not so. After extensive wooing by Republicans, Mahone voted on March 14 to block a Democratic committee slate. The next day, Republicans made freshman Mahone chairman of the Agriculture Committee and, with the tie-breaking power of Vice President Chester Alan Arthur, installed a GOP committee slate.

But as Republicans moved on to the patronage jobs, the hardball intensified. Democrats managed to deprive Republicans of the 39-seat quorum needed to conduct business. They hoped to strike a deal to retain their control of those lucrative offices in exchange for proceeding on presidential nominees. The White House was growing impatient.

All of a sudden, a rift appeared in GOP ranks. Powerful Republican Roscoe Conkling got into a battle with Garfield over nominations affecting his state. Conkling and a junior GOP colleague resigned from the Senate, fully anticipating that the legislature would immediately re-elect them to send a message to Garfield. That did not happen.

Instead, the resignations left Democrats with a two-vote majority. But instead of trying to re-take control of the committees, Democrats settled for control of the Senate's officers, a situation that continued through the rest of the 47th Congress.

— *Andrew Taylor*

1995, should make in order for the Senate to peacefully assemble in January.

Republicans say that unless they get a one-vote margin in committees, for example, presidential nominations could be bottled up in committee. And while the issues at stake may seem relatively unimportant to the casual observer, they are critical to the Senate's inside players.

"I think a chairman simply has to have a one-vote margin in order to effectively exercise control over the committee," said John W. Warner, R-Va., chairman of the Armed Services Committee. "Staffing, space, those things can be worked out. But at some point there are times when somebody's got to take the gavel, strike it, and call for a vote and have some assurance that that vote can carry."

During the week of Dec. 4, the GOP conference unified behind a position that committee chairmen should have a one-vote edge in their panels to reflect the presence of a Republican vice president to preside over the Senate and cast tie-breaking votes.

"If I'm going to be chairman, I want to have one more member," said Banking Committee Chairman Phil Gramm, R-Texas.

But Democrats also dug in: "The only thing that I feel very strongly about is that the committee ratios reflect the Senate makeup, and that means 50-50," Daschle said.

Assuming Bush and his running mate, Dick Cheney, are inaugurated on Jan. 20, Cheney would cast a tie-breaking vote as president of the Senate, even on a resolution to organize the Senate and make committee assignments. "They have an organizing capability with a vice president who can cast a tie-breaking vote," allowed Byron Dorgan, D-N.D. "But of course there's unlimited debate on a resolution to organize."

"It appears that this is going to take a lot longer than anybody contemplated," said a senior GOP aide. "This is going to take a good damn long time."

All Lott would offer as he briskly paced from Daschle's office to his own after their Dec. 7 session was a terse comment: "We talked about the general parameters. We're going to think about it, come back and have some more meetings with some specifics."

Complicating matters is that Republicans will not be able to garner a majority to push through the key resolutions establishing committee rosters and ratios until Jan. 20. An anomaly in this year's elections is that Vice President Al Gore will be the deciding vote in the Senate from Jan. 3-20. The Senate typically organizes on the opening day of a Congress by unanimous consent of all senators.

Democrats have a simple, potent argument: that a 50-50 body should have a 50-50 split on committees.

Democrats point to the comparable experiences of state legislatures that have found themselves evenly divided. Usually, the experience in the states has been one of power-sharing, including divvying up committee chairmanships, sharing presiding duties and allowing both parties to have ample agenda-setting opportunities.

Traditionally, the makeup of committees has mirrored the makeup of the entire Senate. The essential difference between the two sides is the significance of the 51st vote of the vice president. Democrats say the vice president is not an actual member of the Senate, which is true. They then argue that this means he should not be considered when extrapolating committee ratios.

"We fully expect that the American people would understand — and the Republicans would eventually understand — that if you have 50 percent of the members of the Senate, it requires a fair share of the opportunity to be involved in the schedule . . . committee memberships and other issues," Dorgan said.

Republicans counter that the dynamic of the committees should mirror that of the floor. Under this reasoning, the chairman represents the equivalent of the vice president and would cast

Parties Name Fundraisers

Senate Republicans and Democrats chose new leaders for their campaign committees when leadership elections were held on Dec. 5.

Among Senate Republicans, Bill Frist of Tennessee was elected to lead the National Republican Senatorial Committee, replacing Mitch McConnell of Kentucky.

Frist raised more than $4.3 million for his 2000 re-election campaign, discouraging potential Democratic opponents such as Rep. Harold E. Ford Jr. from challenging him. Nearly $1 million of that money came from political action committees that traditionally have supported Republicans.

Including his 1994 election, Frist has done well raising money from corporate sources throughout the South and the nation. Some of his leading contributors include casino operators Harrah's Entertainment Inc. and Gaylord Entertainment Co., along with Memphis-based FedEx Corp. and Bell-South Corp.

Senate Democrats elected Patty Murray of Washington to chair the Democratic Senatorial Campaign Committee, replacing Robert G. Torricelli of New Jersey.

For her first Senate campaign in 1992, Murray raised $1.5 million, less than a third of which came from political action committees. But in 1998 Murray topped $5.3 million, collecting more from the business community than her Republican opponent, Rep. Linda Smith (1995-99). Murray's leading PAC contributors have been unions and women's groups, as well as liberal interest groups such as the Sierra Club and the National Committee for an Effective Congress. However, she also has ties to business contributors, including Washington state's Boeing Co. and Microsoft Corp.

In the House last month, Republicans re-elected Thomas M. Davis III of Virginia to another term as head of the National Republican Congressional Committee, which broke its fundraising records in the 1999-2000 election cycle. The committee raised at least $117.4 million, easily topping its 1995-96 effort of about $100 million.

Democrats have not yet chosen a replacement for Patrick J. Kennedy of Rhode Island, who has said he would not return as chairman of the Democratic Congressional Campaign Committee.

— Derek Willis

the deciding vote in committee markups.

And Senate precedents suggest that Republicans have history working in their favor.

Complicating Republicans' problems is that some of their own current chairmen — including Commerce Chairman John McCain, R-Ariz., and Appropriations Chairman Ted Stevens, R-Alaska — have said they would be willing to preside over evenly divided panels. (They have also signaled, however, that they will follow Lott on any procedural votes.)

"I think that we're pretty united, more so than they are," said Sen. John B. Breaux, D-La.

Republicans and Democrats easily re-elected their top leaders at party caucuses Dec. 5.

The closest contest of any of the leadership races was for chairman of the Republican Policy Committee, the fourth-ranking leadership post. Incumbent Larry E. Craig, R-Idaho, a Lott confidant, faced a late challenge by Pete V. Domenici, R-N.M.

Craig won that race on a 26-24 vote. ◆

The Deal Is Easy, the Details Aren't

At the beginning of each Congress, the Senate must vote on a resolution that organizes the chamber by specifying such things as the ratio of Republicans to Democrats on each committee as well as the proportion of money that will go to each party on each committee. When Republicans and Democrats agreed in principle to share power because of the 50-50 party split, they left the specifics undecided, setting up committee-level sparring that set a tone that lasted well beyond the end of 50-50.

For some of the chamber's "Old Bulls" it was a snap. But for many others, the latest test in the ticklish process of getting a 50-50 Senate up and running — implementing the landmark power-sharing agreement in each committee — has proven anything but easy.

That a handful of powerful committee staff aides and their elected principals are battling over seemingly trivial questions such as office space has so far paled in significance to the legislative issues facing President Bush and the new Congress. The delays have yet to affect the Senate's agenda or Bush's in the traditionally slack few weeks of a new Congress and administration.

But when lawmakers return Feb. 26 from a weeklong recess, these organizational questions will assume greater urgency as the Senate faces a critical deadline to pass a measure to keep funds flowing to the Senate's committees. Without agreement on administrative and organizational issues, the funding resolution may stall, and the very committees that hold the latchkeys to so many Bush agenda items, such as education, might have to temporarily close their doors.

After prodding by Majority Leader Trent Lott, R-Miss., at a Feb. 13 meeting, some of Lott's unhappy chairmen made progress at the bargaining table. But bitter divisions over office space and how much influence panel Democrats will have over the agenda have several key committees, including Finance and Judiciary, stuck in the mud.

March 1 is the deadline for the Senate to pass a resolution to finance the operations of every committee. Democrats acknowledge that they are using the committee funding resolution deadline as leverage to prompt agreements on staff funding, allocation of office space and influence over the topics of upcoming hearings and markups of legislation. (The hard-and-fast deadline is March 10, after which staff paychecks would halt.)

"It is in the interest of both Republicans and Democrats to get this resolved . . . so that you are in a position to move the funding resolution," said a Senate Democratic aide.

The ongoing talks come several weeks after the historic 50-50 pact (S Res 8) passed by the Senate on Jan. 5. Under that accord — which was only grudgingly accepted by many GOP chairmen — Democrats claim an equal number of committee seats and an equal share of committee staff budgets and office space. Typically, the majority controls two-thirds of committee budgets and gets far nicer and more spacious office digs.

Committee by Committee

The 50-50 agreement between Lott and Minority Leader Tom Daschle, D-S.D., capped weeks of secret negotiations between the two leaders. Implementing it on the committee level, however, has required a far larger set of negotiations involving committee chairmen, their ranking Democrats and their top staff.

Like the original Lott-Daschle accord, the only way to implement a 50-50 plan on committees is through bipartisan agreement between the chairman and ranking member. This has required separate talks on the organization of the Senate's 16 standing committees, as well as select committees such as Intelligence.

Lott and Daschle mostly left it to their numerous subordinates to work out the details in a bevy of separate talks. The results have been mixed.

One problem is that the requirement that staff budgets and space be evenly split means Republican aides have to give up office space to make room for an influx of Democratic staff.

"Space may be a bigger problem than almost anything else," said a Senate GOP leadership aide.

How well the individual committee negotiations have gone has, not surprisingly, depended on the dynamic of the assorted committees, the personalities involved and the politics of the committee agenda.

The Governmental Affairs Committee, for example, which has a broad investigative and oversight mission but typically produces relatively little legislation, has been a trouble spot. The panel held contentious hearings in 1997 on political fundraising scandals involving President Bill Clinton, and top Democrat Joseph I. Lieberman of Connecticut has asked for authority to call hearings and issue subpoenas that would give him, in theory, the ability to scrutinize the Bush administration. Chairman Fred Thompson, R-Tenn., is stoutly resisting.

Problems have been kept to a minimum on other committees such as Agriculture, Appropriations, Budget, Commerce and Foreign Relations, where the agendas are less partisan and the chairmen and top Democrats have good relationships.

"It's a work in progress," said Rules and Administration Committee Chairman Mitch McConnell, R-Ky., whose panel is responsible for allocating space and drafting the committee funding resolution. "Each committee is dealing with it differently, based on the personalities of the chairman and ranking member, how well they get along."

For committees with a greater legislative focus such as Armed Services, Judiciary and Banking, Democrats have been seeking guarantees that they will be able to get their issues and legislation onto the committee agenda. A key question is whether greater Democratic influence over the agenda — hearing schedules, witness lists and markup rosters — is written into committee rules or handled informally.

"We want there to be a way for Democrats as a group to be able to call for hearings, to be able to call for and get consideration of agenda items," said a Democratic committee staff director. "There are a million ways to do it. You don't have to do it in the rules."

Most chairmen are strongly opposed to rules changes that guarantee

By Andrew Taylor / Feb. 17, 2001

Democrats an equal voice in setting the schedule, and Republicans have been bristling at what they see as a coordinated campaign by many — though not all — ranking Democrats to erode the authority of GOP chairmen.

"They're demanding rules changes to create co-chairmanships," griped a GOP leadership staff aide.

The March 1 deadline to pass the committee funding resolution is also

Helms and Biden have come to a "gentlemen's agreement" that allows Biden to call for Foreign Relations Committee hearings on issues he chooses.

the deadline by which committees are supposed to adopt the rules that will govern them for the 107th Congress. In the past, the matter was routine because the majority could impose its will. Many committees adopted the same rules over and over, but the 50-50 dynamic is causing some ranking members to try to revisit the rules. And since it takes a majority of a committee to adopt its rules, Democrats now have more influence to get changes.

'Get This Done'

Lott told his chairmen, many of whom disliked the 50-50 deal with Daschle, to "work it out" with their ranking Democrats, said Lott's chief of staff David Hoppe. "And in a lot of cases they have, but there are a number of cases where they haven't, and so Lott says, 'Look, it's time to get this done,' because . . . when we come back [from the recess] it'll be pretty close to March 1st."

Said another aide present at the meeting, "He said, 'I know lots of you have not even met [with ranking Democrats]. Sit down with them, work it out and get it solved.'"

So far, the behind-the-scenes maneuvering has yet to create any legislative logjams. In one of the few public protests, however, top Judiciary Committee Democrat Patrick J. Leahy of Vermont criticized the lack of progress at a Feb. 15 scheduled markup of a bill to overhaul bankruptcy laws. Leahy told his colleagues it was premature to act on the bankruptcy bill before deciding how the committee should be arranged "to take into account the 50-50 membership in the Senate and our 9-9 membership here on this committee."

For ranking Foreign Relations Committee Democrat Joseph R. Biden Jr. of Delaware, who enjoys a very good relationship with Chairman Jesse Helms, R-N.C., the key question "was whether or not we institutionalize who can call hearings on what subjects.

"And we just made a gentlemen's agreement that if there's anything I care about, that we'll have hearings on it," Biden said. "But we didn't write it into the rules."

The same is true for the Commerce, Science and Transportation Committee, where Chairman John McCain, R-Ariz., and ranking Democrat Ernest F.

Hollings of South Carolina, have a smooth relationship. No written agreements were required between the two to assure evenly balanced hearings and an equal split of the budget. "[McCain's] word is his bond," said Hollings.

Other panels that have successfully reached accords — including Agriculture, Appropriations, Budget and Environment and Public Works — feature chairmen and ranking members who have long, established relationships.

At Appropriations, where Chairman Ted Stevens, R-Alaska, and ranking Democrat Robert C. Byrd of West Virginia have a peas-in-a-pod relationship unsurpassed by any other chairman and ranking member, everything is fine — no rules changes, no written agreements. (The GOP staff is less happy; at least two marquee Capitol offices will be handed over to the Democrats.)

At Budget, Chairman Pete V. Domenici, R-N.M., and new ranking Democrat Kent Conrad of North Dakota quickly agreed to largely preserve the prerogatives of the chairman but allow Conrad to hire new staff aides — including a two-man press operation — to combat the bully pulpit of the White House.

Domenici and Conrad also signed an agreement to lock in staff budgets for the duration of the 107th Congress, regardless of whether the 50-50 Senate flips to 51-49 in favor of either party because of death or other reasons.

The potential for such a shift is not entirely academic, as 98-year-old Republican Strom Thurmond of South Carolina has recently pared back his work schedule and spent time in the hospital.

And at Environment, staunch conservative Chairman Robert C. Smith, R-N.H., and the Senate's number two Democrat, Harry Reid of Nevada — who forged a close relationship on the Ethics Committee — reached a deal during the week. "We'll sit down in the next two or three weeks and actually negotiate a hearing schedule," said top Reid aide Eric Washburn.

On the other side of the spectrum is Intelligence, where a battle over staff hiring has spilled into public view. In a tiff first reported in the Capitol Hill newspaper Roll Call, Intelligence Committee Chairman Richard C. Shelby, R-Ala., who has broad power over staff hiring, fired a senior Democratic aide without consulting the incoming ranking member, Bob Graham, D-Fla. ◆

Procedure and Consequence

The Senate is an institution governed by precedent rather than rules. But precedents for how to handle legislation are open to interpretation, which makes the Senate's parliamentarian an important figure in the operation of the chamber. That's why the majority likes to choose its own.

Senate Majority Leader Trent Lott already had trouble trying to run the 50-50 Senate. Now, the Mississippi Republican will have to shepherd President Bush's agenda through the Senate with a parliamentarian originally appointed by Robert C. Byrd, the Democrats' master strategist.

Lott's unprecedented decision to exile his party's own parliamentarian, Republican Robert B. Dove, cast a spotlight the week of May 7 on the crucial role of the traditionally unseen job of the Senate's top umpire.

Dove's forced retirement added to the unpredictability of the already tumultuous and evenly divided Senate. Even as the Senate handed Bush his biggest win to date in passing his budget (H Con Res 83) mostly intact on May 10, ample evidence is building that Lott has his hands full.

Beyond the questions it raised about Lott's leadership style, the eruption that led to Dove's firing dramatizes the crucial role special filibuster-proof procedures will play in the coming weeks as Republicans seek to make the best of Bush's dwindling honeymoon period.

It was Dove's inconsistent rulings on the critical budget process that led to his dismissal.

The 53-47 vote on Bush's budget also served as a potent reminder that the procedural protections available to the budget — "reconciliation" in the argot of congressional budgeting — are vital to the success of this president. Unless a bill is protected by special rules governing the reconciliation process, it effectively needs 60 votes to pass.

Victory on the budget contrasted with floor action on Bush's landmark education bill (S 1), during which Democrats won a series of floor votes that made the plan significantly less appealing to Bush's conservative party base. On vote after vote, lawmakers approved spending increases that demonstrated the strength of a center-left coalition in Congress with an appetite for spending far beyond Bush's budget limits.

The next severe test of the 50-50 dynamic will come as the Senate turns to Bush's tax cut bill later this month.

Finance Committee Chairman Charles E. Grassley, R-Iowa, and top panel Democrat

By Andrew Taylor / May 12, 2001

Lott, left, and House Budget Chairman Jim Nussle, R-Iowa, celebrated the Senate's passage of the budget resolution, but the tight 53-47 vote showed that reconciliation protection will be vital to the future of the bills needed to carry out the plan outlined in the resolution.

Max Baucus of Montana unveiled a draft bill May 11, but its course through the 10-10 committee could be a wild one. Senate Minority Leader Tom Daschle, D-S.D., has rejoined the panel and is poised to be a force during consideration of amendments the week of May 14, and committee conservatives such as Phil Gramm, R-Texas, are grumbling that the plan does not follow Bush's closely enough.

At the same time, Lott and Daschle remain at an impasse over how to organize the Senate's half of the conference committees, which resolve differences between the House and Senate. The two have been negotiating since January, and until they reach agreement, most bills are blocked from going to conference. (Story, p. 73)

A Critical Time

The timing of Alan S. Frumin's return to the parliamentarian post — he served as parliamentarian for eight years until Democrats relinquished control of the Senate in 1995 — presents Republicans with another complication in negotiating the tortured path of Bush's tax agenda. Some of the most important parliamentary decisions of the year are about to be made.

The Senate will soon take up the pivotal tax cut bill. As a reconciliation bill, the tax cut is safe from filibuster, but as a trade-off for that protection Senate rules place strict limits on what can be in the bill. The parliamentarian determines not only what can be included in a reconciliation bill, but also which floor amendments will be subject to a point of order that can only be overcome with 60 votes.

Under the "Byrd rule," written by the cagey West Virginian in 1985, "extraneous" provisions that have little impact on the budget cannot be included in reconciliation, and it is the parliamentarian who decides which provisions are "extraneous." Now, the rule will be enforced by Byrd's protégé Frumin, instead of Dove, who had a long association with former GOP Leader Bob Dole, R-Kan. (1969-96)

Those calls can be difficult and complicated, and they often have major consequences for legislative strategy and tactics.

In fact, it was a series of budget-related rulings that appears to have cost Dove his job. Dove disappointed Republicans with several rulings that rolled back the GOP's ambitious plans to take advantage of reconciliation procedures to advance Bush's budget and tax plans through the 50-50 Senate.

Republicans complained that the enigmatic Dove flip-flopped on prior decisions after being pressured by Democrats such as Byrd. Those inconsistencies, Republican leaders charged, made it all but impossible to plan a floor strategy and tactics.

"Dove's problem is that he can't give you a yes or no answer," said a GOP senator who was at the center of a recent battle. "And he tends to be pushed by people who visit with him."

Republicans have stewed for weeks as Dove issued parliamentary advice they thought conflicted with prior rulings.

But they are not likely to have better luck with Frumin, who associates say is more skeptical of reconciliation-related shortcuts than was Dove.

They point out that Frumin gave former Majority Leader George J. Mitchell, D-Maine (1980-95), bouts of heartburn by putting a damper on talk of using budget reconciliation to advance President Bill Clinton's universal health care plans.

"There are people around the leader who get dissatisfied about the rulings the umpire makes."

—Ted Stevens, R-Alaska, speaking of former Parliamentarian Robert B. Dove, above

The Last Straw

The final episode for Dove came May 3 as GOP negotiators were trying to wrap up conference talks on the fiscal 2002 budget resolution. Dove decreed that the design of a proposed special emergency fund that would have allowed Congress to appropriate money above the budget resolution cap ran counter to the Budget Act.

The decision would have made the entire budget resolution subject to the 60-vote point of order.

Republican leaders wanted to give the Budget Committee authority to approve emergency appropriations, taking considerable power from the Appropriations Committee, something Dove ruled could not be done under the fast-track reconciliation procedures governing consideration of the budget resolution.

Although it is not clear precisely how events unfolded, shortly after Dove's decision on the emergency fund, Lott ordered him dismissed. The move did not compliment Lott, whose penchant for control and predictability have been hallmarks of his almost five-year stint as majority leader. After Lott's action came to light, Republicans looked, even to one another, as if

they had fired a referee for the way he was calling the game.

"There are people around the leader who get dissatisfied about rulings the umpire makes," said Appropriations Committee Chairman Ted Stevens, R-Alaska. Stevens was in the middle of the episode, having won Dove over to his opinion that the emergency spending provision was subject to the burdensome point of order.

Several GOP senators and aides acknowledged that the ruling that prompted Dove's dismissal was in fact a correct one.

Dove had been in trouble with Lott for some time, and the majority leader had indicated to fellow Republicans that if Dove were fired Frumin would not be his replacement. But after considering what a Lott aide said was a "full list" of potential successors, including the top aide to partisan GOP Whip Don Nickles, R-Okla., Lott had little choice but to follow Senate custom and install the deputy parliamentarian, Frumin. The selection was assured when Dove declined to stay on the job temporarily, said several senior GOP aides.

A Senate GOP officer would only say that Frumin was not Lott's first choice but that he was the only real option under the circumstances.

In a May 9 speech in which he praised Frumin's appointment, Byrd said it was important to avoid "the crass politicization" of the parliamentarian's office and to "reject any tendency to use the office of the parliamentarian as a tool for partisan advantage."

Beyond the rulings themselves, GOP leaders had lost faith that they could predict how Dove might rule.

"The fact of the matter is that if you cannot expect consistency from the parliamentarian, which is so critical to the functioning of the Senate, it creates a serious number of difficulties in managing the Senate," a Senate GOP leadership aide said last month.

At one point, in the week before Senate floor consideration of the budget, Dove issued a ruling that gave Democrats a glimmer of hope that they could force Republicans to muster 60 votes to bring the budget resolution to the floor. Republican strategists found ways around that, but GOP leaders were left seething.

In addition, Dove appeared to change his mind on the core question

No Deal on Conferences

The impasse hardened between Senate leaders over the makeup of conference committees the week of May 7, and that suits Democrats just fine.

"We're content with the current circumstances," said Minority Leader Tom Daschle of South Dakota. "I don't have any problem with not having conferences ever, if that's [Senate Majority Leader Trent Lott's] decision."

Daschle and Mississippi Republican Lott have spent much of the year trading proposals on how to settle the last remaining organizational disagreement of the 107th Congress, and until they do, most of the bills passed separately in the House and Senate cannot be reconciled for consideration by President Bush.

With the Senate split 50-50, the normal rules that give the majority party the upper hand on committees, conferences and the floor do not apply.

From the beginning, Republicans have argued that they deserve one-seat majorities on the Senate side of conference committees, to reflect the majority status they have with Vice President Dick Cheney's tie-breaking vote. Democrats want equal representation on the conferences, to reflect the even split among the 100 senators.

"I have to be satisfied, and of course [Lott] has to be satisfied," said Daschle, whose latest offer would have let Lott break ties on all conference committees if the top Democrat on the panel "certified" that Republicans had made "a good-faith effort" to negotiate.

"I can't go any further than that," Daschle said.

The budget resolution (H Con Res 83) was not affected by the fight because of the special rules governing it. But bankruptcy overhaul legislation (HR 333, S 420), ready for conference since mid-March, remains trapped.

Although Lott and Daschle were close to an accord late last month, no progress has been made recently.

Daschle blamed Republicans, saying some are unwilling to accept any conditions on Lott's authority to break ties in conference committee votes. Some Republicans have complained that Lott gave too much ground when he agreed to a 50-50 split on standing committees, and they will not let him make the same mistake again.

If the stalemate continues, one option would be for the House and Senate to take up each other's bills and pass them again, substituting an amendment that would represent, for practical purposes, a conference agreement. In the case of the bankruptcy bill, the House would take up S 420, substitute the text of a House-Senate agreement, and send the bill back to the Senate, which could then vote to concur with the House action and send the bill to Bush.

This procedure is most commonly used for less controversial bills, and has the potential to vest leverage in the more nimble House. The Senate must reopen the possibility of lengthy debate if it wants to make further revisions to a House-passed product.

— *Matthew Tully*

and Lott and Secretary of the Senate Gary Sisco, who is responsible for the parliamentarian's office, declined comment on the circumstances of Dove's firing.

"It's a personal matter," Lott said.

Daschle appeared to approve of the decision to dump Dove, about whose rulings Daschle had previously complained.

Troubles Ahead

The entire episode cast a harsh new light on the trials of managing the 50-50 chamber at the same time that Republicans sat nearly helpless during floor consideration of Bush's landmark education bill.

"There's a left-of-center coalition that's controlling the floor right now," said Judd Gregg, R-N.H., one of the GOP point men on the education bill. Among the liberal Democrats who won amendments were Paul Wellstone of Minnesota, Edward M. Kennedy of Massachusetts and Barbara A. Mikulski of Maryland.

"I've been in the majority and I've been at 50-50," said Christopher S. Bond, R-Mo. "And the majority's better."

And more battles lie ahead.

Bush's first roster of 11 judicial nominees on May 9 earned praise from Democrats, but in the same breath they announced they will use the full power of their parity in the Senate to enforce the longtime Senate tradition of respecting the opinions of home state senators.

Bush mostly avoided confrontation with his first batch of picks, but problems later seem assured. Among the tools Democrats have said they are willing to employ is denying the Judiciary Committee the quorum required to report a nominee to the floor. Unlike bills, nominations have to pass through committee to have any realistic chance of a floor vote. (*Judges, p. 123, 128*)

As for Lott, he admits he would like to see things go more easily:

"People say, 'Have you changed?' No, the situation's changed. I would prefer to have things move along more smoothly and predictably. But the main thing is to get your work done on the big issues. Eventually, we're going to get an education bill. We're going to get tax relief. We won't get a whole laundry list of things done, but we'll get the big things done." ◆

of whether the budget resolution can allow tax cuts to advance under reconciliation protection at all. In 1996, he ruled that reconciliation could be used to cut taxes, but after heavy lobbying from Byrd earlier this year decided he was no longer willing to affirm his own 1996 ruling on the matter.

A senior Lott aide said Dove was

fired because of this pattern. But many concede that Dove was correct in the disputed ruling regarding the budget resolution, and that all sides contributed to the confusion about what he had decided and what some of the nuances associated with it meant. Still, it was the last straw.

Dove declined to be interviewed,

Another Senate Deal, Another Set of Details

Not long after the dust had settled from the fight over organizing a 50-50 Senate, the chamber flipped to Democrats, which required passing a whole new organizing resolution. Negotiations focused on, and temporarily broke down over, the handling of judicial nominations, which must be confirmed by the Senate after being approved in the Judiciary Committee. Republicans ultimately conceded on June 29 that they had no precedent to support their position in the deal, but until then they fought bitterly.

Republicans concede that Majority Leader Tom Daschle has a winning hand as the 51-49 Senate tries to clear key procedural hurdles and get on with its business.

Now all they want from the South Dakota Democrat is the right to surrender on their own terms.

The usually mundane and obscure steps of "organizing" the Senate took a dramatic turn — at least in the arcane world of Senate precedent and procedure — June 14 when Republicans publicly broke off talks and declared an impasse on a resolution to establish new committee rosters.

Saying the talks had stalled over the kind of assurances Democrats would give that President Bush's Supreme Court nominees would be considered on the floor, Republican negotiators instead demanded that the matter be put to a vote.

Specifically, Republicans want to vote to lock in a 120-year practice under which the Senate has given floor votes to high court nominees, even if they are rejected by the Judiciary Committee. Republicans also want a vote to require that senators who block a judicial nominee from their state with a "blue slip" reveal that action to the public.

"All we're asking for is an assurance that a procedure that's been in effect for 120 years be in effect for the 107th Congress," said Phil Gramm, R-Texas, one of five GOP negotiators who reported the impasse with Daschle at a June 14 news conference. "I think the proposal that we've made, which is to go forward with what we agree on and simply have votes on the two things we differ on, is eminently reasonable, and I'm still hopeful that it might yet be accepted."

Daschle has taken a firm line in reorganizing the Senate to give Democrats an edge on Senate committees to reflect the change from 50-50 to 51-49. He promises fair treatment of Bush's judicial nominees but is unwilling to give explicit guarantees. He also says that the reorganizing should be achieved "through negotiations and discussions, rather than with potentially divisive votes."

The imbroglio has the potential to stall committee action on scores of Bush executive branch and judicial appointments, as

Hatch, left, and McConnell are part of the GOP's negotiating team that decided it has offered Democrats all it can to settle disputes on the reorganization.

well as critical legislation, such as the president's $6.5 billion request for supplemental appropriations for the current fiscal year.

But both sides expressed hope that the matter would not blow up the Senate, and that it could be peacefully resolved the week of June 18. "Nobody gains from chaos," Gramm said. "A continuing impasse helps nobody."

A Good Start, but Then . . .

The announced deadlock came near the end of a week in which the promising start of negotiations had dissolved into rumors of hard feelings. Bickering over committee office space and impolitic handling of the decision to install Democratic Whip Harry Reid of Nevada in the plum Capitol suite occupied by GOP Whip Don Nickles of Oklahoma seemed to sour the atmosphere. And injecting the question of nominations raised the specter of potentially destructive debate about the treatment of President Bill Clinton's judicial nominations.

Minority Leader Trent Lott, R-Miss., demurred from directly participating in the discussions. He had endured criticism for his secretive handling of the 50-50 negotiations that gave Democrats parity on committees,

By Andrew Taylor / June 16, 2001

Quick Contents

Republicans still want a written guarantee that President Bush's Supreme Court nominees will not languish in the Judiciary Committee, but Democrats are only willing to promise to be fair. Now the GOP wants to settle the matter on the floor of the Senate.

and the defection of James M. Jeffords, I-Vt., from the GOP, which cost Republicans the majority.

Instead, Lott named a "gang of five" Republican veterans to negotiate: Gramm, Pete V. Domenici of New Mexico, Orrin G. Hatch of Utah, Mitch McConnell of Kentucky and Arlen Specter of Pennsylvania.

The negotiations started well, according to insider accounts. Daschle immediately agreed to GOP requests that Democrats obtain their one-seat edge on every committee (except for the equally divided Ethics panel) by adding a Democrat, rather than by bumping Republicans. And Daschle agreed to enforce accords by former GOP chairmen and ranking members that committee staff and office space would remain equally divided for the duration of the 107th Congress.

While questions of committee ratios, staff and space would be dealt with in the resolution itself, Republicans pressed for a memorandum of understanding that the Senate would follow past practice and precedents to allow every Supreme Court nominee to be voted upon by the full Senate. They sought comparable assurances for lower court nominees, provided they had not been blackballed by home-state senators or deemed unqualified by the American Bar Association.

Daschle countered with an offer to conduct a colloquy in which he would note the precedents on nominations but not explicitly bind majority Democrats to follow them.

Republicans took umbrage at the notion of a colloquy, which, according to Hatch, does not carry the same "weight" as a signed memorandum. They responded by narrowing their focus on nominations to Supreme Court picks. At the same time, however, they aggravated Daschle by insisting the nominations issue be addressed in the text of the organizing resolution itself.

"We've tried to narrow the focus to get results," Lott said June 13. "[Daschle] makes a proposal; we respond with a broader proposal. He comes back with a broad proposal, but ignores a lot of what we did; we come back with a smaller proposal that he considers a step back."

With the realization that Daschle was unwilling to give them the assurances on nominations that they wanted and that they had little leverage to

force them, Republicans instead sought an exit strategy. They came up with the idea to put the issue to a vote.

Daschle said it was inappropriate to make the organizing resolution a public battle, which left some Republicans scratching their heads. After all, it was only six months ago that Daschle had made it plain he was willing to play hardball to get his way on organizing the 50-50 Senate.

Republicans said floor votes on organization would not be divisive, but would merely express a willingness to agree to disagree.

"We dealt in such good faith . . . that we wanted the thing to end on a good high note," Gramm said. "And we thought the way to do it was to agree on what we'd agreed on and to just have the two votes. I'm surprised he's not doing that."

Said GOP Conference Chairman Rick Santorum of Pennsylvania: "If Sen. Daschle and the Democrats don't like what we're proposing, vote it down. What's the impasse? We're not demanding this as a condition of organizing the Senate."

Out of the Shadows

The process of organizing the Senate is usually trouble-free and unnoticed by anyone other than Senate insiders. Organizing resolutions simply outline committee ratios and rosters. But that changed when last year's elections produced an evenly divided Senate. The long-negotiated resolution (S Res 8) that got the unprecedented 50-50 Senate running addressed a bevy of other issues, such as committee staff ratios, office space and floor procedure.

The historic 50-50 power-sharing deal was the product of difficult negotiations in December and January between Daschle and Lott. The agreement gave Democrats equal seats on Senate committees, as well as equal staff resources and office space.

Lott took extraordinary heat at the time from some fellow Republicans who thought he had conceded too much. Most GOP chairmen thought they should have retained a one-seat edge on their committees, and an 1881 precedent appeared to support that demand. (*Box, p. 67*)

But Daschle held firm, and Lott opted to avoid a protracted battle over organizational issues, largely to allow the Senate to get on with its business and

not distract from the start of the Bush administration.

Just as 50-50 was unprecedented, so too is the mid-session shift of the majority from GOP to Democratic control. Under the 50-50 agreement, a new organizing resolution is required.

Senate committee rosters presently include only holdovers from the 106th Congress; no freshmen officially have committee slots, and more senior senators who have switched to more prestigious committees, such as Finance or Appropriations, have temporarily lost those positions. Democrats are chairmen, but in most instances, they fail to control a majority of their committees.

Republicans entered the talks believing Democrats' desire to replenish committee rosters gave them an opportunity to press for guarantees that Bush's nominees would not be unfairly held up in committee. They cited statements by liberal Democrats pledging to take an aggressive stand against Bush judicial appointees as justification.

But Daschle's position from the start was that there was nothing to negotiate beyond committee rosters, staff budgets and office space. Judicial confirmations are controlled by the majority.

"There's nobody in our caucus who believes we should change the rules," said a Democratic leadership aide. "Daschle's made it clear that he's willing to say publicly that we will, as we have in the past, treat nominees fairly and in good faith."

Still, Democrats remember well how Republicans stalled Clinton's nominees, and that has cemented their resistance to GOP demands. They have made a point of saying that Robert H. Bork and Clarence Thomas, both nominated to the Supreme Court by GOP presidents, still got floor votes after failing to win committee approval. Bork lost, but Thomas was confirmed.

For example, Judiciary Committee Chairman Patrick J. Leahy, D-Vt., said 62 of Clinton's judicial nominations never even got a committee hearing.

"I've been here 25 years. I get a little bit tired of getting lectured by senators who, for example, put secret holds on or held up people," Leahy said. "I've seen some of the most unfair, unjust, sneaky, underhanded things [done] to Clinton nominees.

"And," Leahy said, "I have a proven track record" of treating GOP nominees fairly. ◆

The Vote That Never Happened

Before legislation can go to the floor for consideration by the House of Representatives, rules for the debate must be approved. The length of time to be spent on the issue and the amendments that will be considered are decided in advance, which can make the rule on legislation as significant as the legislation itself. When the campaign finance bill reached the House, advocates of the bill said the rule for debate that was approved by the Rules Committee was designed to kill their bill, so they fought back.

The campaign finance debate ended before it began. Meehan, center, and Shays, right, said the rules of debate were designed to defeat their bill.

Give it a weekend, Sen. John McCain said. Let everyone settle down for a few days and try again next week.

That was July 12. McCain, an Arizona Republican, had just watched the best shot he had seen in years at rewriting the laws of the campaign finance system fall with a thud on the House floor, tangled in a dispute over the rules for debate.

The fight had been nasty. The mood afterward was gloomy. McCain did his best to maintain a can-do optimism for his cause and for the coalition that had come so close to seeing it through.

"I hope when things cool off, as they will over the weekend, that we can bring this up again," he said. "Come the beginning of next week, I hope we can all sit down and work out a way to have a fair consideration of this bill."

But it could be a long time before campaign finance legislation is back. Republican House leaders made clear that they are in no hurry to give it a second chance. And Democratic advocates, who were fighting doubts and divisions within their own coalition right up to the final hours, cannot say with certainty they have the votes to pass their bill if it does return.

Meanwhile, a stack of tardy appropriations bills, among other legislation, await action.

"Right now, I have no plan to bring it up," said Speaker J. Dennis Hastert, R-Ill.

Minority Leader Richard A. Gephardt, D-Mo., said he will meet with members on his side to decide how to proceed. If the GOP leadership is not willing to revisit the issue, Democrats may begin collecting signatures on a "discharge petition" to force the bill (HR 2356), which was cosponsored by Martin T. Meehan, D-Mass., and Christopher Shays, R-Conn., back to the floor of the House.

Shays said he also might try to organize sympathetic Republican votes to block consideration of other matters until they get their debate. But Gephardt said he hopes the debate can go on without such tactics.

"I'm happy to meet with anybody at any time to talk about a way to do this," he said.

After being elevated to a populist cause in McCain's failed presidential bid in 2000, campaign finance had stalled abruptly on a piece of procedural arcana. The issue itself became secondary as both parties veered away from a showdown on the merits of two competing bills. Instead, a vicious fight over how to bundle technical amendments tore at Republicans and, at least for that moment, fortified Democrats who before that were struggling to unite behind their bill.

In the end, 208 Democrats were joined by 19 Republicans and one Independent to defeat the rule for floor consideration of the Shays-Meehan bill.

By John Cochran / July 14, 2001

Under Ney, who with Armey emerged from a July 12 meeting, Republicans proposed a campaign bill attractive enough to tempt some Democrats.

Against the Grain

The defeat of the campaign finance rule required a number of party switchers.

REPUBLICANS	Jim Leach, Iowa	Mark Souder, Ind.
Charles Bass, N.H.	Frank A. LoBiondo, N.J.	Fred Upton, Mich.
Sherwood Boehlert, N.Y.	Constance A. Morella, Md.	Zach Wamp, Tenn.
Michael N. Castle, Del.	Tom Petri, Wis.	Frank R. Wolf, Va.
Greg Ganske, Iowa	Marge Roukema, N.J.	
Lindsey Graham, S.C.	Joe Scarborough, Fla.	**DEMOCRATS**
Amo Houghton, N.Y.	Christopher Shays, Conn.	James A. Traficant Jr.,
Nancy L. Johnson, Conn.	Rob Simmons, Conn.	Ohio

The moment could prove pivotal for the larger campaign finance debate. McCain, who emerged victorious from the Senate's recent battle over the issue, is perhaps the only clear winner, with considerable power to shape how the public views the moment. By the House's action, he claimed a new outrage to take with him on the road.

Democrats, with Gephardt in the lead, gambled by deciding to block debate rather than fight under a rule they believed was unfair. They now must fight for real for the Shays-Meehan bill — or risk criticism that they were only after a political issue.

Republicans gambled, too, and they have tied themselves to the rhetoric of "reform" by backing new restrictions on unregulated "soft money."

No Backup Plan

Both sides seemed stunned by the sudden collapse of a debate that had such promise. Neither offered a clear Plan B. For all concerned, the focus turned instantly to fixing blame for the failure to get the debate under way.

McCain, Gephardt and others said the Republican leadership had stacked the rules against them, forcing the confrontation that brought the day down with a crash. Hastert,

Majority Whip Tom DeLay, R-Texas, and other GOP leaders said Democrats killed the debate to avoid the embarrassment of watching their favored bill, which would ban soft-money contributions to national political parties, go down to defeat.

One thing was undeniable: A day full of dramatic twists, reversals and standoffs left members exhausted, battered and angry.

"This is pretty intense," Rep. Albert R. Wynn, D-Md., said at one point. "The stakes are high."

Few issues are of greater personal significance to lawmakers than rewriting the laws that govern how they fund their own campaigns. The House had been moving toward what promised to be a cliff-hanger between two rival pieces of campaign finance legislation.

One was McCain's preferred bill, legislation mirroring the one (S 27) that he and Russell D. Feingold, D-Wis., had pushed to passage in the Senate on April 2 after two hard-fought weeks. The House version is sponsored by Shays and Meehan, who outmaneuvered the Republican leadership twice before to drive a nearly identical bill through the House, in 1998 and 1999.

That measure (HR 2356) would ban soft money to national political parties and restrict the ability of labor unions, for-profit corporations and nonprofits to directly fund "issue advertising" — which the bill's proponents call thinly veiled campaign spots — close to Election Day.

The bill would allow state and local parties to raise limited soft-money contributions for get-out-the-vote and voter registration efforts as long as they did not name a federal candidate. Members of Congress and national political parties would be forbidden from helping in those efforts.

Against that legislation the Republican leadership pitted a less restrictive bill (HR 2360) with provisions designed to drive apart the coalition that got Shays-Meehan through the House in the past.

That rival bill — written by Ohio Republican Bob Ney, chairman of the House Administration Committee — would cap soft-money contributions to national political parties at $75,000 per year and forbid the money from being used for anything except generic voter registration and get-out-the-vote activities. It would put no restrictions on soft-money fundraising at the state and local level.

Ney's bill aimed directly and purposefully at fears within the 38-member Congressional Black Caucus, whose members mostly had supported a soft-money ban in the past. Those members said such a ban might hamper voter-mobilization efforts in minority communities. The 18-member Hispanic Caucus, also all Democrats and past supporters of the Shays-Meehan bill, shared those concerns.

Proponents of Shays-Meehan faced a twofold task: In a narrowly divided House, they could ill afford to lose votes from their original coalition of backers, but they could not make wholesale changes that would leave the bill too different from McCain-Feingold and risk losing Senate support. Every change to the bill had to be vetted with the Senate sponsors and leadership, in an effort to avoid a conference committee to reconcile House and Senate versions. Shays and Meehan feared a conference would give opponents another chance to kill the bill.

As the clock ticked down, Shays and Meehan worked to fine-tune their bill by asking the House Rules Committee to bundle 14 changes into a single "manager's amendment."

The changes included striking one of the restrictions Shays and Meehan had placed on the soft-money fundraising done by state and local parties.

In a July 11 meeting that slipped past midnight, the House Rules Committee refused to let Shays and Meehan bundle their changes. Each of the 14 amendments would require its own vote. Shays, Meehan and their supporters were stunned, and accused the Republican leadership of trying to bring down the bill with a complicated, obstacle-strewn rule.

At a news conference the following morning with McCain, Feingold and others, Shays said he was profoundly disappointed. He had said repeatedly since the Senate passed McCain-Feingold in April that he was confident Hastert would give his bill a fair shot.

Asked at the news conference if the Speaker had broken that promise, Shays looked down for a few pregnant moments.

"I had a distinguished senator say we're going to get screwed," Shays finally said. "I said no. But he was right."

McCain, standing to his right, broke in with a wry crack: "I would never use such language."

Hastert was clearly annoyed by what Shays had said, telling reporters he had "bent over backwards" to accommodate the Connecticut Republican. Hastert said he had promised a full, fair debate just after the July Fourth recess, and that's what Shays would get.

"I stuck by that commitment," he said.

Hastert, however, was under pressure from other Republicans to change the rules of debate in response to Shays' concerns, and he was working on a rewrite even as the debate began. Negotiations were going on behind the scenes, with Shays moving between the Speaker's office and Gephardt's.

When the floor debate on the rule finally began, just before 2 p.m., Democrats lined up to criticize it. Meehan said Republican leaders were standing in the way of a straightforward debate on the bill.

"What this is really about is technicalities designed to kill a bill that would end soft-money abuse," he said.

New York Republican Thomas M. Reynolds, a member of the Rules Committee, defended the rule, saying Meehan and Shays would get the opportu-

"What this is really about is technicalities designed to kill a bill that would end soft-money abuse."

—Rep. Martin T. Meehan, D-Mass., cosponsor of the bill

nity to make every change to the bill that they had requested.

"The Speaker pledged a fair, open and timely debate on this measure, and as has been the hallmark of his leadership, today he made good on that commitment," he said.

Majority Leader Dick Armey, R-Texas, attacked Shays' demands to make so many late changes to his bill with one amendment as "unreasonable" and "arrogant."

A Compromise Undone

By that point, however, Hastert had offered to give Shays what he wanted. In return, Ney would get one amendment of his own, the nature of which would be determined later. Gephardt demanded to see Ney's amendment and to have time to discuss it with his caucus before he would agree to support the new rule.

Some Republicans agreed that the original rule was unfair and vowed to oppose it. Among them were Lindsey Graham of South Carolina, Zach Wamp of Tennessee and Michael N. Castle of Delaware. Some of those Republicans and others, including Fred Upton of Michigan, also met with

Gephardt and McCain.

"Shays felt shafted, and we're trying to redress that with a fair rules process," Upton said.

But at the same time, a larger group of Republican conservatives demanded that Hastert stick with the original rule. Their opposition forced a pause in the floor action, driving the Republican Conference behind closed doors in the basement. By many accounts the meeting was a bruiser.

"This is hardball politics today," Graham said later.

Before that caucus, an angry John Shadegg, R-Ariz., vowed to bring down any new rule. The public deserved to hear full debate on every change Shays and Meehan wanted to make in their bill, Shadegg said.

"We believe the original rule was eminently fair," he said. ". . . You don't back off of a position you've taken."

In the end, Republicans said they would not concede to Gephardt's demand to review Ney's amendment, saying they were running out of time. Gephardt did not really want an agreement, they said, and was just trying to obstruct the process.

Republicans poured out of their conference at about 5:30 p.m. Minutes later, the rule went down, and the finger-pointing on both sides began.

"After a long and strenuous path to try to pass campaign finance reform, it's pretty apparent that the Democratic leader of the House of Representatives decided to scuttle the attempt to do it," Hastert said. ". . . It's pretty clear Mr. Gephardt doesn't want the result. He'd rather have the issue for a campaign issue. That's sad."

Shays said he could have lived with breaking the changes to his bill into a few amendments, but not 14.

"I knew when they did it in 14 parts that the fix was on," he said. "This was designed to be a process that would simply not allow for fair debate."

What cards either side was left holding when the debate fell apart — and what it might portend for any future debate on the issue — was unclear.

Gephardt may have been making headway with the Black Caucus. After a last meeting July 12, members said they were waiting for a written document that would have promised that the Democratic National Committee, the Democratic Congressional Campaign Committee and the Democratic Senatorial Campaign Committee

Mild-Mannered Rebel Shays Takes Leaders' Attacks in Stride

For years, Connecticut Republican Christopher Shays has led the fight against his leadership to push for a broad campaign finance overhaul. But the nasty battle over the issue the week of July 9 put him in the middle as never before.

Majority Leader Dick Armey, R-Texas, attacked him on the floor. Other GOP leaders and their aides branded Shays as a Democratic collaborator.

"Shays is not interested in negotiating because he doesn't have the sign-off of [Minority Leader Richard A.] Gephardt," John Feehery, spokesman for House Speaker J. Dennis Hastert, R-Ill., told reporters in the midst of the day's maneuvering. "The Speaker has tried to work with Shays, but he doesn't have the sign-off of Mr. Gephardt."

But Shays, known as one of the most mild-mannered members of Congress, stuck to his position. Asked about potential retribution from his leadership, he said: "I don't care."

Shays proudly touts a long list of issues on which he routinely goes against the prevailing winds of his party. He supports environmental protection, gun control and abortion

Shays endured stinging criticism from his own party, but he vows to keep fighting.

rights, and he has opposed efforts to eliminate family-planning funds from both domestic and foreign spending bills.

Shays also was one of only four House Republicans who opposed all four articles of impeachment against President Bill Clinton. In total, he voted more frequently with Clinton than all but a handful of his GOP colleagues; in the 106th Congress, he backed Clinton almost half the time

— ranking him as one of the president's top 10 Republican allies.

Shays was one of a sizable minority of Republicans who bucked their leadership and sided with Democrats in 1996 and in 2000 in support of increasing the minimum wage. He also was in the minority of Republicans who supported Clinton's 1994 anticrime bill, which included a ban on certain semiautomatic, assault-style weapons.

Shays is deliberate and patient when making his case. Although not shy about challenging his opponents, he usually does so without appearing strident. On July 13, Shays said he bore no grudge against his leadership.

"There's nobody I respect more than Denny Hastert," he said.

Shays also had kind words for Armey: "I really like Dick Armey. I really like the guy."

But he vowed to do "anything and everything" to get his campaign finance bill (HR 2356) back to the floor for debate, even if that means rallying other Republicans to stymie his leadership on other issues.

"This bill will come to the floor of the House again," Shays said. "And we will vote on it."

— *John Cochran and David Mark*

would devote about 15 percent of their money to get-out-the-vote efforts.

Daschle stopped by that meeting. So did Howard Wolfson, the executive director of the DCCC.

Gephardt "said some things that gave us some comfort," said Maryland Democrat Elijah E. Cummings, vice chairman of the caucus.

The chairman of the Hispanic Caucus, Silvestre Reyes, D-Texas, said he thought most of his members were poised to support Shays-Meehan.

But Wynn, a prominent member of the Black Caucus, had decided to cosponsor the Ney bill. Other caucus members said they planned to vote against both.

Democratic Caucus Chairman Mar-

tin Frost of Texas opposes the restrictions the Shays-Meehan bill places on members of Congress getting involved with state and local party fundraising.

The day before the debate, he sent out a letter to members warning them about it and said he would vote against the bill unless it was changed.

At the same time, efforts to win over Republican freshmen, many of whom McCain campaigned for, may have come to little.

All but one, Rob Simmons of Connecticut, voted with the Republicans for the GOP rule. And Simmons opposed it only as a favor to Shays.

"As I sat there and watched the thing go down," Simmons said. "I figured this is not going to win, so I might

as well stick with Chris Shays."

Meehan said he is convinced that he and Shays had made great progress shoring up support for their bill in the final days and hours. Gephardt said the same.

Ney, who argued throughout the week that his alternative bill was pulling votes away from Shays-Meehan, said the fight over the rule shows he was winning.

"We have beaten Mr. Gephardt on the vote," Ney said. "Everyone knows it."

But Feingold, like McCain, played cheerleader as the week drew to a disappointing close. "We're going to win," he said. "We're going to win sooner than it may feel right now." ◆

Congress and the Making of Public Policy

The main job of Congress is to write and approve legislation that sets national policies on everything from how much tax money to spend on the military to ensuring market competition in industries where a single company might be able to consume all its rivals. Most of the time Congress spends on its legislative business is devoted to the federal budget, which is broken up into 13 appropriations bills that must be passed every year in order to keep government functions funded and operating. But even within the seemingly small universe of dollars and cents, Congress has ways to wield great authority in setting national policy. The most obvious is in the decision Congress makes about which programs to fund and which programs not to fund, be they social projects such as adult literacy programs or scientific operations such as research at the National Institutes of Health. Congress also can set policy by putting conditions on the use of federal money, as it has done by threatening to withhold highway construction money from states that do not enact certain speed limit laws or drunk driving standards. In addition, since appropriations bills must be passed each year, they become popular vehicles for controversial changes in federal policy on such things as gun control or abortion. These provisions, which have nothing at all to do with the federal budget, are called policy "riders."

Beyond the budget is a wide world of policy questions for Congress. Industries seek policy changes or additions to aid their business in all manner of ways, from the easing of tax requirements to the opening of trade relations with countries or regions of the world. For Congress, the making of public policy is a complex equation. To begin, there may be differing views within the House and Senate on how much federal involvement is necessary to resolve a particular problem. Traditionally, Republicans have favored less government involvement while Democrats have favored more, but that generalization sometimes dissolves when it gets down to the details of a particular policy proposal. It is true, though, that every policy proposal has a constituency that is pushing for it. Often, there is constituency in opposition. In the end, these groups introduce complex political considerations that quite often are more determinative of the outcome than the abstract values of fairness, equity or actual legislative needs.

Being Bold in the Chair

Few committees in Congress have as wide-reaching jurisdiction as the House Commerce Committee, which lays claim to an abundance of influential economic issues. The ability of that committee to stay current with America's fast-moving economy depends in large part on its chairman, Rep. Billy Tauzin of Louisiana.

One of the maxims of K Street is that the best bill on Capitol Hill is usually a dead one. For risk-averse business lobbyists, who have thrived on gridlock, the new chairman of the House Energy and Commerce Committee has a simple message: "I want to move bills."

With Billy Tauzin of Louisiana wielding the gavel, the cavernous Rayburn Building hearing room of the oldest legislative committee in Congress — created 206 years ago — will be a very different place than during the past six years of Republican control. No one expects a continuation of the deliberative stewardship of the previous GOP chairman, Thomas J. Bliley Jr. of Virginia. Instead, there are plenty of reasons to expect that Tauzin will run the committee much more in the style of its most recent Democratic chairman, John D. Dingell of Michigan. During his 14 years at the helm, Dingell built a remarkable fiefdom through a combination of ruthless expansionism and shrewd deal-cutting.

"He is much more activist than his predecessor," Dingell says in describing Tauzin. "He and I will probably agree more than Bliley and I would."

Once known primarily as a fierce champion of his state's oil and gas industry, a mainstay of the "old" economy, Tauzin's desire to be at the center of the Next Big Debate has prompted him to become pivotal on topics central to the success of the "new" economy. In the 107th Congress, he sees himself as a principal decision maker when it comes to balancing competition and regulation as the preferred incubators of electronic commerce.

But in the next two years, Tauzin aspires to act not only on that question but also on almost every front that is made available to him by his panel's expansive range of jurisdiction:

• **Telecommunications:** He wants to liberate the local Bell telephone companies from current restrictions, including on their ability to offer long-distance service and thereby be conduits of the Internet.

• **Health care:** He wants to have an important hand in the next version of legislation to protect the rights of patients in managed-care medical insurance plans.

• **Consumer protection:** He wants to push for a law to enhance the privacy of online shoppers.

• **Energy:** He wants to be the House's principal figure now that the debates over federal fuel and electricity policies are climbing up the national agenda.

• **Environment:** He wants to rewrite the superfund statute (PL 96-510) to increase businesses' flexibility for dealing with their hazardous wastes and to limit their responsibility for the waste problems they inherit from others.

Tauzin's approach is rooted in a view that the Republican Party often should embrace rather than fear aggressive moves to write legislation to shape the behavior of American industry — or at least be willing to use the bully pulpit of Capitol Hill to try to change corporate behavior. During his nearly 21 years in Congress, his preference has increasingly been for a deregulatory approach, especially since

By Alan K. Ota / Feb. 3, 2001

switching parties in 1995. He still often sounds like the populist Southern Democrat he once was, especially when he can frame the debate as being about consumer protection. But his career has been marked as much as anything by a desire to be a playmaker, building coalitions to win support for his point of view and often shifting his point of view in the process.

To the consternation of some conservatives, for example, he initially responded to the Firestone tire recall last year with a series of hearings at which he heaped criticism on Bridgestone/ Firestone Inc. and Ford Motor Co. After that, he persuaded GOP leaders to work for enactment of his legislation (PL 106-414) setting new rules for the disclosure of product safety information.

In typical fashion, Tauzin sought to trump the philosophical case against the bill advanced by deregulatory purists among the Republicans with two other arguments, one to appeal to the affected business and the other to his colleagues. To the auto industry, he said his proposal was far preferable to alternatives then gathering steam in the Senate. To fellow Republicans, he argued that only holding hearings would be perceived by the public as too weak a response — especially three months before Election Day. Consumer advocacy groups such as Public Citizen say the law is toothless, but Tauzin sees it as a model for his future consumer protection campaigns. He said he was determined not to cede such issues to the Democrats, who have been the more regular allies of consumer watchdog groups.

"Where I go off is when something is broken, when the system is not working," Tauzin said. "It's part of where I come from. . . . It is a Southern tradition to be passionate. Passion is what touches people."

The 'Cajun Ambassador'

Even his rivals for power in the House say Tauzin has several advantages as he seeks to advance his agenda.

Since quitting the Democratic Party for the GOP, he has displayed an ability to toggle between the parties, neither calling his new fealty to the Republican leadership into question nor angering his old colleagues across the aisle.

His animated and back-slapping style — he calls himself the Cajun ambassador to Congress — belies an intense competitiveness and a diligence when it comes to learning the nuances of policy. (Biography, p. 84)

"Billy tries to keep that a secret, but he is a serious legislator," says Majority Leader Dick Armey, R-Texas, who held a series of debates across the country with Tauzin in 1997-98 on how to overhaul the tax code. (Armey favored a flat income tax, Tauzin a national sales tax.) "Some people may miss the point about how good he is."

When stalking for votes and trying to flush out the positions of wavering Republicans, he can be as methodical as his most potent political ally in the House, Majority Whip Tom DeLay, R-Texas. This year, Tauzin will be especially well-positioned to advance his measures, because he will be not only a committee chairman but also one of DeLay's deputy whips. (DeLay, p. 37)

"Billy is very good at explaining to members how a vote may relate to their future in the Congress," says Roy Blunt, R-Mo., the chief deputy whip. "I don't think anybody . . . has a better sense of policy and politics. He is very good at figuring out what needs to be done and how to get it done. It's rare to have proficiency in both areas."

The formidable campaign fundraising operation Tauzin

set up to help his campaign for the chairmanship should now pay additional dividends. Having traveled the country in the past two years to raise an estimated $8 million for other GOP candidates — and having collected $800,000 from business interests while spending $1.3 million on a campaign in which he lacked major party opposition — Tauzin is poised to call in a host of chits this year.

Tauzin has cultivated a power-sharing relationship with the six men who will chair the subcommittees of Energy and Commerce, who he expects will uniformly be with him as he advances his agenda. "I used to be a one-general army. Now, I have six generals," he said in an interview Jan. 18.

The remark is a clear reminder of one of Tauzin's more famously flamboyant stunts: his uncanny evocation of George C. Scott's portrayal of Gen. George S. Patton in an inspirational GOP fundraising video. More routinely, however, Tauzin is apt to put more of a down-home spin on his charm offensive. He has been known to make a pot of gumbo available in his office. He makes recipes from his book, "Cook and Tell: Unique Cajun Recipes and Stories," a centerpiece of his fundraisers. He entertains lobbyists and colleagues at his hunting lodge, a mobile home near a wildlife preserve on Maryland's Eastern Shore. And like several other members (Dingell among them), he has decorated his office with hunting trophies — one of them an alligator head, its jaw stuffed with Mardi Gras beads.

Tauzin's legislative salesmanship has captured the attention of K Street, where he is seen — for better or worse — as a catalyzing force. "He's a wheeler-dealer. He wants to be in the room when the deal is cut. He doesn't just want to give speeches," said former Sen. J. Bennett Johnston, D-La. (1972-97), now an energy industry lobbyist.

"The strength of Billy is that he understands how to move things," said David K. Rehr, president of the National Beer Wholesalers Association. "Everyone knows he is for-

Tauzin, here in 1985, now is a prime playmaker on the "new economy" issues before Congress. But he has not lost an interest in energy, the topic central to his state's economy, on which he made his early mark. He has joined Bush in advocating oil drilling in the Arctic National Wildlife Refuge.

midable. If you're with him, that's a blessing. If you're against him, it's a curse."

Critics suggest, however, that Tauzin's zeal to cut deals could lead him to either enrage the more conservative Republicans in the House or to lose control of the size and shape of whatever legislation he is trying to shepherd. "There are mixed feelings among business lobbyists. They are not sure exactly what will happen this year," said Frank Torres, a lobbyist for Consumers Union.

Tauzin responds to his critics by saying he will make sure that whatever deals he strikes are acceptable to the House GOP leadership. "We need to develop packages of reform that Tom DeLay can easily pass on the floor. The worst thing that happens to Tom is when he gets a package that he can't even sell to the Republican team."

Tauzin's counterpart across the Capitol, John McCain, R-Ariz., chairman of the Senate Commerce Committee, sees a bit of his own maverick style in Tauzin. "Things that were not on the table before," McCain said in a Jan. 30 interview, "are on the table now. He is open to discuss things. He is courageous."

Turf Battle With Oxley

Tauzin's arrival at the center chair on the Energy and Commerce dais is not a surprise. Almost from the start, he was perceived as the favorite in his campaign against Michael G. Oxley of Ohio to succeed Bliley (1981-2001), who retired after reaching his six-year limit as chairman. Instead of cinching the victory outright — in the vote of all House Republicans, for which he had been preparing for two years — Tauzin was compelled to accept the prize while paying a higher-than-expected price: Two of Energy and Commerce's most highly prized slices of legislative jurisdiction — over securities and insurance — were transferred to a new Financial Services Committee, with Oxley as the chairman. *(Story, p. 54)*

David C. King, a public policy professor at Harvard University and author of the 1997 book "Turf Wars: How Congressional Committees Claim Jurisdiction," says that the outcome was a significant setback for Tauzin, who now will be under pressure to prove he can be a strong defender of his panel's legislative prerogatives.

"Prior chairmen have had great success in expanding the turf of that committee," King said in a Feb. 1 interview.

"With the loss of territory, the war is not over for Tauzin. There's going to be a lot of other battles. He's going to have to prove his toughness and prove that he can win these fights."

But his allies say Tauzin will be a ferocious defender of the committee's remaining turf, pointing to his ongoing effort to prevent other panels — Oxley's, first and foremost — from impinging on his committee's pre-eminence in laying ground rules for the new economy. Speaker J. Dennis Hastert, R-Ill., settled one such skirmish Jan. 20, when he made public an agreement under which Tauzin will keep jurisdiction over the bookkeeping standards for business and all online commerce except the sale of securities. Oxley will have jurisdiction over a new generation of online stock exchanges and their competition with traditional stock markets.

Even before that scuffle ended, Tauzin was moving to put in place a decentralized committee power structure he says is designed to develop and move bills quickly.

Under Bliley, subcommittee chairmen were required to work in consort with the committee's staff director, James E. Derderian, who assigned staff employees to work on projects blessed by Bliley. Derderian has been replaced by David V. Marventano, a former Se-

curities Industries Association lobbyist and chief of staff for former Rep. Bill Paxon, R-N.Y. (1989-99), and the subcommittee chairmen will be able to hire their own staff directors and develop their own bills. They will meet weekly with Tauzin to coordinate their efforts. "We are moving away from an authoritarian structure. We are going to emphasize teamwork," says James C. Greenwood, R-Pa., the new chairman of the Oversight and Investigations Subcommittee.

"Staff directors will be loyal to subcommittee chairmen; it's an important change," said Cliff Stearns, R-Fla., chairman of the new Subcommittee on Commerce, Trade and Consumer Protection.

Internet Privacy

Looking for a relatively quick and politically painless first victory this year, Tauzin is expected to move on two areas outside the jurisdiction of his committee. He will renew his efforts on behalf of a repeal of the 3 percent excise tax on telephone service, a proposal in the purview of the House Ways and Means Committee. And he hopes bipartisan legislation he helped to write (HR 50), which would set a national uniform poll closing time, becomes a part of any electoral overhaul package.

Tauzin, shown at right in 1995, made the cause of satellite broadcasters his own in drafting the cable television regulation law of 1992, one of his first forays into high-tech lawmaking. He switched parties in 1995 after the GOP promised he could keep his seniority on the Commerce Committee. At the start of the 105th Congress, he cemented his position as a steward of high-tech legislation by becoming chairman of the Telecommunications Subcommittee. Since then, he has become a critic of much of the 1996 rewrite of telecommunications law.

As he begins marking up bills in his own committee, Tauzin will face a series of challenges that will test his ability to simultaneously move his own agenda, show the regulatory restraint that most Republicans want and maintain the trust of the businesses that backed his rise to the chairmanship.

One of the first key tests will come on the question of whether the federal government should restrict the ability of online vendors to collect personal information about their customers. The debate came to nothing last year.

This year, Tauzin has promised to move what he sees as middle-ground legislation by November. It aims to enhance consumer privacy predominantly by giving incentives to businesses that restrict their own data collection.

Trade groups representing a broad spectrum of industry have shown little enthusiasm for passage of any sort of privacy protection legislation. "We don't want a knee-jerk reaction of regulation. We need to be very careful of overreach. We do not want legislation that would unduly place restrictions on businesses," Lonnie Taylor, chief lobbyist for the U.S. Chamber of Commerce, said Jan. 10.

Some online businesses say Tauzin's proposal, still in draft form, could become a vehicle for a more regulatory approach — such as a requirement that they obtain customers' consent before collecting personal data, such as Internet browsing and buying habits.

"What we don't want is a train wreck where we have to put all our creative people to work figuring out what the legislation is, as opposed to doing what they do best," Robert Herbold, chief operating officer of the software giant Microsoft Corp., said at a Jan. 19 news conference.

Floyd Kvamme, a partner in the Silicon Valley venture capital firm Kleiner Perkins Caulfield & Byers and a Bush administration adviser on high-tech issues, said Tauzin's proposal has been tepidly received because the industry is sharply divided. "There are two schools of thought. Some want a bill. Some don't. I personally lean toward a moratorium, legislation that would prevent further legislation temporarily in this area." Kvamme said Jan. 19.

As a first step, some high-tech executives said, Congress should prevent states from creating their own restrictions, maintaining that such a patch-

The Tauzin File

Rise from Chackbay
Born Wilbert Joseph Tauzin II on June 14, 1943, in Chackbay, deep in the Cajun country of southern Louisiana. Nicknamed "Billy" by a grandfather, who ran a dance hall and was a member of the Parish Police Jury, akin to a county council. Received B.A. in 1964 from Nicholls State University and J.D. in 1967 from Louisiana State University, where he befriended classmate John B. Breaux. Married since 1993 to Cecile Bergeron; has five grown children from his previous marriage. In the state House from 1971 to 1980, he rose to be floor leader for Gov. Edwin W. Edwards. Elected to the U.S. House as a Democrat in a 1980 special election to succeed GOP Rep. David C. Treen (1973-80), who had been elected governor. Named to the Energy and Commerce Committee in 1981. Finished fourth in a 1987 race for governor. Re-elected eight times as a Democrat and three times as a Republican in the 3rd District, which Bill Clinton carried twice and George W. Bush carried with 52 percent in 2000.

A Break and a Rivalry
In 1993, broke with Clinton over the president's advocacy of an energy tax. Voted for the plan as part of a deficit reduction bill but excoriated the president for failing to provide political cover for oil state Democrats. Early in 1995, helped found a conservative coalition of House Democrats and arranged for it to be named after a Louisiana pop culture icon, the blue dog of painter George Rodrigue. In August 1995, switched to the Republican Party after winning a promise that he could keep his seniority on the Commerce panel. In 1996, became the first member of Congress to change party affiliations and then run unopposed for re-election. In 1997, in the opening round of a battle for panel leadership with Michael G. Oxley of Ohio, a subcommittee that both wanted was split: Tauzin got control of telecommunications issues; Oxley hazardous waste and finance. In January, their rivalry climaxed when GOP leaders picked Tauzin to chair Energy and Commerce but allowed Oxley to take the panel's securities and insurance jurisdiction with him and become the new chairman of Financial Services.

Legislative Accomplishments
Pushed a provision (PL 97-35) repealing a 1978 ban on natural gas burning by utilities. Led campaign to stymie legislation designed to limit retail fuel price increases by forcing producers to renegotiate gas contracts with utilities. Helped push into law (PL 99-499) a renewal of the superfund hazardous waste cleanup program financed partly by a crude oil tax that was higher on imports than on domestic crude. Wrote provision in cable television regulation law (PL 102-385) barring program vendors from discriminating against satellite broadcasters. Prime sponsor of law (PL 104-67), enacted over Clinton veto, to limit lawsuits by disgruntled investors. Wrote curbs on wetlands protections in bill that House passed, but Senate killed. The next year, promoted bipartisan overhaul of safe drinking water law (PL 104-182). Pushed enactment of measure (PL 106-414) requiring auto industry to give data on product liability problems to federal regulators.

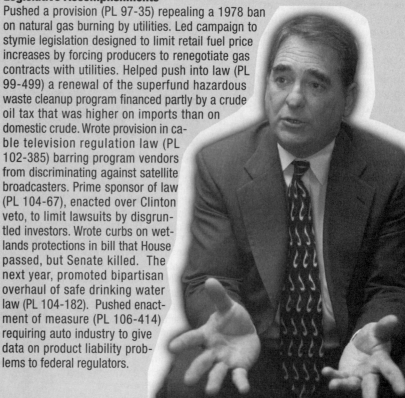

work would be difficult to enforce. "We would be comfortable with privacy legislation as long as it includes federal pre-emption of conflicting state laws and regulations," Meg Whitman, president of the online auction service eBay Inc., said Jan. 19.

A New Telecom Law?

Another fractious battle looms over Tauzin's bid to rewrite the telecommunications law (PL 104-104) enacted five years ago. The law was designed to spur competition through deregulation, and Bliley was content to wait out the evolution of the industry. Tauzin said the desired outcome has not happened to his satisfaction.

With Dingell, Tauzin is working to draft a package of proposals to hasten development of high-speed Internet services over both telephone and cable television lines. As in the 106th Congress, its central element would be to back away from a centerpiece of the 1996 law: the requirement that the Baby Bells open their local markets to competition before being allowed to offer long-distance services in that state. Tauzin and Dingell want to drop that caveat and let the local phone companies into the long-distance data transmission business immediately, predicting that this will drive down retail prices for high-speed Internet access.

Their effort this time will have additional and influential backing from Michael K. Powell, the new chairman of the Federal Communications Commission.

The proposal, however, continues to face opposition from established long-distance carriers AT&T Corp. and Worldcom Inc., and their powerful allies in the Senate, including Majority Leader Trent Lott, R-Miss., and Ernest F. Hollings, D-S.C., the ranking member of the Senate Commerce Committee.

The Baby Bells say the current federal restriction on their offering data transmission service is particularly unfair, since their main potential competition, cable television providers, are regulated only by local authorities.

Tauzin opposes proposals to require cable companies to make their lines available to others who want to transmit data, a move for what is known as "open access," which would curtail cable TV's current competitive advantage.

One potential compromise would be to provide tax incentives to companies that install fiber-optic lines that could carry the Internet or entertainment programming. Sen. John D. Rockefeller IV, D-W.Va., has introduced such a proposal (S 88), and others, including Rep. Cal Dooley, D-Calif., have similar proposals in the works. Tax breaks "may be the last resort," Tauzin said, "but the first resort ought to be policies that encourage competitive offerings."

Another Energy Deal

Tauzin chaired the Telecommunications Subcommittee from 1997 through 2000 and is sure to keep a focus on those issues. But this year he expects that energy policy may occupy the largest piece of his time.

Oil and gas refining is the main industry in his House district along the Gulf coast, and Tauzin said that for now he backs the administration's argument that California should try to solve its current crisis of electricity shortages itself, without further federal intervention. President Bush laid out the rough outline of his plan — emphasizing measures to encourage oil and gas development — in a short telephone call to congratulate Tauzin on Jan. 4, minutes after he was named to his chairmanship.

"There is a big job for us to do" Tauzin recalled Bush as saying. "We need to find out what's gone wrong with the electric power system in California. And we need to fix it quickly before it becomes a major crisis."

He and Joe L. Barton, R-Texas, chairman of the Subcommittee on Energy and Air Quality, will visit California this month. But for now, Tauzin said, any legislation he would back would not include price controls. He has opposed proposals similar to a measure (HR 238) by Anna G. Eshoo, D-Calif., and Duncan Hunter, R-Calif., to authorize the Energy Department to cap wholesale energy prices.

In this "gas-guzzle, high-tech economy," Tauzin said, "what we have is a failure of supplies to meet demand. . . . We lack refining capacity in this country. And we lack electric power generation capacity."

Patients' Rights Redux

On managed care — sure to be revived as a premier consumer issue again this year — Tauzin has not yet tipped his hand on what he would prefer. In any case, his panel will probably play a secondary role in the House to the Ways and Means Committee and its new chairman, Bill Thomas, R-Calif., who has been the House GOP's leading voice on health care policy. (*Other chairmen, p. 59*)

Tauzin voted against the patient protections package by Dingell and Charlie Norwood, R-Ga., the House passed in 1999, although he voted for all three more-limited Republican options. Tauzin said he

Tauzin has taken over the Energy and Commerce chairmanship with the retirement of Thomas J. Bliley Jr., here at a 1997 markup. For much of its 206-year history, the panel has been the prime exerciser of this clause in the Constitution: "Congress shall have the power to regulate commerce with foreign nations, and among the several states." While using that power to regulate the cables and wires that are the current conduits of commerce, the committee continues to maintain jurisdiction over such previously powerful mediums as railroads and trucks.

feared the Norwood-Dingell bill would increase claims against small businesses for behavior that more properly should be attributed to health maintenance organizations.

Greg Ganske of Iowa, a leading GOP advocate of the Norwood-Dingell bill on the Energy and Commerce panel, said he holds out hope that Tauzin will alter his position this year. "In the last session, Billy was competing for a chairmanship. A lot of pressure is on those guys to toe the line," Ganske said in a Jan. 17 interview. "This year, I am hoping things will be different. He is a strong individual."

Tauzin said he is eager to have a hand in drafting this year's measure. "We need to have a resolution of disputes before people get to court. That's the big concern I have with Charlie's bill," he said. "But I've told him from day one that he doesn't have to run off with his own version. We can work out something in the committee and we will."

Money Politics

While pursuing the chairmanship during the past two years, he entertained lavishly at the Republican National Convention in Philadelphia, hosted a fishing trip for the benefit of the National Republican Congressional Committee (NRCC) in Islamorada, Fla., and also hosted more than 90 fundraisers for other Republicans, one-third of them in the candidates' districts. A typical appearance featured a feast of jambalaya and other Louisiana delicacies — sometimes prepared by his cousin Jimmy Gravois, from recipes in the campaign cookbook — and a raconteur's turn by Tauzin, who revels in telling tall tales and jokes involving "Boudreaux," a fictional Cajun bon vivant.

Some of this self-promoting largess was paid out of the $1.7 million contributed in 1999-2000 to Tauzin's campaign and to Bayou Leader PAC, his leadership political action committee.

"Billy Tauzin is coming into office as the chairman of one of the premier committees in Congress with a satchel full of IOUs," said Larry Makinson, a senior fellow with the Center for Responsive Politics, a nonprofit group that monitors political cash. "The industries that invest in him are going to be looking for some kind of return. He's in a prime position to deliver."

Tauzin rejects any hint that his legislative agenda will be driven by con-

tributors. "I wasn't born rich, never got rich and probably never will be rich," Tauzin said. "I've got to raise money for my campaigns. Nobody who contributes to me can get me to vote a certain way on a bill."

On Tauzin's most recent annual congressional financial disclosure form, for 1999, he listed assets of between $161,000 and $465,000, mainly in retirement accounts, life insurance, and property. He supplemented his congressional salary with income from his property in Maryland, including annual membership fees — to pay for upkeep and to keep the waterfowl fed before they are shot — of about $2,000 he collects from a dozen or so members of his three-year-old Long Point Hunt Club.

Asked if any club members are lobbyists with business in his committee, Tauzin mentioned three: Ward H. White of BellSouth Corp.; Wallace Henderson, a former aide who now presses the interest of telecommunications energy and financial services companies; and former Rep. Lloyd Meeds, D-Wash. (1965-79), an energy industry and railroad lobbyist. Tauzin said the arrangement was blessed by the House ethics committee in 1997.

In raising money for the 2002 election, Tauzin is expected to concentrate his efforts on the wide array of industries under his panel's purview. He is expected to work closely with Thomas

M. Davis III, the NRCC chairman and a new member this year of Energy and Commerce, where he is expected to focus on the concerns of his northern Virginia constituents.

Tauzin became a key ally of the businesses of the new economy in the infancy of the Internet age — he said by happenstance. At the urging of an accountant friend in Louisiana, in 1993 he developed legislation to restrict lawsuits by disgruntled investors against companies that do not perform up to expectations, their investment bankers and financial advisers. High-tech companies, whose stocks were then the particular targets of such suits, gravitated to the idea. Over President Bill Clinton's veto, a revised version of Tauzin's proposal became law (PL 104-67) six years ago.

Three years later, he says he drew quizzical looks when he first sought campaign cash from the corporate leaders of high-tech manufacturers.

"They wanted to know why I was coming to visit Silicon Valley. I was hurt that they really didn't know what I had done," Tauzin recalled. "Then it dawned on me. . . . These were the most forward-looking people I had ever met in my life. . . . All they understand is tomorrow. They are not interested in yesterday." ◆

Tauzin, above in 1998 and at right at this year's presidential inauguration, made fundraising a central element of his rise to the chairmanship. He helped to raise an estimated $8 million for other GOP candidates in the past two years, often by hosting fundraisers that featured the cooking of his cousins Jimmy Gravois and Deany Gravois. The three, at left, also collaborated on a book of Cajun recipes and stories.

Privacy, the Internet and Congress

Congressional action always has lagged behind the market forces of the U.S. economy, and that fact has been particularly acute in the digital sector. But advances in computer marketing techniques have raised a host of troublesome privacy questions that have forced Congress to consider regulating the Internet industry whose growth fueled much of the prosperity of recent years.

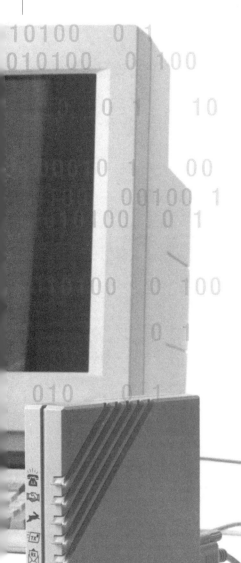

Americans want the convenience of one-click shopping on the Internet. They want their physicians and pharmacies to have up-to-date and accurate records. They want cutting-edge 911 capabilities on their cell phones.

They also want their privacy. They want all the new conveniences without making themselves more vulnerable to tracking by criminals, businesses and even the government.

The difficulty of accommodating both these demands has made privacy one of the most vexing technology policy issues facing Congress.

Over the past few years, lawmakers have generally been reluctant to impose potentially burdensome new rules on the booming digital economy for fear of chilling development of the new products that American consumers have so embraced. Instead, Congress has taken a position of non-interference, essentially hoping the technology industry would police itself.

The 107th Congress could well bring a change in that thinking. A growing number of policymakers appear convinced that some government regulation is necessary, especially in the areas of online privacy, electronic surveillance and medical and financial record-keeping. Even some executives in the regulation-averse technology industry are, for the first time, urging Congress to pass limited privacy laws, worried that the lack of federal standards will lead to a confusing patchwork of state regulations.

"The issue has been bubbling up for some time, but in the last Congress we kept asking ourselves, 'What is the appropriate role to take? What are we legislating?' " said Rep. Anna G. Eshoo, D-Calif., who represents most of Silicon Valley and is sponsoring an Internet privacy bill. "It's moving from the back burner to the front burner, and we will probably establish some kind of a

By Adriel Bettelheim / Feb. 24, 2001

floor [for privacy standards] in this Congress."

Lawmakers are expected to tackle the issue through narrowly focused legislation instead of one or two comprehensive privacy bills. That approach would preserve committees' jurisdictions, although privacy advocates warn it also places the United States at a disadvantage to Europe and Canada, where more sweeping measures have been enacted.

"Congress tends to deal with privacy problems one by one," said Chris Hoofnagle, staff counsel for the Electronic Privacy Information Center (EPIC), a group of privacy advocates. "The problem is, some of the bills don't assure fair information practices and place the burden on the consumer to prevent the information that is being collected from being used. The attitude sometimes is, 'If this isn't a clearly unfair practice, it isn't a problem.' "

Regulating cyberspace has been a humbling exercise to date. Congress could not find a comfortable middle ground when debating whether to tax e-commerce or regulate Internet content. Lawmakers in 1998 deferred on the taxation issue by settling on a three-year moratorium on Internet-specific taxes. And laws passed in 1996 and 1998 to restrict indecent material on the Internet were blocked by courts on the grounds they violated free speech. In the 106th Congress, lawmakers introduced about 200 privacy measures, but failed to agree on any wide-ranging legislation.

A Wish List

A coalition of more than a dozen groups representing consumer, civil liberties, educational, library and labor interests outlined its privacy wish list Feb. 12. The coalition — which includes the American Civil Liberties Union, the Consumer Federation of America and the United Auto Workers — wants Internet companies to both openly disclose their information-gathering practices and to give consumers a handy way to prevent that information from being shared.

The technology industry is not of one mind on the need for legislation, but is signalling it may be receptive to congressional efforts to clarify ground rules for proper conduct in cyberspace. For example, the American Electronics Association (AEA), the nation's largest high-tech trade group, in January suggested a set of minimal privacy standards it could support, but stressed that any Internet privacy bill must pre-empt state laws.

Major companies such as Hewlett-Packard Co. have taken similar positions. But industry groups such as the Information Technology Industry Council (ITI) are taking a harder line, saying they have yet to see privacy legislation they can support.

"We are not allergic to federal legislation, but we're trying to ask questions: What is the scope of the bill, is it just targeted at the Internet, does it place new burdens on buyers and sellers [in cyberspace]," said ITI President Rhett Dawson.

"It's a very complex and sensitive issue, and members of Congress are looking at it with fresh eyes and getting sobered by the experience."

Legislation in the Works

Lawmakers already have introduced at least 18 privacy bills in the 107th Congress, and the Congressional Privacy Caucus, which includes House and Senate members of both parties, is planning March hearings on one subject of immediate concern — "Web bugs," a variety of tracking software that advertisers can surreptitiously use to monitor consumers' Internet habits.

Separately, Reps. Asa Hutchinson, R-Ark., and James. P. Moran, D-Va., have reintroduced a bill (HR 583) to establish a bipartisan commission to study and make policy recommendations on a wide range of privacy issues. In the last Congress, supporters could not muster the two-thirds majority needed to pass the measure without debate.

Perhaps nowhere is the privacy issue more immediate than in health care. New Department of Health and Human Services rules to safeguard medical records so roiled providers and insurers that they persuaded the Bush administration to delay implementation, which had been set for Feb. 26,

and to reopen them for revision. (*Story, p. 90*)

Consumers' concerns about information security are profound. Polls indicate Americans are increasingly wary of online marketers and believe that information they provide to businesses might be misused.

Surveys of separate groups of 1,200 and 1,000 adults by the consulting firm Wirthlin Worldwide in 2000 and 2001 found many of them were worried about providing personal information over the Internet. When asked to rate their concern on a scale of 1 to 10, with 10 being "extremely worried," nearly half categorized their level of concern a 9 or 10.

Regulators, meanwhile, are urging Congress to take a more activist approach. The Federal Trade Commission (FTC), which polices online commerce, reversed an earlier position and concluded last year that self-regulation by the technology industry has not done enough to protect consumer privacy. In a May 2000 report to Congress, the FTC recommended that lawmakers pass a privacy law that ensures a minimum level of privacy protection and establishes "basic standards of practice for the collection of information online."

The FTC based that recommendation on a survey of heavily visited U.S. commercial Web sites. The study found most of the sites that collected personal information did not notify consumers that the information was being collected and did not offer an "opt-out" feature, which allows customers to explicitly direct site operators not to share the information with third parties.

Some of the consumers' and regulators' concerns may be linked to highly publicized instances of electronic surveillance, such as online marketer DoubleClick Inc.'s in-depth tracking of consumers' online habits and last year's disclosure that the FBI's Carnivore software can "wiretap" e-mail.

Lawmakers say these subjects frequently come up for discussion in town meetings with constituents.

"I represent a lot of people who work for telecommunications companies, and while they salute the technology, the prospect for invasion of privacy online or on the phone is driving them absolutely bananas," said Rep. Rodney Frelinghuysen, R-N.J., a sponsor of four privacy bills.

The range of privacy measures being

Click-and-Tell Policies

According to a May 2000 study by the Federal Trade Commission, Web sites' policies on collecting and sharing personal information vary widely. For instance, only 41 percent of the sites surveyed at random by the agency told visitors what personal information they were collecting and gave them choices as to how it would be used.

Random Sample*

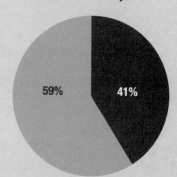

Most Popular Sites**

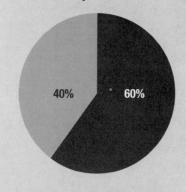

 Informed consumers about information collection policies.

Did not inform consumers about information collection policies.

* Surveyed 335 sites, selected at random, that had at least 39,000 unique visitors per month.

** Surveyed 91 of the Internet's 100 busiest sites.

SOURCE: Federal Trade Commission

introduced suggests that lawmakers have different perceptions about what to do first. Sen. John Edwards, D-N.C., for example, has proposed legislation (S 197) that would require advertisers to warn consumers when they use Web bugs or other tracking software.

Other lawmakers are focusing on the potential for criminals to steal people's Social Security numbers in order to use their identities to make purchases, take out loans and engage in other financial transactions. Rep. Ron Paul, R-Texas, has proposed a bill (HR 220) that would prevent Social Security numbers from being used for anything other than Social Security or tax purposes.

A related bill (HR 91) by Frelinghuysen would place restrictions on how Internet service providers can use customers' Social Security numbers.

The first stop for most efforts dealing with electronic commerce is likely to be the House Energy and Commerce Committee and the Senate Commerce, Science and Transportation panel, whose chairmen are both receptive to moving privacy measures this year.

House Energy and Commerce Chairman Billy Tauzin, R-La., has indicated he would like to move legislation by this summer that would discourage the extensive collection of personal information. Tauzin's Senate counterpart, John McCain, R-Ariz., unsuccessfully pushed legislation in the last Congress that would have required Web sites to disclose their data collection practices and give consumers a chance to opt out. *(Tauzin, p. 81)*

The House and Senate Judiciary committees also will weigh in, particularly on electronic surveillance matters that may affect law enforcement and the way the federal government collects personal information.

House Judiciary Committee Chairman F. James Sensenbrenner Jr., R-Wis., warned in January that turf battles could break out on several fronts as the panels jockey for primacy on matters relating to the Internet. *(Story, p. 59)*

Tracking the Customer

One area of early consensus may come on the issue of wireless phones and what technology experts call "location privacy."

This is a difficult area for lawmakers because it will require Congress to find a balance between encouraging the use of a new technology and limiting how

it is applied for commercial purposes. Enhancements will soon allow many of the nearly 106 million people who use cellular phones or pagers to be located when they dial 911 in an emergency. But some lawmakers say that technology would enable marketers to determine when a person drives past a store or fast-food establishment and send a message urging him to pull over for a special promotion.

Such concerns led Rep. Rush D. Holt, D-N.J., to propose legislation (HR 113) that would prohibit sending unsolicited commercial messages on wireless systems.

A bill (HR 260) by Frelinghuysen would require wireless service providers to disclose how they use location information and require the providers to obtain a customer's written consent before it can be collected and used.

Congress may end up working on parallel tracks with the FTC, which began exploring the issue in December. The Cellular Telecommunications & Internet Association also has asked the Federal Communications Commission (FCC) to issue location privacy rules that could apply to both telecommunications vendors and Internet service providers.

As in the 106th Congress, much attention is expected to be focused on the complicated issue of online profiling and the way marketers track consumers' Web surfing and purchasing habits. Congress will have to decide whether to layer new regulations on the still-evolving business of Internet commerce.

Interest in the subject has been heightened by the advent of Web bugs — nearly invisible pieces of software buried on Web pages that tell online marketers the computer addresses of users visiting their sites.

Privacy advocates also have uncovered instances where a computer code was manipulated to allow the sender of an e-mail message to see what was written when the message was forwarded with comments to other recipients.

Tauzin and John D. Dingell of Michigan, ranking Democrat on the House Energy and Commerce Committee, may collaborate with Robert W. Goodlatte, R-Va., and Rick Boucher, D-Va., on legislation that would require consumers to be given notice that personal information was being collected and also give them the chance to opt out of having it shared with third

parties. The legislation also would preempt state Internet privacy laws — a provision widely viewed as a prerequisite for any high-tech industry support.

"Even those of us who are not supportive of massive government regulation of privacy believe there has to be a baseline standard," Goodlatte said. "The public is concerned, and there are always going to be entities that do not comply with self-regulation and go beyond the scope of what is reasonable."

Tauzin spokesman Ken Johnson said it was "very possible" that the Commerce panel chairman would move a bill in the next several months, but that the Louisiana Republican was exploring other options. The panel's Telecommunications, Trade and Consumer Protection Subcommittee will hold privacy hearings in March.

The kind of bill Goodlatte envisions would resemble legislation (HR 237) Eshoo already has introduced with Rep. Christopher B. Cannon, R-Utah. That bill, in turn, mirrors the legislation McCain promoted last year to require disclosure of Web sites' information practices, as well as an opt-out mechanism for consumers.

State vs. Federal Laws

Such proposals remain controversial because they could nullify strong state privacy laws and replace them with weaker federal standards. Privacy groups such as EPIC say these proposals are being prepared at the behest of the technology industry, which they say is really less interested in establishing national privacy standards than in ducking tougher laws that could evolve at the state level.

Such laws could include "opt-in" provisions. These are features that would require consumers to give explicit consent to having their personal information shared, thereby putting the burden on the Web site operator. Many businesses dislike opt-in requirements because they could hinder their ability to compile consumer databases.

"Most in the privacy community will speak against anything that prevents states from passing stronger legislation," said EPIC's Hoofnagle, who rejects the argument that it would be nearly impossible for Internet companies to navigate 50 different state laws. "We want to spur states to do stronger laws. The experience suggests that industry can comply with the strongest law."

HHS Reopening Medical Privacy Rules To Consider Industry's Objections

In a move that will reopen the partisan debate over sensitive medical privacy regulations, agency officials said Health and Human Services Secretary Tommy G. Thompson has decided to heed industry concerns and consider changes to the final rules published Dec. 28 by the Clinton administration.

Thompson will call, in the Federal Register, for new comments on the first-ever federal medical privacy standards as early as Feb. 26.

Agency officials were drafting a statement Feb. 23 in which Thompson was expected to say the administration "should be open to the concerns of all those who care strongly about health care privacy. After we hear those concerns, our commitment must be to put strong and effective patient privacy protections into effect as quickly as possible."

Thompson's decision, which follows industry demands for a far more business-friendly policy, dramatically changes the debate over the complex regulation. Democrats had hoped the issue would be resolved when the Clinton administration issued the regulations. Instead, years of continued haggling could be in store.

The new comment period, which will last 30 days, gives industry executives a new opportunity to argue for changes that could fundamentally alter several major provisions of the regulations. Thompson said he would assess the comments before determining whether revisions are in order.

The delay "creates an opportunity to ensure that the provisions of this final rule will indeed work as intended," Thompson said.

Although lawmakers declined to comment until official notice to reopen the rules is filed, the decision is certain to enrage Democrats who have been calling for swift implementation of the rules.

The regulations "should be implemented as scheduled to keep our commitment to Americans that their personal medical information is just that — personal," Sens. Edward M. Kennedy of Massachusetts, Patrick J. Leahy of Vermont and four other Democrats had written in a Feb. 15 letter warning President Bush not to delay or revise the regulations .

Health care lobbyists immediately applauded Thompson's move. When she learned of it, American Association of Health Plans President Karen M. Ignagni called the decision a "responsible step."

"This rule, in fact, differed from the guiding principle that was outlined in the original proposed rule in significant ways that may reduce, not improve, consumers' access to quality health care," Ignagni said Feb. 23.

Industry Maneuvers

Thompson's decision came after health care lobbyists had succeeded in delaying the regulations — which had been scheduled to become effective Feb. 26 — for nearly two months by pointing out that the Clinton administration had failed to formally file them with Congress and the General Accounting Office.

The 1996 Congressional Review Act (PL 104-121) requires agencies to file rules at least 60 days before they are set to become effective. After the regulation was formally filed on Feb. 13, a new effective date of April 14 was set, with enforcement to begin in 2003.

The Clinton administration's apparent omission was discovered during the debate over pre-emption, but are being careful not to weigh in too early and antagonize Congress or the high-tech industry. The National Governors Association, for example, has not taken an official position on Internet privacy bills, although it says states have a constructive role to play.

Liability Concerns

Industry officials also worry that federal legislation could include provisions that would give consumers the right to sue Internet companies if their personal information is misused, or that would give the FTC broad power to define what constitutes misconduct in the collection of personal information.

"It's a very worrisome prospect, especially when the legislation only applies to personal information collected on the Internet, but not on phone lines or the mail," said ITI's Dawson.

Financial privacy also will consume lawmakers' attention, driven by concerns about the exchange of sensitive personal information among banks, insurers, brokerages and other institutions. The practice was made easier by the 1999 financial services overhaul, which allowed banks to establish affiliates that sell a wide variety of products.

Legislation (S 30) by Sen. Paul S. Sarbanes, D-Md., would require financial institutions to obtain consumers' consent before they share personal information with affiliates. This would prevent banks from automatically passing information about customers to

Technology industry executives insist that federal standards are necessary because of the myriad possibilities for privacy legislation at the state level.

They point to states including Florida, Illinois, Maine, Maryland and Vermont, which all passed laws governing the release of personal financial information that are more comprehensive than federal standards included in the 1999 financial services overhaul (PL 106-102). That law did not pre-empt tougher state laws.

"Any legislation considered by Congress should be explicitly and solely designed to pre-empt the enactment of a crazy quilt of onerous, contradictory new state laws," said William T. Archey, president and chief executive officer of the AEA.

State officials are anxiously watching a series of meetings by industry lobbyists throughout January and early February. Three times a week, health care lobbyists met to pore over the rules, searching for technicalities that would persuade the agency to delay or change the rule. Lobbyists say the regulations are too vague, would cost their industry billions of dollars to implement and do little to protect consumers from prying eyes.

"There are a number of reasons to take another look at this," Alan Mertz, executive vice president of the Healthcare Leadership Council, a coalition of health care interest groups, said Feb. 20. "Our intention is not to rescind the whole rule entirely. We just want it fixed."

Nearly every health care insurer and provider would be affected by the regulations, which for the first time would give patients access to — and some control over — their medical records.

A hospital, for example, would have to obtain a patient's written consent before using information in his or her file to carry out routine treatment. Patients also would be able to make copies of their records and suggest changes, something most state privacy laws do not allow them to do.

Providers, insurers and others that do not comply would face civil and criminal fines. An individual or company selling confidential medical information could face penalties of up to $250,000 and 10 years in prison.

Patient Care Issues

Several health care trade groups wrote Thompson on Feb. 1 to complain that key provisions in the regulations were "unworkable and could seriously disrupt patient care."

Perhaps the group's greatest concern is a provision that was not in a draft of the regulations issued Oct. 29, 1999. It would require patients to sign specific consent forms before providers could use or disclose personal data for treatment or payment.

Pharmacists, in particular, say the consent requirement would create inconvenient delays. For example, when a physician phoned in a prescription for a sick child, pharmacists fear they would not be able to fill it until a parent came to the pharmacy to sign a consent form.

"Thirty-five to 40 percent of all prescriptions are picked up by someone other than the patient," Carlos R. Ortiz, director of government affairs for CVS Pharmacy, told a Feb. 13 congressional briefing. "There will be chaos at our pharmacy counters, and you will be getting phone calls from constituents about getting their prescriptions filled in a timely manner."

Some health care executives also are frustrated by the structure of the rules, which would provide a floor of federal protections that states could supersede. The result, they say, would be a patchwork of state and federal privacy guidelines.

However, privacy groups are cheering most elements of the new regulations. Advocates say Americans are increasingly concerned about breaches of medical privacy, such as hackers downloading confidential records from databases.

Privacy advocates also are concerned about scientific developments that can now tell patients more details than ever about their genetic makeup. Unless new safeguards are added, consumer groups fear that employers or insurers could use genetic information about patients to discriminate against them.

"We have mapped the human genome, but people are afraid to get tested. The Internet can deliver cutting-edge research and health care services, but people are unwilling to trust their most sensitive information in cyberspace," Janlori Goldman, director of Georgetown University's Health Privacy Project, told a Senate Health, Education, Labor and Pensions Committee hearing Feb. 8.

"We will never fully reap the benefits of these astounding breakthroughs until privacy is woven into the fabric of our nation's health care system," she said.

— Rebecca Adams and Adriel Bettelheim

---

subsidiaries that sell securities or insurance.

Sen. Richard C. Shelby, R-Ala., wants to expand protections in the 1999 law to prevent banks from selling customers' Social Security numbers. "Looking back, we had a bite at the privacy apple when we did the [financial services] modernization bill. Unfortunately, I think we bit into a worm," Shelby told a housing and finance group Feb. 15.

Sen. Patrick J. Leahy, D-Vt., is likely to trigger this year's first airing of the privacy debate on the Senate floor shortly after the Presidents Day recess. Leahy is expected to offer an amendment to a bankruptcy overhaul bill (S 220) that would prevent companies that file for bankruptcy or go out of business from selling consumer infor-

mation they have compiled.

The measure was prompted by an incident last year in which the Internet toy seller Toysmart.com attempted to sell personal information on the shopping habits of its customers and their children after it filed for bankruptcy. After consumer groups complained, Walt Disney Co., the majority owner of the company, agreed to buy and destroy the information. The fate of Leahy's measure depends less on its merits, however, than on whether Republicans are willing to add it to the bankruptcy bill.

The privacy debate is also moving into other arenas. Some lawmakers believe Congress should enact laws to prevent workplace discrimination or insurance decisions based on health records containing genetic informa-

tion. Critics say the Americans with Disabilities Act (PL 101-336) already prevents workplace discrimination based on one's genetic profile, and that such measures could prompt a flood of lawsuits.

Such concerns have intensified since the recent publication of the entire sequence of the human genome. Knowing a person's genetic profile could yield clues about current afflictions and whether a person is prone to cancers or other gene-based diseases.

Rep. Louise M. Slaughter, D-N.Y., has put forth legislation (HR 602) that would bar insurers from using genetic information in coverage decisions. A companion bill (S 382) has been offered by Sen. Olympia J. Snowe, R-Maine. ◆

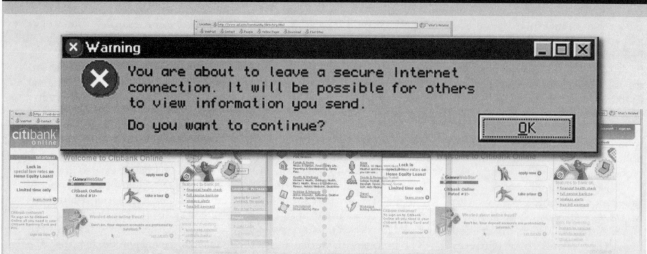

Key Areas for Privacy Legislation

The 107th Congress is expected to consider privacy measures in 2001 that would cover several areas, including Internet tracking technology, wireless-phone ads and the sharing of personal medical records. Some lawmakers, for example, want to curb the use of software that can follow a PC user's Web-surfing habits and trace his e-mail, while others are focusing on protecting consumers' Social Security numbers. Here are the major privacy issues facing Congress and some of the bills that have been offered to address them:

▶   **Online information:** Lawmakers are considering a variety of proposals dealing with how Web sites collect personal information. Sen. John McCain, R-Ariz., and Rep. Anna G. Eshoo, D-Calif., have proposed legislation (HR 237) that would require site operators to post their privacy guidelines and give consumers a chance to opt out of sharing information. They also want to establish a federal baseline for privacy protection that could pre-empt stronger state laws. Sen. John Edwards, D-N.C., has introduced a bill (S 197) that would place controls on the use of "Web bugs" and other tracking technology that can give companies detailed information about a person's Internet use.

▶   **Wireless advertising:** Reps. Rush D. Holt, D-N.J., far left, and Rodney Frelinghuysen, R-N.J., want to limit the transmission of unsolicited advertising to consumers' cell phones. Holt's bill (HR 113) and Frelinghuysen's measure (HR 260) would limit marketers' ability to track phone users and transmit ads based on their locations.

▶ **Identity theft:** Several bills would restrict business use of Social Security numbers. Frelinghuysen has introduced a bill (HR 91) to make it harder for Internet scammers to commit identity theft by stealing Social Security numbers. And Sen. Paul S. Sarbanes, D-Md., left, has introduced a measure (S 30) that would restrict how banks trade customers' personal information with affiliated companies.

▶ **Student Web surfing:** Sen. Christopher J. Dodd, D-Conn., and several other lawmakers have proposed a measure (S 290) that would require school districts to notify parents when classroom computers use technology that could collect data on children for commercial purposes. That includes Internet content filters, which are utilized by many schools to block objectionable material but can also track users' surfing habits.

▶ **Medical records:** Health and Human Services Secretary Tommy G. Thompson, left, heeding the concerns of GOP lawmakers and health care interest groups, will re-open the rules-making process for medical privacy regulations issued in December by the Clinton administration. The health care industry complained that the rules, as written, could allow medical providers to withhold treatment if patients do not consent to share their medical information.

— *Adriel Bettelheim*

Welfare Overhaul's Next Wave

In 1996 the Republican Congress and Democratic President Bill Clinton agreed to replace the unlimited welfare system created by Lyndon Johnson's "Great Society" programs with one that puts recipients of federal aid on a timetable. The new system put a premium on moving welfare recipients into work programs, and in the growing economy of the late 1990s welfare rolls dropped substantially. But the time has come to reauthorize the 1996 law, and Congress considers again the long-term feasibility of welfare-to-work.

An instructor at Philadelphia's Transitional Work Corporation talks to welfare recipients about the skills they will need to succeed — an issue Congress will face when it reauthorizes the 1996 welfare law.

It was just a sentence buried under a mountain of budget proposals, but that one line in President Bush's first budget may have captured the essence of the coming debate in Congress over the future structure of the welfare system.

In the fiscal 2002 outline he sent to Capitol Hill on Feb. 28, Bush said states should be encouraged to set up tax credits to reward people who give money to private charities. No problem so far; lawmakers from both parties say charities should get more help.

The catch is how Bush proposed paying for the tax credits. He wants to let states dip into a pot of money that used to be politically untouchable: the funds for Temporary Assistance for Needy Families (TANF), the program commonly known as "welfare."

With that proposal, Bush stepped squarely into the heart of the congressional debate over the upcoming reauthorization of the 1996 law (PL 104-193) that wiped out the old welfare system and built a new, time-limited one in its place.

Congress is just starting to turn to the task, but the outlines of the debate are already clear as lawmakers take a good hard look at the biggest social policy change of the 1990s.

Many Republicans will argue that the battle against welfare dependency is essentially over — caseloads have dropped by more than 50 percent, and there are 6.9 million fewer people on the rolls — and that lawmakers should feel

free to spend TANF money on other things. Democrats and some moderate Republicans will argue the opposite: The remaining welfare recipients have more serious problems that will require just as much federal spending, if not more, to help them leave.

Without saying a word officially, Bush may have picked an early fight with Democrats.

By allowing states to spend welfare funds on other initiatives, the Bush proposal would set "a dangerous precedent," said Benjamin L. Cardin of Maryland, the ranking Democrat on the House Ways and Means Subcommittee on Human Resources. "We should be moving in the opposite direction." Administration officials did not respond to requests for comment on the proposal.

Five years ago, the welfare overhaul produced a flood of emotional and bitter exchanges. Rep. John Lewis, D-Ga., called it "mean" and "downright lowdown." House Majority Whip Tom DeLay, R-Texas, called the criticisms "one last, desperate attempt by the minority to cling to the status quo."

Those kinds of exchanges are unlikely to be repeated this time, because welfare has largely disappeared from the political debate. When Bush first ran for governor of Texas in 1994, "welfare reform" was one of his biggest themes. In his presidential campaign last year, he barely mentioned it.

But the question Congress faces is still important to millions of poor families: What comes next?

Among Republicans, the ideas include toughening work requirements, encouraging marriage and curbing out-of-wedlock

By David Nather / March 17, 2001

93

births and creating a greater role for faith-based social services. The faith-based proposals are in keeping with the direction Bush has signaled, but they come at a time of growing doubts on Capitol Hill.

Democrats, meanwhile, will try to ease the program's time limits and shift the emphasis to reducing poverty, not just caseloads.

The reauthorization will be many lawmakers' first look back at the decision to end welfare as an entitlement, available to all families poor enough to qualify, and replace it with a block grant that limits every poor family to five years of federal assistance — after which adults are expected to go to work.

For both parties, the terms of the debate have changed. For Republicans, the task will be to preserve and build upon a welfare overhaul that they consider one of their greatest successes.

"If it ain't broke, don't fix it," said Rep. Wally Herger, R-Calif., the new chairman of the Human Resources Subcommittee, which has jurisdiction over TANF and held its first reauthorization hearing March 15.

"I think it's exceeded everybody's expectations as the most successful legislation in memory," said Rep. E. Clay Shaw Jr., R-Fla., one of the authors of the 1996 law.

For Democrats, the goal is no longer to fight time limits or work requirements, but to make sure poor families are being treated fairly within the boundaries of the new system. They want to call attention to the story they see behind the plummeting caseloads and declining poverty rates: the single mothers who have been unable to leave welfare or thrive in their new jobs.

"The best you can say is that some people are doing as well as can be expected under the circumstances, and others are doing worse," said Sen. Paul Wellstone, D-Minn., who voted against the 1996 overhaul.

Already, some state and local welfare-to-work programs are experimenting with new ways to help "hard-to-serve" welfare recipients — those who have no high school diploma, little or no work history, little knowledge of English, or more serious problems such as mental illness or substance addiction. The lessons of these programs

Sinuon Mel said a transitional work program taught her job skills. Now she is studying for a high school diploma.

could become important as Congress looks for ways to deal with the changing face of welfare.

They could be particularly important to moderate Republicans, who appreciate the overhaul's successes, but are mindful that many poor families have not shared in them.

"We definitely want them to get into the work force. We're not going to go back on that," said Nancy L. Johnson, R-Conn., who chaired the Human Resources Subcommittee in the 106th Congress and remains on the panel. "But we want them to move out of that minimum wage job and up the economic ladder. Not enough states are paying attention to that."

The Other Strands

The TANF reauthorization must be done by October 2002, when the program expires. At the same time, lawmakers will be debating what to do about the other major strands of the safety net for poor families. Food stamps, child-care assistance and transitional Medicaid health insurance coverage for welfare recipients who have gone to work all must be renewed by the same date.

Smaller pieces of the 1996 welfare law, including a contingency fund for

states with high unemployment rates and grants to help states with rapid population growth, must be reauthorized by October 2001.

The broad numbers have made the overhaul look like an unqualified success. Those numbers, however, do not tell the whole story.

Overall poverty rates are lower than they have been since 1979. In 1996, 13.7 percent of Americans were officially classified as poor, with an income of no more than $13,874 for a family of three; by 1999, that had fallen to 11.8 percent. The trend held up for children and for every major racial and ethnic category. (*Chart, p. 95*)

Most low-income mothers who have left welfare have found jobs, and never-married single mothers — the people most likely to stay on welfare for long periods, according to numerous studies — are moving into the work force in record numbers and earning more than ever.

"The good news is that we have a program that even the critics would admit has worked very well," said Herger.

But some critics say the overhaul left too many people behind. "I think people feel like the problem has been solved — which they shouldn't, because a lot of people have been hurt," said Peter Edelman, one of three Department of Health and Human Services (HHS) officials who resigned in protest in 1996 when President Bill Clinton decided to sign the legislation.

Edelman and other foes of the 1996 law say their greatest fear has been realized: Many families that have left welfare are still struggling. They cite a December study by the Urban Institute, a Washington think tank, that said about a third of former welfare recipients had to skip meals or eat less. About 46 percent said they had been unable to pay rent or utility bills at some point within the previous 12 months.

Many other former recipients have not found jobs. Pamela Loprest, a senior research associate at the Urban Institute and the author of the study, said about a quarter of former welfare recipients had no earnings after leaving the system. Some probably shifted to disability payments, she said, but about 17 percent could not be found.

Those people "are the big concern,"

The Changing Face of Welfare

Welfare Rolls Decline

Since the 1996 welfare overhaul, nearly 6.9 million fewer people are on the rolls, a decline of 54 percent.

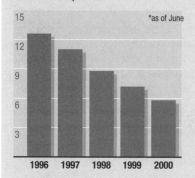

*as of June

(bar chart: 1996, 1997, 1998, 1999, 2000)

Poverty Rates Fall

Supporters of welfare overhaul say it has contributed to a drop in the percentage of people living below the overall poverty level — $13,874 for a family of three in 1999.

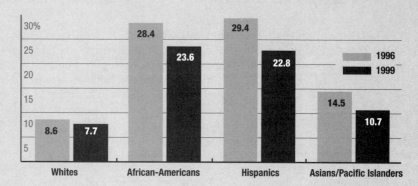

	Whites	African-Americans	Hispanics	Asians/Pacific Islanders
1996	8.6	28.4	29.4	14.5
1999	7.7	23.6	22.8	10.7

SOURCE: Department of Health and Human Services, U.S. Census Bureau

Former Recipients Struggle

The Urban Institute interviewed 1,206 adults who stopped receiving welfare between 1997 and 1999. Here are some of its findings from a study released in December 2000.

Employed: 64 percent

Unemployed but worked recently: 10.8 percent

Never employed: 17 percent

Returned to welfare: 21.9 percent

Median hourly wage: $7.15

Median annual earnings*: $16,320

Has to eat less or skip meals: 32.7 percent

Could not pay mortgage, rent or utility bills at some point in last 12 months: 46.1 percent

Adults without health insurance: 37 percent

Children without health insurance: 17 percent

* Assuming 12 months employment

SOURCES: Urban Institute, U.S. Census Bureau

A counselor at a Philadelphia work program helps clients fill out time cards.

CQ PHOTO/SCOTT J. FERRELL

---

said Loprest. "We don't have a good picture of what's happened to these people and how they're surviving."

Even employers who are trying to make the new system work warn Congress not to declare victory too quickly.

"It's easy to gloss over the fact that there are still some major challenges," said Dorian Friedman, vice president of policy at the Welfare to Work Partnership, a national coalition of businesses that promise to hire former recipients. "A lot of the people who have left the rolls and gone to work are still poor."

The biggest unknown is what will happen as more families start running into the time limits on federal TANF benefits. So far, an estimated 60,000 people have hit time limits in 21 states.

No studies have looked specifically

at how those people have fared, because the limits have kicked in too recently, but news reports from those states suggest many recipients have gotten extensions. Some mothers who lost their benefits ended up "broke, sick and depressed," according to a report in The Tampa Tribune in October 1999, a year after Florida's limit on welfare benefits took effect.

Over the next two years, the first time limits will kick in for families in another 27 states and the District of Columbia. States can continue benefits to children and even entire families if the states pick up the tab themselves, but it is not clear how many will do so.

It is also not clear how much of the welfare overhaul's statistical success has been due to the booming economy.

Supporters say prosperity alone cannot explain the drops in welfare caseloads or poverty rates, because neither declined in the mid-1980s, when the economy was also strong.

"This has very little to do with the economy," said Rep. Shaw, "and everything to do with the tremendous success of welfare reform."

Still, "there's a concern that an economic downturn could reverse a lot of the gains that we've achieved," said Elaine M. Ryan, acting executive director of the American Public Human Services Association, which represents state human services administrators.

Moderate Republicans, Democrats and state officials all believe they will have a battle on their hands to prevent conservative Republicans from cutting

Private Group Tries to Ease Toughest Welfare-to-Work Cases

PHILADELPHIA — A block from city hall, the Transitional Work Corporation helps "hard-to-serve" welfare recipients, those who are having the toughest time finding work.

The job of this public-private partnership is to reconcile the message of the new system — everyone who can work should — with the reality that many welfare recipients are about to hit the program's five-year time limit and cannot simply be thrown into the job market and expected to succeed.

This is one of the key issues Congress will face when it turns to reauthorization of the 1996 welfare overhaul (PL 104-193): How to make sure people who leave the welfare rolls get the help they need to survive.

The Philadelphia program strikes a balance that, in the eyes of its supporters, shows the solution does not have to be complicated. After participants enroll, they get a part-time job at a city government office or nonprofit organization. They typically work 25 hours a week, aided by mentors in the workplace and job coaches at Transitional Work offices.

That, plus skills training at the program's offices, is supposed to give former recipients the experience they need to move to a permanent job in the private sector six months later. In

the meantime, they receive allowances for such essentials as child care, clothing and transportation.

Since the program began in October 1998, officials say, it has placed more than 3,100 welfare recipients in transitional jobs. Of those, 1,084 have gone on to permanent, unsubsidized jobs; another 521 are currently working in transitional jobs. The remainder dropped out, said officials, either because they did not follow the rules or because late-term pregnancies left them unable to work.

The lesson for Congress, according to those who run the program and those it has helped, is that the nation's remaining welfare recipients need a chance to gain skills before they can move into the work force. Further, subsidies for health insurance, child care and transportation may have to be continued long after former recipients have landed jobs.

"Everybody should go to work," said Richard Greenwald, the corporation's president and chief executive officer. "But you've got to support them."

In other words, the program's counselors say, lawmakers must recognize that many newly working mothers are not earning enough to survive without Medicaid, food stamps and child-care assistance.

"All of the support systems are taken away one by one," said Achée O'Quinn, who steers low-income mothers off welfare and into jobs. "A lot of them are tempted to go back."

Which Comes First?

Before 1996, most welfare recipients were placed in education and training programs to prepare them for the workplace, but critics said those programs dragged on forever.

By the time Congress passed the 1996 overhaul, the consensus had shifted: Welfare offices were told it was best to place recipients in a job — any job — quickly. That approach may have helped shrink welfare rolls, but employers say it also gave them a lot of unprepared workers.

"[Employers] expect to train the workers in the hard skills that are necessary to do the job," said Dorian Friedman, vice president of policy at the Welfare to Work Partnership, a national coalition of businesses that have promised to hire recipients.

But when they get applicants who do not know how to deal with coworkers or customers, she said, "employers don't feel like that is their problem. . . . By the time an applicant comes to them for a job, that stuff should have been taken care of."

The Philadelphia program's solu-

TANF funds.

Ever since former House Budget Committee Chairman John R. Kasich, R-Ohio (1983-2001), wrote a non-binding budget resolution for fiscal 1999 that called for TANF cuts, the money has been tempting fiscal conservatives.

"I don't think the states are going to get a pass on [TANF cuts]," warned one Senate Republican aide. "Obviously, state budgets have been relatively healthy."

But state officials say they need the funding because the people still on welfare are more likely to have multiple problems, such as mental illness and substance abuse, and thus will be

more expensive to move off the rolls.

"The people who are left on the rolls have a lot of problems, and they need help," said Rep. Johnson, who vowed to fight any TANF budget cuts.

The Players

When welfare legislation begins moving in committee, it will be handled by a cast that is relatively new to welfare policy.

In the House, Herger plans to focus the hearings on "ways to make welfare reform work even better." That could include deciding what to do for welfare recipients who have not been able to find jobs, he said, and ways to "help

families stay together and make sure children have two parents."

Herger also brings a longtime pet cause to the debate: eliminating welfare fraud. He is likely to revive a 1999 proposal to crack down on prison inmates who "illegally receive hundreds of millions of dollars in welfare payments each year."

In the Senate, the Finance Committee has a new chairman, Republican Charles E. Grassley of Iowa, who says the question of how ex-welfare recipients are doing will be critical when the panel starts to write its reauthorization plan.

"We need to know as much as possible about how these former welfare re-

"Everybody should go to work," says Richard Greenwald, president and CEO of the Transitional Work Corporation. "But you've got to support them."

tion is to put welfare recipients to work in a transitional job while they receive training in computers, English and math and learn how to deal with customers and co-workers.

Those who have been through the Transitional Work Corporation program say the approach works.

"When they said, 'You've only got five years' [before welfare benefits end], I said, 'Oh my God, what am I going to do?'" said Sinuon Mel, a former welfare recipient. She said she had no work skills and no high school diploma when she joined the program; now she is getting computer skills training and practicing for her general equivalency diploma while doing clerical work in the program's offices.

The nonprofit corporation stretches its budget to rent expensive office space a block from city hall. Program officials say they want to send a message: Everyone in the program is now in the economic mainstream.

The difficulty, however, is not limited to getting that first job.

Keeping it, and staying afloat financially, can be just as hard.

For example, when a low-income mother leaves welfare for work, she remains eligible for food stamps if her family's income is low enough. She can also get Medicaid for up to a year and child-care assistance through the Child Care and Development Fund, a federal-state program.

The problem, say caseworkers, is that many people who leave welfare are never informed they can continue to receive temporary Medicaid coverage. As a result, Medicaid enrollment dropped for the first time in years shortly after the welfare overhaul began.

Many former welfare recipients also have trouble getting food stamps, say state officials, because federal rules make it tough to keep families on food stamps automatically after they have lost welfare benefits.

For example, when some 3,700 Ohio families hit their welfare time limits in October, the Department of Agriculture told state officials they would have to determine eligibility on a family-by-family basis.

"[Welfare reform has] brought a part of the population out of the house that wouldn't normally be out of the house," said Elmore Johnson, the Transitional Work Corporation's vice president for employer services. "[But] they can't leave them halfway. . . . There should be enough money to support their families."

— *David Nather*

cipients got back in the work force, if they stayed on the job, and how far they've moved to self-sufficiency," Grassley said in a statement.

Johnson and Cardin, who are well-versed in the complexities of welfare policy, and Shaw, who has the institutional knowledge of the debates that shaped the 1996 law, also are expected to play important roles in any discussions of welfare overhaul.

There are also some lawmakers who may not be centrally involved in the committee work but are likely to take an active role in floor debate. They include Sen. Sam Brownback, R-Kan., who believes reauthorization efforts should focus on faith-based organizations that could set up mentoring programs for people who are having the hardest time leaving the rolls.

"This is part of compassionate conservatism," said Brownback. "I would hope we would see more of these steps taken, because we've reduced the welfare rolls a lot."

Lawmakers also will hear from a colleague who has seen welfare firsthand: Rep. Lynn Woolsey, D-Calif., who relied on government aid to supplement her wages when she was a single mother raising three children in the 1970s.

"My fear is that the debate will be about, 'Well, who are these people who are still on welfare? Maybe we should punish them more,'" said Woolsey. "You know what? We're just going to hurt children."

The fact that Bush has not given more clues about his ideas could be a problem for Republicans, who are working with a GOP White House for the first time in eight years and are trying to coordinate their policies with the new administration.

Bush indicated that welfare will not be a back-burner issue when he selected former Wisconsin Gov. Tommy G. Thompson to run HHS, which oversees TANF. As governor, Thompson imposed strict time limits on welfare, but he also argued that states should spend more on services such as child care, health care and transportation that low-income mothers need when they join the work force.

However, in testimony at a March 14 hearing of the Ways and Means Committee, Thompson had little to say about the subject. "We really haven't put that much emphasis on TANF reauthorization yet," he said.

Thompson is not the only one keeping his silence. One House GOP leadership aide said welfare overhaul is "not on our radar screen yet."

Democrats have no shortage of ideas for smoothing the rough edges they see in the new system. Among other things, they want bonuses to states that reduce poverty and exemptions from time limits for welfare recipients who work part time.

They say they are more focused on welfare than Republicans because they expected to take the House back in 2000. "We had to figure out what we were going to do," said Jim McDermott, D-Wash., a member of the Ways and Means Human Resources Subcommittee. House Republicans "can't do anything because they haven't heard what [Bush] wants."

The Issues

Democrats have begun to accept the general idea of time limits, and Republicans have promised to look more closely at people who are not faring well under the new rules. All signs, however, indicate that the two sides will continue to talk past each other on most of the issues. These areas are likely to be the biggest flashpoints:

• **Funding.** The biggest concern of moderate Republicans, Democrats, and state officials will be to maintain the current funding for the TANF block grant, set at $16.5 billion a year through fiscal 2002.

Democrats also are likely to push for more child care funding, a move that is likely to be resisted by both conservative Republicans and moderates such as Johnson. New workers need to be helped with transitional services, Johnson said, but "all of this should be able to be done with the resources we're already providing."

• **Work requirements.** For conservative Republicans, one goal will be to strengthen employment guidelines.

Under the 1996 law, states had to move at least 50 percent of their welfare recipients into jobs or "work activities" such as subsidized employment, on-the-job-training and community service by fiscal 2002. But they could also satisfy the requirement if people simply left the rolls — and so many did so that those who remained did not have to work.

As a matter of principle, however, Republicans believe people should work in exchange for welfare benefits — so they may push for new work requirements for those who have not left.

"Just the threat of a work requirement was moving people off of welfare" even before the 1996 law took effect, said one House Republican aide.

• **Stopping the clock.** One major goal for Democrats will be to change the time limit for people who are working. In 1999, 28 percent of welfare recipients were working but did not earn enough to get by without TANF benefits. Under the 1996 law, that assistance counts against their five-year time limit.

Another likely Democratic objective will be to create more exceptions to the five-year limit for people who have been unable to leave welfare and are about to lose their benefits.

The 1996 law allows states to exempt 20 percent of their caseloads from the time limit because of "hardship." But some Democrats and advocates for the poor believe if the remaining welfare recipients have more serious problems than the ones who left, the 20 percent exemption will not be enough.

"Some people in that other 80 percent are going to be pushed off a cliff," said Wellstone.

• **Faith-based initiatives.** The debate will offer Republicans a chance to expand on Bush's call for more faith-based initiatives.

The welfare overhaul already allows federal funds to be used for welfare-to-work programs run by religious groups, a concept Bush wants to expand to a broader range of social services. When Bush outlined his faith-based initiatives proposal during the presidential campaign, he called it "the next bold step of welfare reform."

Brownback sees it the same way. "We need to do more than just say, 'Go get a job,'" he said. "But we don't think the old way helped either — just give them a little bit of money and hope everything works out. You've got to work with them on the inside, and then you've got to hold their hand when they get on the outside."

• **Reducing poverty.** Democrats want to do more to reduce poverty. Cardin said the reauthorization proposal he plans to introduce later this year will include bonus payments to states that do the best job of lowering poverty rates.

"Yes, we want people to move off of welfare. Yes, we want two-parent families. Yes, we want families to stay together," said Cardin. "But we also want families out of poverty, and right now that is not an objective of welfare reform."

• **Reducing out-of-wedlock births.** Some conservatives believe the key to trimming welfare dependency further is to keep low-income women off the rolls. They say that means doing a better job of reducing births among unmarried women and promoting marriage.

"What we have is a kind of national neurosis where we don't talk about why child poverty exists or why the welfare state exists," said Robert Rector, a senior research fellow at the Heritage Foundation, a conservative think tank. "Both of them exist because of the erosion of marriage."

Such statements make some conservative Republicans nervous because they fear efforts to encourage marriage could lead to new government programs. Others, however, say there is nothing wrong with the message itself.

"What would be the single biggest thing we could do to reduce child poverty? Maintain intact homes," said Sen. Jeff Sessions, R-Ala. "When you split up a family, there will never be as much money as when families stay together."

• **The needs of Hispanics.** One significant change in the welfare rolls since 1996 has been the growing proportion of Hispanic women receiving aid.

The reason Hispanic women are not leaving the rolls as quickly as white and African-American women is that many lack basic job skills, said Eric Rodriguez, director of the Economic Mobility Project at the National Council of La Raza, an advocacy group. And they are often sent to English classes instead of skills training programs.

To address the issue, La Raza wants Congress to shift away from the 1996 law's "work first" philosophy and put more emphasis on education, training and better access to transitional services.

"The job isn't done," said Friedman of the Welfare to Work Partnership. "There's still a lot more that lawmakers can do." ◆

Dealing After the Rhetoric

Every policy debate is influenced by political considerations, but the impact of those concerns rises and falls depending on whether or not it is an election year. An update of the bill that provides federal money for education had been attempted by Congress in years past, but it wasn't until after the election of 2000 was behind them that lawmakers could begin serious negotiations. The education bill passed the House and Senate in the summer of 2001, but the deal began coming together in the spring.

Most senators who were involved in last year's education overhaul debate knew it was little more than an election-year test drive. This year, the stakes are much higher: This education bill is almost certain to become law.

The Senate is expected to take up its bill (S 1) to reauthorize the 1965 Elementary and Secondary Education Act (ESEA) beginning the week of April 23 and remake it in the image of President Bush's education overhaul plan. The House may not be far behind. The Education and the Workforce Committee could mark up its overhaul bill (HR 1) as early as the week of April 30 if it can work out a bipartisan compromise by then, according to GOP aides.

This time, Congress will be forced to think about the real-world consequences of its actions, unlike last year — when the two parties were slugging it out in the election campaigns and had little incentive to compromise on anything.

If the Bush administration and Senate Democrats can work out a funding increase everyone can live with, there could be a bipartisan compromise that would cut the floor debate time and improve the bill's chances in the 50-50 Senate. ESEA programs currently receive about $17.5 billion. Bush wants to

By David Nather / April 21, 2001

boost that by $1.6 billion, but Democrats say the increase should be about $15 billion.

If they cannot work out their funding differences quickly, the Senate could be stuck on the education bill for a long time.

"Historically, ESEA takes two or three weeks" even under the best circumstances, said one Senate GOP leadership aide. "This is going to be one of the longest amounts of time we'll spend on any bill this year."

All sides are clearly trying to prevent a repeat of last year, when the ESEA debate sank under the weight of political posturing: vouchers and block grants for the Republican base, new programs and gun control amendments for Democratic constituencies. This year, the dueling press conferences have not disappeared, but the goal is no longer to win votes. It is to strike a deal.

Bush tried to nudge the negotiations along in an April 18 speech at Central Connecticut State University, saying he and Senate Democrats had "agreed on some core principles" for the education overhaul in talks prior to the April recess, including a consolidation of many ESEA programs and greater state and local flexibility.

In return, Sen. Edward M. Kennedy, D-Mass., who has persuaded other Democrats to hold their fire on most education issues, held an April 19 press briefing to remind Bush that Democrats still want more

Quick Contents

Senate Democrats and Republicans are near agreement on several key provisions of a bill that would reauthorize the Elementary and Secondary Education Act while remaking it to President Bush's liking. The key to a quick deal may hinge on both sides holding down the big floor amendments.

The Dealmakers

Feeding the Right: Sen. Judd Gregg, R-N.H.

The point man on vouchers last year, Gregg knows they have little chance in the Senate this year. He will likely settle for federal aid for a more limited form of private education: tutoring services.

Taming the Left: Sen. Edward M. Kennedy, D-Mass.

Kennedy has played the role of partisan warrior for the last few years, but he also knows how to tone down the rhetoric when he wants to cut a deal. This year, he is toning it down.

Toward the Center: Sen. Joseph I. Lieberman, D-Conn.

The former vice presidential candidate may have forced Kennedy to move to the center, some analysts say, by offering Republicans another high-profile Democrat they can deal with.

Attempting a Comeback: Sen. James M. Jeffords, R-Vt.

Jeffords was upstaged by Gregg last year, but gained a stronger voice this year with his push during the debate over the budget resolution for more special education funding. Now, he must decide what to do with that clout.

money to back up the overhauls before they will close the deal. "It's nonsense to think that we can reform our schools on the cheap," he said.

For the most part, however, both Kennedy and Sen. Judd Gregg, R-N.H., have played it low-key this year in leading the charge for their ideological bases. Gregg has lowered his sights on private school vouchers, while Kennedy — who has been told by Bush that greater funding could follow if senators reach a bipartisan deal — has been keeping partisan fire to a minimum in hope of winning more money.

If the deal is sealed, the big floor amendments may end up as little more than token gestures. Republicans are still expected to offer an amendment to add private school vouchers, but they are not holding their breath for it to succeed. A tentative compromise would allow parents to use federal funds to pay for public school choice and private tutoring services, but not private school tuition. (*Chart, p. 101*)

Even Bush is sending new signals that he will not fight for private school vouchers. In his April 18 speech, he talked about "consequences" for failing schools and "options" for the parents of children in those schools, as he has all year. But the only options he mentioned were "charter schools or public school choice or private tutoring programs" — not private schools.

Democrats, meanwhile, are likely to offer amendments to preserve the three-year-old class-size reduction program, which would be merged into a block grant with teacher quality programs under the Senate bill, and the school renovation program created in last year's omnibus appropriations bill (PL 106-554).

And no agreement can prevent senators from offering amendments to champion their favored causes. Kennedy said some Democrats may insist on offering proposals left over from the Senate Health, Education, Labor and Pensions Committee markup, including an amendment by Jack Reed, D-R.I., to authorize $25 million to buy new books for school libraries.

If that happens, Republicans say, all bets are off. "We have as many good ideas on education as they do," the leadership aide warned.

Most education groups believe, however, that the floor battles will not get out of hand and that ESEA will be reauthorized this year. That is why they are

paying such close attention to what the Senate does with the bill — and the consequences that can be expected after it becomes law.

Of those, none is attracting as much attention as Bush's proposal to measure the progress of schools and their students through annual testing.

It is the centerpiece of his plan to hold every level of the education system accountable for its results, from the states down through the school districts to the schools and the children they teach. By requiring annual state testing in reading and math for children in the third through eighth grades, Bush hopes to have test scores in every state that will show which children are falling behind and which schools need help.

There is nothing new about standardized testing. As of 2000, 48 states had testing programs in place to determine whether students were meeting state education standards. However, only 13 states were testing students every year in reading and math between the third grade and the eighth grade, according to the Council of Chief State School Officers, which represents state education commissioners and superintendents.

The Consequences of Failure

What is new, however, is the idea of federal consequences for failure. Bush wants to award bonuses to states that do the best job of raising test scores, but he also wants to penalize states with low test scores.

Low-performing schools in poor neighborhoods, for example, would lose a portion of their federal Title I funds. Under the original Bush plan and the House Republican bill, parents could use the funds to pay for private school tuition — a kind of limited voucher. Under the proposed Senate compromise, the funds could be used to pay for private tutoring services.

More than any other piece of the Bush overhaul plan, the testing proposal is being pummeled from all sides.

Suburban parents say their children are already being tested enough. In Scarsdale, N.Y., for example, some parents have threatened to boycott the state science tests by keeping their eighth-graders home on exam day. Urban parents have a different concern: They say their children are not getting the help they need to pass the tests.

Liberal Democrats and educators say

standardized tests are being overused, while conservative groups such as the Family Research Council and the Home School Legal Defense Association fear a slide toward a national test.

Powerful state organizations such as the National Governors' Association and the Council of Chief State School Officers say the system should be built on the tests that are already offered rather than requiring new ones.

"This has been created in a very rapid period of time without much thought about how this would actually work," said Gordon Ambach, executive director of the Council of Chief State School Officers.

Even the education analysts who support annual testing — believing it to be the best way to determine how different groups of students are performing over time — say Bush's proposal is in danger of being watered down to the point where it no longer means anything.

"The real question is whether . . . we're going to see any significant changes at all," said Chester E. Finn Jr., assistant secretary of education under President Ronald Reagan and now president of the Thomas B. Fordham Foundation, a conservative think tank.

These crosscurrents of pressure from constituents, lobbyists and education analysts are forcing lawmakers to dive into the details of testing — and causing considerable agonizing about how the final language should read. "How do you walk the fine line between knowing what's happening and allowing some creativity?" said one Senate Democratic aide.

Putting Tests to the Test

In the Senate, the bill has been carefully structured to allow school districts within a state to use different tests, and for different tests to be used from one grade to another, as long as they are approved by the Department of Education.

The only rule of thumb Education Secretary Rod Paige would use in approving those systems, according to spokeswoman Lindsey Kozberg, is whether the tests show how well students are doing in meeting their state's education standards. "We're going to focus on results," she said.

The prospect of a mix of exams bothers advocates of testing, who say it will be virtually impossible to measure

The Outline of an Agreement

When the Senate floor debate begins on the education bill (S 1), Democrats, Republicans and the Bush administration will be trying to reach agreement on a bipartisan plan. The amount of funding is still in play and several details have yet to be worked out, but many key provisions have been solidified:

STRAIGHT A'S

▶ Demonstration programs would be established in seven states (25 school districts) to allow the use of funds from "formula-driven" programs such as Title I aid to disadvantaged schools for any educational purpose, as long as better academic results were achieved.

▶ The programs would run for five years under Department of Education supervision. They would be terminated in any state or district that did not meet annual progress standards for two years or exceed them for three years.

▶ Title I funds would have to be targeted to poor schools under the current formula unless a state could prove to the Department of Education that it had a better method of steering the money to them.

ACCOUNTABILITY

▶ Students would be tested in reading and math annually in grades 3 through 8, as Bush proposed, to determine which schools needed help. States would choose the tests that were used.

▶ The following steps would be used to improve schools that did not meet "adequate yearly progress" standards, as determined by individual states:

Year One: Technical assistance would be available to improve the school.

Year Two: Parents could send their child to a better-performing public school, but federal funds could not be used for transportation.

Year Three: Federal funds could be used for private tutoring services or for transportation to another public school.

Year Four: The school would be reopened under a different structure or new faculty.

PORTABILITY

▶ Parents of children in underperforming schools could use federal funds for public school choice and state-approved private tutoring services — but not for private school tuition.

▶ Tutoring services could include before-school, after-school, weekend and summer programs. They could be run by for-profit businesses, school districts or community-based organizations.

▶ Tutoring programs would have to be based on the most effective methods (as determined by scientific research). Poorly performing programs could be declared ineligible by the state.

▶ Federal funds could come from Title I, the Title VI Innovative Education Program Strategies block grant and the 21st Century Community Learning Centers program, which funds after-school initiatives. State matching funds would be required.

students' progress as Bush wants because the tests will not be covering the same material.

"You could end up with this fruit salad of tests, and you won't be able to tell if Sally is doing better in the fourth grade than in the third grade," said Amy Wilkins, principal partner at the Education Trust, a nonprofit organization that advocates tougher education standards.

"People will say, 'This is ridiculous. We're not learning anything. We're just testing for the sake of testing,'" said Diane Ravitch, a research professor at New York University and assistant secretary of Education under former President George Bush.

Some state officials, however, believe it is not necessary to offer identical tests region to region and year to year.

Frank Shafroth, director of state-

federal relations at the National Governors' Association, said the only thing that matters is covering the same concepts "so you have a way to compare how students in Philadelphia are doing relative to students in Pittsburgh, even if the tests aren't identical."

Conservatives, meanwhile, are wary of Bush's assurances that the testing requirement will not lead to a national test. Although Bush insists states could pick their own tests, he would use the National Assessment of Educational Progress tests in reading and math, which are conducted by the Department of Education's National Center for Education Statistics every other year as a check to make sure state tests are not too easy.

The concern is that such a move could easily turn the progress test into a national exam. In testimony before the House Education and the Workforce Committee on March 29, Family Research Council president Kenneth L. Connor said the group was concerned that using the Education Department exam to check the results of state test scores "may lead to a national curriculum and a de facto national test."

House Republicans have already bowed to Connor's concerns: HR 1 would allow states to use other tests as a confirming score. The Senate bill would use the Education Department test as the only checkpoint, but conservative groups are trying to persuade Republicans to offer an amendment to change that.

If states are allowed to choose other tests, Ravitch said, "[the Education Department's test] will be dead" because it is currently an optional exam and states will abandon it. "You'll have a race to the bottom to find the easiest state test," she said.

For critics of standardized testing in general, the only relevant fight is to stop the testing plan altogether.

The National Center for Fair and Open Testing, a Cambridge, Mass.-based educators' group, is mobilizing supporters to defeat the Bush testing plan. The group says the rewards and penalties would create all the wrong incentives, steering teachers toward easy subjects — and possibly away from the schools where students need the most help.

"The tendency will be to find the easiest things to test and drill the students on them," said Monty Neill, the group's executive director. "That's no way to improve education." ◆

Congress and the President

Nearly everything Congress does must be signed by the president, making him a fact of everyday life in the House and the Senate. Although a large part of the relationship between Congress and the president is settled by laws regarding veto power and executive orders, the most significant connection between them is political and shapeless. It is more often the veto threat — not the veto itself — that wields the most influence for a president with Congress, as President Bush demonstrated in the debate on a patients' rights bill. Following the landslide Republican victories in 1994, former President Bill Clinton was famously put on the spot in a news conference to explain his relevance in Washington in light of such sweeping GOP gains. At the time, Clinton weakly insisted that the Constitution assured his relevance with its list of concrete duties for the chief executive, but upon recovering from the shock of those election day losses, Clinton soon demonstrated that the relevance of the president is measured in political, not just constitutional, terms. For example, it was Clinton's shrewd political maneuvering on the overhaul of the welfare system — long a Republican ambition — that got that bill into law. Clinton used the credibility the Democratic Party had on social issues to lay claim to the conservatives' goal of putting time limits on welfare payments to force people into job training programs. There is nothing in the federal code or Constitution explaining how a president does that.

In many ways, the balance of power between Congress and the president is a zero-sum game. The more power the president has in that relationship, the less Congress has, and vice versa. The president and Congress need one another, but even when they are of the same party there is a constant tug for a greater share of the power. In the opening months of the 107th Congress, President Bush used a mix of compromise and threat to effectively steer some legislation through Capitol Hill. But at the same time, his effort to leave Congress out of the discussion about reforming the military's structure brought him congressional opponents, who exerted their full authority on budget matters to impose themselves on the policy debate.

The Presidency Bush Inherits

President Clinton ended his second term more popular than he was when he entered the White House, despite the eight years of tumult. His political style involved cutting deals with his enemies despite the disapproval of his allies, leaving George W. Bush a legacy of ad hoc leadership that he will have to work hard to reform into the corporate, orderly style he prefers.

George W. Bush enters the White House in a seemingly enviable position. His party controls Congress, the nation remains prosperous, and America steers the global agenda. But Bush inherits a presidency fundamentally weakened by both historical trends and the style of his immediate predecessor.

Confronted by an increasingly assertive Congress, rampant partisanship, a public increasingly comfortable with divided government and a scandal-obsessed media, former President Bill Clinton resorted to a variety of tactics to retain power and keep the upper hand over a fractured, sometimes hostile legislative branch.

Clinton embraced an unusually broad agenda but staked out positions on what often seemed like an ad hoc basis, using poll-tested ideas and shifting coalitions in an attempt to dominate the debate between the White House and Capitol Hill.

He hands Bush what might be called an "improvisational presidency," in which the executive turns to tactical maneuvers and cunning when he cannot persuade Congress to go his way.

Central to Clinton's strategy was the use of longstanding presidential prerogatives, such as:

• **Administrative fiat.** When the president could not achieve legislative victories, he used executive branch agencies to issue myriad orders and regulations. These include recent directives setting time limits on how long managed-care plans can take to render decisions on medical claims, and placing roadless areas of national forests off limits to development.

• **The veto.** After Republicans seized control of Congress in 1995 and threatened to take away the president's ability to set the national agenda, Clinton used the veto to provoke showdowns over discretionary spending, winning increased funding for his top priorities and advancing a progressive agenda.

• **The bully pulpit.** Clinton adapted the presidency to the new information age, using campaign-like appearances built around themes such as economic opportunity. He used frequent speeches and public appearances to co-opt GOP positions on crime, welfare and the budget, and to assert his role as symbolic leader during crises, such as the aftermath of the Oklahoma City bombing.

By Adriel Bettelheim / Jan. 20, 2001

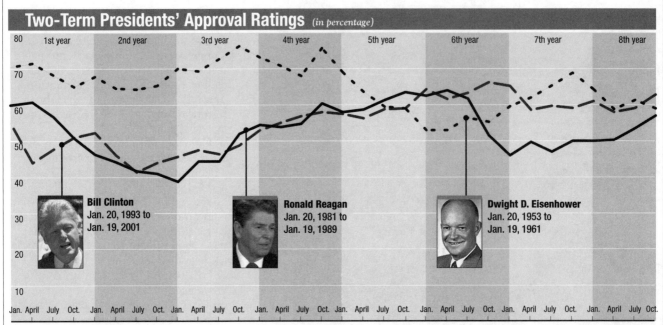

Two-Term Presidents' Approval Ratings *(in percentage)*

Bill Clinton
Jan. 20, 1993 to
Jan. 19, 2001

Ronald Reagan
Jan. 20, 1981 to
Jan. 19, 1989

Dwight D. Eisenhower
Jan. 20, 1953 to
Jan. 19, 1961

SOURCE: Gallup Organization

Bush is expected to employ a more controlled, corporate style of governing that is less hands-on and delegates considerable executive authority to Cabinet members. However, experts say he will have to use the president's clout to communicate clearly with the GOP-led Congress and score early successes.

"The new administration will have to be focused from the get-go," said Marshall Wittmann, senior fellow at the Hudson Institute. "You build power by scoring incremental successes, and Bush begins with an advantage, because Republicans . . . have a tendency to look to the executive branch for leadership. It's a kind of monarchy-driven party."

Many observers say the presidency has become more about narrow tactical and political successes than the kind of institutional authority over foreign and domestic affairs that presidents wielded during the Depression, World War II and the Cold War — a brand of clout historian Arthur Schlesinger Jr. called the "imperial presidency."

"The presidency has shrunk, in part because of the removal of an immediate national security threat and the increased prominence of economic issues like trade in national security matters," Thomas E. Mann, senior fellow in government studies at the Brookings Institution, said in a Jan. 9 interview. "There's simply less opportunity to dominate policy-making."

Intent on taking the initiative in ar-

eas once thought to be the exclusive domain of the president and his Cabinet, Congress in recent years has forced the president to improvise on an issue-by-issue basis and prevented him from assembling permanent working majorities in the House and Senate. Washington's countless interest groups have contributed to this by inserting themselves into national debates and applying intense lobbying pressure on individual votes.

Faced with such pressures, the president gradually has become a "designator and certifier," in the words of Charles O. Jones, professor emeritus of political science at the University of Wisconsin-Madison. Jones said the president is apt to identify fundamental problems and float potential solutions without always worrying about the details of how they could be enacted into law.

"Clinton never was a natural-born legislator or lawmaker, but he was a natural and instinctive campaigner," Jones said. "He was able to enhance his relatively weak political position by persuasively identifying and explaining what the issues were. And there was almost no issue too small to attract his interest. He was the ultimate policy wonk."

Reagan's Lament

America's last two-term president, Ronald Reagan, lamented at the end of his second term that he had been reduced to outlining broad terms of debate because the institution of the pres-

idency had been weakened. Reagan was dismayed that his administration's ability to dominate events, so evident during the legislative successes of his first term, slipped away as the Iran-Contra affair and an aggressive Democratic Congress put him on the defensive.

But if Reagan sounded glum about the power of the presidency as he left the White House, Clinton was sanguine and boastful as he completed his final year in office. Blessed with a still-vibrant economy and consistently high job-approval ratings, Clinton viewed his institutional clout as an extension of the prosperous times. He also took pride in the public's apparent renewed belief that government could be an agent of positive change.

In a series of January appearances across the country that amounted to a kind of victory lap, Clinton fairly bragged about how he had conceived a "third way" for government to skirt partisan divisions and operate more effectively to make a difference in people's lives. While critics have long derided this approach for lacking any true convictions, Clinton depicted it as pragmatic and forward-looking.

"The American people chose a vital, common-sense center eight years ago," Clinton said in a Jan. 11 address in Dover, N.H., site of one of his first 1992 campaign successes. "It seemed very foreign back then to Washington. I can remember political writers who spent the previous umpty-ump years in Washington saying, 'I don't know what this guy believes. Does he believe anything? I mean, you've either got to be a conservative or a liberal.'

"Guess what? That's now the new consensus in Washington. People now believe that this is the right direction. It's even basically the landscape against [which] the last election was fought in such a close fashion. There is a consensus that we have to find ways to continue to change consistent with our basic values and our common community and humanity."

The question now is whether Bush will be able to adapt Clinton's model to claim more executive power. As he is the leader of the first unified Republican government in half a century, some in his party are urging Bush to pursue early legislative victories on tax cuts and other issues.

But with a narrow margin in the House and a 50-50 Senate, an excessively bold agenda or assertive style could quickly result in gridlock — and not just between Republicans and Democrats. Some GOP lawmakers on Capitol Hill, such as incoming House Ways and Means Committee Chairman Bill Thomas, R-Calif., are signaling that the new president should not take for granted their support in enacting his sweeping $1.3 trillion tax-cut plan.

Wittmann questioned whether the more controlled, corporate style of governing that Bush is expected to embrace will erode goodwill. "Republicans during the Clinton years hungered for the White House bully pulpit to get their message out," Wittmann said. "It will be interesting to see whether Bush is as articulate as Clinton in developing and communicating his goals, and whether he uses television and the range of media outlets to get the party's message out."

The Job and Its Powers

Presidents have always enjoyed considerable latitude in defining their job and their powers. While the Founding Fathers clearly spelled out the roles and responsibilities of Congress in Article I of the Constitution, the presidency was characterized in grand but somewhat vague terms that were more open to interpretation. Was the "chief executive" or "commander-in-chief" a supreme leader, or just one vital part of a plan built around separated institutions sharing power?

The matter was much-debated dur-

ing George Washington's first administration. Treasury Secretary Alexander Hamilton took the first view, arguing that the president had a constitutional duty to exercise broad executive prerogatives, such as making treaties with foreign nations and directing domestic fiscal policy. Secretary of State Thomas Jefferson differed, taking more of a strict, constructionist view that the president could only go as far as the legislative branch would allow.

Jefferson's view has prevailed up to current times, except for a brief period of presidential dominance. It was perhaps fitting that Jefferson, who was elected president by the House of Representatives in 1801 after a tie vote in the Electoral College, regarded Congress — not the public — as his primary constituency, though he still held considerable political power as the head of the majority Democratic-Republican party.

Two decades later, Democrat Andrew Jackson challenged the status quo by building the first modern political party organization. Jackson set up a spoils system, installing allies in patronage jobs and triggering intense power struggles, especially with opposition Whigs in the Senate. The party system allowed Jackson to appeal directly to the public (not unlike Clinton) and go around their elected representatives. However, Jackson personally subscribed to the doctrine of states' rights, and most of the presidential perks he

amassed were lost by the succession of weak presidents that followed him until the Civil War.

Abraham Lincoln used political patronage to pass a constitutional amendment abolishing slavery, striking deals with three House members through his secretary of war to allow Nevada to enter the union and provide the necessary votes to pass the 13th amendment. As the Civil War raged, Lincoln also was forced to seek an overarching source of national power. His solution was to assert that the president was entitled to "war power" through language in the Constitution designating him commander-in-chief — a power Franklin D. Roosevelt would claim during World War II. Lincoln used executive fiat to free slaves and station federal troops in the reconstructed South.

In the 20th century, Theodore Roosevelt adapted Lincoln's model, arguing the president did not need specific constitutional authority to act at home or on foreign soil. This unusually activist president intervened in labor disputes and took on large industrial trusts. Roosevelt also benefited from a change in thinking following the Spanish-American War that led the once-isolationist U.S. government to pursue more foreign policy objectives. During his tenure, Roosevelt presided over the building of the Panama Canal and got involved in disputes in Cuba and the Dominican Republic.

Woodrow Wilson refined the model

Clinton Admits False Statements

On his last day in office, President Bill Clinton finally admitted that he lied in the cases that led to his 1998 impeachment.

"I tried to walk a fine line between acting lawfully and testifying falsely, but I now recognize that I did not fully accomplish this goal and that certain of my responses to questions about Ms. Lewinsky were false," Clinton said Jan. 19, referring to his sworn denials of an affair with former White House intern Monica Lewinsky.

His admission — part of a deal with Independent Counsel Robert W. Ray — spares Clinton further proceedings in the protracted in-

vestigation that began with the Whitewater land deal. Clinton agreed to a $25,000 fine and a five-year suspension of his Arkansas law license.

"This matter is now concluded. May history and the American people judge that it has been concluded justly," said Ray, who took over from Kenneth W. Starr in late 1999.

It did not satisfy former House Speaker Newt Gingrich, R-Ga.: "This is a guy who will spend all of his life explaining that nothing he ever did wrong was wrong — and it all depends on how you define the word 'wrong.' It's a trivial ending to a relatively trivial presidency."

of the strong president further, becoming the first chief executive to propose and draft legislation. Wilson, setting the stage for presidents like Reagan and Clinton, also employed modern "spin," holding frequent news conferences, directly lobbying Congress and assessing public opinion. This helped win passage of bills creating the Federal Reserve and Federal Trade Commission.

When the United States entered World War I, Congress expanded Wilson's authority by giving him expanded war powers. But Wilson failed to convince the public of the need to join the League of Nations after the war, and his efforts to win Senate ratification of the treaty creating the entity were unsuccessful.

Wilson may have adapted the presidency for modern times, but Franklin D. Roosevelt reshaped the office. Elected by a shell-shocked country during the Depression, Roosevelt racked up enormous victories as Congress ceded broad authority to the executive branch in the areas of banking, housing, agriculture, public works and fiscal policy. In his first year in office, Roosevelt saw most of his then-radical New Deal initiatives win passage by the House and Senate. Roosevelt also was able to gain unprecedented emergency authority, first in providing relief programs during the Depression, and later in military planning during World War II.

Roosevelt's tenure created an expectation in the post-war era that the president should be a kind of chief legislative leader. Dwight D. Eisenhower was criticized during his first year in of-

fice for not offering a legislative program — a situation he quickly corrected. Congress even helped centralize power in the White House by creating the Council of Economic Advisers in 1946 and a National Security Council the following year. With the federal bureaucracy growing and the United States getting more involved in global affairs, the president assumed multiple roles. The Marshall Plan to rebuild Europe, the Bretton Woods agreement on an international gold standard, and the decision to commit troops in Korea all were executive branch initiatives, carried out with congressional deference.

The spell of unchallenged White House primacy effectively ended during the administration of Lyndon B. Johnson. Despite Johnson's landslide victory, Senate Foreign Relations Committee Chairman J. William Fulbright, D-Ark. (1945-74), in 1965 refused to accept the president's decision to send 22,000 troops into the Dominican Republic to deal with an army revolt and rebel strife — despite having recently given Johnson de facto power to fight a war in Vietnam through the Gulf of Tonkin resolution. Fulbright broke with precedent by openly questioning the need for such unilateral force. The move led to more congressional inquiries about foreign policy objectives, culminating in Fulbright's televised 1968 hearings into the legitimacy of the Vietnam military commitment.

This trend continued when Richard M. Nixon took office, and Congress began a lengthy review of U.S. overseas commitments and "executive agreements" that presidents had struck

with foreign governments. This tendency of Congress to use investigations and inquiries to assert its power continues to this day.

Political scientist James P. Pfiffner attributed this fundamental shift, in part, to the breakdown of political parties beginning in the 1950s.

"Presidential hopefuls began to depend less on political parties and more on their own resources and public popularity," Pfiffner wrote in 1991. "As a result, once they were in office, they could no longer depend on a governing coalition based on a political party apparatus in the states and within Congress. The increase of ticket-splitting further separated the political fates of presidents from their party colleagues in Congress."

Nixon's years were highlighted by bitter power struggles with Congress that surpassed those between Clinton and congressional Republicans. In his memoirs, Nixon recalled throwing down a gauntlet to Congress to defy his grabs for influence over foreign and domestic policy. One tactic Nixon employed was the refusal to release congressionally appropriated funds for programs he thought were wasteful or unnecessary. Democrats who controlled the House and Senate not only resisted his drive for autonomy but passed legislation restricting it. After Watergate, Gerald R. Ford and Jimmy Carter were unable to stop the trend of Congress encroaching on powers previously claimed by the White House.

The legacy of these years is seen in a variety of laws reasserting congressional power. The War Powers Resolution (PL

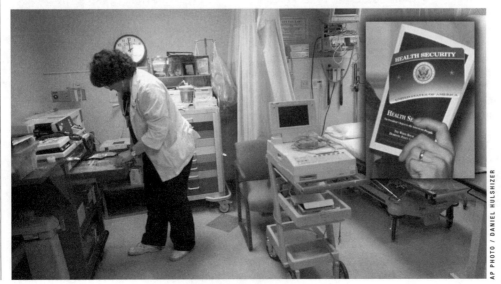

After overreaching with his sweeping 1993 health care reform plan (inset), Clinton never struck a deal with Congress on a meaningful health care package that would have helped hospitals like the Medical Center of Ocean County, N.J., which closed its acute-care ward (left).

AP PHOTO / DANIEL HULSHIZER

93-148), passed in 1973 over Nixon's veto in response to Vietnam, forced the chief executive to obtain congressional approval for any extended military engagements, though virtually every president has skirted it, including Clinton in ordering interventions in Haiti and the Balkans. In 1974, Congress passed the Jackson-Vanik amendment linking trade policy with the Soviet Union to human rights. The 1974 Budget Act (PL 93-344) changed the federal budgeting process and put Congress in the driver's seat. It created the Congressional Budget Office, giving the legislative branch its own economic forecasts and deficit estimates that sometimes challenged the assumptions of the White House Office of Management and Budget (OMB).

Post-Watergate reforms also changed Congress, weakening the seniority system and opening up committee markups to the public. While this took away power from a relatively small group of committee chairmen, it also made it more difficult for the president to win congressional support for his proposals, because the administration was forced to deal with multiple power centers in the House and Senate. Gradually, the president had to be more nimble and entrepreneurial to get what he wanted.

Riding a huge Electoral College victory and a surprise GOP takeover of the Senate in 1980, Reagan won significant legislative victories in his first year, including passage of a unorthodox plan to restructure the budget and cut individual and business taxes. Reagan also consolidated White House control over Cabinet agencies by issuing executive orders requiring that all regulations be cleared by OMB. While this was depicted as a way of reducing federal interference in commerce and local affairs, it also had the effect of paring the influence of congressional oversight committees.

But after early budget and tax victories, Reagan administration officials decided to pursue an ideologically rigid agenda largely designed to embarrass Democrats who opposed them. This backfired when the economy slowed, and congressional Democrats fought Reagan's efforts to spend more on defense without raising taxes.

Reagan was unable to get Congress to embrace his social agenda, which included proposed constitutional amendments banning abortion and allowing school prayer. And Congress began asserting its war powers role when Reagan sought an extended deployment of U.S. Marines in war-torn Lebanon. The Iran-Contra scandal diminished

By his second year in office, Clinton could rely neither on the majority of Democrats nor on a bipartisan coalition to win votes. The dilemma contributed to the crushing defeat of his administration's ambitious plan to reform health care and led to the GOP takeover in the mid-term election of 1994.

Reagan's public standing during his final two years in office and effectively ended his conservative revolution.

Heightened partisanship and an assertive Congress frustrated the administration of George Bush — first in the refusal of the Senate to confirm his choice of former Sen. John G. Tower, R-Texas (1961-85), as defense secretary. Then in 1990, Bush was embarrassed when GOP House members refused to support a bipartisan budget deal that appeared to break his campaign vow of "no new taxes." The prevailing view among analysts is that Bush was permanently hurt by placing foreign affairs over domestic issues and by failing to set clear a legislative agenda.

The Lone Crusader

Unlike his immediate predecessor, Clinton had an extremely broad domestic agenda when he arrived in Washington. But he quickly encountered problems dealing with Congress. Running as a "New Democrat," Clinton had defied his party's liberal base on issues such as welfare, crime and the budget. This deprived him of some of the party loyalty normally accorded to new presidents on Capitol Hill.

Though Clinton was able to personally mobilize Democratic support and pass his 1993 deficit-reduction plan without a single GOP vote, his collaboration with Republicans on passage of

the North American Free Trade Agreement (NAFTA) further alienated his base. By his second year in office, Clinton could rely neither on the majority of Democrats nor on a bipartisan coalition to win votes. The dilemma contributed to the crushing defeat of his administration's ambitious plan to reform health care and led to the GOP takeover in the mid-term election of 1994.

After the Republicans took control of Congress, Clinton began to scale back his legislative initiatives and use the appropriations process and power of the veto to achieve his legislative goals. This approach enabled Clinton to save pet projects such as the AmeriCorps National Service program, which makes grants to states, localities and nonprofit groups to enable volunteers to engage in community service and earn stipends for college tuition.

The program, created in 1993, was a target of conservative Republicans in Congress, who derided it as wasteful and questioned why people should be paid to volunteer. GOP leaders made several attempts to delete funding for the program in the appropriations bill for the departments of Veterans Affairs and Housing and Urban Development. In response, Clinton either refused to sign any version of the bill that did not restore funding, or compromised with the GOP on an amount that would allow the program to meet its target of placing 25,000 volunteers in the field.

After the failure of his sweeping health care plan, Clinton pursued health measures that were more modest in scope during his second term. He won inclusion of a new children's health-care initiative in the Balanced-Budget Act of 1997 (PL 105-33) that was funded in part by an increase in federal cigarette taxes. Later, he unsuccessfully sought a Medicare buy-in for early retirees and an expansion of Medicaid and the state Children's Health Insurance Program.

Kenneth M. Duberstein, a Republican lobbyist and former chief of staff to Reagan, said Clinton's general persuasiveness on Capitol Hill was diminished by his improvisational approach and failure to build lasting relations with the GOP. Another factor was Clinton's campaign-style approach and "war room" tactics — something Duberstein said Bush would be wise to avoid.

"You have to make a priority of 'going steady' with Congress and making them working partners in governing," Duberstein said. "Clinton didn't do the depth of bipartisan cooperation that is fundamental to being a successful president, particularly on issues like health care and the budget. He learned many lessons since his early years, but he never fully earned the trust of the Republican Congress."

If Clinton's legislative options were at times limited, he still was able to exercise his presidential powers and considerable political skills to great effect in cajoling and even bullying Congress. He was helped by key political advisors — such as Dick Morris, creator of the "triangulation" strategy of staking out the middle ground of debates — and an increased capability of pollsters and consultants to gauge what the public believed in.

"Here's a fellow who could really read polls for what was behind them," said University of Wisconsin political scientist Jones. "He could give life to issues that otherwise would be difficult for the public to get interested in, things like school uniforms, emergency call numbers, having community policing in your neighborhood."

Executive Actions

During Clinton's final months in office, the executive branch seemed like a rulemaking machine, issuing directives to make federal programs more accessible to non-English speakers; implement new workplace safety rules;

place roadless areas of federal lands off-limits to logging and development; create new national monuments, and speed up decisions on managed-care claims.

These unilateral regulations conveniently bypassed a recalcitrant Congress and eliminated the need for lengthy hearings and public-comment periods. They also gave the president's opponents an unpalatable choice: put up with the rules or face the arduous task of devising legislation to undo them.

"Clinton was really successful creatively using executive orders and pushing the envelope, in part because there is a lot of wiggle room in administrative law," Harvard University political scientist David King said. "It's an option when a president cannot rely on incremental policymaking that gets him past cloture," the 60 votes necessary to cut off debate in the Senate.

The president's most notable use of the executive order came in September 1996, when he set aside 1.7 million acres of environmentally sensitive Utah canyonlands as the Grand Staircase-Escalante National Monument. The move delighted environmentalists but was bitterly condemned by many western Republicans and some Democrats, who charged it was a brazen federal land grab made without regard to local concerns.

Clinton designated at least a dozen additional new monuments and expanded two existing ones, citing executive powers granted to Theodore Roosevelt under the 1906 Antiquities Act. The U.S. Forest Service issued controversial regulations during his final

weeks in office banning development in roadless areas of national forests, and the Interior Department issued new rules dealing with bonds and the permitting of hard-rock mining.

Former White House Chief of Staff John D. Podesta said these environmental orders reflected a fundamental shift in strategy following the Newt Gingrich-led Republican revolution, as the president moved from vetoing environmental provisions in annual spending bills to taking the offensive and crafting new rules to block GOP initiatives.

Collectively, the presidential actions were the most assertive use of executive orders since Reagan's decision to subject regulatory actions to OMB review. But they served to remind future presidents that Congress, with no centralized power base, frequently is unable to respond to complex or controversial issues with detailed statutory language. Instead, it is more likely to set benchmarks and timetables in legislation and allow the executive branch to work out the technicalities.

Sometimes Clinton overreached. The Food and Drug Administration in 1996 determined that nicotine was a drug and argued it had the statutory authority to regulate tobacco products, especially relating to children and young teens. However, the U.S. Supreme Court ruled in a 5-4 vote in March 2000 that only Congress could confer such power.

Observers do not expect Bush to show a similar appetite for sweeping executive orders because the GOP-controlled legislative branch initially

Prodded by businesses looking to expand overseas, Clinton worked with GOP leaders to win passage of a trade agreement with China in 2000, seven years after a similar bipartisan effort established a North American free trade zone. But the administration often had to struggle to get Congress to go along with other foreign policy initiatives.

AP PHOTO / CHIEN-MIN CHUNG

will roll out bills to implement his agenda, as custom dictates. However, Bush has said he may use the executive order to negate some Clinton administration efforts. One likely target: Occupational Safety and Health Administration workplace safety standards that require a wide range of employers to set up programs to prevent repetitive stress injuries. Business groups claim the regulations will cost them billions of dollars.

Veto Power

Republicans began the fiscal 2000 appropriations cycle in early 1999 intent on limiting what they said was Clinton's penchant for more new spending and tax increases. The GOP appeared determined to stick to budget caps set two years earlier, hoping there would be enough left for an election-year tax cut.

Then something familiar happened. Using the power of the veto, Clinton rejected five of 13 spending bills that Congress sent him, forcing the GOP into showdowns over spending priorities. In the end, Republicans caved in to many of the president's goals, including more subsidies for hiring teachers and community police; the release of back U.S. dues to the United Nations, and nearly $500 million in new funding to purchase environmentally sensitive and culturally significant land.

After failing to veto a single measure from the Democratic-controlled Congress during his first two years, Clinton repeatedly used the veto to block GOP initiatives, cloaking his actions in the reasoning of responsible governing. But unlike past presidents, Clinton went beyond simply preventing measures from becoming law by advancing a progressive agenda through what appeared to be defensive measures.

"Republicans tried to use their majority in Congress to shrink those parts of the government that most mattered to Clinton, and he used the veto to stop it," said Brookings' Mann.

Some see the presidential veto strategy as part of a larger drama pitting Clinton's concept of an activist government against the GOP's vision of a more limited federal bureaucracy.

"Standing against Republicans during the government shutdown [of 1995-96], he staged a morality play reminding middle-class voters what they gained from government," Clinton's former speechwriter Michael Waldman writes in his book, "POTUS Speaks: Finding the Words that Defined the Clinton Presidency."

"The drip-drip of Rose Garden events, announcing incremental steps on issues such as child care, crime, health care and consumer protection,

> *After failing to veto a single measure from the Democratic-controlled Congress during his first two years, Clinton repeatedly used the veto to block GOP initiatives, cloaking his actions in the reasoning of responsible governing.*

all sought to restore confidence that government could do something."

Clinton clearly benefited from his personal popularity and ability to convince the public the legislation being vetoed could have serious consequences. His 1995 veto message nixing the Republican budget plan stated the GOP legislation "would hurt average Americans and help special interests" by cutting deeply into Medicare, Medicaid, nutrition programs and tax credits for the working poor.

It is unlikely that Bush will resort to such rhetoric, at least in the early part of his administration. With extremely tight margins in Congress and a comparatively limited agenda, Bush is likely to sign whatever Congress passes. But if control of one or both houses of Congress passes to Democrats after the 2002 elections, observers believe Bush may follow his father's model and begin blocking measures, or using veto threats to prompt serious bargaining on taxes, education and other top-priority issues.

The Global View

Though he was leader of the last remaining superpower and embraced the global economy through landmark trade agreements, Clinton leaves an ill-defined legacy for his successors in foreign affairs, in the opinion of many experts.

His early endorsement of NAFTA, the creation of the World Trade Organization and, later, a pact promising permanent normal trade relations with China all helped spur global economic growth and control inflation. His moves to bail out the Mexican economy and shore up the International Monetary Fund also demonstrated that the United States would remain internationally involved rather than sit by and watch as other entities foundered.

His advocacy of sustaining a strong dollar in the face of big trade deficits countered the popular belief that a weaker dollar would narrow the gap by improving exports. Indeed, the move allowed the U.S. economy to continue to flourish with low inflation, and to be insulated from inflationary pressures in the rest of the world.

However, Clinton also had notable failures on his watch. He could not regain fast-track authority to negotiate trade pacts after the authority expired in 1994. His administration's pursuit of protectionist policies in behalf of narrow U.S. interests such as banana and beef exporters appeared at odds with his free-trade stance. And the 1999 World Trade Organization meeting in Seattle ended up a debacle, as environmental and labor protesters stole the stage.

Experts say Clinton suffered from not having a foreign policy framework and by exercising his presidential powers on an ad hoc basis. Global trade, security and diplomatic matters usually got low priority compared to his domestic initiatives.

"It's difficult to say he did something different," Anthony H. Cordesman, senior fellow in strategic assessment at the Center for Strategic and International Studies, said in a Jan. 17 interview. "He was pragmatic on trade and followed a policy that was pretty close to the Bush administration. In other areas, he enunciated ambitious doctrines but did not always follow through."

On military matters, Clinton's most immediate legacy consists of the peacekeeping and humanitarian missions in Haiti, Somalia, Kosovo and Bosnia. Despite congressional criticism that the missions focused on humanitarian goals instead of national security interests, the president asserted his prerogatives, aware that Congress, except in the rarest of circumstances, will not order U.S. troops back.

Incoming Secretary of State Colin L. Powell is skeptical of using force in diplomatic hot spots, and he and other Bush administration officials have broached the idea of withdrawing some U.S. forces from the Balkans and asking for more help from America's allies.

Clinton had success eliminating nuclear warheads from the Ukraine and other former Soviet republics and winning 1997 Senate ratification of a chemical arms pact. But his failure to reach any significant arms control agreement with Russia and his repeated inability to broker a Middle East peace settlement raised questions about what many saw as an improvisational approach to foreign affairs.

"He didn't come up with an approach to the world that will last after him," Richard N. Haass, director of foreign policy studies at the Brookings Institution, said at a Jan. 9 forum. "He didn't give the American people a handle, a philosophy, a doctrine, a policy that will essentially guide them through the second decade of the post-Cold War world."

State of the Union Appeal

Just days after the public learned about Clinton's affair with White House intern Monica Lewinsky, the president in January 1998 delivered a 72-minute, State of the Union address that effectively shifted the focus from his personal behavior to his leadership.

With scandal swirling, the president in effect told the American people that, if they liked his policies, they should keep him in office. Clinton's approval ratings in overnight polls remained around 60 percent. And his call in the same speech to use surplus revenues to "save Social Security first" became a centerpiece of domestic policy debates.

Clinton's most lasting effect on the presidency may be how he changed the way the chief executive speaks to the nation. A born kibbitzer who took instinctively to the podium, Clinton gave more speeches than any of his predecessors — approximately 550 per year, compared to 320 for Reagan and 88 for Harry S Truman. He also found new settings to reach out to average Americans, holding town hall meetings over which he presided like a talk show host. He also used visual images and themed events to make policy debates real — for example, signing the welfare-overhaul bill while flanked by a struggling mother of three who made ends meet working in a supermarket.

Some of this was born of necessity. The profusion of cable channels and Internet sites that sprang up during Clinton's tenure created what has been called a "virtual presidency," in which every Rose Garden pronouncement was instantly beamed to millions of people. In such an environment, the White House felt it had to constantly feed a voracious news machine and, in a perverse way, struggle to be heard when it made a really important announcement.

"He has to speak more often, and always to make news, no matter how small," former speechwriter Waldman wrote. "Speeches are no longer thunderbolts hurled from Olympus. Instead, they are a steady purr, one of two or even three a day. The White House is not just the object of news coverage by news networks — in effect, it has itself become a 24-hour, cable news channel. It is expected to

generate programming."

The ubiquity of the commander in chief gives him a tremendous advantage over Congress, which by nature is decentralized into 535 fiefdoms and cannot speak with one voice. Even when Gingrich and his revolutionaries synchronized their 1994 agenda as the "Contract With America" and tried to dictate terms of the debate, or when independent counsels subpoenaed administration figures in connection with the various scandals surrounding him, the president held the upper hand, speaking with one voice at a lectern bearing the seal of his office.

It remains to be seen how much Bush will warm to the task. More the competent manager than the improvisational policy wonk, Bush almost certainly will not think out loud in the way that Clinton did. The former Texas governor's everyman appeal translated into significant currency on the campaign trail, and his tendency to delegate kept him seemingly above the partisan fray during the disputed election. But exactly which persona he will project is still an open question.

"I still don't know who Bush is and what he wants," said Brookings' Mann. "Is he the pragmatic unifier, or a conventional conservative Republican who's happy to give loose rein to his party base? He really has not adapted his transition or agenda to the extraordinary circumstances of the election."

Also unknown is how much Bush will adapt sophisticated polling techniques to the job at hand. Clinton was obsessed with polls and regularly used

surveys to identify issues that resonated with swing voters. From this came tactics such as the decision to use the loaded word "risky" to characterize GOP plans to use the surplus for tax cuts.

It is unlikely that Bush will take such a campaign-like approach to his message — and almost certain that he will be more hands-off. Greater priority will be placed on honing an easily communicated agenda, and less effort will be directed at spin wars. Yet the nexus of public opinion and political strategy may be exploited early in his administration, perhaps to gauge whether to embark on plans to enact his entire $1.3 trillion tax-cut plan or promote controversial policies like school vouchers.

Uniqueness of the Time

Bush comes to the White House at a unique time. With three consecutive years of budget surpluses, he will not be immediately burdened by the deficit politics that plagued his recent predecessors. There also are no looming crises on the foreign or domestic fronts, though many forecasters are predicting an economic slowdown. And despite narrow margins, he will be the first GOP president since Eisenhower to work with a Congress controlled by his own party.

Though he will not have the authority of presidents who governed in times of war, Bush still has a chance to wield considerable clout if he runs his presidency in sync with the times. Just as Clinton used well-calibrated centrist

policies to establish the mien of a competent, responsible leader, Bush may be able to stake out positions or themes that confer a similar mantle on institutional authority, experts say.

"As the first truly post-imperial president, George W. Bush has the chance to demonstrate that his pledge to be a healing 'uniter' — made long before the nation experienced the 35 tortuous days that followed the election — can help to overcome the divisions in Congress and the electorate, the poison in our politics and our rattled nerves," historian Michael Beschloss wrote recently in The New York Times.

"If he does, he may prove himself a stronger president than anyone might have imagined." ◆

CQ PHOTOS / SCOTT J. FERRELL

Led by Georgia Rep. Newt Gingrich (far left), the GOP captured control of Congress by running a well-crafted, issue-focused campaign in 1994. Clinton's eventual success at derailing Republican priorities stirred bitter partisanship, which erupted in 1998's impeachment. The House Judiciary Committee, and then the House, passed articles of impeachment for Clinton's conduct in an affair with a White House intern that he tried to cover up. Clinton was acquitted in a Senate trial, but Washington never fully recovered from the bitter partisan atmosphere of the episode. Bush and Cheney on inauguration day (far right) campaigned on a pledge to return "honor and dignity" to the White House, but also vowed to "change the tone in Washington."

Political Capital, the Precious Commodity

A president's ability to persuade Congress to do as he wishes is far more useful than any executive order he can sign without consulting the legislative branch. But in the American system of balanced power, persuasion comes when those being persuaded believe it is in their best political interest to go along, and that happens when the president has the political capital to bend others to his will.

From left, Senate Majority Leader Trent Lott, R-Miss., House Speaker J. Dennis Hastert, R-Ill., Bush and Vice President Dick Cheney met at Bush's Texas ranch last December.

He is not coming to the rescue of any domestic or foreign crises, and he has no landslide victory to strengthen his hand. But President Bush ascends to power with one strong and potentially decisive advantage in dealing with Congress: a Republican majority that needs him more than he needs them.

That is the dominant view on Capitol Hill as Bush begins his presidency with an agenda crowded by ambitious campaign promises, a shortened transition period, a perilously thin margin of Republican control in Congress, and the lingering bitterness of an electoral victory many Democrats consider tainted.

These factors could limit Bush's most important source of power — that intangible sense of political authority presidents use to get the votes they need in Congress, a commodity that ebbed and flowed dramatically through the Clinton administration.

In the eyes of lawmakers from both parties, Bush begins with a limited amount of political capital to spend on winning votes on tough issues. If Bush spends it right, he can generate more with legislative victories. If he spends it unwisely, insisting on support for unpopular measures, he could simply run out.

Most believe Bush can build on the inherent advantage he has in facing a GOP-led Congress that is expected to be hungry for legislative successes, but only by starting small.

That means smaller tax cuts, they say, not the entire $1.3 trillion he promised through 2010; a rewrite of education policy, but probably without the limited school voucher plan he proposed; and a "lockbox" to keep Congress from spending the Social Security trust fund, but not the big overhaul that would add private savings accounts to the nation's most popular entitlement program.

"If he wants capital, he's going to have to earn it," GOP Rep. Jack Quinn of New York said on Jan. 17. "Nowadays, it just doesn't get handed to you."

Political capital is hard to define,

and members of Congress have different ideas about where it comes from. Some believe it derives largely from the margin of victory in the presidential election, an interpretation that could hurt Bush given his loss of the popular vote.

Others say the sources of political capital for a president can be anything from public approval ratings to legislative successes and the risks he takes in office. It can come from solidarity between a president and his political party, and even minor things such as courtesy calls to members of Congress.

Whatever the source, presidents need it to get members of Congress to cast difficult votes. If Bush wants Democrats to vote for bigger tax cuts or for a missile defense program they have opposed, he will have to spend political capital.

If he wants conservative Republicans to vote for a bigger federal role in education than they would like or to pass the Patients' Bill of Rights that faltered in the last two Congresses, he will have to cash in even more.

That is why the interests of congressional Republicans are so important. The good news for Bush, according to lawmakers and analysts, is that Republicans have every incentive to cooperate with him and stay out of trouble.

Balance of Power

One look at congressional election trends explains why. Republicans have held their majority in Congress through three elections since 1994, but they have lost seats in the last two elections and almost lost the Senate in the last round.

In the next round, Republicans will be trying to keep control of Congress in a midterm election — where the president's party traditionally loses seats.

"If the Republicans control everything in sight and have to go back to the voters with no accomplishments, it hurts them," Rep. Robert E. Andrews, D-N.J., said on Jan. 17.

That does not mean Bush can as-

By David Nather / Jan. 20, 2001

sume he has the backing of congressional Republicans. Some already have signaled their independence, as Senate Republicans did at a Jan. 19 confirmation hearing for Bush's choice for Health and Human Services Secretary Tommy G. Thompson when they suggested Bush's plan to provide prescription drug coverage to seniors might be too limited.

Ultimately, though, lawmakers and political scientists do not expect any major Republican uprisings against Bush.

To some Republican lawmakers, Bush has served the party immeasurably simply by putting the White House back in GOP hands — and by making a strong case for its core causes, such as tax cuts, to jump-start the suddenly slowing economy. That is why they believe Bush is flush with political capital.

"He's actually, I believe, gained capital on the Hill since the election," GOP Rep. Mark Souder of Indiana, one of the party's self-described social conservatives, said on Jan. 17. "Every Republican is incredibly impressed by how he's managed the economic debate."

Rep. Johnny Isakson, R-Ga., a member of the House Education and the Workforce Committee, said Bush has credibility in the education debate because of the solid improvement in Texas students' test scores when he was governor. Texas and North Carolina are the two states that have had the most success in using standards-based education overhauls to raise math scores, according to a July 2000 study by RAND, a nonprofit public policy research organization.

Isakson said that could help Bush when the time comes to convince Republicans to approve an annual testing requirement — pushing the boundaries of the long-held GOP view that the federal government should not set education rules.

Other Republicans, however, say Bush begins his tenure lacking enough authority to put his entire campaign agenda before Congress, and must therefore focus on scoring a few quick legislative victories.

"I don't think there's any question that he starts out with a disadvantage" because of the compressed transition and critical comments by Bill Clinton in his final days, incoming House Budget Committee Chairman Jim Nussle, R-Iowa, said on Jan. 17.

Nussle was referring to comments Clinton made at a Democratic rally in Chicago on Jan. 9 that questioned the legitimacy of Bush's victory.

Although senators increasingly are of the mind that Bush's tax cut plan should pass as a single bill, Nussle suggested Bush should build momentum by signing two piecemeal tax cuts Clinton vetoed last year: repeals of the so-called marriage penalty and the estate tax.

Quinn, a moderate Republican who depends on labor support to hold his seat, suggested Bush could start by signing the minimum wage increase that foundered last year. Since the deal was negotiated before he took office, Quinn said, "Bush could sign it and say [to critics], 'Hey, it wasn't on my watch.'"

Real Bipartisanship?

It will be quite a trick, however, to woo the Democrats — especially in the 50-50 Senate, where Bush would have to pick up 10 Democrats to overcome a filibuster. Some Democrats warn that Bush will have to work harder than he has so far to build political capital with them.

"He has to reach out to the whole range of opinions, not just the people who agree with him," said Democrat Jack Reed of Rhode Island, a member of the Senate Health, Education, Labor and Pensions Committee.

Reed said in a Jan. 18 interview that one area where Bush fell short was his Dec. 21 education meeting in Austin, when Bush invited 19 House and Senate members from both parties to the governor's mansion to discuss education overhaul proposals but did not include Sen. Edward M. Kennedy, D-Mass. — the ranking Democrat on the Senate Health, Education, Labor and Pensions Committee.

Bush's relations with Democrats continue to be hampered by the way he became president. While many prominent Democrats have urged the party to put the election behind them, many Democratic supporters remain convinced Bush was, in effect, chosen by the Supreme Court when it halted the Florida recounts.

"I think he's got to acknowledge that he was put in the White House through a very questionable procedure," Democratic Rep. Eddie Bernice Johnson of Texas, chairwoman of the Congressional Black Caucus, said in a Jan. 17 interview.

Bush scored points with Democrats who attended his education meeting in Austin. Andrews, a member of the House Education and the Workforce Committee, attended the event and said Bush seemed to make a real effort to solicit a range of opinions, going around the room and asking for each lawmaker's views on improving schools.

In order to get his education package through Congress, however, Andrews said he told Bush the voucher plan would have to go.

"He needs to decide whether he's going to try to build an [education package] that gets the entire Republican Party and 10 percent of the Democrats, or whether he's going to build an [education package] that gets 80 percent of the members from both parties," Andrews said.

One lesson Bush can take on political capital comes from his father, who learned after the Gulf War that personal popularity and political capital are not necessarily the same thing. At one point in March 1991, President George Bush scored an 89 percent approval rating, the highest ever measured by a Gallup poll.

But the next two years were no more productive for Bush in his relations with a Democratic Congress than the previous years had been, according to Congressional Quarterly's vote analysis at the time.

Still, some think former President Bush made a mistake by not pushing harder.

"You've got to use your capital in order to gain more," Rep. Robert T. Matsui, D-Calif., said on Jan. 17. "You can't just sit on it." ◆

Fiscal Discipline in a Time of Plenty

The political landscape is shaped to a large extent by the condition of the federal budget. Tight resources produce one kind of politics, scarce resources produce another. President Bush arrived in Washington proposing an austere budget at a time when the politics on Capitol Hill were driven by record surpluses.

Now that he has put his ambitious agenda before Congress, President Bush confronts some hard truths about turning a campaign vision into a fiscal blueprint for the nation.

On Capitol Hill, his Republican Party is beset with the competing agendas of several economic policy cliques: Tax cutters, debt hawks, domestic spending moderates and defense boosters. Each must be listened to, and many must be mollified, for Bush's deep tax cuts and the rest of his program to have a fighting chance of becoming law. And with the GOP in control of the White House and both sides of the Capitol for the first time since 1954, the party will have a hard time affixing blame elsewhere if they fail.

The first and perhaps most perilous test of its stewardship will come this spring with votes on the fiscal 2002 budget resolution, a document that has been relatively inconsequential in the last several years. Adopting the measure will be unusually pivotal, because doing so will compel Republicans to find the balancing point among all their fiscal factions.

And the GOP hierarchy is already realizing it will have to make do almost entirely with votes from its own party. That is because the budget resolution is among the most high-profile vehicles available for the minority party to define its differences with the majority.

"I don't know that anybody thinks it's going to be easy, because we anticipate we won't get any Democratic votes for the budget," Sen. Sam Brownback, R-Kan., said Feb. 7. "So we've got to hold everybody together, and there are different factions in the caucus. Some that want to do debt buy-down. Others that want an aggressive tax cut. That has to be resolved. How do you keep everybody together given the disparate desires among the group?"

The budget resolution does not have the force of law and so it is not submitted to the president for his signature. Instead, it is supposed to dictate the parameters for the rest of the year on appropriations, by setting caps for defense and all other discretionary spending in the coming fiscal year. It also effectively limits the scope of any tax measure. The budget accomplishes this by dictating the maximum bottom line in any "reconciliation" legislation, the measures to balance tax and spending policies against expected revenue.

Such bills are given special procedural protections: a shield from a filibuster, a 20-hour limit on debate and restrictions on amendments. In the evenly split Senate, these advantages will be essential to enact anything like the tax package that Bush ceremonially presented to Congress on Feb. 8. Without an adopted budget resolution, the chances for the broadest and deepest tax cut in 20 years all but disappear.

During the previous six years of Republican control, the budget resolution was generally drafted more than anything as a political statement — to underscore the GOP's stated commitments to tax cuts and spending restraint. The budget rarely led to fiscal policy changes. President Bill Clinton vetoed a series of ambitious tax measures. And, aided by appropriators from both parties, he routinely demanded and won far more spending than the Republican budget blueprints purported to allow.

But the success or failure of Bush's first year in office, and to some extent his entire term, will be imperiled if his tax cuts stumble even before they cross this initial threshold. A narrow GOP majority should be able to push the budget through the House; the climactic vote is more likely in the Senate, where there are 50 Republicans and the tie-breaking vote of Vice President Dick Cheney.

Drafting has not yet begun, but already Budget Committee Chairman Pete V. Domenici, R-N.M., sees little hope of sending to the Senate floor a bipartisan document. That is because no committee Democrat is expected to vote for language making available $1.6 trillion for tax cuts in the next decade, the figure Bush wants. "I have no game plan for a budget that I could get out with Democratic support," he said Feb. 6.

The budget resolution could grant procedural advantages to supporters of tax cuts, but it also gives tax cut opponents an additional shot at sinking them. And this group includes more than just old-school liberals, with their expansionist view of government, and fiscal watchdogs, who proudly oppose almost anything that would slow the reduction of the national debt. The chance to oppose a budget providing for Bush's tax cut may also prove irresistible for a third group: senators torn between their convictions and their political situations. Voting "no" on something as amorphous and "inside baseball" as a budget resolution this spring may be politically easier than opposing the tax cut reconciliation bill later.

Obstacles to Republican Governance

In some ways, having the same party in control of Congress and the White House should smooth the way for the opening stage in the budget process. Republican leaders generally are united behind Bush's tax cut plan. And they have the rhetorical power of the White House to help sell their message not only to to the public, but also to fence-straddlers in their own party.

The exercise should also energize Republicans, said former House Speaker Newt Gingrich, R-Ga. (1979-99). "Get up every day and realize you're governing," he urged his colleagues in a Feb. 7 interview. "You're not opposing. You're not fighting. You're not anti-Democrat. You're governing . . . For some of our members that's a big change."

But that advantage is matched by other, more problematic dynamics:

• Democrats consider the budget resolution their strongest line of defense against an excessively deep tax cut. If the Re-

By Daniel J. Parks with Andrew Taylor / Feb. 10, 2001

Senate's Key Tax Cut Players

A complex set of political crosscurrents awaits the budget resolution that will carry President Bush's tax plan in the Senate. Neither party can be assured of all its votes as headstrong factions, empowered by the 50-50 party split, seek the small compromises that could determine the viability of the plan. Nobody can be ignored.

Here is a look at some of those factions:

APPROPRIATORS

Stevens   Byrd

In the recent past, appropriators such as Ted Stevens, R-Alaska, and Arlen Specter, R-Pa., only reluctantly agreed to the spending levels in budget resolutions, knowing that final negotiations with President Bill Clinton would bring more money. President Bush is not likely to provide year-end increases, which could make appropriators much more fussy about what they accept. Top Appropriations Democrat Robert C. Byrd of West Virginia is now on Budget.

TAX CUTTERS

Gramm   Brownback

Tax-cut enthusiasts like the GOP's Phil Gramm of Texas have a long tax cut wish list, including elements missing from the Bush plan, such as capital gains rate cuts. Sam Brownback, R-Kan., and Don Nickles, R-Okla., are among those who want greater "marriage penalty" relief. Majority Leader Trent Lott, R-Miss., has been cautious but also said "we could probably do more" than Bush's $1.6 trillion. Still, moderates are unlikely to support anything higher.

DEMOCRATS UNDER PRESSURE

Cleland   Baucus   Landrieu

Four Democrats face a tough choice on Bush's tax cut plan because they are up for re-election in 2002, and hail from states Bush carried by wide margins in the November election. The list includes Max Cleland of Georgia, Max Baucus of Montana, Mary L. Landrieu of Louisiana and Tim Johnson of South Dakota. Cleland faces even more pressure because home-state Democratic colleague Zell Miller has endorsed the Bush plan.

DEFENSE HAWKS

Warner   McCain

Bush has angered the defense hawks on Capitol Hill by deciding to postpone for a year the Pentagon budget boost he promised. He wants to use Clinton's Pentagon budget for fiscal 2002 instead. Pentagon supporters such as John W. Warner, R-Va., who is chairman of the Armed Services Committee, and John McCain, R-Ariz., could be a wild card in the budget resolution negotiations as they can be expected to press for additional defense spending.

REPUBLICANS TO WATCH

Voinovich   Snowe   Collins

The universe of Republicans who have opposed earlier tax bills is small, including George V. Voinovich of Ohio, Olympia J. Snowe and Susan Collins, both of Maine, and Specter, each of whom voted against a 10-year, $792 billion tax bill in 1999. This year, they are more supportive but are pressing for conditions. Voinovich insists on a clause to guarantee debt reduction; others want a "trigger" that will halt tax cuts if surpluses do not materialize.

GATEKEEPERS

Domenici   Lott

Budget Chairman Pete V. Domenici, R-N.M., who has chaired the committee off and on since 1981, has the unenviable task of trying to rally all 11 panel Republicans behind a budget blueprint. If he cannot, he can bring one directly to the floor after April 1. Lott makes decisions regarding timing for floor debate and always plays a key role in assembling the requisite majority of the full Senate.

publicans can put a tax package before the Senate that is filibuster-proof, they are more likely to pick up Democratic supporters on a straightforward vote on the measure.

• Moderates are well aware that with Congress so narrowly divided, each vote can be crucial. So at least for now, many moderates are holding out for a deal to their liking. For the GOP, the 50-50 Senate leaves no margin to lose maverick Republican votes as long as Democrats are united.

• Republicans will be under new political pressure this year to live with whatever discretionary spending limit the budget promises. In recent years, GOP leaders promoted budgets with unrealistically low caps, and grumbling moderates and appropriators generally went along, knowing that the pressure from Clinton's veto threats would prompt them to produce more generous spending bills. Once that happened, the floodgates opened, and members of both parties piled on additional spending.

But if Congress exceeds its self-imposed spending limits this year, both the GOP majority and Bush will be open to charges of ineffective leadership and poor fiscal management. It would be an inauspicious start for a party eager to prove that it is best able to keep government running smoothly and the economy humming. "We've got a president of the United States who says once we set the caps we're going to stay with them," said Senate Majority Whip Don Nickles of Oklahoma. "So I think it's critically important."

The Appropriators

To reach an agreement on discretionary spending, GOP leaders will have to balance the demands of conservatives — some of whom balked against even an inflationary increase for fiscal 2001 — against the party moderates and appropriators who, knowing the spending limits will probably be taken more seriously this year, will press harder than ever for more generous funding levels.

"The budget resolution in the last couple of years has not been worth the paper it's been written on," said Nickles, who was among those who held out a year ago for the tighter spending limits that the party was ultimately forced to jettison. "It hasn't been enforced. Congress, Democrats and Republicans, ignored it, appropriators ignored it. The budget process has not worked."

James W. Dyer, staff director of the House Appropriations Committee, noted that the budget will have to leave room for the new spending that Bush will request. "So you say to yourself, 'Well, how do we accommodate these increases while at the same time demonstrating that we are the conservative party?'" Dyer said Feb. 7. "You'll have this huge debate, it seems to me, over the efficacy of the congressional budget resolution and whether or not it's going to be another document just

Bush's tax plan faces a deadlocked Senate Budget panel. Conrad, left, at a Feb. 6 hearing, and the other 10 Democrats will oppose it; Domenici and the other 10 Republicans will endorse it.

like we've had over the past six years that kind of died once it passed the House, or whether or not it has the staying power to help us in the fall. And it's a tough call."

The last time the budget process worked more or less as designed was four years ago, when the landmark deficit reduction deal between Clinton and Congress was turned into a budget resolution, and the two reconciliation bills it provided for — one for spending cuts, the other for tax changes — became law.

But a year later, Congress failed to agree on a budget resolution for the first time since the modern budget process was adopted in 1974. Although both chambers passed resolutions, House and Senate Republicans were deeply divided over spending levels and how large a tax cut should be included, with the Senate GOP generally favoring a more moderate course.

The Mavericks

In the Senate, where each vote can be decisive, a few budget mavericks have recently moved from the back benches into the headlines.

Republican tax cutters gained their first ally across the aisle on Jan. 22, when Democrat Zell Miller of Georgia announced his support for Bush's tax cut, saying that he thought the economy needed a boost and that a gesture of bipartisanship was in order. But the GOP almost as quickly was preparing to lose one of its own: George V. Voinovich of Ohio.

Although Voinovich said Feb. 8 that he is not committed to opposing the Bush tax cut, he laid out a set of conditions that GOP leaders are extremely unlikely to accommodate. Voinovich said he will insist on "ironclad" mechanisms to limit discretionary spending. He also said he wants all of the surpluses in the Social Security and Medicare hospital trust funds as well as specific amounts of the remaining "on budget" surpluses dedicated to debt reduction.

Voinovich also stated unequivocally that he would not settle for promises of future action from his leadership, and that to win his vote on tax cuts his demands must be enacted first. That would seem all but impossible, since the budget resolution does not carry the force of law.

John McCain of Arizona, another

frequent thorn in the side of Senate GOP leaders, also remains uncommitted. He criticized the size of Bush's tax cut during their contest for the 2000 Republican presidential nomination, but since then McCain has said a slowing economy might make him reconsider. "When circumstances change, you have different views," he said Feb. 6, "but I still want to see their proposals."

The Moderates

Many of the moderates in the Senate Republican caucus are similarly withholding judgement.

"I think everybody is still looking at the numbers and trying to figure out their comfort level," said Olympia J. Snowe of Maine. Added Lincoln Chafee of Rhode Island, "I want to keep an open mind. I'm a debt reduction hawk."

As their potential clout in the debate has increased, the ranks of those claiming to occupy the middle ground has swollen. The bipartisan Centrist Coalition, of which Snowe and Chafee are members, counts nearly one-third of the Senate as members.

Making matters more complicated for the GOP, the economic slowdown has not yet triggered any groundswell of public support for a tax cut that might help move wavering moderates. In a Jan. 5-7 Gallup Poll, 65 percent of respondents listed cuts in federal incomes taxes as a high priority, but a dozen other topics — from Medicare solvency to improving race relations and environmental quality — received more mentions as a high priority.

And while Alan Greenspan's Jan. 25 endorsement of tax cuts boosted the hopes of Bush and GOP leaders, it appears to have had little overt effect in wooing Democrats or Republican moderates.

Like Voinovich, some moderates are pushing for mechanisms that would ensure a steady reduction of the government's debt. Many are promoting the use of "triggers" that would condition each year's phase-in of the tax cuts to the attainment of debt-reduction milestones. The administration and many congressional Republicans have spurned that idea, and they have suggested little in the way of potential compromises

that might pull more moderates on board.

Meanwhile, Democratic centrists in the House were drawing their line in the sand as well. Charles W. Stenholm of Texas, a leader of his party's fiscally conservative wing, said Feb. 6 that he is particularly concerned that the president will not include an increase in defense spending in his budget proposal. Bush is preparing to propose holding defense spending to $310 billion next year, the level in Clinton's final budget proposal — frustrating and surprising defense hawks of both parties.

Stenholm's concern about the president's defense decision has a different focus. If the budget does not account for promises Bush has made to the military for new spending, that would be "a totally unrealistic baseline," because the increases likely will come in future years, Stenholm said.

The GOP Right Flank

While Senate Republicans worry about their ability to move a $1.6 trillion tax cut, some of their counterparts in the House are pressing for even larger tax cuts, which almost certainly would doom any budget resolution that embodied them. The House's Republican Study Committee — formerly the Conservative Action Team, or CATs — on Feb. 7 unveiled a plan for a $2.2 trillion tax cut. They argued that returning more of the surplus to taxpayers was the only way to restrain spending.

Rep. Mark Foley, R-Fla., a Ways and Means Committee member, described the proposal Feb. 6 as a "stalking horse" intended to eventually make a $1.6 trillion tax cut look like a compromise. He urged the conservatives to back away from the plan, saying that he and some other Republicans "already have heartburn at $1.6 trillion."

Foley urged his party's leaders in the House to concentrate on achievable goals over the long term, rather than on muscling to passage a budget resolution providing for steep tax cuts. "I think they can pass any bill out of the House we want," Foley said. "The Senate is the kiss of death on some of this legislation."

The Democratic Left Flank

Making life more complicated for the GOP, most returning Democratic

members of the Senate Budget Committee are either fiscal policy hawks — such as Ernest F. Hollings of South Carolina and Russell D. Feingold of Wisconsin — or traditional liberals such as Ron Wyden of Oregon and Paul S. Sarbanes of Maryland. Neither camp has ever been enamored of tax cuts. And the four new Democrats on the panel — Hillary Rodham Clinton of New York, Debbie Stabenow of Michigan, Robert C. Byrd of West Virginia and Bill Nelson of Florida — are expected to stand with Daschle and the committee's ranking Democrat, Kent Conrad of North Dakota, in their opposition to the $1.6 trillion Bush proposal.

As the ranking Democrat on the Appropriations Committee, Byrd is expected to push particularly hard against any budget with tight spending caps.

The membership on Senate committees is evenly split between the parties under the power sharing agreement worked out last month between Daschle and Majority Leader Trent Lott, R-Miss. But even if a GOP package fails in committee on an 11-11 tie, Lott has the parliamentary power to put it before the Senate.

The wavering support among Republican moderates — and the possibility that a big tax cut is possible if the party does not overreach — has even some of the Senate GOP's most ardent tax cut enthusiasts bending to pragmatism. Robert C. Smith of New Hampshire said efforts to push for a larger cut than Bush's could undercut the president. Budget Committee member Phil Gramm of Texas said the party can try for larger cuts next year if the surplus picture continues to improve. Fellow budget panelist Christopher S. Bond of Missouri said, "At this point we have to make sure we can get something through."

In an apparent effort to shore up public support for tax cuts, Republicans plan for the House to vote Feb. 13 on a bill (HR 2) that would prevent Social Security and Medicare trust fund surpluses from being tapped for any other purpose. The House passed similar legislation in 2000, but it failed to stir much public notice and died for lack of action in the Senate. ◆

The Veto Threat

The first time President Bush issued a formal threat to veto legislation was in the midst of the Senate's debate on a patients' bill of rights, legislation that would give patients in health maintenance organizations (HMOs) more leverage in disputing treatment decisions. The Senate seemed to ignore Bush's unequivocal threat and passed the bill he opposed, but this looming veto became pivotal when the bill reached the House in August.

At 11:55 a.m. on June 21, a fax machine whirred to life in the Capitol and delivered a White House position paper that represented President Bush's forceful entrance into the Senate debate on a patients' bill of rights.

In a week consumed largely with procedural matters, Bush's unequivocal promise to veto the bill (S 1052) unless it is substantially rewritten could well have been the most important development of the early debate.

But more than that, Bush's veto promise — and the fact that it came on the first bill pushed onto the agenda by the Senate's newly minted Democratic majority — opened a new chapter in his relationship with Congress. A veto is a president's ultimate tool for blocking legislation he dislikes. Successfully employing veto threats to affect legislation as it moves toward his desk, however, is a far more complicated matter.

In vowing to veto the Senate bill, Bush instantly triggered a fresh round of calculating for Democrats and Republicans. It takes a two-thirds vote of both House and Senate to override a veto, a virtually impossible task in the closely divided 107th Congress.

Now, congressional Democrats pushing the patients' bill of rights measure face a choice. Do they call Bush's bluff and pass a bill that he promised to veto? Or do they address his concerns before sending him the bill and ensure a Bush signature? Or, as Republicans did so often in their dealings with former President Bill Clinton, do they seek a political advantage from a veto rather than compromise on the issue?

But the White House has questions to consider, too. Chief among them is whether to remain as inflexible as that first statement promises.

"It's absolutely essential that [the White House] carry through on the veto threat, either behind the scenes in negotiations or to actually do it if the bill comes out in the way he doesn't like," said James Thurber, professor of government at American University. "If it's a frivolous threat, then it hurts you in the future."

Sooner or later, every Congress and every president confronts these very basic questions about legislative strategy and tactics.

Expect more veto threats now that the congressional agenda is turning to issues put forward by Senate Democrats. At the same time, the White House has made it plain that it is eager to use the veto to keep in check Congress' appetite to spend money as it turns to the fiscal 2002 appropriations cycle.

"It's a discipline that we welcome," said House Majority Whip Tom DeLay, R-Texas.

Influence of the Veto

Vetoes of popular legislation can erode a president's approval ratings, but they also allow the chief executive to dictate outcomes. On the patients' rights legislation, whether Bush's veto promise has any immediate impact on the ongoing legislative process remains to be seen.

Republican lawmakers and Bush aides expressed hope that the president's position would prompt middle-of-the-road senators to forge a compromise.

"That's the only chance we have of getting a bill done," said Sen. Pete V. Domenici, R-N.M. "I think some Democrats would get on board if [Bush] said, 'That's my final offer.'"

In the House, where a similar patients' rights bill in 1999 attracted 68 Republican votes despite the opposition of GOP leaders, those same leaders now are using the veto promise to try to rally the troops around yet another compromise bill unveiled by House leaders the week of June 18.

"The threat of a veto has us picking up votes like mad over here," DeLay said.

As for Democrats, who benefited from Clinton's usually adroit use of the veto, the tables have turned. Now they are issuing the same plaintive pleas that Republicans made during six years under Clinton.

"We would hope . . . that the president would work with us and not against us to help protect patients all around this country," said Sen. John Edwards, D-N.C., a lead sponsor of the patients' rights bill. "I think that it's unproductive that on the first day of full debate he issues a veto threat instead of working with us."

Proponents of the bill vowed that Bush's veto promise would not cause them to compromise at this stage. "We do our job, he does his job," said Sen. Tom Harkin, D-Iowa. "We do what we think is best . . . . If he wants to veto it that's his business." After a veto, Harkin said, "We'll see if we can work something out."

Democrats also point to the way Bush handled a patients' rights bill when he was governor of Texas. He vetoed the first bill the legislature sent him but let a second become law without his signature in 1997.

"He let it become law down in Texas, then he took credit for it in the campaign," said Sen. Edward M. Kennedy, D-Mass. "There weren't all that many differences between the first bill that he resisted and the second one that he accepted."

Democrats cite the Texas example as evidence that Bush might ultimately sign whatever he receives.

There is a natural tendency for Congress to test a president to see whether he actually carries out a veto threat. Clinton was nearly always resolute in making good on his veto threats, often to the amazement of Republicans, who thought they had boxed him in on issues such as taxes, overhauling welfare and the budget. Clinton never seemed to take political heat for his vetoes, even when killing volatile legislation such as measures to

By Andrew Taylor / June 23, 2001

Republicans hope Bush's forceful veto threat will make Democrats more willing to deal. Minority Leader Trent Lott, R-Miss., did radio interviews during the debate.

outlaw a gruesome late-term abortion procedure.

"The fact is, Bill Clinton vetoed welfare reform . . . and that was a lot more popular than a patients' bill of rights," said a former House leadership aide, now a lobbyist. "If [Bush] is really interested in not being controlled by the Hill, I think it's in his interest to let it be known that he will veto [the patients' rights bill]."

Democrats dispute that. "Why wouldn't you test him?" said veteran Rep. John P. Murtha, D-Pa. "I would doubt very much that he'd veto the bill. It's a very popular bill."

A Tougher Stand

Bush's strong stance on the patients' rights bill differs starkly from his hands-off approach on a controversial bill (S 27) to overhaul campaign finance laws. On that measure, the administration failed to issue a standard "Statement of Administration Policy" or "SAP," specifying the president's official views before Senate passage.

Instead, Bush offered a statement of principles, and when the Senate promptly ignored many of them — voting down some offered as amendments — the White House signaled that Bush would likely sign whatever bill Congress sent him.

So congressional insiders watched Bush closely on patients' rights. "The

president's advisers have already demonstrated that we can't count on the veto on many issues that have concerned our members for years," said a Senate GOP aide.

At one point, conservatives feared Bush would be less than forceful in his handling of patients' rights, which might embolden Democrats and erode Republican resolve. Instead, the SAP was remarkably strong.

In fact, White Houses usually give themselves more wiggle room. Veto threats are rarely issued in the president's name; relying instead on "senior advisers" who "recommend" vetoes. Such statements do not necessarily bind the president, and the extent of changes required to win a signature often are left open to interpretation.

The June 21 SAP left no such leeway. It said "the president will veto the bill unless significant changes are made to address his major concerns," then listed the changes.

"They don't come any stronger," said a former Clinton administration official in the Office of Management and Budget. A senior GOP aide wandering outside the Senate chamber clutched the SAP and waved a Churchillian "V" sign — except the "V" stood for veto, not victory.

"That's not as wise as something that leaves more freedom for negotiation," Thurber said. "It's better strategy

to leave a way out in case you can't get exactly what you want."

The congressional agenda is increasingly moving toward issues upon which the White House and various congressional factions will have to sort out their differences.

More to Come?

Early signs have been mixed. For example, Senate Appropriations Committee Chairman Robert C. Byrd, D-W.Va., stuck closely to Bush's $6.5 billion fiscal 2001 supplemental appropriations request when moving a draft bill through his committee June 21.

It was a different story just a day earlier when the House Agriculture Committee approved a $5.5 billion farm aid plan (HR 2213). GOP Chairman Larry Combest, R-Texas, had promoted a larger, $6.5 billion plan — opposed by the administration — and it fell to panel Democrats, led by fiscal conservative Charles W. Stenholm of Texas, to bring the measure back in line with the administration's wishes.

Prior to the Senate patients' rights debate, the only instance in which Bush had threatened a veto involved a State Department authorization bill (HR 1646) that passed the House on May 16. Bush opposed language to reverse the White House's "Mexico City" policy, under which U.S. aid cannot go to international family planning groups that advocate abortion. The House narrowly voted to reverse the committee and support the administration.

The veto prognosis for a patients' rights bill is mixed, too. "I'm not so sure that he wants to take this issue on as his first big veto," said Rep. Jim Leach, R-Iowa. "That may be why the Democrats want to put him in that box."

"He wants to sign a bill. He campaigned on it," said Rep. Robert L. Ehrlich Jr., R-Md. "Politically, he can afford to do the right thing [and veto the bill] because it's early in his term. He's going to come back and say, 'Look, I like most of this bill; here's the provision you need to fix and I'll sign the bill.'" ◆

Congress and the Courts

Congress intersects with the third branch of government — the court system or judicial branch — in several ways. The courts can be the referee for disputes between political rivals, as happened with the Supreme Court's decision in the 2000 presidential race, and they can interpret the laws Congress passes while simultaneously setting limits on the authority Congress has to pass legislation. For example, it was a decision by the Supreme Court in 1987 that cemented Congress' wide latitude to use its spending authority to direct other governments, such as states, to set particular policies. In that case, Congress threatened to withhold federal highway money from South Dakota unless the state raised its lawful drinking age from 19 to 21. More recently, Congress has felt pressured in the 107th Congress to pass legislation on a patients' bill of rights in part because state courts have been slowly carving out a case-by-case set of protections for patients that could become the standard if Congress fails to use its authority to set a national policy.

But the most direct relationship between Congress and the courts has been the "advise and consent" role the Senate plays in confirming a president's choice for federal judgeships. By choosing the men and women who take lifetime seats on federal district benches, federal appeals courts and the Supreme Court, a president can shape the interpretation of law far beyond his term in office. But he cannot do so without the support of a Senate majority, and in recent decades, the confirmation process for judicial nominees has been swept into the highly charged, partisan rhetoric of the day. The escalating use of the "advise and consent" role as a political tool against an opposition party president seemed to reach new heights with President Clinton, who had enormous difficulty winning confirmation from a Republican Senate for many of his nominees. Democrats have taken control of the Senate in the 107th Congress, which has Republicans fearful that President Bush's nominees will face similar obstacles. Whether Democrats block Bush's choices for the federal judiciary, the threat itself has become a defining element of relations between the president and Congress.

Nominating Judges: President vs. Senate

Before Democrats took control of the Senate, they made clear their intention to use every ounce of leverage they could muster to influence President Bush's choices for federal judgeships. The Senate must confirm a president's selections for the federal district and appeals courts, as well as for the Supreme Court.

During much of Bill Clinton's presidency, Democrats fumed as Senate Republicans turned many of his judicial nominees into a new kind of political hostage.

So when Republican George W. Bush ascended to the presidency this year, the question was whether those Democrats, now at parity in the Senate, would opt for statesmanship — or retaliation.

The answer is becoming clear, and it looks like payback time.

With Bush expected to send his first batch of judicial nominees to the Senate in the next few weeks, Democrats are warning that they will exact a price if they are left out of the process of picking and confirming judges.

Sen. Patrick J. Leahy of Vermont, top Democrat of the Judiciary Committee, made clear his view of what is at stake for Bush in the dispute over how judges are confirmed.

"I'm trying to avoid a situation," he said after a contentious committee meeting, "where the vice president would have to be coming up here constantly to break ties."

As a veteran of the wars over judges during Clinton's presidency, Leahy has long feared the situation he finds himself in today: Dozens of vacancies on the federal bench, which Clinton was blocked from filling by a Republican-led Senate, will go to conservative judges selected by Bush as Democrats fight to keep from being locked out of the process.

The power to choose judges for lifetime appointments is one of the most significant prerogatives of the president, allowing him to direct judicial philosophy — and therefore the interpretation of federal law — long after he has left office.

The first skirmish in the new fight came over a piece of baby blue paper. Republicans hope to use this bit of legislative arcana to make it easier for Bush to have his choices approved in the Senate over the objections of Democrats.

The blue slip, as it is called, is used by senators to record their opinions on judicial nominees from their home state after the names have been formally submitted by the White House.

Near the top of the page it says, "No further proceedings on this individual will continue until blue slips are returned by home state senators." Senators sign their names on a line across the bottom.

At a closed-door Judiciary Committee meeting on April 24, Chairman Orrin G. Hatch of Utah told the panel he intends to enforce a policy under which only one senator's approval could be enough to allow a nomination from his or her state to proceed. Democrats declared Hatch's announcement an unfair change in policy since the days when a single senator could use the blue slip to sink Clinton's picks.

More than an hour of debate did not resolve the issue, and afterward Leahy issued his warning. The remark reflects the depth of Democrats' anger over the issue, but more significantly it reveals how little trust there is between the two parties on the way Bush's judicial nominations will proceed. Other Democrats have departed from Senate etiquette by threatening to filibuster Bush's nominations.

"I'm willing to do whatever I need to do to protect our rights," said John Edwards, D-N.C.

All nine Democrats on the Judiciary Committee sent White House Counsel Alberto R. Gonzales a letter April 27 emphasizing the importance of the issue, and offering suggestions on how the White House should consult with them.

"There are a number of senators who were treated very badly by the last Republican Congress on how their judges were handled," said Joseph R. Biden Jr., D-Del. "I am certain there is a yearning on the part of more than a handful of Democrats" to treat Bush's nominees the same way, he said.

Clinton's power to shape the judiciary was significantly weakened by a concerted Republican effort to block his nominations. The atmosphere around appointments developed an unusually partisan tinge, with Republicans accusing Clinton of choosing liberal activists and Clinton accusing Republicans of delaying women and minority candidates.

Democrats and scholars believe the extended delays suffered by so many Clinton nominees, combined with the willingness of Republicans to prevent votes on many others, shifted the balance of power so that the Senate now has a much greater say in nominations.

The challenge for Bush will be to reassert his authority, perhaps by making the case for his nominees in public, while at the same time easing combative tensions. Republicans and Democrats from previous administrations say that to be successful, Bush must make the confirmation of his judges a high priority in his administration.

Judicial nominations are "an important part of any administration's legacy because appointments are for life. A president can put his or her stamp on the judiciary for a lot longer than he or she can the executive branch," said C. Boyden Gray, White House counsel to former President George Bush.

Bush's Tightrope

Those looking for indications of how Bush will approach the process will be watching to see if he includes Roger L. Gregory among his first nominations.

Gregory, an attorney from Richmond, Va., is the first black to serve on the U.S. Court of Appeals for the Fourth Circuit. He was one of the victims of the Clinton-Senate feud that began in 1995 and ran through Clinton's presidency.

Gregory was a recess appointment to the bench on Dec. 27 after the Senate adjourned without acting on his nomination. He will have to leave the court if Bush does not

By Elizabeth A. Palmer / April 28, 2001

renominate him and the Senate does not confirm him by the end of this year.

Bush withdrew all leftover Clinton nominations, including Gregory's, on March 19, but it remains possible that Bush will propose keeping Gregory as a conciliatory gesture to Democrats. Gregory has the outspoken support of Virginia's two Republican senators, who have said they are lobbying the White House on Gregory's behalf.

"That would be a phenomenal good-faith gesture that I think would overnight change a bad-faith atmosphere," said Sheldon Goldman, a political science professor at the University of Massachusetts at Amherst who has studied judicial nominations for decades.

But so far, Bush has not shown much interest in good-faith gestures. On March 22, for example, Gonzales sent a letter to the American Bar Association saying the group no longer would be asked to evaluate the professional abilities of judicial candidates.

For almost 50 years, the ABA provided presidents with confidential reviews of potential nominees, but Republicans, who decried the political positions espoused by the ABA, objected to giving the group a unique role in the nomination process. Democrats, more closely aligned politically with the ABA, were outraged.

The recent fight over the blue-slip procedure also reignited partisan passions. Hatch maintained that blue-slip objections will be given "great weight," though they will not necessarily carry the power to kill a nomination. Key in determining how much weight to give a negative blue slip, he said, would be whether the Bush administration had "consulted" with the senator.

"This is a testing time of wills at the very beginning of the administration," Goldman said. "The Bush folks are pushing the envelope and Senate Democrats are responding."

The result, Goldman said, could be "the politics of compromise or the politics of gridlock."

All involved agree that the Clinton years remade the ju-

dicial nomination process, leaving a host of questions open for the new administration. But in a reflection of the degree to which partisanship has come to inhabit this process, the questions differ depending on who is talking.

Said Hatch: "Will the Democrats acknowledge they lost the election and there's a new president?"

A Democratic Judiciary Committee staffer responded: "Is there something wrong with the president ideologically stacking the courts — we'll have to answer that question."

Leahy said Democrats realize things have changed. "George Bush was the one inaugurated. . . . It doesn't mean that Republicans can simply ignore us."

The nominating of judges is an often-overlooked aspect of executive-legislative branch relations, in part because most of the significant action occurs behind closed doors. Names are compiled, vetted and discussed with senators in strict confidentiality. *(Process box, p. 125)*

But while the process rarely breaks out into public view, the way it is handled, especially between an individual senator and the administration, can affect all sorts of other issues.

"It colors a lot of things," said the Democratic staffer.

And while the process may be low-profile, it is high-intensity. Most senators take their involvement in the choice of a judge from their state very seriously and personally. After all, many of those nominated for lifetime seats on the federal bench have had careers long enough and prominent enough to make them either important friends or bitter rivals of their home-state senators.

The 50-50 Senate poses benefits and problems for Bush on this issue. The rules negotiated between the two parties would allow a Bush nominee who had been rejected by the Judiciary Committee to still get a floor vote because Senate Majority Leader Trent Lott, R-Miss., has the power to call up a nomination regardless of the committee action.

That power, combined with a blue-slip process that might not stop a nominee despite objections from a home-state senator, make it unlikely that nominations would be held up at the committee level.

Hatch, left, and Leahy, right, have clashed and compromised more than once this year. But the handling of Bush's judicial nominations has both men and their parties deeply split.

Filibuster Talk

But the even balance also means it will be much easier for Democrats to sustain a filibuster of a nominee, a strategy not typically employed on judicial nominations but one several Democrats said they were prepared to use if necessary.

"I'm very concerned," Hatch said. "We've been able to avoid filibusters on judges, which we must continue or Katie-bar-the-door."

For Bush, the perils of the Senate will require that he demonstrate a strong commitment to his choices early in the process, said Gray, who handled judicial nominations in a Senate then controlled by the opposing party.

"There was some push-back . . . at the beginning," Gray recalled.

The Process of Selecting a Judge

While the Constitution grants the president the power to appoint judges with the advice and consent of the Senate, tradition holds that home-state senators of the president's party have significant say over who is picked for district court judgeships. But the precise details of those arrangements are loosely defined and differ from state to state and year to year. Here are some of the models used.

BIPARTISAN COMMISSION

Wisconsin has one of the most formal systems, in which a 22-year-old commission develops a list of candidates for judicial vacancies. While the party controlling the White House also controls a majority of seats on the commission, Democrats and Republicans are represented on the panel.

DEAL BETWEEN SENATORS

In Illinois, Republican Peter G. Fitzgerald and Democrat Richard J. Durbin have an agreement in which the senator of the party in the White House provides three suggestions, while the senator of the other party provides one. During the Clinton administration, Durbin used a commission but Fitzgerald has not established such a panel.

PRESIDENT'S PARTY CHOOSES

In Indiana, Republican Richard G. Lugar uses the Indiana Federal Merit Selection Advisory Committee to collect judicial candidates, which are sent to the White House. The committee includes Republican leaders and members of the judiciary, academia, religious and civic groups. Lugar does not consult with Democrat Evan Bayh, who during the Clinton administration did not use a committee.

NO FORMAL SYSTEM

North Carolina does not have a formal process in place, at the congressional or state level, to put forth a list of judicial picks.

— *Alecia Marzullo*

"We had some tests of will between us and home state delegations and the Senate leadership and the Judiciary Committee leadership. There were some scrapes, some tests of how much political capital we were willing to expend. Then when they found out that we were willing to expend it, I think they said 'Okay, this is the way it is going to be.'"

His advice to Bush?

"Go for it, get the best slate of judges you can get and don't worry about the Senate being 50-50," Gray said. "I don't think we did it any differently with the Senate [controlled by Democrats] than we would have had the Senate been in Republican hands."

Bruce Fein, an associate deputy attorney general under President Ronald Reagan who was central to Reagan's success at winning confirmation for his nominees, believes Bush also needs to raise the profile of judicial nominations. "If [Bush] thinks that he wants to leave a legacy . . . then he needs to make it a regular feature of his speaking engagements," Fein said.

"One of the things that killed [the nomination of Robert H.] Bork was that Reagan went out and vacationed" at the start of his nomination fight, said Fein. Bork was defeated 42-58 in his bid for a seat on the Supreme Court in 1987.

But giving his nominations a high priority — and visibility —without alienating Democrats will be difficult.

Democrats believe Bush's success will depend on how much he involves them in the process, whether he tells them of his picks or actually seeks their opinion.

There is a "big difference between consulting and informing . . . informing is not consulting," Leahy said. "In a 50-50 Senate, I expect there would be a lot closer consultation."

Former Sen. Paul Simon, D-Ill., (1985-97), who sat on Judiciary, agreed.

"There's nothing like having people come in — to have the president bring in Pat Leahy and a couple other key Democratic members of the Senate Judiciary Committee and say 'I want to

work with you,'" he said.

But even with closer consultation, Democrats may still make it hard on Bush nominees. "It's an interesting situation because there's no question Republicans held the past administration to a standard no other administration has been held to," Leahy said.

The atmosphere Bush inherits grew out of a long, slow decline in relations between Clinton and the GOP Senate.

The Clinton Numbers

Numbers tell the story of how Clinton rivaled Reagan in the volume of District Court judges he was able to get confirmed, even as he lagged well behind the popular Republican in winning confirmation for appeals court judges.

The majority of nominees a president makes are for District Court seats, the trial level court in the federal system, where judges try fact and decide questions of evidence and witnesses.

But appeals court judges, though fewer in number, are of greater significance in the process. There are 11 circuit courts of appeal around the country, with another appeals court located in the District of Columbia. These judges hear appeals of District Court decisions, and their opinions focus on interpretations of law and the Constitution. In addition, the circuit court judges form a pool from which presidents frequently choose Supreme Court nominees. *(Box, p. 127)*

Clinton won confirmation of 65 nominees to the courts of appeal and 307 judges to the District Courts, according to numbers compiled by the Congressional Research Service. Those numbers are similar to Reagan's record of getting 83 appeals court judges and 292 District Court judges approved by the Senate.

But where Reagan won confirmation of 87 percent of those he nominated for the all-important appeals court seats, Clinton's success rate was 61 percent. Reagan's District Court nominees were confirmed nearly 95 percent of the time; Clinton's were confirmed 80.6 percent of the time.

The result is that after eight years of a Democratic administration, Republican appointees still dominate the appellate courts. Of the 12 circuit courts, three have a majority of Democratic appointees, seven are dominated by Republicans, and two are evenly split.

"There's just no question that these

judges make huge decisions on where the country's going to go," said former Sen. Simon. He pointed to a recent decision by a federal judge barring affirmative action at the University of Michigan as an example of the power of the federal bench to shape important legal questions.

Despite his losses, experts say Clinton's push for diversity on the federal bench was successful.

Writing in the March/April issue of Judicature, a magazine on judicial policy, political scientists Rorie L. Spill and Kathleen A. Bratton found that Clinton appointed "more women and minorities to the federal bench than any of his predecessors."

Clinton doubled the number of African-American judges on District Courts and nearly doubled the number of women. The Clinton administration also appointed the first American Indian to a District Court.

"They did a magnificent job in that respect," said Goldman of Amherst. "They broke all records."

Those numbers were achieved by starting with a diverse group of nominees. For appointment to the courts of appeal, 49.2 percent of Clinton's nominations were white men, compared with 70.3 percent of George Bush's picks and 92.3 percent of Reagan's nominees.

But it is the delays and bitter fights over nominees that are likely to be the Clinton administration's bequest to the next president.

"The legacy of the Clinton years is that the confirmation process can no longer be seen as routine but a matter of intense partisan and ideological concern for all the court levels," Goldman and several others wrote in Judicature.

Walking Through Molasses

The Clinton administration had a Democratic Senate during its first two years, and was able to win approval of 127 judges in that time.

Republicans took control of the Senate in 1995, and the administration and the new chairman of the Judiciary Committee, Hatch, worked well together initially. Clinton was able to get another batch of 53 judges through.

The cooperation ended with the advent of a presidential election.

"1996 was a pretty grim year," said Eleanor D. Acheson, who, as assistant attorney general in the Clinton administration, was a key player in the process. "It became a sort of walking-

The Interest-Group Gantlet

At one time, the Senate's job of approving presidential appointments to the federal judiciary drew little outside interest. But in recent years, advocacy groups that specialize in following judicial issues have trained their sights on the process of approving federal judges.

C. Boyden Gray, White House counsel for former President George Bush, said the groups he found more troublesome than influential are solidifying their involvement.

"It slowed things down, it was a burden to have to fight them . . . but I think we did all right," he said. "And I think they're a fixture, they are part of the landscape, and I don't think there's anything anyone can do to change that situation."

Spanning the spectrum from the liberal People for the American Way to the conservative Eagle Forum, a handful of groups work to influence the selection process.

Senate Judiciary Committee Chairman Orrin G. Hatch, R-Utah, is concerned about their impact, especially after the bitter fight over the confirmation of Attorney General John Ashcroft in February. Many of the groups that lobby on judges joined the Ashcroft debate.

"Perhaps trying to keep narrow interest groups from influencing the debate with unfair attacks is like trying to teach lions to be vegetarians," Hatch said in an April 23 speech at Harvard University's John F. Kennedy School of Government. "If, as a part of the process, unaccountable special interests are allowed to brutalize the reputations of fine individuals and their families, it will not be long before some of the best candidates will opt out of consideration altogether."

Groups seeking to influence the confirmation process now use a mixture of television advertisements to generate public involvement, and phone banks to call Senate offices during important debates. Among the more promi-

nent groups are:

• **People for the American Way.** Headed by longtime civil rights activist Ralph G. Neas, this liberal interest group keeps extensive records on the judicial nomination process and issues periodic reports about the makeup of the federal judiciary. In particular, the group has focused on the delays faced by Clinton administration nominees and the effect of President Bill Clinton's effort to diversify the federal bench.

• **The Center for Law and Democracy's Judicial Selection and Monitoring Program.** Thomas L. Jipping, the director of this group, also produces a cable television show called Legal Notebook. The show explores various facets of the legal system, including judicial nominations. The monitoring program is designed to "fight judicial activism," according to its Web page, and issues reports such as "Democrats v. Republicans II: Who's Still More Serious about Judges?"

• **The Alliance for Justice's Judicial Selection Project.** The Alliance, headed by Nan Aron, is an umbrella group comprising women's rights, civil rights, environmental and consumer groups. The project issues periodic reports about the makeup of the courts and the nature of the confirmation process in the Senate.

• **Eagle Forum Court Watch.** The national chairman of this conservative watchdog project is Virginia Armstrong, a political science professor at Hardin-Simmons University in Abilene, Texas. Eagle Forum is led by activist Phyllis Schlafly. The goal of the project, according to its Web site, is to "raise public awareness about the Imperial Judiciary." Among other activities, the members lobby senators on appointments and track Senate floor votes on judicial nominations while working to keep Congress from federalizing more criminal offenses.

— Elizabeth A. Palmer

Supreme Opportunity

One reason appeals court nominees get such intense scrutiny from the Senate is that those courts serve as a farm team for the Supreme Court. True to that tradition, many of the people seen as contenders for a Bush administration nomination to the high court are sitting on the appellate bench.

Although none of the nine Supreme Court justices has announced an intention to depart, speculation continues that one or more might take advantage of a Republican president to retire.

Justice Sandra Day O'Connor, 71, is the focus of speculation because she has served nearly 20 years on the court and has had health problems. Chief Justice William H. Rehnquist, a member of the court since 1972, also is mentioned.

Rehnquist, 76, fed the rumors when, in a rare interview on the Charlie Rose show in February, he said, "I think, traditionally, Republican appointees have tended to re-

tire during Republican administrations. . . . It's not invariable. But there's surely a slight preference for that."

Bush, who may find it easier to get a conservative nominee approved to replace a conservative justice such as Rehnquist, will be pressured to put the first Hispanic on the high court. Emilio M. Garza, a judge on the 5th U.S. Circuit Court of Appeals, is a possible candidate, as is White House Counsel Alberto R. Gonzales.

If Bush should have to replace O'Connor and wanted to nominate a woman, another judge on the 5th Circuit, Edith Jones, could be a candidate. But Jones is more conservative than O'Connor and could face a tough fight in the Senate.

Of course, Bush could avoid a confirmation fight if he chose one name that has been bandied about: Senate Judiciary Committee Chairman Orrin G. Hatch, R-Utah.

— *Elizabeth A. Palmer*

through-molasses kind of process."

For all of 1996, Clinton was able to win confirmation of just 20 judges. Four years earlier, when his predecessor, George Bush, was in a re-election year and faced a Senate controlled by the opposite party, Bush won confirmation of 66 nominees.

Acheson and others hoped that when the election ended, things would pick up again. But in 1997, conservative Republicans, who feared that Hatch would go easy on Clinton nominees, tried to wrest away some of his authority in the judicial nomination process. Though Hatch ultimately kept his power, it did force him into a more antagonistic position toward the administration for the remainder of Clinton's presidency.

"I took a lot of abuse" for defending Clinton's nominees, said Hatch. Despite the best efforts of conservatives to block Clinton's judges, he said, "they didn't make any difference — I was able to do what was right."

In the last few years of the Clinton presidency the number of judges confirmed was relatively constant, and in comparison with previous presidents,

relatively low: 36 in 1997, 64 in 1998 35 in 1999 and 37 in 2000.

Virtually none of Clinton's nominees were rejected. Senate Republicans prevented them from being voted on, in committee or on the Senate floor.

Vital to their success was the blue slip, which some senators simply refused to return. During the Clinton era, Hatch almost always refused to hold a hearing on a nominee unless he had received a positive blue slip back from both home state senators.

This blocked Clinton from getting judges on the bench, but spared senators from casting many votes. Of the 106 nominations Clinton made to the court of appeals, for example, the Senate returned 38, or nearly 36 percent, without any final action. Of the 96 nominations to the same courts made by Reagan, just nine — 9.4 percent — were returned. The number of Clinton District Court nominees returned was nearly five times that for Reagan picks.

During the eight years of the Clinton presidency, just one judicial nomination, that of Ronnie L. White of Missouri, was rejected. The Senate rejected his nomination to be a District

Court judge in 1999 on a party-line 45-54 vote.

While Republicans had a strategy for challenging Clinton, observers on both sides of the aisle believe Clinton's manner of dealing with judicial nominations contributed to the problem.

Both the Reagan and Bush administrations looked for conservative jurists who had a "shared similar philosophy," Fein said, about the proper role of government and methods of constitutional interpretation.

When Democrats won control of the White House, both sides fully expected Clinton to chose liberal judicial activists.

"Clinton made a very deliberate decision . . . not to nominate red-flag people that would be really unacceptable to the vast majority of Republicans," Goldman said. "He went out of his way not to antagonize them."

Acheson said the Clinton administration did not agree with the way Republicans had handled the process. "There was a very deep concern that a very damaging thing had been done with this Luke Skywalker- Darth Vader division . . . the notion that this really is a battle between darkness and light."

But while Clinton sometimes cut deals to get judges through, he did not use the heft of his office to make an all-out push for his nominees. Critics say this was an indication that Clinton did not expend enough political capital, which left his nominees vulnerable to the antics of opposing senators.

Fein said the Reagan administration regularly discussed judgeships in policy negotiations. If the administration needed more votes on its plan to sell AWACS radar surveillance planes to Saudi Arabia, and a senator wanted some consideration on a judgeship, the Reagan team would sometimes say, "All right, we'll bend on that one," Fein said.

Acheson says that while "we didn't sort of bully through [judges], it's hard to know what we would have achieved if we would have done that."

"I can't say that I recall an experience where a senator, either Democrat or Republican, said 'if this, then that,' quid pro quo on nomination, either threat or promise," she said.

But the administration's philosophy also meant no penalty was imposed on senators who delayed the process.

Said Fein: "I don't know of anybody on the Republican side who got retribution for blocking judges." ◆

An Easing of the Bitterness

When President Bush submitted the names of his first 11 judicial nominees, the sniping between Democrats and Republicans abruptly eased. But Democrats were not backing off from earlier threats to obstruct the path of nominees they disliked; they simply realized they had the power they needed without talking about it. And that was before they retook control of the Senate.

Tensions eased between Hatch, left, and Patrick J. Leahy, D-Vt., but Democrats still may oppose Bush judicial nominations by using their power in the 50-50 Senate.

Even before President Bush formally announced his first group of judicial nominations May 9, Senate Democrats called a press conference to respond to his choices.

Instead of angrily lambasting Bush, as many had expected, Democrats calmly praised him.

"I'm pleased that the White House has chosen to work with us on the first group of nominations," said Minority Leader Tom Daschle, D-S.D., who only the week before had threatened to block nominations on the Senate floor to secure Democrats' rights to object. "We are pleased that by and large there are no blue-slip problems."

But mixed with their conciliatory language, Democrats announced in no uncertain terms that they would take full advantage of their authority in the 50-50 Senate to scuttle future nominees they do not consider acceptable.

They also exalted in a partial victory for having driven Bush to at least postpone three nominations that had been under consideration.

"What we've made clear today is that Democrats in the Senate will not be railroaded into rubber-stamping of judges over the course of the next year who may have a very hard ideological cast to them," said Charles E. Schumer, D-N.Y.

The tone of the press conference was so unexpectedly cordial that when asked about it, Senate Majority Leader Trent Lott, R-Miss., quipped, "Aren't they whining? I must not be doing my job."

Bush nominated 11 people to seats on the courts of appeal. The nominees are generally young, conservative and ethnically and racially diverse. The group includes three judges supported by President Bill Clinton, three women, one Hispanic

and two African-Americans. *(Nominees, p. 130)*

At first glance it appears that just one of the nominees — Terrence W. Boyle, who was chosen for a seat on the U.S. Court of Appeals for the 4th Circuit — may face serious confirmation problems.

For weeks, Senate Democrats have been ratcheting up their rhetoric on the judicial nomination process in anticipation of the first batch of Bush choices. Many believe Republicans used the so-called blue-slip process, which allows senators to register their opinions of home-state judges, to unfairly block Clinton from winning confirmation of dozens of judges.

While Clinton named nearly as many judges to the bench as did President Ronald Reagan, a much higher percentage of Clinton's picks were sent back to the White House without final action. *(Story, p. 123)*

Now that a Republican occupies the White House, Democrats want to be sure they have the same authority they say their GOP counterparts exercised over the past six years.

Escalating Rhetoric

The battle became so intense on May 3 that Democrats on the Judiciary Committee refused to allow the panel to vote on two Justice Department nominees until the unrelated quarrel was settled.

Democrats were demanding a promise from Judiciary Committee Chairman Orrin G. Hatch, R-Utah, that a single home-state senator could use the blue slip to block a judge's nomination. Hatch refused.

By the time Bush made his announcement, however, Democrats had dropped the angry threats and were calmly confident they would retain their rights.

In part, this was the result of a decision by the Bush administration to postpone several nominations that had upset Democrats, particularly that of conservative Rep. Christopher Cox, R-

By Elizabeth A. Palmer / May 12, 2001

Calif., to the U.S. Court of Appeals for the 9th Circuit.

But it also seemed to be a realization on the part of Democrats that with the evenly divided Senate, they have the power to prevent any judge from being considered. They decided they no longer need to ask for their rights from Republicans, but can assert authority on their own.

Daschle and Schumer said that while they appreciated the way Bush handled his first batch of nominees, they will now begin to scrutinize each nominee's record and background.

"The blue slip policy will continue because we on the Democratic side wish it to be so," said Schumer.

In offering his first set of nominations, Bush took two steps that scholars and observers had said would help smooth the process with the Senate: He gave the process high visibility, and he renominated Roger L. Gregory, a black judge who had been nominated by Clinton but never was considered by the Senate.

Bush announced his picks from the East Room of the White House at his only scheduled public appearance of the day, providing a setting typically reserved for Supreme Court nomina-

tions.

"A president has fewer greater responsibilities than that of nominating men and women to the courts of the United States," Bush said. "A federal judge holds a position of great influence and respect, and can hold it for a lifetime."

Bush called on the Senate to evaluate his nominees fairly. "Over the years, we have seen how the confirmation process can be turned to other ends. We have seen political battles played out in committee hearings — battles that have little to do with the merits of the person sitting before the

Bush's First Judicial Choices Highlight An Influential Conservative Court

In recent years, no other single court has affected the jurisprudence of the U.S. Supreme Court as much as the conservative U.S. Court of Appeals for the 4th Circuit. It has supplied a string of cases the high court has chosen to hear, and its rulings have often highlighted the philosophical split on that court.

When President Bush introduced his relatively small slate of judicial nominations May 9, he lavished attention on the 4th Circuit.

Three of Bush's 11 nominees — one quarter — went to the Richmond, Va.-based district that is representative of the struggle between parties for control of the courts, and the influence those courts can have on law and society.

The three nominees are South Carolina District Court Judge Dennis W. Shedd, North Carolina District Court Judge Terrence W. Boyle and Roger L. Gregory, a Richmond lawyer who is currently serving a one-year term on the court. The court hears cases from Maryland, North Carolina, South Carolina, Virginia and West Virginia. (*Nominees, p. 130*)

In its 1999-2000 term, the high court considered nine cases that originated from the Richmond bench, only one fewer than the enormous

9th Circuit that is based in San Francisco and covers nine states and two U.S. territories.

While the Supreme Court reversed nine of those 10 decisions of the liberal 9th Circuit, it split nearly evenly on the 4th Circuit cases, affirming four and reversing five.

The decisions by the 4th Circuit have been pivotal in the Supreme Court's campaign to redefine the limits of congressional power.

The 4th Circuit won plaudits from many conservatives for its decision rebuffing federal involvement in crime control as outlined in the Violence Against Women Act (PL 103-322). The Supreme Court upheld the circuit court's decision by a 5-4 vote on May 15, 2000, in *United States v. Morrison.*

The Supreme Court agreed with the 4th Circuit's view that crime control is the province of states and that Congress does not have the authority to provide remedies for victims of crime. A provision in the law that was struck permitted victims of gender-based violence, such as rape, to sue their attackers in federal court.

The Supreme Court also affirmed the 4th Circuit's decision barring the Food and Drug Administration from regulating tobacco. In its March 21 decision, *FDA v. Brown and William-*

son Tobacco Corp., the court held that the agency could not regulate tobacco because Congress had not explicitly granted the agency that authority.

But the court did overturn one of the 4th Circuit's most controversial rulings last year. In *Dickerson v. United States*, the Supreme Court held 7-2 that suspects must be warned of their rights when being questioned, a ruling that upheld the high court's landmark 1966 decision, *Miranda v. Arizona*. The lower court had used a law passed by Congress to rule that the warning was not a constitutionally protected right.

There are 15 authorized judgeships on the court: five are vacant, including the seat Gregory temporarily holds with the recess appointment he received from former President Bill Clinton. Of the 10 permanent judges on the panel, six were appointed by Republican presidents and four by Clinton. If all three of Bush's picks win confirmation, the balance would be eight Republican nominees and five from Democrats.

Two members of the 4th Circuit have also been mentioned as possible Supreme Court nominees: Chief Judge J. Harvie Wilkinson and J. Michael Luttig.

— *Elizabeth A. Palmer*

committee . . . I ask for the return of civility and dignity to the confirmation process."

Bush renominated Gregory to a seat on the U.S. Court of Appeals for the 4th Circuit. Clinton chose Gregory for that seat, and when the Senate adjourned last year without acting on his nomination, Clinton gave Gregory a one-year recess appointment.

With the new nomination by Bush, Gregory could be confirmed to a lifetime seat on the court. He is strongly supported by Virginia's two Republican senators, John W. Warner and George F. Allen, and many Democrats who believe Gregory was not treated fairly.

"It seems to me that President Bush held out the olive branch" with the nomination, said Jon Kyl, R-Ariz.

Others named by Bush include members of the Federalist Society, a group of conservative and libertarian lawyers and scholars. Bush had said he would seek conservative thinkers for vacancies on federal courts.

"Every judge I appoint will be a person who clearly understands the role of a judge is to interpret the law, not to legislate from the bench. . . . My judicial nominees will know the difference. Understanding this will make them more effective in the defense of rights guaranteed under the Constitution, the enforcement of our laws, and more effective in assuming that justice is done to the guilty and for the innocent."

Other Bush nominees include Miguel A. Estrada, who would be the first Hispanic on the U.S. Court of Appeals for the District of Columbia, and Utah law professor Michael W. McConnell, who was chosen for a seat on the 10th Circuit.

Also nominated for the D.C. Circuit was John G. Roberts Jr., a partner at Hogan and Hartson who had previously been nominated for the appellate court by former President George Bush.

But it is another judge first nominated by the former president that could become the focal point of the fight over nominations. That would not be anything new for Terrence W. Boyle.

Tarheel Standoff

Nowhere has there been a fiercer confrontation between a state's senators over nominations to the courts than the battle in North Carolina be-

Bush's Judicial Nominees

On May 9, President Bush nominated the following 11 people for positions on the U.S. courts of appeal:

Terrence W. Boyle, 55, nominated to the U.S. Court of Appeals for the 4th Circuit. Currently U.S. District Court judge in North Carolina, he is a former aide to Sen. Jesse Helms, R-N.C.

Edith Brown Clement, 53, nominated to the U.S. Court of Appeals for the 5th Circuit. Currently U.S. District Court judge in Louisiana, she presided over the insurance fraud trial of former Gov. Edwin Edwards.

Miguel A. Estrada, 39, nominated to the U.S. Court of Appeals for the District of Columbia. Currently a partner with Gibson, Dunn and Crutcher, he worked in the Justice Department's office of the Solicitor General during the Clinton and Bush administrations.

Roger L. Gregory, 47, nominated to the U.S. Court of Appeals for the 4th Circuit. Currently serving a one-year term on the court, he is the first African-American to serve on the 4th Circuit.

Michael W. McConnell, 45, nominated to the U.S. Court of Appeals for the 10th Circuit. Currently a professor at the University of Utah College of Law. An expert on religion and the constitution, he has argued nine cases before the Supreme Court.

Deborah L. Cook, 49, nominated to the U.S. Court of Appeals for

the 6th Circuit. Currently a justice on the Supreme Court of Ohio, she is a member of the conservative Federalist Society.

Priscilla Richman Owen, 46, nominated to the U.S. Court of Appeals for the 5th Circuit. Currently a justice on the Supreme Court of Texas, she served on the Texas court with White House counsel Alberto R. Gonzales.

Barrington D. Parker Jr., 56, nominated to the U.S. Court of Appeals for the 2nd Circuit. Currently a U.S. District Court judge in New York, he presided over the trial of reputed mob boss John A. "Junior" Gotti.

John G. Roberts Jr., 46, nominated to the U.S. Court of Appeals for the District of Columbia. Currently a partner with law firm of Hogan and Hartson, he was a law clerk for Chief Justice William H. Rehnquist.

Dennis W. Shedd, 48, nominated to the U.S. Court of Appeals for the 4th Circuit. Currently a District Court judge in South Carolina, he is a former staffer for Sen. Strom Thurmond, R-S.C.

Jeffrey S. Sutton, 40, nominated to the U.S. Court of Appeals for the 6th Circuit. Currently a partner with Jones, Day, Reavis and Pogue. Sutton argued, and won, a case before the Supreme Court that states that discriminate against the disabled cannot be sued in federal court.

tween Republican Jesse Helms and Democrat John Edwards.

Boyle's story began long before Edwards was elected to the Senate in 1998. In October 1991, Boyle was nominated to the 4th Circuit, but he never received a hearing by the Senate Judiciary Committee, then chaired by Joseph R. Biden Jr., D-Del. His nomination was returned to Bush when Congress adjourned at the end of 1992.

Boyle was an aide to Helms, who has blocked every nomination from North Carolina for the 4th Circuit since then. Helms argued that the court did not need any additional

judges.

Helms was supported by the 4th Circuit's chief judge, J. Harvie Wilkinson III, who said in an interview last year that he did not need more people. "My view is that we're doing a fine job with the personnel that we have," he said. "We're on top of our docket."

Wilkinson said May 10 that he stands by his previous statements. There are currently five vacancies on the 4th Circuit; Bush has sent the Senate nominees to fill three of them.

While Helms said he still thinks the court does not need additional judges, he said he is supporting Boyle's nomination because it would right a wrong.

Now Edwards has taken the position that putting Boyle on the bench would be unfair to the Clinton nominees that Helms kept from being seated. Edwards has vowed to prevent all of the circuit's open seats from going to conservative judges.

"In the interest of fairness, the right thing is to consider Judge Wynn and Ms. Gibson," he said May 7.

Those two nominations — North Carolina appeals court judge James A. Wynn Sr. and University of North Carolina-Chapel Hill law professor S. Elizabeth Gibson — were sent to the Senate by Clinton but were never considered by the Judiciary Committee because of objections by Helms. Wynn would have been the first African-American to serve permanently on the panel.

Wynn said in a May 9 interview that "it was an honor for me to be nominated." But, he added, "it has been a disappointing process for quite some time."

He said he had talked to Helms when the problem arose and was told there was no need for additional judges on that bench. "I simply had to accept that there was nothing I could do," he said.

Edwards said May 10 he is still in negotiations with the White House and may not automatically block Boyle's nomination if some agreement can be reached about the other vacancies on the court.

"Judge Wynn, I think, is the natural choice," he said.

Consulting?

Daily contact between Edwards and the White House was only one sign that the Bush administration was paying increased attention to the role Democrats will play in the nomination process.

While Bush is expected to pick the majority of his judges from the ranks of conservatives and the Republican party faithful, he ignores the concerns of Democrats at his own risk.

At least three nominations that had been expected to be announced on May 9 were not included. All three come from states where both senators are Democrats. Even Republicans acknowledge there is little they can do to move a nomination if both of the state's senators object.

So when Barbara Boxer, D-Calif.,

came out early against the nomination of Cox for the 9th Circuit, all eyes turned to Dianne Feinstein, D-Calif. She has declined to publicly discuss the nomination, but sources said its postponement was a sign she would oppose having Cox seated on the bench. Also delayed was another expected nomination for the 9th Circuit, Los Angeles County Superior Court Judge Carolyn Kuhl.

Another nominee for the 4th Circuit, Peter D. Keisler, was pulled from the list because of opposition from Maryland's two Democratic senators, Barbara A. Mikulski and Paul S. Sarbanes. Keisler, who would have been appointed to the seat traditionally reserved for Marylanders, is not a member of that state's bar, and both senators said they had not been adequately consulted about his nomination. "Neither of us is interested in helping him along," said Sarbanes.

Neither Democratic senator from Louisiana was consulted before Bush nominated Edith Brown Clement to the U.S. Court of Appeals for the 5th Circuit. But John B. Breaux said he did not expect to be involved in the process until after Bush made his first choice and the matter was before the Senate. Mary L. Landrieu said, "I want to work with the administration, but I'm not going to be a rubber stamp."

Carl Levin, D-Mich., said he simply will not consider Bush nominees for the two Michigan vacancies on the U.S. Court of Appeals for the 6th Circuit, unless Bush chooses two women who were nominated by Clinton but never were acted on in the Senate.

"They are not that interested in consultation," Levin said of the White House. "They are apparently willing to dig themselves into a deeper hole."

Michigan's other Democratic senator, Debbie Stabenow, said the administration had asked for a meeting, and an administration source said they had been trying to get together with the senators for several weeks.

Democrats took heart in the delayed nominations. "Let us hope that the initial signals from the White House that they understand our resoluteness and will not try to roll over us will continue," said Schumer.

Schumer and other Democrats attributed the postponements, at least in part, to their new strategy to use existing rules to block nominations, with or without the assent of Republicans.

"They were on the list and ready to go until we came up with this policy," Schumer said bluntly. "It's only the ability of the 50-50 Senate that could do it."

A Blocking Strategy

Under the Democrats' strategy, if either of the home state senators objects to a judicial nomination, Democrats on the Judiciary Committee will prevent that nomination from getting a vote.

There are at least two ways Democrats can block a nomination. The most obvious, and the one they would prefer not to use, is to simply not show up for a meeting. Because the committee is divided 9-9 along party lines, at least one Democrat must attend for there to be a quorum to do business.

That is the rule which prevented the committee from voting on two Justice Department nominees May 3. One of those nominations, that of Larry Thompson to be deputy attorney general, was approved May 10. The other nomination, of Theodore Olson as solicitor general, was postponed again at the same meeting after allegations surfaced that Olson had been part of a coordinated campaign by a right-wing magazine to ferret out scandals involving Clinton.

Democrats can also effectively filibuster a judicial nominee in committee. Under committee rules that were approved in March, a majority of the committee must vote to close off debate before a vote can occur.

At least one member of the minority must vote with the majority, which means if minority members are unified in their opposition to a nomination, they can stop it from leaving the committee.

The 50-50 rules give Lott the power to pull legislation or nominations out of committee and on to the floor if they have been defeated, but he cannot do so if there has been no vote.

All nine Democrats on the Judiciary Committee sent Hatch a letter saying that if he did not enforce the blue slip policy as they say it existed during the Clinton years, they would.

"The Democratic members of the Senate Judiciary Committee are committed to enforcing those policies and practices," they wrote.

Said Schumer: "It will have the same effect as if Senator Hatch enforced the blue slip, which we think he should do but we don't think he will do." ◆

Congress and the Bureaucracy

It is a natural consequence of a large, slow-moving entity like the federal government to have decisions of the past accumulate into obstacles for the present. Even in this era of smaller government, new priorities and new agendas seldom replace the old ones. Instead, with each turnover in the White House or in Congress, the new priorities are simply added on top of the old ones, building a bureaucracy of government activities that can slow the federal work to a crawl. A prime example of this was the decision by Congress, as requested by President Franklin Delano Roosevelt, to establish Social Security as a "mandatory" expense of the federal government. For the first time in its history, Congress pledged to set aside whatever money was necessary each year to fund retirement benefits for elderly Americans, creating an entitlement to that money for which citizens could sue if they were denied. This decision did more than elevate economic conditions for many senior citizens; it set about changing government budgeting forever, opening the door for other mandatory spending programs, including Medicare and Medicaid. As a result, mandatory spending now consumes about two thirds of the total the government has to spend each year. The need to maintain these programs, track their past costs and forecast their future costs has made mandatory spending a self-sustaining reality of government.

One of Congress' roles is to provide oversight for federal agencies, to scrutinize these bureaucracies. Regularly, congressional committees hold hearings to evaluate the effectiveness of this federal agency or that one. But even when problems are found, bringing about change is difficult. A critical weakness in Congress' effort to deal with bureaucracy — to say nothing of trying to shrink it — is the simple demand of having to create a new budget each year. Writing and passing such an enormous budget annually requires that large portions of it be replicated from years past and updated but not scrutinized; the priorities of the new year are added to the priorities of last year.

Federal Regulations in a GOP Capital

The president has the authority to create a wide range of regulations by executive order, but Congress can play a role by passing legislation that limits executive input by detailing the way federal agencies implement that legislation. Republicans controlled the House and Senate when this story appeared, creating a dynamic that offered President Bush especially wide latitude to use his executive powers. Since then, Democrats have retaken the Senate, which could give them some options for opposing Bush's rules.

Talk about efficiency. Even before tough new air conditioner energy-conservation standards were published by the Clinton administration in January, several major manufacturers began a concerted lobbying campaign to change the rules.

Then George W. Bush became president, and the effort took on greater momentum. The industry won sympathy from important GOP lawmakers such as Senate Majority Leader Trent Lott of Mississippi, Senate Finance Committee Chairman Charles E. Grassley of Iowa and members of the Texas congressional delegation. They petitioned White House aides and officials from the Office of Management and Budget (OMB), which oversees regulations. And they enlisted the support of career Department of Energy officials who, according to industry leaders, had recommended increasing air conditioner and heat pump efficiency by 20 percent instead of the 30 percent that outgoing Secretary Bill Richardson had ordered.

Within weeks, the drive paid off. On April 13, Bush political adviser Karl Rove told reporters that the administration would increase the efficiency standards by 20 percent. The industry was satisfied, but environmentalists were furious.

A new form of regulatory activism appears to be taking hold in the Republican-controlled government. GOP lawmakers, who for years were chafing under President Bill Clinton's regulatory agenda, are moving to undo his policies. And industry lobbyists — aware of the difficulties of trying to shepherd legislation through the evenly divided Senate — are pushing hard for the administration to use its executive powers to lessen the government burden on business.

In the Reagan years, Republicans complained of the "iron triangle" — an unbreakable alliance among Democratic committee chairmen, agency officials and interest groups that worked in concert to achieve common goals, whether it was funding for special projects or protecting specific constituencies. Reagan OMB directors David Stockman and James C. Miller III made it part of their mission to break the triangle.

Now, it appears, the old iron triangle has been turned on its head. Environmentalists and consumer activists say they fear the formation of a new triad — composed of industry officials, the White House and GOP committee chairmen — that leaves them out of the equation.

"It's fair to say they haven't been seeking us out for advice on how to proceed," said Debbie Sease, legislative director for the Sierra Club.

Today's triangles may not have the permanence or secrecy that characterized the networks of the past. But many regulatory experts predict that the new dynamic will control the rule-making process in more than 50 federal agencies. Corporate lobbyists, mindful of the Republicans' thin margin of control in Congress, are expected to make their case directly to the White House and to political appointees at the agencies, where they are likely to find a sympathetic ear.

"There's a new level of belief that agency regulations are likely to be more helpful than harmful," said Roy Blunt, R-Mo., House chief deputy whip. "For the past eight years, no one ever thought that could be the case. It's mind-boggling to be able to call former House staffers who are now in the

By Rebecca Adams / May 5, 2001

A Regulatory Timeline

▲ 1970-74:
President Richard M. Nixon signs an order creating the EPA and legislation establishing the Occupational Safety and Health Administration, the Consumer Product Safety Commission and the National Highway Traffic Safety Administration.

▲ January 1976:
President Gerald R. Ford promises in his State of the Union address to cut red tape and address "the petty tyranny of massive government regulation."

▲ 1977-80:
President Jimmy Carter deregulates the airline, trucking and railroad industries. He also issues an executive order calling for regulatory agencies to be more sensitive to the concerns of those being regulated.

Carter signs the Paperwork Reduction Act (PL 96-511), which directs the Office of Management and Budget (OMB) to eliminate unnecessary federal paperwork requirements. In addition, the bill creates the Office of Information and Regulatory Affairs within OMB.

Carter also signs the Regulatory Flexibility Act (PL 96-354), which requires federal agencies to consider cost-benefit analysis when writing rules.

White House or at an agency to see what they can do to help us."

He and other Republicans say that the administration is simply following the model created by Clinton, who they argue pursued a policy of aggressive regulation, especially in the areas of environment, health and workplace safety.

"I think it's appropriate for this White House to use the administrative side as aggressively as the previous administration," said Sen. Judd Gregg, R-N.H., a member of the Governmental Affairs Committee.

Gregg expects one of the main tools that Republicans will use to change regulatory policy will be OMB's Office of Information and Regulatory Affairs (OIRA), which monitors every major regulation that agencies issue. The nominee to head that office, Harvard professor John D. Graham, is known as an expert on and advocate of risk analysis, a tool researchers use to evaluate the relative harm that can come from various threats to human health and the environment.

Risk analysis is controversial because critics say that it can be used to undermine or undo regulations that society needs. But others say it can be useful to avoid imposing burdensome regulations on business when the risk is not really that great. "There's a distinct possibility that the agency will be used very effectively," said Gregg of New Hampshire.

'Just Wait'

While Republicans often criticized the Clinton administration for changing policy by administrative fiat, that approach is likely to be tempting for the Bush administration given the current balance of power.

"What you'll soon see is that the president will soon go wild with executive orders, even though he complained about it when Clinton did it, because the Senate is such a difficult place for him to navigate," predicted David C. King, professor of public policy at Harvard's John F. Kennedy School of Government. "That's the area in which the president does have an upper hand that he's not likely to lose soon . . . because undoing administrative actions requires consensus, not simply complaint, from Congress."

That sentiment is echoed by Robert E. Litan, director of economic studies at the Brookings Institution. "It's just so much easier to do things administratively," he said. "The fact that it's a 50-50 Senate makes that even more true."

As the Bush administration has revised or killed Clinton policies, Democrats say they are exploring ways to pressure the administration to back off.

"It's not easy," said Joseph I. Lieberman of Connecticut, ranking Democrat on the Senate Governmental Affairs Committee. "We still have the right to pursue litigation and use the power of investigations and public exposure. The problem is that anything we do legislatively faces a presidential veto."

The Democrats' challenge is likely to become greater as Bush appointees — many of whom come from the private sector, conservative think tanks and trade groups that vigorously opposed Clinton policies — fill agencies and take full control of the regulatory process.

"If you think it's been rough so far, just wait," said William Kovacs, U.S. Chamber of Commerce vice president for technology, environment and regulatory affairs. He predicts big fights over some of the environmental issues, such as clean air standards that were left unresolved in the Clinton years.

Business groups and their congressional allies have a long list of goals. Among them:

• They expect the Occupational Safety and Health Administration to take a cooperative rather than confrontational approach in getting businesses to improve work conditions. Republicans have long argued that this agency is so overbearing and punitive that businesses are afraid to seek its help in addressing problems.

• The health care industry and House Ways and Means Committee Chairman Bill Thomas, R-Calif., have long sought to overhaul procedures used by the Health Care Financing Administration (HCFA), which regulates Medicare and Medicaid, and curtail its power. Now that top hospital lobbyist Thomas A. Scully has been nominated to head the agency, Thomas and the industry are more likely to get what they want.

• The Bush administration is preparing a national energy plan, scheduled to be released in the next few weeks, that is expected to contain a number of proposals that can be accomplished by administrative action, such as allowing

▲ **FEB. 17, 1981:**
President Ronald Reagan issues an executive order barring agencies from issuing a major rule unless OMB decides its benefit outweighs its costs. It also requires OMB approval before a rule can be published.

▲ **JANUARY 1985:**
Reagan issues an executive order requiring OMB to approve agencies'

annual regulatory agendas.
▲ **1986:**
Reacting to complaints that the Office of Information and Regulatory Affairs overruled too many agency decisions and allowed industry groups excessive influence over rulemaking, Congress includes language in the final omnibus continuing resolution (PL 99-591) requiring its administrators to be

confirmed by the Senate. The law also restricts the agency's oversight functions to the "sole purpose" of reviewing information-collection requests contained in proposed regulations.

▲ **JANUARY 1992:**
President George Bush imposes a moratorium on new regulations and instructs agencies to change existing rules or programs that create regulatory burdens.

increased drilling on public land and easing regulatory restrictions on energy producers. Other agencies are considering low-profile ways to help ease the regulatory burden on businesses.

Undoing Clinton's Rules

During his final weeks in office, Clinton issued a number of rules that Republicans say were traps deliberately set to put Bush in politically difficult positions. Clinton signed off on more than 50 regulations after the election, prompting Bush spokesman Ari Fleischer to call him a "busy beaver" in his final days. Republicans note that it is not unusual for incoming presidents to conduct a broad review of last-minute rules signed by their predecessors.

"Some regulations that the Clinton administration put forward were blatantly political," said Rep. Christopher Shays, R-Conn. "And I believe that some of them were done to stiff this administration."

The rules for tighter efficiency standards for air conditioners, issued Jan. 22, were designed to force manufacturers to make their products more energy-efficient by 2006. After intense lobbying by environmentalists and one manufacturer of air conditioners that use less energy, Richardson proposed raising the standard by 30 percent. But that was controversial, especially because the department had considered a 20 percent increase, which the industry had said it could accept.

The companies, arguing that the 30-percent rule would jeopardize profits,

began lobbying. The air conditioning industry hired outside consultants such as Baker, Donelson, Bearman & Caldwell, a Washington lobbying firm headed by former Senate Majority Leader Howard Baker Jr., R-Tenn. (1967-85). The industry's trade group, the Air-Conditioning and Refrigeration Institute, flew company executives to Washington to contact lawmakers representing areas with large factories, such as Texas. And the group found and publicized a Clinton administration Department of Justice memo questioning the wisdom of the regulation.

"We called everyone we could," said David F. Lewis, vice president of government relations for Lennox Industries Inc., a Dallas-based company. "We wore out a lot of shoe leather."

He said industry officials met with Lott and Sen. Thad Cochran, R-Miss., telling them that the rule could hurt air conditioning manufacturing facilities in Mississippi and other states. They also told lawmakers and administration officials that the industry would consider challenging the regulations in court if they were not overturned.

Officials from Lennox as well as Trane Co. and Carrier Corp. also persuaded Grassley, Rep. Joe Knollenberg, R-Mich., and other lawmakers to send letters to the administration urging officials to reverse the rules, saying American jobs were at stake.

Those actions got attention. After Bush took office, his administration called for a new rule that would implement the 20-percent standard.

When the Bush administration De-

partment of Energy announced the change in the Federal Register, it directly cited the trade group's efforts. The department said that it was "of the view that [the association] has raised some substantial questions" about the Clinton standard.

Environmentalists criticized the action, especially because a day earlier they were pleased that the Bush administration had kept in place a Clinton rule, accepted by industry, requiring tighter energy efficiency standards for clothes washers and water heaters.

Bush must still decide on other Clinton policies, including one to control water runoff by farms and loggers. It is on hold until a National Academy of Sciences study is completed this year. Once it is released, the agriculture and forestry industries will lobby for new regulations that would limit costs to comply.

Thus far in his term, Bush has already signed legislation (PL 107-5) to kill a Clinton ergonomics rule opposed by many major business groups, who argued that it would cost too much to implement. He has also signaled his intention to reverse or revise Clinton regulations, including one to toughen cleanup standards for hardrock mining operations.

Bush also stoked public criticism by reneging on a campaign pledge to regulate carbon dioxide and by rejecting the Kyoto Protocol on global warming.

Perhaps the most controversial move was reversing a Clinton rule to reduce

▲ **SEPTEMBER 1993:** President Bill Clinton issues an executive order allowing agencies to issue regulations only when benefits "justify" costs. All major rules must be submitted for OMB review, but only those with an annual economic effect of $100 million or more require its approval.

▲ **1996:** Congress passes the Small Business Regulatory Enforcement Fairness Act (PL 104-121), which requires agencies to help small businesses comply with rules and allows for waivers of civil fines. The law includes language establishing the Congressional Review Act,

which requires agencies to submit new rules to Congress and the General Accounting Office and gives lawmakers an expedited way to reject them.

▲ **JAN. 20, 2001:** On his first day in office, President George W. Bush orders a 60-day hold on the effective dates of all published Clinton regulations not yet in effect so the new administration can review them.

▲ **MARCH 7, 2001:** Congress passes a resolution (S J Res 6) repealing ergonomics rules issued by the Clinton adminstration; Bush later signs it into law (PL 107-5).

the levels of arsenic in drinking water. The rule, issued in December, would have lowered the amount of arsenic permitted in drinking water to 10 parts per billion from 50 parts per billion. EPA Administrator Christine Todd Whitman announced March 20 that the rule would be withdrawn, leading Democrats and some GOP moderates to complain that the administration was out of touch with the public. Some political scientists believe the issue may have tipped the political scales.

Bush's regulatory strategy will be labeled in two categories, "Before arsenic and after arsenic," said Gary Bass, director of OMB Watch, a group that monitors the agency.

George C. Edwards III, professor of political science at Texas A&M University and director of the Center for Presidential Studies in the Bush School of Government and Public Service, said that outcries like the one over arsenic may force the White House to voice more concern about the environment.

"They got a negative reaction to the first regulatory decisions on environmental protection," Edwards said. "It's not what they actually meant . . . and they've been playing catchup ever since. That fact may temper them."

Complaints from environmental activists — and moderate Republicans, who fear a backlash from suburban voters in 2002 — have caused the White House to become more wary about overturning Clinton rules — and more savvy about explaining any changes. Bush announced several pro-environment moves the week of April 16, including decisions to uphold Clinton rules restricting wetlands development and lowering the levels at which factories must report lead emissions.

The White House also has upheld Clinton regulations involving complex medical privacy rules and tougher emission standards for diesel engines. But those actions have not muted criticism. Consumer groups point out that the Bush administration agreed to change the privacy regulations largely because health industry groups protested that the rules would make it tougher to dispense prescriptions and treat patients.

The president's decision to uphold Clinton's diesel fuel emission standards pleased automakers as well as environmental groups. According to energy industry lobbyists and environmentalists, however, the administration is quietly

conducting a study that could lead to the rules being relaxed.

Observers predict the administration will always have a strong conservative and pro-business ideology at its core, but they say it is now presenting a more cautious public face to stem concerns.

Graham's Role

GOP lawmakers are encouraging the administration to consider the costs and benefits of any new rules on business, including rules that were proposed during the Clinton years. The focus of that effort will be the OMB's regulatory affairs office.

"This administration will take a responsible, conservative approach," said Sen. Rick Santorum, R-Pa. "We'll do it in a way that's supported by the evidence, and not to appease interest groups."

OMB and Congress have a long history of conflict. During Republican administrations, Democrats charged that OMB officials were delaying, changing or killing regulations ordered by Congress and written by government experts. The agency would write a rule, OMB would put it under "review," sometimes indefinitely, and lawmakers would protest.

Reagan beefed up the agency's oversight power by issuing an executive order in 1981 that required agencies to prove that a regulation's benefits would "outweigh" its costs — a standard Democrats said was often tough to prove. Later, Reagan banned agencies from issuing any regulatory policies that were not approved by OMB at the start of each year.

Democratic chairmen in the House were outraged by Reagan's actions, and John D. Dingell, D-Mich., then head of the House Energy and Commerce Committee, routinely called officials to Capitol Hill and demanded that they explain regulatory decisions.

"Dingell would beat up on me all the time," said Christopher DeMuth, president of the American Enterprise Institute and an administrator of OMB's regulatory affairs office under Reagan.

In 1986, the Democratic-controlled House forced a showdown by deleting funds for OMB's regulatory division from the fiscal 1987 budget. Lawmakers restored the money after OMB director Miller and Wendy Lee Gramm, head of the regulatory affairs office, agreed to make the rule-making process more transparent by disclosing White

House documents related to regulatory decisions.

In the first Bush administration, Democrats pushed through a number of bills to strengthen clean air standards. And in each case, the Democratic-controlled Congress, aware of OMB's power, was very specific about how the agencies were to implement the laws such as amendments to the 1990 Clean Air Act (PL 101-549).

"We had to write a lot of detail in the law because we were afraid to leave it up to EPA," said Henry A. Waxman of California, ranking Democrat on the House Government Reform Committee. "We had to mandate things that otherwise would be [optional] if you had confidence that the people administering it had the same goals in mind as the authors."

After Clinton took office in 1993, he tried to open the regulatory process further when he issued an executive order requiring the White House to document any closed-door meeting between OMB officials and outside groups on a regulation. The order, which also required the cost of a regulation to "justify" its benefit, is still in effect.

With the GOP controlling the White House and Congress, Dingell said he may use discharge petitions — which members may sign if they want to bring a bill from committee directly to the floor — to publicize the issues. But he realizes his options to force real change on a GOP administration are limited.

"I will still do what I can," Dingell said. "But I [could] do a lot more if I were still chairman."

Blocking Regulations

The White House and Congress have several weapons beyond writing a new law that they can use to kill or alter regulations. They include:

• **Reopening a rule.** The 1946 Administrative Procedures Act allows the White House to reopen the rule-making process by soliciting new public comments, as it did in February with the medical privacy regulation. After considering the comments, the president can either modify a regulation or allow it to take effect without changes.

• **Enforcement.** They can also limit the funds available to agencies to enforce regulations. Bush has proposed cutting the funds of nine agencies and the EPA in his fiscal 2002 budget, which could affect the enforcement of a variety of labor, environmental, health and public safety regulations.

• **Congressional review.** Congress can reverse a rule through the Congressional Review Act (PL 104-121). Conservative lawmakers successfully used it for the first time ever in March to kill the ergonomics regulation.

The White House can indirectly reverse a regulation through the courts — either by mounting a weak defense of a rule written by a previous administration or by seeking a settlement with plaintiffs whose arguments it supports. This tactic is a gamble because judges can be unpredictable and their rulings can be appealed. But since the creation of numerous health and safety laws in the 1970s, legal challenges to regulations have become a common tool of both business and public-interest groups.

"One of the best ways to get rid of a regulation is to get a friendly lawsuit," said Jim Tozzi, deputy administrator of the regulatory office under Reagan.

For example, the administration tacitly encouraged a suit brought by the timber industry and western state officials against a Clinton regulation that blocked road building in 58.5 million acres of national forests.

In the suit, the Boise Cascade Corp., a major timber company, argued that the rule was not legal because the Clinton administration did not follow the proper procedures in writing it. Environmentalists had been watching the case to see whether the Bush administration would mount a vigorous defense of the rules. But on May 4, the administration announced a compromise under which the rule would go forward, but could be changed to allow forest plans to be written on a case-by-case basis, with input from local officials.

The judge in the case, U.S. District Court Judge Edward J. Lodge, had indicated that he thought the Clinton process was "grossly inadequate." He must decide by May 12 whether to block the rules.

Environmental groups, which cited the roads issue to attack Bush's environmental record, said the administration's plan was actually an effort to undermine the regulation. The groups had used an advertising campaign that features bucolic images of forests and wildlife, then shift jarringly to pictures of trees falling to the sound of chainsaws. A narrator says timber companies are trying to destroy the nation's forests, and that Bush may let them. The ad effort, by the Heritage

> *The White House can indirectly reverse a regulation through the courts — either by mounting a weak defense of a rule written by a previous administration or by seeking a settlement with plaintiffs whose arguments it supports. This tactic is a gamble because judges can be unpredictable and their rulings can be appealed.*

Forests Campaign, released new ads the week of April 30 calling on Bush to strongly defend the rules.

The White House is also said to be considering settlements in several lawsuits that seek to overturn Clinton regulations, including rules to phase out the use of snowmobiles in national parks and to reintroduce grizzly bears to areas in Idaho and Montana. In another suit, business groups are seeking to kill more stringent reporting requirements for lead emissions. In this case, Bush kept the Clinton rule, which required more businesses to report their lead emissions.

Environmental Defense and the Natural Resources Defense Council are joining as many suits as possible in defense of the Clinton rules. The groups say they will fight hard to prevent settlements.

Political Fallout

Democrats say they expect a political backlash from the Bush administration's regulatory decisions.

"We have an election in two years," said Sen. Barbara Boxer, D-Calif. "Let the people decide whether President Bush is being reasonable."

This month, the Sierra Club is running ads criticizing Bush on the environment. A coalition of environmentalists is also issuing daily faxes, e-mails and calls to supporters to generate concern about Bush's energy policy.

Bush's moves on the environment have "invigorated us to try to find ways to stop the administration," said Patty Murray, D-Wash., chairwoman of the Democratic Senatorial Campaign Committee.

A Democratic party television ad released April 29 attacks Bush's arsenic decision and criticizes a proposal by the Department of Agriculture, later scuttled, that would have ended testing of school lunch meat for salmonella.

The ad features a young girl asking, "May I please have some more arsenic in my water, Mommy?" A boy follows with the question, "More salmonella in my cheeseburger, please?"

Administration officials call the ad unfair — Rove called it "laughable" — particularly since the salmonella proposal was never an official position.

"This administration will be judged over the totality of its record," Rove said on NBC's "Meet the Press" April 29.

In the meantime, such ads can be expected to continue as the two parties battle over the role and scope of the regulatory process in getting federal policies changed. And just as industry can effectively mobilize its allies in Congress and the agencies, experts say, so can their adversaries.

"We're seeing a fundamental shift in power," said Harvard's King. "When there are shifts like this, there is always some turmoil. . . . It's natural." ◆

Managing Agencies: Congress and the INS

Federal agencies often become targets for criticism from the public and from Congress, and a recent example is the Immigration and Naturalization Service. It can take years for legal residency applications to be processed, and the population of illegal immigrants in the United States continues to grow, suggesting that the INS has not been proficient at either helping legal immigrants or stopping illegal ones.

AP PHOTO / LESLIE MAZOCH

The dual role of the INS to monitor U.S. borders, as this Border Patrol agent does in Brownsville, Texas, and to process requests to enter legally, could be divided by Congress.

It is never night in Nogales, Ariz. The bright stadium lighting that illuminates this town, which shares its name and an international border with Nogales, Mexico, burns 24 hours a day as part of the U.S. government's strategy to deter illegal immigrants from crossing into the United States.

The strategy also includes 30 low-light cameras pointed at the border, and more than 20 public safety announcements on television and radio warning of the dangers, from snakes to dehydration, that await those hoping to sneak across the desert into the United States.

But at the same time, the Immigration and Naturalization Service (INS), operator of this broad program, is helping a non-profit coalition called Humane Borders maintain aid stations across some of the more treacherous parts of Arizona's southwestern boundary. Large blue flags will mark locations

By Elizabeth A. Palmer / March 31, 2001

where immigrants crossing illegally can get water and other life-saving assistance.

Conflicting missions are a way of life for the INS, the agency charged with protecting U.S. borders as well as the people who seek to cross them. This year, a Republican president and a fleet of new leaders in Congress seem likely to generate momentum for a restructuring that splits the agency in two, a longtime goal of INS critics.

The complex politics of immigration are soon to be unleashed in Congress, where the immigration agency has become the new IRS — a symbol of wrong-headed bureaucracy that is slow to respond to problems and often seems to value process and paperwork more than people.

President Bush plans to offer a legislative package soon that would divide the agency into two separate offices, one responsible for enforcement of border laws, the other for citizenship processing.

"There's got to be a significant reorganization of INS because that's the most dysfunctional federal agency at the present time," said F. James Sensenbrenner Jr., R-Wis., the new chairman of the House Judiciary Committee, which deals with immigration issues.

"I just look at my own casework load in Wisconsin, where I now have six times as many INS cases versus IRS cases," he said in an interview. "And southeast Wisconsin is not a big immigration district."

The Bush plan also is likely to become a target for those who would like to make substantive changes to immigration law, a politically dynamic topic that has often been a sticking point for pivotal year-end legislation. Last year, the fiscal 2001 appropriations bill that included funding for the departments of Commerce, Justice and State (PL 106-553) was delayed into December because of a fight over an amnesty program for illegal immigrants.

This year, the proposals range from improving immigration standing for some Central American immigrants — a provision that failed to be included in the flurry of deal-making that closed out the last Congress — to repealing a law that allows indefinite detention of immigrants who have committed a crime.

One issue that won the attention of then-candidate Bush during the presidential debates is the use of secret evidence to detain and deport immigrants who are in the country legally.

Dozens of people have been imprisoned by the INS without even knowing the evidence against them. Bush has said he opposes this practice, and a bipartisan group of House members on March 28 introduced legislation to change the way the evidence is handled. (*Evidence, p. 140*)

There is widespread support in Congress for doing something about the INS, driven in part by such high-profile failures as the mistaken release of Angel Maturino Resendiz, who used the

Political Adversaries Unite to Push For Repeal of 'Secret Evidence' Law

Many minority groups worked hard to defeat the nomination of former Sen. John Ashcroft to be attorney general because they thought he was too conservative to sympathize with their needs, but one group, the Islamic Institute, actively supported his bid.

The key to the group's position was that Ashcroft supports the repeal of a provision of immigration law that permits the government to use confidential evidence against immigrants in asylum and deportation cases without disclosing it to the defendant.

The evidence often involves suspicion of terrorism, and the provision, which permits the government to detain people without sharing its evidence, has been disproportionately leveled against immigrants of Arab descent, according to opponents.

President Bush and Ashcroft have said they think the law is unfair, and on March 28, a bipartisan group of House members introduced the Se-

cret Evidence Repeal Act of 2001 (HR 1266).

It may be one of the bills attached later this year to the Bush proposal to split the Immigration and Naturalization Service. *(Story, p. 139)*

The cosponsors come from the ends of the political spectrum, from Bob Barr, R-Ga., and Thomas M. Davis III, R-Va., to David E. Bonior, D-Mich. The House Judiciary Committee approved a similar measure last year, but it saw no further action.

At issue is the use of classified evidence during political asylum and deportation cases to prevent a would-be immigrant from entering the country or to deport one who is already in the United States.

Advocates of repeal say immigrants are unfairly held in detention for long periods because they cannot prove their innocence without knowing the evidence against them.

The October 2000 Judiciary Committee report on legislation that

would have repealed the use of classified evidence concluded that it was overwhelmingly directed at Arab immigrants suspected of being terrorists. "As a general matter, the use of secret evidence has undermined the confidence of the Middle Eastern community in law enforcement," the committee's report found.

"The use of secret evidence in immigration proceedings not only violates basic principles of fundamental fairness, but it is also blatantly unconstitutional," said Barr.

The bill would require that a federal judge review the classified evidence and draft a non-classified version for the immigrant and the immigration judge hearing the case.

Bonior said he thinks chances are "very good" that the bill will be approved given the support shown by the Bush administration. "I'm confident that it is going to happen this session," he said.

— *Elizabeth A. Palmer*

---

name Rafael Resendez-Ramirez. In the United States illegally, Resendez-Ramirez was detained and then released by the INS several times, including in 1999 in the middle of a killing spree that had made him the subject of a nationwide manhunt. He was convicted of killing nine people.

"Resendez is a poster child for all that is wrong at the INS and Department of Justice," Rep. Lamar Smith, R-Texas, said when Resendez was convicted of murder last year.

But problems with the INS, and immigration policy in general, may run deeper than the inherent conflict in one agency's bureaucratic structure.

The Republican Party, for example, is deeply splintered on many immigration issues. While its conservative wing believes in strictly controlling immigration and limiting the number of foreign-born residents and the benefits to which they might be entitled, others in the GOP are themselves first-generation Americans with strong ties to im-

migrant communities.

"We as a country are deeply conflicted about immigration," said Doris Meissner, the INS commissioner during the Clinton administration. "We don't know what we think about it."

She said any agency "trying to function where there is that ambivalence in the body politic is going to have a problem."

The Bush administration has yet to name an INS commissioner, a decision that is likely to speak volumes about its intentions on immigration issues. Bush has been seen as more supportive of immigrants and immigration than some in the conservative wing of his party.

The uncertainty over what is to come runs deeper because, in addition to a new administration, the Congress organized with a new cast of committee leaders. And although they have been in Congress for a while, it is unclear how they will approach immigration issues in their new roles.

During the last decade, the number of immigrants entering the United States reached record levels. In absolute numbers, the 1990s saw more immigrants accepted into the country than ever before. Even as a proportion of the population, the only immigration wave that exceeded the 1990s occurred at the turn of the previous century.

The number of illegal immigrants residing in the country is also high. According to a study by Northeastern University, there are approximately 11 million undocumented workers in the United States. The official government estimate is roughly 6 million.

In 1970, according to James M. Lindsay, a senior fellow at the Brookings Institution, 6 percent of U.S. residents were foreign-born. Today, that number has risen to more than 10 percent.

That change was reflected in the 2000 Census, which showed a large increase in the Hispanic population, especially in relation to other immigrant groups. More than half of the nation's foreign-born population came from Latin America.

The 2000 census found that, for the first time, Hispanics pulled even with African-Americans as the largest minority group in the United States.

The data also shows that immigrants are locating in new areas, such as North Carolina and Nevada, in addition to more traditional places like New York City, California, Florida and Texas.

Congress' attitude toward the INS reflects the deep conflict felt in the political realm about the nature of the immigration boom. While members have been unceasing in their criticism of the agency's shortfalls, they also have doubled the agency's budget in less than a decade.

"The Congress certainly took its liberties in bashing the agency," said Meissner, now a senior fellow with the Carnegie Endowment for International Peace.

Meissner said the INS was "chronically very backward" when she arrived in 1993. At that time, for example, less than 20 percent of staff had computers on their desks, she said. Now virtually all of them do.

Money From Congress

In fiscal 1993, Congress appropriated $1.5 billion for the INS; by fiscal 2001, funding more than doubled to $3.3 billion. In fiscal 1993, there were more than 18,000 authorized positions at the agency; by fiscal 2001, that ballooned to more than 33,000.

In fiscal 2001, the agency's total budget is $4.8 billion, with an additional $1.5 billion coming from fees paid for immigration services.

That "may well be the largest growth in peacetime of any federal agency," said Russell Bergeron, director of media relations for the INS.

The agency processes nearly half a billion people each year through the ports of entry into the United States, and claims to be the federal agency that comes in contact with more people than any other. About half of those are not U.S. citizens.

The increased funding allowed the agency to hire hundreds more Border Patrol agents, modernize and centralize its information collection system and add more application inspectors.

"There's been a tremendous investment made in the infrastructure of the agency," said Meissner.

Some of the chronic problems that have plagued the agency, such as excessive delays in processing citizenship applications, appear to be improving.

Members say they have been inundated with stories from constituents whose relatives or employees have spent years waiting for the INS to complete action on their naturalization application. The agency acknowledged that at the start of fiscal 1999, it took an average of 28 months to process applications; critics said it took twice that long.

Over the last two years, the agency said it has reduced the average time to between six months and nine months, according to its internal estimates. During those two years, the INS processed more than 2.5 million naturalization applications.

From 1993 to 2000, the agency processed 6.9 million applications for citizenship, more than the total in the previous 40 years combined.

"That's really the untold story — the agency does its work much, much better than it ever did before," said Meissner.

There is some disagreement, though, about just how far the agency has come. In its fiscal 2002 budget submission, the Bush administration said it "often takes three years or more for INS to process immigration applications and or petitions."

Bush requested an additional $100 million in appropriated funds for five years for the agency to beef up its processing speed to an average of six months per application. Most of the money available for processing comes from application fees.

Frequently, the fees collected do not provide sufficient money for all the immigration services. That problem is exacerbated by the fact that many who use immigration services, such as those seeking asylum, do not pay a fee.

Judith E. Golub, a lobbyist for the American Immigration Lawyers Association, said of the $500 million proposal: "It's very helpful and it's an encouraging sign, but we're not sure it's enough."

Conflicted Missions?

At the heart of the debate over the efficiency of the INS remains the question of whether its two fundamental missions are so contradictory that they cannot properly coexist under a single roof. Can an agency charged with tracking down and deporting illegal aliens also function as an agency that is supposed to treat would-be immigrants as customers?

Currently, the INS operates 33 district offices around the country. Another nine Border Patrol sectors are positioned along the southwest border of the United States.

Most district offices, which are located in major metropolitan areas and along the border, perform a combination of law enforcement and service activities. Those offices report to three regional service processing centers.

The INS also operates three international field offices in Mexico City, Rome and Bangkok. Agents there help those wishing to emigrate to the United States and aid in investigating international operations that are suspected of smuggling workers.

Legislation to split the agency into separate lines of authority for enforcement and services was approved by a House subcommittee last year but went no further because of Republican disagreements with the Clinton administration over how the restructuring would work.

This year, members are waiting for the Bush administration to supply the details. "I support the concept of splitting the immigration service into two as the president stated during his campaign," said Sensenbrenner. "How that is accomplished and how that is controlled, I'm waiting to get the lead from the administration on."

While Republicans seem agreeable to the central idea of the Bush plan, Meissner and Democrats are more skeptical. Rep. Sheila Jackson-Lee of Texas, ranking Democrat on the Immigration and Claims Subcommittee, said she does not support a complete split of the agency.

"It's imperative that the left hand knows what the right hand is doing," she said.

Meissner said the INS functions "are not basically in conflict" but rather "points on a continuum" of immigration issues.

The parameters of the debate will be established when Bush sends his proposal to Capitol Hill. For now, Jackson-Lee said she is optimistic about dealing with Bush on immigration issues.

"He did not use immigration issues in a negative manner" as governor of Texas, said Jackson-Lee. "He's going to have to get his party to not see immigrants as the enemy." ◆

When the Spending Is Mandatory

The debate over the future of Medicare has been underway for years because demographic projections show that the retirement of the baby boom generation will swamp the program, along with Social Security. But preparing for that future is complicated by the simple fact that Medicare is a "mandatory program" whose expenses Congress must cover no matter how high they go. And they can be very hard to predict.

Conventional wisdom on Capitol Hill has long been that if lawmakers added a prescription drug benefit to Medicare, the government would spend more initially but save money in the long term because the medicines would help prevent illnesses and shorten hospital stays.

Dan L. Crippen, director of the Congressional Budget Office (CBO) recently told lawmakers that it is impossible to predict the behavior of seniors if they were to be given such a benefit. "We believe [the amount of drugs seniors use] will go up . . . but we're not exactly sure how much, and we don't know for sure how quickly the costs would grow after you introduced the benefit, which in some ways is a more important question," Crippen told the Senate Finance Committee on March 22.

He later told the House Ways and Means Health Subcommittee there was no evidence that adding prescription drugs to Medicare would save the program any money. "Most of the studies that suggest there are savings are not very compelling," Crippen said.

Such is the nature of the debate over the future funding and structure of the 35-year-old health entitlement program for nearly 40 million elderly and disabled Americans: As is often the case with Medicare, no one really knows.

Figuring out what the program will cost taxpayers is as much art as science, and legislators have grown accustomed to seeing even the best-researched estimates balloon.

The fact lawmakers must rely on projections that invariably are wide of the mark has only served to complicate the ongoing debate over whether to add a prescription drug benefit to Medicare or to overhaul the entire program. John D. Rockefeller IV, D-W.Va., a member of the Senate Finance Committee, said lawmakers have no other choice but to live with the uncertainty of Medicare cost estimates. "What is your alternative?" Rockefeller said. "Abandon the program?"

That is unlikely. But sometimes Congress has to alter its strategy in order to control Medicare costs. For example, lawmakers cut payments to hospitals, nursing homes, home health agencies and other Medicare providers in the 1997 balanced-budget act (PL 105-33) — and they have been restoring them ever since. Some experts attribute the "givebacks" to lobbying efforts, while others say the reductions went far beyond what Congress had intended.

"[The guesswork] certainly has caused a lot of frustration," said Gail R. Wilensky, chairman of the Medicare Payment Advisory Commission, which advises Congress on Medicare issues. But such uncertainties are a "fact of life in dealing with Medicare. That's the nature of the program."

Patricia Neuman, director of the Medicare Policy Project for the Kaiser Family Foundation, a nonprofit research and philanthropic organization, said analysts who estimate Medicare spending must consider "an amorphous world of assumptions," including new technologies, new drugs and the effect

"It's difficult to know" what Medicare expenditures will be **"with any precision,"** says CBO's Crippen.

By Mary Agnes Carey / April 14, 2001

The Growth of Medicare Outlays

Since Congress established the Medicare program for the elderly and disabled, spending has grown from $3.2 billion in 1965 to $216 billion in 2000. The balanced-budget act and a crackdown on fraud helped contribute to a slight drop in 1999.

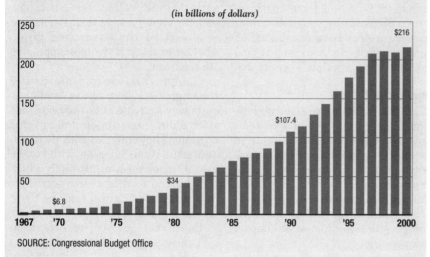

(in billions of dollars)

SOURCE: Congressional Budget Office

that direct-to-consumer advertising has on the elderly.

Neuman says analysts must also consider how changes made by Congress in the Medicare delivery system — particularly the emphasis in recent years on managed care — affect Medicare recipients. "This is educated guesswork," she said. "In the end, [lawmakers] have to trust the CBO to do the best they can."

A Complicated Formula

Trying to determine Medicare spending has never been simple for lawmakers or the federal agencies charged with making such estimates. The misjudgments go all the way back to the beginning of the program in 1965, when experts predicted that Medicare hospital costs would be $5.5 billion in 1980. The figure turned out to be $25.6 billion.

"It's difficult to know" what Medicare expenditures will be in a given year "with any precision," said Crippen.

There are several reasons why getting a precise figure is so hard. New and expensive technologies can drive up costs, and so can the behavior of beneficiaries and the hospitals, physicians, therapists and other professionals who provide medical care.

For example, the elderly use more than three times the amount of health care resources that the under-65 population uses, Crippen said. Seniors are eager to try costly, cutting-edge technologies and drugs designed to treat ill-

nesses common to their age group, such as heart disease or cancer.

Analysts also have found it almost impossible to determine how beneficiaries and providers will react to spending changes. Often, when Congress tries to restrict spending, Crippen said, Medicare recipients and providers figure out how to get around it: If reimbursements for doctors' office visits are cut, the number of visits billed to Medicare increases. Or a patient's simple cold gets billed as pneumonia, which is reimbursed at a higher rate.

"Behavior is a very difficult thing to predict," said Paul Ginsberg, director of the Center for Studying Health System Change, a nonpartisan, private research organization.

Other factors can skew the numbers too. Home health care spending rose an average of more than 20 percent in the 1990s — in part because of several court decisions in the late 1980s that eased eligibility requirements. Lawmakers also hoped that managed-care providers' attention to costs would help cut Medicare spending. Instead, many insurers are leaving the program, citing low reimbursement rates and too much paperwork.

One of the biggest surprises in Medicare spending is that its growth has slowed significantly the past few years. According to CBO, Medicare payments grew an average of 3.4 percent annually in fiscal 1998 through fiscal 2000, compared to 10 percent per year over the previous decade.

"No analyst ever thought they would see a drop in Medicare spending in their lifetime," said Robert Reischauer, president of the Urban Institute and former CBO director under Presidents George Bush and Bill Clinton.

According to an April 2000 CBO analysis, the slower growth was the result of low inflation, slower than projected growth in enrollment and a government crackdown on fraud — as well as the 1997 balanced-budget law.

Hit or Miss Strategies

Strategies that Congress has used over the years to curtail Medicare spending have had mixed results.

For example, in 1983 lawmakers were faced with a forecast in 1983 that the Medicare program could go bankrupt in four years,. So they approved language in a Social Security bill (PL 98-21) that changed the way hospitals were reimbursed for treating Medicare patients.

Instead of billing the program whatever it cost to treat patients, hospitals were given a fixed schedule of prices for treating different types of illnesses. The measure was intended to force hospitals to budget their resources more effectively so they would not spend more treating Medicare patients than they could recover from the program.

Another strategy put into place by Congress at that time was to hold hospitals' payment increases close to the rate of inflation, then about 3.8 percent annually.

But hospitals found new ways to bill for services to get more money from Medicare, said Crippen, and that canceled out any savings gained from keeping payment increases below inflation. "It looks like they came out about even," he said.

Over time, there have been some savings from the changes made in the 1980s. According to a 1998 analysis by the National Bipartisan Commission on the Future of Medicare, the new billing system helped reduce the average hospital stay for Medicare patients from more than 11 days in 1982 to less than seven days in 1997.

The new system also helped keep Medicare payments to hospitals close to the overall inflation rate, a radical change from earlier years, when inpatient hospital services represented the largest single Medicare cost, according to the commission.

The bipartisan panel was created in the 1997 budget bill to develop ways to make the program financially stronger, but disbanded in 1999 when members were unable to reach consensus.

More recently, Congress has struggled with how much to pay home health services and managed-care providers to attract and keep them in Medicare.

Home health care costs began to rise rapidly in 1980 after Congress removed a restriction that limited Medicare recipients to 100 visits a year and did not require beneficiaries to pay any of the costs.

Several court decisions near the end of the decade also contributed to what the bipartisan Medicare commission described as a "liberalization" of the home health benefit. It took on "more of a long term nature rather than its original acute care emphasis," the panel said in its 1998 report.

Home health costs continued to climb in the 1990s, increasing an average of more than 20 percent a year as the number of beneficiaries receiving services and the average number of visits per beneficiary both doubled.

So lawmakers, in an effort to rein in costs, included language in the 1997 balanced-budget law cutting payments for home health visits.

According to the home health industry, the cuts were too deep and have forced dozens of agencies out of business. Since then, lawmakers have delayed a scheduled 15 percent across-the-board rollback in payments to home health services included in the 1997 law. The Senate also voted April 5 to include a "contingency reserve" of $13.7 billion in the fiscal 2002 budget resolution (H Con Res 83). That would effectively repeal the 15 percent cut, which is scheduled to take effect in October 2002.

Congress' strategy with Medicare managed-care providers has not worked any better. Operating under the assumption that Medicare recipients in managed-care plans are healthier than those in the traditional fee-for-service program — and would be cheaper to insure — Congress began in 1997 to tighten reimbursements to some managed-care insurers in areas where costs are high in order to give more money to companies in areas where costs are lower.

But that move has backfired, and managed-care companies have left the program in droves, saying that Medicare was no longer profitable for them.

Over the last two years, Medicare managed-care plans have received about $16 billion in "givebacks" and the industry is pushing for more money to keep plans in the program. So far this year, insurers have terminated 65 contracts with Medicare and scaled back services in another 53 contracts.

Juggling Act

Congress' inability to estimate how managed-care plans would operate in Medicare is yet another example of how difficult it is to know what the impact of legislative changes will be on the marketplace. A similar sense of uncertainty permeates discussions of how coverage of new technologies and the latest prescription drugs would impact Medicare costs.

"These are decisions that have been with the Medicare program since the beginning," said John Rother, legislative and policy director for the seniors' group AARP. "It has been a controversial issue for years — should Medicare be slower or quicker" in approving new treatments for reimbursement, he said.

Such decisions are not always simple. For example, positron emission tomography, also known as "pet scans," can help detect Alzheimer's disease, but since there is no known cure, should Medicare cover a procedure to diagnose it? If so, Medicare costs would certainly rise, because millions of seniors suffer from that condition.

In recent years Congress has decided to broaden Medicare coverage for mammographies and colorectal screening, because breast and colon cancer can often be cured if caught early.

If Congress decides to include prescription drug coverage in Medicare, lawmakers and analysts alike would examine the effect of direct-to-consumer advertising on the elderly.

A September 2000 report by the National Institute for Health Care Management, a nonpartisan research group, found that prescription drugs advertised directly to consumers were the best- and fastest-selling medicines, contributing to a 19 percent increase in pharmaceutical spending in 1999. The group also reported that the 25 most heavily advertised drugs in 1999 accounted for 77 percent of the money spent to advertise prescription medications.

Proponents of such advertising argue that the ads have given consumers more information about their health conditions and diseases, which helps them have more informed discussions with their physicians. But critics say patients often pressure their physicians to prescribe the advertised drug, whether or not it is the most appropriate treatment.

Congress' unease in dealing with the unpredictable nature of Medicare costs may increase as lawmakers consider adding prescription drugs to the program. They struggled with the issue during the 106th Congress, with House Republicans pushing through a bill that looked to the private sector to help provide drug coverage. The Senate did not take action.

Lawmakers are still reeling from CBO figures released March 22 that estimated total spending on prescription drugs for Medicare enrollees would reach $1.5 trillion over the next decade, nearly one-third more than what CBO estimated last year.

Those figures may not be enough to slow the momentum for adding prescription drug coverage to Medicare. Both parties ran hard on the issue last year and are certain to do so again in 2002, either taking credit if a bill passes or pointing fingers if it does not.

Senate Finance Committee Chairman Charles E. Grassley, R-Iowa, said Republicans and Democrats alike have no choice. "The last election was all about prescription drugs. The last election was a mandate to deliver on that," he said.

Ways and Means Committee Chairman Bill Thomas, R-Calif,. who co-chaired the Bipartisan Medicare commission, said his colleagues should focus on prescription drugs in the context of larger changes to the Medicare program.

"It is the 25-to-35-year window that really ought to drive the decisions we're making for fundamental reform, not what it's going to cost this year, next year, five years or even within a 10-year budget projection," Thomas said.

"The current system is not sustainable. . . . If you don't change the current system, but you add prescription drugs to it, that means it is less sustainable than it would be otherwise. That's pretty fundamental stuff, but people don't want to deal with the fundamentals," he said. ◆

Rumsfeld reviews troops with Joint Chiefs of Staff Chairman Gen. Henry H. Shelton, left.

Restructuring the Military

Since the Cold War ended in the late 1980s, the United States has struggled with ways to adapt the military to a world without a superpower foe. But this most entrenched bureaucracy, with its many advocates in Congress, has been very slow to move.

He is challenging nearly every assumption of U.S. military policy, from the lofty satellites that scan the Earth to the training of soldiers who plod through the mud. He has created more than 20 informal panels of experts — the number keeps climbing — that seem to have interviewed everyone with an idea to spin, an ax to grind or a program to protect. And in a town that thrives on leaks, he has managed to keep nearly all of it as secret as a murder case.

Defense Secretary Donald H. Rumsfeld's goal — his marching order from President Bush — is nothing less than the most comprehensive analysis of the U.S. military, its strategy and weapons since World War II.

"We're witnessing a revolution in the technology of war," Bush said in a Feb. 13 speech. "I have given [Rumsfeld] a broad mandate to challenge the status quo."

Whether Rumsfeld's recommendations will be revolutionary or evolutionary remains to be seen. Absent a clear foreign threat, the administration must persuade Congress and the public to buy into a new military vision. So far, that effort has not begun.

Each of the services already has modernization plans and a wish list of advanced weapons. The Army, under the prodding of Chief of Staff Gen. Eric K. Shinseki, has already tak-

en steps to transform itself into a more mobile force. The Navy has more efficient warships on the drawing boards.

The problem has been paying for such changes, given budget constraints and the Pentagon's insistence on maintaining and improving the Cold War weapons it already has.

The idea of an end-run — putting the budget emphasis on sophisticated weapons and technology the military might need for combat in the future — worries some congressional defense specialists.

"I'm all for looking to the future," House Armed Services Committee member Floyd D. Spence, R-S.C., declared during a March 21 hearing, "but a lot of those future threats are threats right now."

After weeks of speculation that Rumsfeld would recommend cutting this or that major weapons system — everything from aircraft carriers to the F-22 fighter and the Crusader cannon — the current sense is that he will not threaten any of the current programs. "What they are going to do is take the Clinton modernization plan and actually pay for it," predicts Loren Thompson, a defense industry consultant.

Except for his May 8 recommendation that the Air Force should be in charge of protecting the nation's space satellites, Rumsfeld is keeping his own counsel.

Among the changes he is thought to be considering:

• Dropping the goal that U.S. forces should be able to win

By Pat Towell / May 12, 2001

two major regional wars almost simultaneously.

• Eliminating up to two-thirds of the nation's nearly 7,300 nuclear warheads, but without first reaching a reciprocal arms deal with Russia.

• Shifting the primary focus of defense planning from Europe to the Pacific, where long-range bombers and ships might be more important than large ground forces.

• Spending less money on tanks, ships and planes designed for the Cold War and European combat and spending more on lighter, more agile weapons, as well as sensors, robot planes and long range, precision-guided weapons.

• Privatizing hundreds of thousands of administrative and maintenance jobs in the military, including personnel who overhaul aircraft and other combat equipment.

Even if, as expected, any reorganization is strung out over months of executive orders and legislative detail — Bush is expected to cover some of the themes in a Naval Academy commencement address May 25 — it could disrupt a half-century of military and industrial routine. Military units would migrate or transform, bases would close or move, jobs would be lost and created, industries would win and lose.

"This is going to be a real crossroads debate," said Kansas Republican Pat Roberts, a member of the Senate Armed Services Committee.

Already, Capitol Hill is restless, a distant spectator to Rumsfeld's ruminations across the Potomac. Senate Republican leaders reportedly were so angry at being left out of the deliberations that they held up confirmation of several of Rumsfeld's subordinates to get his attention.

Said Ike Skelton of Missouri, the ranking Democrat on the House Armed Services Committee, "Those of us who work on national security have some expertise. If they don't want it, they're going to get it — in the form of questions and decisions."

Senate Armed Services Committee Chairman John W. Warner, R-Va., however, said Rumsfeld is staying in touch. "He talks to me regularly on a wide range of issues," Warner said, "but we early on decided there wasn't any real value in me, week-by-week, trying to follow all the groups giving him advice."

Warner's patience did not keep him from issuing a clear warning in response to news accounts suggesting that the review might call for fewer of the big aircraft carriers built in Virginia.

Rumsfeld's first public recommendation, that the Air Force should be in charge of defending space satellites, was a foretaste of the debate to come. He couched the change in management terms. Critics called it the first step in militarizing space.

"I think putting weapons in space may be the single dumbest thing I've heard so far from this administration," said Senate Minority Leader Tom Daschle, D-S.D.

Promises and Portents

Since the end of the Cold War, the defense budget has been cut by one-fourth and the military rolls by one-third. Though Republicans on defense committees repeatedly accused President Bill Clinton of wearing out the armed forces with overseas missions while denying them the money necessary to modernize, Congress itself kept a tight lid on defense spending.

Because Bush had promised the military throughout his campaign that "help is on the way," many in Congress and at

the Pentagon expected a substantial increase in the fiscal 2002 defense budget request, and perhaps a supplemental request for fiscal 2001. Instead, Bush announced a modest budget and a major review of defense policy before any more money would be forthcoming.

The Pentagon, like other agencies in the Bush administration, also began taking on a more corporate flavor. Much of the senior management comes from the defense industry.

For his review, Rumsfeld began creating panels of experts — civilians and retired officers — to address issues as he encountered them. At least one panel, dealing with a highly technical issue, consists of one person writing a report.

Some lawmakers have complained that Rumsfeld is relying too heavily on civilian analysts.

In an April 20 op-ed column, Randy "Duke" Cunningham, R-Calif., a retired Navy fighter ace and member of the House Defense Appropriations Subcommittee, likened the review panels to the civilian experts whose predictions about aerial combat in the 1960s left U.S. fighter pilots illtrained and ill-equipped for dogfights with North Vietnamese MiGs.

Cunningham called on Bush to put aside the civilians' recommendations until he obtained the military leadership's advice about future strategy. "[He] can then overlay the input of academics and civilians never exposed to the realities of actual 'Private Ryan' combat to determine the final vision."

Rumsfeld said his panels have heard presentations from a wide range of people. Moreover, he said, the process is intended simply to help him make up his own mind about proposals which, he acknowledges, will have to make their way through the legislative process.

"Some people think I arrived in this job from the pharmaceutical business with a head full of plans, ready to bring it out, unwrap the cellophane package, and hand them over to the Pentagon," he said during the news conference on space operations.

"I didn't. I am very sincerely trying to figure out what I ought to think about these things," Rumsfeld added. "And I'm getting smart people from all around, inside the government, outside the government, in the Congress, in uniform, out of uniform . . . not to tell them what's going to happen, but to try to figure out what I think maybe ought to happen."

One assumption is that if members of Congress and the service hierarchies with vested interests in the status quo had greater access to the deliberations, they could rev up lobbying efforts to protect any program that seemed threatened. Secrecy is a military advantage.

But the price of protecting his inquiry from that type of outside pressure may be that Rumsfeld is alienating, or at least not cultivating, potential allies.

"That could be a flaw in their scheme," said John D. Isaacs, president of the Council for a Livable World, a liberal arms control advocacy group. "They're avoiding leaks, but they're not building support."

Reading Tea Leaves

It is generally assumed that Bush will propose a smaller increase in defense spending for fiscal 2002 — something on the order of $20 billion to $25 billion — than the $60 billion increase that senior military leaders and congressional defense specialists had hoped for.

Yet Bush and Rumsfeld have created an expectation of

Rumsfeld's Team: No Figureheads

Defense Secretary Donald H. Rumsfeld is relying on the defense industry and policy establishment for his Pentagon management team. Service secretaries have often been figureheads in the past, but Rumsfeld has picked corporate veterans and apparently will use them to help run the department.

■ **Paul Wolfowitz**, 57, deputy secretary of Defense — Former dean of the Johns Hopkins University Paul H. Nitze School of Advanced International Studies (SAIS) in Washington. In the Reagan State Department, he was director of policy planning, assistant secretary of State for East Asian and Pacific Affairs, and ambassador to Indonesia. Under George Bush, he was undersecretary of Defense for Policy. He joined SAIS in 1994. **Confirmed**.

■ **Gordon R. England**, 63, secretary of the Navy — Former executive vice president for combat systems with General Dynamics, which has several shipbuilding subsidiaries, including Electric Boat and Bath Iron Works. He ran a Fort Worth aircraft plant, which built F-16 fighters for both General Dynamics and Lockheed.

■ **Brig. Gen. (ret.) Thomas E. White Jr.**, 57, secretary of the Army — Former vice chairman of Texas-based Enron Energy Services. A West Pointer with 23 years in the Army, much of it in tank units, White was executive assistant to Gen. Colin L. Powell when Powell was chairman of the Joint Chiefs of Staff. He joined Enron in 1990.

■ **James G. Roche**, 61, secretary of the Air Force — Former corporate vice president of Northrop Grumman Corp., running its electronic sensors division, a key ingredient of the new military. A former Navy destroyer captain, he was a Democratic staff director at the Senate Armed Services Committee and a protégé of Andrew Marshall, director of the Pentagon's Office of Net Assessment. He has used the study of military battles to help train corporate executives.

■ **Dov Zakheim**, 52, undersecretary of Defense and comptroller — Former CEO of SPC International Corp., a consulting firm on defense and high technology for domestic and foreign clients. He held several positions in the Reagan Defense Department, including deputy undersecretary for planning and resources, and in 1997 was a member of former Defense Secretary William S. Cohen's defense reform task force. **Confirmed**.

■ **Douglas J. Feith**, 47, undersecretary of Defense for Policy — Managing attorney with Feith and Zell, in Washington. A leading critic of many arms control agreements, he served from 1984-86 as deputy assistant secretary of Defense for negotiations policy and was special counsel to assistant secretary of Defense Richard Perle from 1982-84.

■ **David S.C. Chu**, 56, undersecretary of Defense for personnel and readiness — Former vice president of the RAND Corp. in charge of its Army research division. He was director of program analysis and evaluation in the Reagan Defense Department and assistant secretary of Defense for program analysis and evaluation in the George Bush administration.

■ **Edward C. "Pete" Aldridge Jr.**, 62, undersecretary of Defense for acquisition, technology and logistics — Former president and CEO of The Aerospace Corp., a nonprofit research and development company designing and testing missiles and satellites for the Air Force. Trained as an astronaut, he was Air Force secretary in 1986-88 and has held several Defense Department posts. **Confirmed.**

■ **Powell A. Moore**, 63, assistant secretary of Defense for legislative affairs — Former chief of staff for Sen. Fred Thompson, R-Tenn. A one-time press secretary to Democratic Sen. Richard Russell of Georgia (1933-71), he worked in the White House for Presidents Richard M. Nixon and Ronald Reagan. He also was an assistant secretary for legislative affairs in the Reagan State Department. He was a vice-president of Lockheed Corp. in 1983-85, and was a consultant until he joined Thompson's staff in 1998. **Confirmed.**

■ **William J. Haynes II**, 43, Defense Department general counsel — Former partner of Jenner & Block, a law firm with headquarters in Chicago and offices in Washington. A Texas native, he was Army general counsel from 1990-93 in the George Bush administration.

■ **Victoria Clarke**, 41, assistant secretary of Defense for public affairs — Former general manager of the Washington office of the public relations firm Hill & Knowlton. She served as assistant U.S. trade representative for public affairs and private-sector liaison from 1989-92, and was press secretary to GOP Sen. John McCain of Arizona from 1983-89.

radical change. During and since his campaign, Bush endorsed the idea that high-powered computers, sophisticated sensors and precision-guided weapons are altering the way wars will be fought and are rendering large warships, tanks and short-range fighter planes obsolete.

"Powers are increasingly defined not by size, but by mobility and swiftness," Bush said in his Feb. 13 speech. "Advantage increasingly comes from information. Safety is gained in stealth, and force is projected on the long arc of precision-guided weapons."

Moreover, it became known early in February that Andrew Marshall, an iconoclastic Pentagon analyst and leading proponent of this "revolution in military affairs," would play a key role in the defense review.

One way of doing what Bush has forecast with modest means would be to save money elsewhere in the defense budget — reduce the size of the military and cut overhead by privatizing maintenance, closing surplus bases and scaling back what the Pentagon planned to spend upgrading older weapons.

The Bush team will probably have to propose cuts in existing weapons programs and Pentagon operations anyway, just to accommodate budget limits. Beyond that, the administration may need to make a few dramatic cuts to make the point that it is intent on change.

"For the world to treat this review as serious, they do have to make some changes," Isaacs said. "They need some scalps on the wall."

Though it is not clear what Rumsfeld will recommend, several key issues are on the table:

Necessary Nukes

President Bush has hinted strongly that he will unilaterally reduce the number of U.S. nuclear weapons. The Center for Security Policy, a conservative group that advocates hard-line foreign and defense policies, said that too large a reduction might undermine the deterrent effect of the U.S. arsenal and even tempt a hostile state to attack.

Senate Republicans last year blocked a provision that would have allowed the president to cut the nation's nuclear arsenal below 6,000 warheads because they did not want to give Clinton any leeway to strike an arms deal with Russia.

Conservatives' reservations about arms reductions would be assuaged if the Bush administration launched an effort to develop a small nuclear weapon designed to burrow deep underground before exploding. Advocates argue that such weapons could destroy concrete-hardened headquarters and bunkers storing nerve gas and germ warfare weapons while causing relatively few casualties above ground. A provision of the fiscal 2001 defense authorization bill (HR 4205) requires the Pentagon to study the feasibility of such a weapon.

But developing any new nuclear weapon would arouse fierce opposition from arms control advocates. Besides wanting to preserve the moratorium on nuclear weapons tests that has been in effect since 1993, arms controllers worry that policy-makers might be tempted to use a relatively small nuclear weapon that promised surgically precise results and few civilian casualties.

Bush opposes the Comprehensive Test Ban Treaty, which the Senate rejected in 1999, but has said he favors continuation of the current test moratorium.

While welcoming the possibility of nuclear arms reductions, some arms control advocates bitterly oppose Bush's notion of making cuts unilaterally rather than through a negotiated treaty: "In rejecting formal treaties, Bush abandons agreed verification procedures that will become increasingly important" as U.S. and Russian nuclear arsenals get smaller, said Spurgeon M. Keeny Jr. of the Arms Control Association.

Where to Fight

Since 1990, U.S. policy has been to maintain a military large enough to win two major wars almost simultaneously — for instance, in the Persian Gulf and Korean peninsula. The rationale is to dissuade a hostile state from taking advantage of U.S. engagement in one place to attack in another.

Republicans criticized Clinton for jeopardizing the armed forces' readiness to fight two wars, saying that his penchant for deploying troops overseas on peacekeeping and other missions disrupted training schedules and wore down equipment.

But critics of the two-war goal insist that it is unrealistic and that the military should be designed and tested against the standard of winning one major war while carrying out several of the non-war missions that have become routine.

On May 8, Rumsfeld seemed to throw his lot with those calling for a new standard when he discussed a report that one Army division had been judged unready for war. His answer was reminiscent of arguments made by the Clinton administration.

The division, Rumsfeld said, "was in Bosnia, and it was doing that very well. And indeed the president and the Congress and the country said, 'Go to Bosnia; that's your job right now.' . . . Mightn't we want to size our forces also for some other things, like a Bosnia or a Kosovo or a non-combatant evacuation in some country or maybe one or two or three of those things?"

There has been speculation that Rumsfeld will recommend shifting the Pentagon's focus from Europe to the Pacific, where China may pose a more serious threat to U.S. allies than Russia poses to NATO. Pentagon futurist Marshall has urged such a shift for years.

While it might cause diplomatic problems in Europe and Asia, such a change might have relatively little impact on the Pentagon's deployments or weapons purchases.

"Most of the shift has already happened," said Michael O'Hanlon of the Brookings Institution, who noted that the two major wars that are the focus of current plans are both in Asia. "There's only so much further they can go with this. A lot of what you would need against China would be traditional: carrier air power, anti-submarine warfare, attack submarines, minesweepers, etc., which we already have."

Revolution or Evolution

Though Bush and Rumsfeld have adopted the rhetoric of those, like Marshall, who speak of a revolution in military affairs, the armed forces insist that their existing modernization plans are moving in that direction, while they also upgrade existing weapons.

Marshall's acolytes complain that because defense budgets have been too tight to fund both the future military and the current one, transformation has been shortchanged in favor of marginal improvements in the current armed forces. They call on the services to "skip a generation" of weapons, a phrase Bush has echoed, but without explaining which current programs he would terminate.

Each of the programs thought vulnerable, however, promises some significant improvement:

• The Navy's DD-21 destroyer would be cheaper to operate than the existing Aegis destroyer, since it would have only one-third as many crew members.

• The Joint Strike Fighter is expected to be much stealthier and only slightly more expensive than the current version of the F-16.

• The Army's Crusader self-propelled cannon is too heavy to airlift comfortably, but once on the ground it is faster and more powerful that the weapon it would replace.

According to sources, the Rumsfeld advisory panel that took the most comprehensive overview of conventional weapons has recommended that at least the cannon and the fighter remain on track. If the new destroyer is delayed, it may well be because more time is needed to develop some of its more novel features. ◆

Congress and Interest Groups

The job of members of Congress is to make yes or no decisions. Support this bill or not. Vote for this provision or vote against it. But in the act of deciding, a member of Congress is almost never alone. He or she is in the constant company of a multitude of people representing an array of interest groups that have a stake in the outcome of votes on this bill or that provision. These lobbyists are an integral part of America's system of public lawmaking, representing the specific wishes of particular industries or sometimes even large individual companies. A small change in the wording on a bill that updates tax laws can have million-dollar consequences for companies.

But interest group politics has developed into a science that has made it the scorn of nearly everyone, including those involved. Interest groups, such as trade associations for the technology sector or trucking industry, have become extremely adept at maneuvering in the system. They make campaign contributions to influential lawmakers and then use that support as leverage for their views. Interest groups do not just state a case for or against legislation, they often draft their preferred bill language, which has on many occasion become part of the final law. Critics of interest groups say their influence has become too great, that it is disproportionate to the constituencies they represent. At the same time, however, Congress is designed to bend to parochial needs. A member of Congress whose district is home to, say, a few defense industry contractors, can hardly be expected to do anything less than heed the advice of the interest group representing those companies.

Strength in Numbers for Lobbying

The picture of lobbyists in a free-for-all, fighting one another to gain individual advantage for their position in Congress does not always hold true. There have been times when varied lobbying groups have united, despite their differences, to press a common agenda.

Last month, some of the most powerful groups representing American business joined together to devise a strategy for this year's big tax debate. They included giants such as the U.S. Chamber of Commerce, the National Association of Manufacturers, the National Association of Wholesaler-Distributors, and the National Federation of Independent Business.

Their aim: to push for passage of a tax bill that includes no special provisions for big business.

Has corporate America's appetite for special provisions in President Bush's $1.6 trillion tax cut package been quelled so quickly?

Hardly. The Tax Relief Coalition will probably only be able to hold itself together as long as the Bush administration is able to restrain Congress from writing specific provisions into the president's bill. If it suddenly became clear that lawmakers were willing to open the bill up to special-interest tax breaks, the group would probably splinter instantly, or continue as a shell of its former self.

But for now, the coalition's willingness to come together around a tax cut in which their members have no proximate self-interest illustrates the new lengths to which the old practice of coalition lobbying has been taken.

With the tax package poised to become the defining issue of Bush's first year in office — and, perhaps, of his entire presidency — interest groups from across the political spectrum are dusting off old umbrella organizations or starting new ones. In some cases, groups that have little direct interest in the tax cut are lining up on either side of the bill for fear that if they don't join the battle, they might be at a disadvantage in future struggles over issues of great importance to them.

Such coalitions long have abounded on an array of other issues, from those that want to stop new workplace injury regulations to those that encourage development of broadband data transmission technology. Coalition politics was in full force during the confirmation process for Attorney General John Ashcroft.

But the tax bill is expected to bring the phenomenon to a new level. One advocate suggested it would be "the World Series of lobbying."

Another, R. Bruce Josten, chief lobbyist for the U.S. Chamber of Commerce, put it this way: "If you look at Congress, it's one pile of money, 535 hands."

An alliance of unions and other liberal organizations— including the National Association for the Advancement of Colored People (NAACP) and the Sierra Club — is forming to defeat the Bush plan outright. Other coalitions of business or community organizations are seeking changes. *(Box, p. 152)*

With the first portion of the tax package headed to debate on the House floor the week of March 5, now is prime coalition-building time.

"The next month is really critical for us to gain visibility for this idea at the local level and to get the idea into the heads of key members," said Deepak Bhargava, director of a coalition that will seek to expand Bush's child credit proposals so that those with low incomes can more readily claim the benefits.

Keeping an Eye on Each Other

Coalitions are essentially groups of groups, which tend to collect relatively scant dues from already organized trade or community organizations. This is different from established "taxpayer" groups trying to influence this year's tax debate — such as the Americans for Tax Reform or the Club for Growth — which solicit members and donations from the public and attempt to get what they want in part by donating to candidates.

When the Tax Relief Coalition was organized, it quickly became clear that participants would have to refrain from actively pushing their own interests. "It's implicit that you're going to check your own parochial appetite at the door," one lobbyist said on condition of anonymity.

In this case, the coalition allows members to keep an eye on their competitors: as long as one industry is willing to put off active lobbying for special provisions, others know their competitors do not have an advantage.

Coalition-building can also stretch the lobbying dollar, because membership is generally just a fraction of the cost of launching a full-scale effort on one's own. Business and taxpayer groups that sign on to the Tax Relief Coalition will be asked to pay just $5,000, for example. With 60 organizations already expressing an interest in membership, the dues could finance advertising campaigns and a considerable lobbying effort.

Some coalitions are more than happy to flaunt their membership, but those who monitor special interest lobbying in Congress say a lack of regulation too often allows these umbrella groups to mask their true identities.

"It's very easy to point at a company that's lobbying or contributing and say, 'We know why you're doing that,' but joining groups with very innocent sounding names is a way for them to engage in these activities without having fingers pointed at them," said Steven Weiss, communications director for the Center for Responsive Politics.

Peter Eisner, managing director for the Center for Public Integrity, sees the current popularity of legislative coalitions as "a trend that comes right out of the presidential and congressional campaigns" of the past decade, in which interest groups have often joined together to purchase "issue advocacy" advertising or otherwise work for their preferred candidates.

The problem, for Eisner, is not so much that public officials may not know who these groups really are, but that essentially unattributed information gets spread in the public domain.

"When a member of Congress needs to know who's supporting a position, their friends and lobbyists out there will let them know what that group is," Eisner said Feb. 21, but "there

By Lori Nitschke / March 3, 2001

is an inherently deceptive quality . . . that certainly is not in the best interest of the public."

A prime example of the confusion that coalitions are capable of causing came during the electricity deregulation debate of the 106th Congress. Two of the groups that advertised the most in the debate portrayed themselves as having competing legislative goals, but The Washington Post found that the two were actually funded primarily by the same nine

And if it becomes clear that room will be made for considerable additions to the package, these coalitions could fall apart.

While those now working to unify various political and economic segments do not want to publicly concede that their bonds are anything less than rock-solid, some say in private that their unity would be challenged if it becomes clear that gains could be made by going it alone.

That is part of what happened to the Tax Reform Action Coalition in 1986. Founded by many of the same groups that have organized this year's Tax Relief Coalition, that alliance attempted to pave the way for the major tax code overhaul that President Ronald Reagan made a top priority of his second term.

As Reagan's bill and his pledge to substantially cut income tax rates went through a number of versions, some in the coalition went their own way. The Chamber opposed the measure after it became clear that corporations would see little of the cut. The NFIB took a temporary leave to push its own priorities. Others in the coalition, while ostensibly backing Reagan's bill through all the

Unable to meld their disparate goals into an alternative tax agenda, a coalition of liberal groups instead is bound by a broad goal: to stop the Bush plan. Announcing the formation of Fair Taxes for All on March 1 were, from left, AFL-CIO President John Sweeney, Nancy Duff Campbell of the National Women's Law Center, People for the American Way President Ralph G. Neas and Democracy 21 President Fred Wertheimer.

utilities. Their goal appeared to be to cloud the debate so that no legislation would move, which is precisely what happened.

While advertising campaigns are the most expensive and visible manifestation of legislative unions, some alliances are little more than "letterhead coalitions" that write to Congress and offer up the occasional newspaper opinion article. Some organizations, such as the NFIB, limit their participation in such groups, believing they accomplish little. *(NFIB, p.152)*

Strong Bonds?

Do coalition efforts pay off?

In this year's tax debate, that will depend largely on Bush's success at imposing discipline on congressional tax writers. He and his top economic advisers have made considerable inroads in convincing business leaders that the success of Bush's presidency rests on corporations' ability to curb their appetites — at least at this time. Members of Congress likely will be a harder sell. Some already warned that the administration needs to be more flexible about opening up the bill.

twists and turns, spent little energy to see it enacted.

Applying lessons from that debate to this year's has its limits. Reagan's goals were to eliminate special tax breaks as well as to cut taxes. And, because the country was then deep into deficit, he insisted that the bill remain revenue neutral — a zero-sum game that pitted business groups against each other, since a victory for one might be offset with a loss for another.

Regardless of the differences, Clint Stretch, a partner at the accounting firm Deloitte & Touche and a veteran of many tax bills, believes that the ties that bind many of the new or renewed coalitions are not that much stronger.

"Back in the old days, it was much more of a free-for-all with everybody for themselves," he said. "And in some ways one suspects it still really is."

Members of Congress most frequently exposed to the efforts of tax coalitions appear to be of two minds about their effectiveness.

"Individual lobbying is preferable," said Benjamin L. Cardin of Maryland, a House Ways and Means Committee Democrat, "because you get to see more of a face on the issue."

But for Dave Camp of Michigan, a Republican on the panel, coalitions can have sway if they can connect their efforts to

For Small-Business Federation, Personal Approach Gets Best Results

When Dan Danner hires new lobbyists, he gives them a simple mandate: Wear out your shoe leather.

For the National Federation of Independent Business (NFIB) and Danner, its senior vice president for federal public policy, the key to successful lobbying is being nearby whenever decisions are made. Forging yet another alliance with like-minded organizations takes second place.

"Although we do participate in coalitions, it is more important for [lobbyists] to be face to face with members and staff," Danner said in a Feb. 27 interview. "There's a temptation to do coalitions for coalitions' sake, and we absolutely do not."

That is not to say that the NFIB does not join, or even lead, coalitions. But its strategy of carefully picking alliances while continuing to push its own lobbying efforts has generally paid off. The 58-year-old group, which now represents the interests of 600,000 small-business owners, will have the luxury of playing defense during this year's tax debate. While President Bush's proposals include little for corporate America, it has plenty for small business.

Ending the estate tax has long been the top NFIB priority and is one of the issues that has prompted the group to participate in a coalition this year. Those advocating the repeal Bush has proposed already are facing a tough task. The idea is coming under attack from insurance companies, charitable groups, state officials and even some billionaires who say they

should not be exempt. In addition, it will compete with other ideas for either spending the $266.6 billion a repeal would cost the Treasury, or devoting that money to other tax cuts.

Bush's proposal to cut personal income tax rates would give most small-business owners a tax break. More than half of small businesses are organized as sole proprietorships, S Corporations or other entities whose profits are taxed at personal, rather than corporate, rates.

While the NFIB is widely credited for its well-organized team of ambitious lobbyists, it is not the only group that represents small firms. The National Association of Manufacturers and the U.S. Chamber of Commerce represent many businesses that earn far less than the Fortune 500. NFIB members tend to be smaller, on average employing five people.

Because it is made up exclusively of such firms, the NFIB sometimes has an advantage over bigger and better-financed competitors. It does not have a divided agenda. Its members pick their top priorities in organization-wide plebiscites several times a year. They almost never show interest in one issue — trade — that has occupied much of the Chamber's and the manufacturers' time in recent years.

Grass Roots

NFIB forces often are warmly received on Capitol Hill, where many lawmakers also have personal ties to small businesses and so retain a soft spot for them. Forty-four members of

Congress have been members of the federation or are married to one, by the NFIB's count. President Bush belonged during his days running an oil exploration concern in West Texas.

And the owners of small businesses are much more eager than corporate CEOs to leave their offices for a few days to try and buttonhole lawmakers and agency officials in Washington.

"You have virtually a grass-roots army of small-business guys," said Bruce Josten, legislative director for the Chamber. "There's not a virtual army of the big guys."

Josten ticks off a list of issues he must worry about that the NFIB does not — trade, bankruptcy, class action litigation, funding for the Export-Import Bank — because he also represents larger corporations.

"People think things come maybe automatically easier to us just because of who we are," the NFIB's Danner said, but "a lot of it is persistence and hard work."

He points to the end of the 106th Congress. Though few lobbyists remained at the Capitol throughout the last day of the lame-duck session, on Dec. 15, the NFIB kept three of its staff there until 8:30 that night. By sticking around, they were able to clear Senate roadblocks to an obscure tax bill that embodied one of the top small-business priorities of the year. As a result, Congress cleared and President Bill Clinton signed the legislation (PL 106-573), which allows those who sell their businesses in installments to pay capital gains taxes

his constituents. "To me, the real strength is that tie to home," he said.

If getting a piece of a tax bill is akin to playing in baseball's October finale, many coalitions are still in spring training.

Bhargava, whose coalition is called the National Campaign for Jobs and Income Support, is spending many of his days on Capitol Hill, attempting to win sponsors for a proposal to make the child tax credit "refundable," meaning it could be claimed by families who do not earn enough to owe income tax. Bush wants to double the credit, which has been $500 since its cre-

ation (PL 105-34). It is now refundable only for low-income filers with at least three children.

Bhargava's work is imperative to the broader goals of the organization directed by Steve Kest, the Association of Community Organizations for Reform Now (ACORN). That group, which works to advance the interests of minority and low-income families through community organizing, sees a fully refundable credit as a boon to those it serves. Bhargava's group estimates that if the credit is not made refundable, the parents of more than 16 million children would be unable to claim it because they do not earn enough

Visits to the Hill are a central NFIB tenet. Blankenburg, left, went to the Longworth Building on March 1 to meet Darrell Issa, R-Calif., and his aide, Sandra Wagner.

throughout the sale, not in the first year of the sale as an earlier law had required.

A number of the group's other tax priorities were not met last year, and are not in Bush's proposal, either. Among them are repealing a 0.2 percent employment tax that funds programs for those who have been laid off, and a proposal to allow the self-employed to begin deducting all their medical insurance costs from taxes immediately, instead of in 2003 as the law now provides.

Dan Blankenburg, the group's tax lobbyist in the House, said the NFIB is prepared to forgo action on those desires again in the name of helping Bush's proposal. "We're not going to run to the Hill and ask for a whole plethora of provisions," he said.

Always a loyal Republican ally, the group has joined the Tax Relief Coalition, which is now aiming to stem the tide of business interest in adding to Bush's package.

The NFIB works on legislative pro-posals with few congressional Democrats, although it has recently forged ties with some of the party's conservatives and moderates. Still, of the $1 million that the federation's political action committee donated to congressional candidates in the past two years, 96 percent went to Republicans.

Training Ground

Blankenburg is a classic example of the type of young, ambitious and inexpensive lobbyist the NFIB seeks. Before coming to the federation a year ago, at age 28, he had been a legislative aide to Rep. John Shimkus, R-Ill.

Most of the lobbyists the group hires have had four or five years of experience on the Hill, Danner said, and they tend to stay at the NFIB only two to three years. The quick turnover is due partly to the salary structure — the pay is only slightly better than many Hill legislative aides receive, or between $50,000 and $75,000, one former employee estimates. Many NFIB lobbyists also par-

lay their experience into other positions in the advocacy business.

Alumni populate K Street, the new administration and the offices with the best views from the Capitol.

Nelson Litterst, a former top House lobbyist for the NFIB, is now lobbying the House on behalf of the president. Litterst's predecessor at NFIB, Ralph P. Hellmann, left to serve as director of policy for Speaker J. Dennis Hastert, R-Ill. Brian Reardon and Jim Hirni, former federation tax lobbyists, also returned to the Hill. Reardon is the deputy staff director and chief economist for the Senate Republican Policy Committee. Hirni is the new legislative director for Sen. Tim Hutchinson, R-Ark.

Alumni with prime positions in the private sector include John J. Motley III, senior vice president for government and public affairs for the Food Marketing Institute; Kent Knutson, manager of federal government affairs for Microsoft Corp.; Kelly Smith, director of federal government relations for Circuit City Stores Inc.; and Mark W. Isakowitz, who has started his own lobbying firm known as Fierce and Isakowitz.

High turnover can take its toll on the federation — Danner currently has two openings on his nine-member team — but the NFIB also benefits from its well-placed alumni. Sorting out whether the group is successful because of its efforts, or because it represents a politically popular group, can become a chicken-or-egg argument.

Both seem intrinsic in the group's success, said Clint Stretch, a lobbyist for the accounting firm Deloitte & Touche. "Small business is right up there after motherhood and apple pie," Stretch said. "And, the NFIB is very good at what it does."

— *Lori Nitschke*

to owe that much income tax.

ACORN joined the coalition that Bhargava directs to leverage its political power. "In order to be effective in influencing policy, you really need reach in as many of the 50 states and 400-odd congressional districts as possible," Kest said. ACORN has chapters in half the states and 100 House districts.

Another liberal coalition, even newer than Bhargava's, has a far broader aim: To stop Bush's bill altogether. Its organizers say about 150 liberal groups have expressed interest in joining. A main player in the effort, Ralph G. Neas

of People for the American Way, says many of this coalition's members were in an alliance earlier this year that sought to block Ashcroft's confirmation as attorney general.

The coalition's organizers concluded it would be futile to try to forge an alternative from the disparate goals of its members.

A similar practicality underlies the aim of the Tax Relief Coalition. If one of its four founding member groups had chosen instead to launch a full-scale drive to make room for its own priorities in the tax bill, it is unlikely the business

Tax Debate Coalitions: A Sampler

NAME	GOAL	MEMBERSHIP
Tax Relief Coalition	To see Bush's proposal enacted without change	Founders include the National Association of Wholesaler-Distributors, the National Association of Manufacturers, the U.S. Chamber of Commerce and the National Federation of Independent Business. Letters have been sent inviting 250 business and taxpayer organizations to join. Dues of $5,000 each will go toward advertising, most likely in Capitol Hill publications.
Fair Taxes for All	To kill the Bush plan	Includes an array of liberal advocacy groups such as People for the American Way; labor unions including the AFL-CIO and the American Federation of State, County and Municipal Employees; Democracy 21, which favors campaign finance changes; the NAACP; the Sierra Club; the National Council of La Raza; and the National Women's Law Center.
Coalition for Jobs, Growth and Competitiveness	To add tax cuts for corporations to Bush's package	Led by the American Council for Capital Formation and longtime tax lobbyists Charls E. Walker and Mark Bloomfield, its members include the Securities Industry Association, the American Forest and Paper Association and the American Chemistry Council. The group has decided not to actively push its agenda unless it is clear the tax bill will be opened up to such amendments.
National Campaign for Jobs and Income Support	To amend Bush's plan to make the child credit refundable	ACORN and several regional community groups — including a federation from the Pacific and Rocky Mountain states and New England's Northeast Action — want to allow those with incomes so low that they do not owe any or much income tax to qualify for the child credit. Other groups that support the effort but are not now part of the coalition include the Children's Defense Fund, the National Council of La Raza and the AFL-CIO.
Americans Against Unfair Family Taxation; Family Business Estate Tax Coalition	To enact Bush's estate tax repeal	Both have long been in existence and have the same stated goal, although the Unfair Family Taxation group has been more willing to compromise in recent years. It is run by the Food Marketing Institute and includes the National Association of Convenience Stores, the National Association of Broadcasters and the National Beer Wholesalers Association. The Family Business group is run by the National Federation of Independent Business and includes the American Farm Bureau Federation, the National Cattlemen's Beef Association, the National Association of Manufacturers and the Newspaper Association of America. Many groups belong to both efforts.
Americans for Sensible Estate Tax Solutions	To scale back Bush's proposed estate tax repeal	This new group — hoping be known by its acronym, ASSETS — is still soliciting members and has not released a full list of those who have joined. Founders include the Association for Advanced Life Underwriting. Organizers are eager for more academics and charitable fundraisers to join; so far, the group's backers include University of Texas economist James K. Galbraith and Iowa State University agricultural economist Neil Harl. The coalition has contracted with former Sen. Alan K. Simpson, R-Wyo. (1979-97), to provide legislative advice.

community would have coalesced.

"Our goal is to mobilize grass roots on behalf of the package," said Dirk Van Dongen, president of the Wholesaler-Distributors. "We welcome into membership in the coalition any organization or corporation that will take the pledge" to support Bush's package

For a brief time, it appeared that the Tax Relief Coalition, which is seeking to bind together the business mainstream, might go head-to-head with another alliance on the core question of whether to press hard for pro-business changes and additions to the Bush plan.

The securities, chemical and forestry and paper industries had launched the Coalition for Jobs, Growth and Competitiveness on Feb. 6 to push for three additions: a package of tax incentives for retirement savings; a provision to allow individual corporations a choice between reduced income tax rates or faster depreciation schedules; and a five-year phase-in of lower taxes on international transactions.

The group, run by the Washington-based American Council for Capital Formation, which advocates policies to ease access to capital, has since been convinced by the administration to downgrade its efforts. "We're now in a research mode," Mark Bloomfield, the group's president, said Feb. 22.

What that means, he said, is that the new coalition will put off active lobbying on its proposals to signal support for Bush's plan. But it will continue to build economic arguments for its own proposals, Bloomfield added, and "to the extent to which the bill gets in trouble and the administration opens it up, then we want to be ready to do those sorts of things."

The group appears well-positioned to know if and when that opportunity will present itself: Alumni of the Council for Capital Formation board include Treasury Secretary Paul H. O'Neill and White House Chief of Staff Andrew H. Card Jr. ◆

The Trade Balance for Bush and Congress

Expanding trade with other nations is always a top goal for presidents, but in trying to achieve it no president can afford to ignore the concerns of organized labor at home. As Republicans and Democrats have grown to near-equal standing in Congress, organized labor, which fears the loss of jobs when trade deals are made with countries that have lower costs of living, has gained strength by being able to influence a decisive group in Congress.

Cheney campaigned at Weirton Steel Corp. in West Virginia vowing to enforce trade laws, but the flood of foreign steel into the United States has industry champions hoping for a more aggressive stand.

When Vice President Dick Cheney campaigned at a West Virginia steel mill last October, he promised workers at the Weirton Steel Corp. that a Bush administration would "vigorously enforce" laws that prevent foreign producers from unfairly "dumping" their product on the U.S. market at below-cost prices.

Like many other U.S. steel giants, Weirton was in the throes of a dismal year. Inventories were piled high, demand had gone soft and prices were dropping. A month after Cheney's visit, Weirton temporarily laid off 2,800 workers, and at the end of the year the company posted a loss of $85 million.

The painful market conditions of last year are not likely to improve for steel in 2001, and now the question of how to address the ailing industry's problems with import competition is emerging as the first big obstacle in getting the new Bush administration's trade agenda off the ground.

President George W. Bush inherits from his predecessor a last-minute recommendation to investigate possible violations of trade laws in the steel sector, and increasingly strident calls from the industry and its champions in Congress to go beyond

By Julie R. Hirschfeld / Feb. 24, 2001

Cheney's campaign pledge and address the troubles that have plagued steel for decades.

"Even though it may create tensions within the administration, there really is, in terms of the steel industry, a need for the Bush administration to intervene quickly," Democrat John D. Rockefeller IV of West Virginia said Jan. 4 at a Senate confirmation hearing for Commerce Secretary Donald L. Evans.

Beyond expressing concern about the issue, administration officials have been vague about their plans. However, the tensions Rockefeller referenced are already clear. To gain congressional support for the ambitious free-trade agenda the White House has outlined — including securing broad trade negotiating authority for Bush and continuing efforts to reach hemispheric and global pacts — the administration will have to convince lawmakers that U.S. producers will not be left behind.

"I think this will be viewed as a test case," said Roger B. Schagrin, a lobbyist and international trade lawyer in Washington who represents several large U.S. steel producers.

Schagrin said the conflict will be illustrated by the upcoming congressional debate over granting Bush "fast track" — statutory authority to negotiate trade agreements and submit them to Congress for an up-or-down vote within 90 days.

"People are going to be resistant to just unfettered fast track unless they're assured there's an opportunity to rectify imbalances . . ." Schagrin said. "I think [the Bush administration is] going to find it's a tough road, and it should be a tough road. "

Striking a Balance

As they confront those concerns, however, U.S. officials also must ensure that whatever action they take is not so protective that trading partners see it as a breach of global trade rules.

"Anyone who cares about the steel industry needs to think about a measure that can pass [World Trade Organization] muster; I'm hoping to make that connection," said Phil English, R-Pa., in an interview Feb. 13.

English, who serves on the House Ways and Means Trade Subcommittee, is crafting legislation that would strengthen U.S. trade laws by making it easier for industries to prove they have been hurt by a surge in imports or by dumped imports.

Some in the steel community insist that concern about U.S. trade relations not keep Congress from making a sweeping effort to rescue the ailing industry. The United Steelworkers of America (USWA), a labor union representing 139,000 U.S. and Canadian employees, wants Congress to pass a four-pronged legislative package — slated for introduction during the first week in March — that includes import quotas, the creation of a retiree health care fund for steelworkers, heftier loan guarantees for steel companies and incentives for consolidation within the industry.

"There's no such thing as free trade; it doesn't work," Gary Hubbard, a spokesman for the steelworkers' union, said Feb. 15. "We're not looking to build a wall around America in terms of trade . . . but ourselves and the textile unions have been hurt the most by these agreements, and we have to protect ourselves. We feel that existing trade laws don't deal with the problem."

Members of the Congressional Steel Caucus are working with the union to draft the bill, arguing that the state of the steel industry demands more than enforcement of existing laws. "The great free enterprise system is not perfect," says Peter J. Visclosky, D-Ind., the vice chairman of the House Steel Caucus. "To the extent our trade law is

Byrd Law Bogs Down

Legislation passed in the waning days of the 106th Congress that would allow steel companies to collect a share of U.S. duties on steel imports is facing obstacles at home and abroad.

As Congress eyes new measures to help the struggling steel industry deal with foreign competition, falling prices and the effects of two decades of downsizing, the challenges confronting the "Byrd amendment" — so named for Sen. Robert C. Byrd, D-W.Va., who engineered its passage — illustrate how difficult that job will be.

Federal agencies are working through the perplexing technical aspects of the legislation, which was inserted into the fiscal 2001 agriculture spending bill (PL 106-387) during conference negotiations, as supporters in Congress scramble to defend it against accusations from U.S. trading partners that it violates World Trade Organization (WTO) rules prohibiting subsidies for domestic industries.

"We are struggling with the important aspects of this bill," Jeff Laxague, a special assistant in the U.S. Customs Service's office of regulation and rulings, said at a Feb. 8 forum on the measure. The agency is laboring to compile rules for implementing the program— including procedures for distributing the tariff payments — which must be vetted by the Treasury Department's enforcement office before the program can be launched.

Confusion over how to set up the program has slowed its creation.

"We're not sure what the best way is to administer this provision," said Laxague, who hopes the rules are completed this month.

The law allows individual producers or industry groups who file complaints with the International Trade Commission (ITC) alleging trade abuses such as "dumping" — selling artificially low-priced imports in the United States — to get a share of the proceeds if the ITC

finds an injury and imposes penalties. Those duties are deposited in the U.S. Treasury, and the Byrd measure would allow interested parties who remain in the steel business to apply for some of the money.

The Congressional Budget Office has estimated the measure will cost about $39 million annually, and Laxague said more than 2,000 applicants could be eligible under existing anti-dumping and countervailing duty orders.

In a meeting Feb. 12, Republican Sen. Mike DeWine of Ohio, who introduced the bill in 1999, urged Commerce Secretary Donald L. Evans to support the measure, which Evans called "an appropriate law" at a news conference the next day. DeWine also plans to meet with Treasury Secretary Paul H. O'Neill and U.S. Trade Representative Robert B. Zoellick to press them to back the law.

DeWine and more than 20 other Senate and House members submitted comments Feb. 9 to Zoellick's office urging a "strong defense" of the law in the face of foreign opposition.

The provision "doesn't change the standard of how anti-dumping and countervailing duties are assessed," DeWine aide Stan Skocki said at the Feb. 8 forum. "We don't really see it as being a problem down the road."

But the European Union and 10 other countries have contested the law in the WTO, saying it subsidizes the U.S. steel industry and encourages anti-dumping cases.

In a January speech, David H. Phelps, president of the American Institute for International Steel, a coalition of steel importers, exporters and industry consumers, called the measure a "threat to free trade" and "an embarrassment to U.S. trade policy."

"It seems only in the U.S. are subsidies to the steel industry growing," he said.

—Julie R. Hirschfeld

being violated, we should try and squeeze those who are violating it."

But there are limits to the amount of pressure Congress can exert. A steel import quota bill similar to the one advocated by the union this year passed the House overwhelmingly in 1999 but died in the Senate. Lobbyists and lawmakers active on steel issues note that opposition from the Clinton administration, which said the bill violated international trade laws, and from agricultural interests, who feared countries would target their sector in retaliation, rendered the bill "dead on arrival" in the Senate.

That leaves members of Congress and steel interests hoping they have better luck persuading the Bush administration to police trade law violations than they had with President Bill Clinton, who waited until the penultimate day of his tenure to suggest the International Trade Commission investigate whether foreign imports hurt U.S. producers. Such a probe could lead to penalty tariffs — but only if the Bush administration decides to pursue it.

"Only your initiation of this review will give people confidence that a meaningful remedy will be directed," Rockefeller wrote to Bush in a Jan. 25 letter. "Only comprehensive relief applied to all categories of steel, exported by all countries, will give our industry the chance to rebuild from the financial devastation of the last several years."

Problems, Old and New

Difficult conditions in the steel industry are nothing new, and they have been bound up in U.S. trade policy for more than three decades. The entrance of foreign steel into the market during the 1960s spurred dozens of trade disputes between the United States and Europe, and between the United States and Japan in subsequent years. Ultimately the influx triggered massive restructuring in the industry during the 1980s and early 1990s, as dozens of large, inefficient mills closed, work forces were scaled down and companies invested in new technology.

But those changes did not insulate the industry from continued trade disputes or the Asian financial crisis of 1997 that sent steel prices plummeting.

Touched off by the "Asian flu," which brought in a record amount of cheap steel imports from such countries as Russia, Japan and Brazil, the latest woes of the U.S. steel industry have been vividly illustrated in recent months by a sharp rise in bankruptcies among large steel companies and layoffs of their workers.

According to the United Steelworkers, 14 steel companies have filed for bankruptcy in the past three years — six in the last six months. More than 15,000 steelworker jobs have been lost since January 1998, the union says, 8,400 of them in the last six months. Steel prices are down to their lowest point in 20 years.

At the same time, U.S. imports of foreign steel have climbed steadily in the past decade, rocketing almost 80 percent between August 1997 and August 1998, according to a September 2000 report by the Congressional Research Service.

The Census Bureau, which tracks trade figures, reports that the United States imported some 34 million metric tons of steel last year, an increase of nearly 6 percent over 1999. The American Iron and Steel Institute calls it the second-highest total in history. The group says finished steel imports — such as sheet steel for automobile body parts and appliances, or the wire used in reinforced concrete — were about 26.6 million metric tons in 2000, or more than 8 percent higher than the previous year. *(Chart, p. 158)*

Despite the repeated efforts of steel companies and workers to prevail in trade cases against countries that allegedly market steel in the United States at prices below production costs, industry groups and lawmakers are convinced that trade laws must be changed or the administration must act on its own to stem the seemingly endless stream.

"This is simply the latest, and perhaps the final, spike in the crisis which, if not addressed, will wipe out this industry," Visclosky said on Feb. 13. "I think this is our last opportunity."

Legislating Trade

The rifts in Congress — and potentially in the administration — over the direction of steel policy echo a division within the industry itself about the root causes of the sector's problems and the government's role in solving them.

There are those in the steel industry who want the U.S. government to let the global market dictate its policy.

"Trade protection has not worked in the past, and it will not work again if we try it," David H. Phelps, president of the American Institute for International Steel Inc., said Feb. 20 at a steel forum hosted by the free market-oriented Cato Institute. "Imports come in because people buy them, not because there's some grand, vast conspiracy to undermine the U.S. steel industry."

Advocates for greater intervention, such as the steelworkers' union and the Congressional Steel Caucus, who are pushing a "Steel Revitalization Package," acknowledge that it will be difficult to get an administration that seems focused on lowering trade barriers to embrace legislation that almost certainly would be seen as violating WTO rules. Already, a law Congress passed late last year as part of the agriculture appropriations bill (PL 106-387) is being challenged in the WTO, even as the Treasury Department ponders how to implement it. *(Box, p. 156)*

The hostile climate the steel industry relief effort is likely to face in Washington has begun having an effect.

"I tend not to try to have my clients spend their time on efforts that I don't think will yield results," said one industry lobbyist who asked not to be named. "There's a lot more farm-state senators than there are steel-producing senators, and farm-state senators know perfectly well that when you do something that's WTO-violative, the first thing other countries do is retaliate against your farm exports."

Efforts to help individual companies and workers cope with the social and financial costs of the crisis also could face challenges over WTO rules, lobbyists said. This could be the case for legislation that Senate Steel Caucus Chairman Arlen Specter, R-Pa., plans to introduce that would allow steel companies or workers to seek injunctions in federal court to stop illegal imports.

WTO considerations might also doom a provision in the Congressional Steel Caucus package that would impose a $10-per-ton tax on steel sales to create a Steelworker Retiree Health Care Trust Fund designed to help companies cover the huge "legacy costs" from the restructuring of the 1980s and early 1990s.

"It's important that companies that have legacy costs deal with the consequences," Thomas A. Danjczek, president of the Steel Manufacturers Association, said Feb. 19. "If we're against subsidies, if we're against non-economic capacity, we have to be against it in our own backyard."

One thing most industry players and

How the Trouble Started

In 1998, financial problems in Asia and other parts of the world triggered a flood of low-priced steel exports to the United States that undercut prices for domestic producers. Although foreign steel imports have not reached those levels again, the U.S. steel market continues to suffer with high inventories and low prices that trace back to that surge.

Volume of Imports *(in thousands of metric tons)*

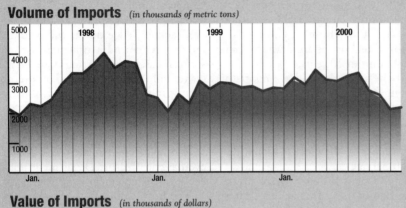

Value of Imports *(in thousands of dollars)*

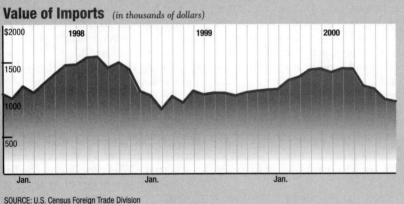

SOURCE: U.S. Census Foreign Trade Division

lawmakers seem to agree on is that regardless of legislative action, the Bush administration should start a broad investigation of the effects of surging imports on the U.S. steel industry, with an eye toward imposing tariffs if injuries are found. The Bush administration has been lobbied hard to do so while members of Congress propose bills — some of which mirror measures they tried to pass last year — that would smooth that process.

'Section 201' Relief

"The major question is whether there can and should be a 201," says Sander M. Levin of Michigan, the ranking Democrat on the House Ways and Means Trade Subcommittee. Levin was referring to a provision in U.S. trade law that allows the president to ask the United States International Trade Commission to investigate whether imports have harmed domestic producers.

Under the statute, investigators do not have to show that the imports were illegal — as anti-dumping and countervailing duty laws require — but that they caused harm to an industry.

Steel-state lawmakers want to change U.S. trade laws by making the process of securing 201 relief easier. A bill (HR 518) introduced Feb. 7 by Ohio Republican Ralph Regula and another being written by English would both lower the standard for determining a "serious injury."

"My hope is that on steel, like on other issues, that there won't be an automatic-pilot response to it. You can be for free trade and also want vigorous action under 201," Levin said. "Trade isn't free when it's subsidized."

While the ultimate decision on whether to pursue an investigation lies with the White House, industry players say it is important for lawmakers to go on record supporting it, through a sense-of-the-Congress resolution or otherwise.

"I think the key lies with the United States Senate, where things are so close

that there's a real chance that something could happen," said Danjczek, of the Steel Manufacturers Association. "201 is political, and therefore political pressure is key."

But even the prospect of using existing laws to address current conditions faces powerful opposition from steel importers. "Our concern with a 201 . . . is it's really putting in place a system that's going to keep alive the very non-economic mills that need to go by the wayside," said Phelps, of the American Institute for International Steel.

Global Implications

Some free-traders go even further, arguing not only that extra industry protections and bolstered trade laws are unnecessary, but that current U.S. statutes should be rolled back.

"In the past, it was OK to sort of throw a bone to the steel industry and put these things in place, but now we have to decide: Do we want to continue subsidizing and supporting steel or do we want to move on and honor our commitments so that we can negotiate a new [WTO] round?" Daniel J. Ikenson, a trade policy analyst at Cato, said Feb. 20. "In order for the administration to advance its agenda, it will need to be willing to discuss some of these issues" at the trade table.

Steel importers already are pushing to make sure laws governing dumped imports and countervailing duties are up for negotiation at the WTO ministerial in Qatar this November.

Such efforts are sure to arouse the ire of domestic steel producers, who say the WTO already does a shoddy job of enforcing the standards. "I think it won't take long for the Bush administration to realize that they won't be able to get free trade agreements when the WTO refuses to allow any of their members to use those rules," Schagrin says. "They don't seem to be able to uphold the bond between liberalizing trade and providing opportunities to rectify the imbalances which come with that."

Other industry players say they hope the steel industry does not become the vivid example of the conflicts of globalization that Schagrin and others predict.

"I'd rather not be the test case. I think this administration does not want to let steel run its trade policy," Danjczek said. "If we're going to get anything out of this administration, we have to play by the rules." ◆

A Case Study in Lobbying

The debate is over a new regulation set in place by the Clinton administration in its closing months. But because it involves new safety rules in the work place — requiring ergonomic considerations to prevent repetitive motion injuries — the regulation emerged as a classic clash between business groups opposed to the regulation and organized labor in support. Congress was, of course, in the middle.

Sen. Ernest F. Hollings, D-S.C., can expect a call any day now from business interest groups that want him to help kill sweeping ergonomics regulations issued by the Clinton administration in November.

Hollings is being targeted because he voted last June to delay implementation of the ergonomics standards, which were several years in the making and have been hotly debated. Now one more debate looms, and it is likely to provoke one of the biggest skirmishes this year between labor and business interests, according to senators and lobbyists.

Both business and labor are launching multimillion-dollar lobbying campaigns to prevail on an issue that GOP leaders want to bring to a vote under the 1996 Congressional Review Act (PL 104-121). That law allows a simple majority in both chambers to pass a resolution of disapproval overturning a regulation within 60 days of receiving it.

Business groups say the regulations, which require programs to prevent repetitive motion injuries at an estimated 6.1 million work sites, would cost too much to implement, particularly with an economic slowdown looming.

But unions are pushing to make sure that the rules, which took effect Jan. 16, will be enforced on schedule beginning Oct. 14. The delay is intended to give businesses time to comply.

Billions of dollars are at stake. The Occupational Safety and Health Administration (OSHA) estimates that the rule will cost businesses $4.5 billion annually, while industry groups argue that the true cost will be closer to $100 billion.

Hollings has not decided how he will vote this time. "I've got some thinking to do about all this," he said Feb. 6.

Republicans, who are nearly united in their opposition to the rules, are determined to act. "The Clinton admin-

By Rebecca Adams / Feb. 10, 2001

The Economics of Ergonomics

OSHA's Rules

The ergonomics rules slated to take effect Oct. 14 would be overseen by the Occupational Safety and Health Administration (OSHA). The agency estimates the rules, which apply to some 102 million workers, would cost employers $4.5 billion a year to implement but save $9.1 billion annually through lower medical and workers' compensation expenses. The rules would:

- Require employers to inform workers about musculo-skeletal disorders, which include conditions such as carpal tunnel syndrome — often caused by computer use — tendinitis, lower back pain and sciatica.
- Require employers to modify job or workplace conditions when they receive a valid complaint and develop programs to avoid future problems.
- Exempt most construction, railroad, maritime and agricultural workers.

Institute of Medicine Study

A study ordered by Congress and released Jan. 17 by the National Academies found a "clear relationship" between activities such as heavy lifting and repetitive movement and the frequency of injuries such as back strains and carpal tunnel syndrome. The study also found that job-related musculo-skeletal disorders:

- Affect about 1 million workers annually.
- Cost employers $45 billion to $54 billion annually in workers' compensation and decreased productivity.
- Result in some 70 million doctor visits annually.

SOURCES: OSHA, National Academies

istration regulation is very intrusive, and very expensive," Don Nickles, R-Okla., assistant Senate majority leader, said Feb. 6.

"I think Congress should have a look at it, and I believe the Congressional Review Act is the proper way to do it," he said. "I believe we would be successful."

President Bush has not said anything publicly about the drive to overturn the ergonomics regulations, but the Senate GOP leadership believes he will sign a resolution of disapproval if it passes. That could take some of the heat off Bush with big business for not including more business-friendly cuts in his tax package.

Sen. Michael B. Enzi, R-Wyo., said he will introduce a resolution to overturn the rules, possibly as early as the week of Feb. 12. "It's the only way to go," Enzi said Jan. 31. "Anything else would take too long."

But Edward M. Kennedy of Massachusetts, ranking Democrat on the

Senate Health, Education, Labor and Pensions Committee, said using the congressional review procedure would be particularly offensive.

"That's using a hammer to swat a fly," Kennedy said Feb. 5. "I don't think using a congressional review would make a great deal of sense."

The biggest test will come in the equally divided Senate. If the regulation is overturned there, GOP leaders will probably be able to use party discipline to deliver the House. Success could also embolden GOP lawmakers to use the review act to attempt to overturn a slew of environmental regulations issued by Clinton.

"If you vote against the disapproval resolution, you're saying you want to hit business owners in your state with an expensive, unnecessary regulation that no one can understand," said a Senate leadership aide Feb. 7. "That's not an easy vote for a Republican or conservative Democrat to swallow."

In June, Arlen Specter of Pennsylvania was the lone Republican senator to vote against delaying implementation of the ergonomics rules. John B. Breaux of Louisiana and Blanche Lincoln of Arkansas were the only Democratic senators to join Hollings in voting for the delay, which was adopted, 57-41, as an amendment to the fiscal 2001 Labor-HHS spending bill (PL 106-554).

A Changing Dynamic

Since that vote, the political dynamic in the Senate has changed considerably, with five Republicans losing their seats in the November elections. That has forced business interest groups to focus their lobbying efforts on conservative Democrats such as Mary L. Landrieu of Louisiana, Max Cleland of Georgia, Max Baucus of Montana and Tim Johnson of South Dakota.

"We absolutely will be contacting every lawmaker we can . . . starting with the ones who supported us in the past and moving from there," Jenny Krese, director of employment policy at the National Association of Manufacturers (NAM), said Feb. 7.

During the week of Feb. 26, dozens of high-ranking executives plan to visit Capitol Hill to kick off a round of intensive lobbying for a vote on the ergonomics rules.

The executives intend to ask lawmakers whether they really want to impose a complex set of regulations on small-business owners, who are already concerned about a sluggish economy. Vice President Dick Cheney and Commerce Secretary Donald L. Evans are also scheduled to address a special NAM meeting.

Organized labor is working similarly hard to assemble a coalition of 51 votes against overturning the rules and already has Specter's support again.

"I see no reason to delay that rule," Specter said Feb. 6.

Labor officials also will try to sway moderate Republicans such as Lincoln Chafee of Rhode Island and GOP lawmakers from states with a strong union tradition, among them Peter G. Fitzgerald of Illinois.

They had hoped to enlist James M. Jeffords of Vermont, chairman of the Senate Health, Education, Labor and Pensions Committee, but Jeffords said Feb. 6 that he would probably be willing to vote to overturn the ergonomics regulations.

Union activists are warning Republicans that dusting off the Congressional Review Act, however attractive it may appear, carries deep political risks.

"This would be a bloodbath on the Senate floor," Peg Seminario, director of occupational safety and health for the AFL-CIO, said Feb. 1. "Do they really want to completely overturn protections for workers and send a message not to try it again? This would be an extreme act, a very bitter fight."

AFL-CIO President John Sweeney said Feb. 5 that he received a warm response when he urged lawmakers at the January House Democratic retreat in Pennsylvania to defend the rules; he is confident that almost all Democrats will support them.

Organized labor also believes that the shifting nature of the debate — from delaying the rules to killing them — bodes well, and is counting on lawmakers' reluctance to use an untested procedure.

"It would really be an outrage to overturn [the rules] completely, especially using this procedure," said Seminario.

Other Options

Even as they lobby lawmakers, both sides are taking advantage of other options. For example, business groups have filed 25 lawsuits seeking to overturn the rules since they were issued in November, and labor unions filed six suits to defend them.

The cases were consolidated in the U.S. Court of Appeals for the D.C. Circuit as part of the first suit, which was brought by the NAM. No trial date has been set.

Sweeney also asked Labor Secretary Elaine L. Chao during a private meeting Feb. 8 to protect the regulations, and labor leaders will have another chance to lobby her the week of Feb. 12, when she is scheduled to attend the AFL-CIO's annual winter meeting in Los Angeles.

Chao is well aware of the tensions surrounding the rules. "This is probably [the most] visible issue in the department," she said at her Jan. 24 confirmation hearing." It's an extremely complicated issue."

Business groups, meanwhile, are studying a possible delaying tactic. They might ask Chao for a temporary stay of the new rules, which would block them from taking effect until all litigation is resolved.

A Labor Department spokesman said Feb. 8 that Chao has limited authority to issue a stay and must show "good cause" to do so.

Chao also could decide to call for new rules — likely to be more business-friendly — that would supercede those business is trying so hard to kill. That would require a new round of deliberations and public comment and could take years to be implemented.

If Republicans are successful in overturning the ergonomics regulations, they might examine other rules issued in the waning days of the Clinton administration.

Many Western GOP senators, for example, would like to overturn regulations that block logging and road-building on some 60 million acres of federal land and impose new requirements on hard-rock mining operations.

"We are looking closely at every single regulation and trying to see what should be done," James. V. Hansen, R-Utah, chairman of the House Resource Committee, said Jan. 31.

Ultimately, however, it all boils down to whether Congress can overturn the ergonomics regulations.

"If we don't have the votes to use the [Congressional Review Act] on ergonomics, we won't have the votes to use it on any other rule for a while," a top Senate GOP leadership aide said Feb. 6. ◆

An Interest Group Wins

Repealing the Clinton administration's rule on ergonomics was an early coup for Republicans in Congress, who managed to team with business lobbying groups to line up the votes so quickly that organized labor could not oppose the move quickly enough to stop it.

For years, Republicans have dreamed about pulling off feats like this one. With little advance warning, they stunned Democratic leaders by swiftly wielding a little-known legislative weapon to dismantle an ergonomics regulation issued in the final days of the Clinton administration.

With the help of an uncommonly united business community, whose cachet is growing in the new GOP era, Republicans succeeded by stealing away votes from centrist Democrats in both chambers. In the Senate, six Democrats joined a unified GOP caucus to support the resolution (SJ Res 6) for repealing the rule. It was passed 56-44 on March 6.

The House followed the next day with a 223-206 vote. Sixteen Democrats voted to repeal the rule, more than making up for the 13 Republicans who sided with organized labor. *(Chart, below)*

Democrats said they felt ambushed by the Republicans' maneuver, the product of close and stealthy strategy planning between Republicans, led by Sen. Don Nickles of Oklahoma, and lobbyists for the business community.

"I'm still trying to figure out what the hell happened," said one Democratic aide after the Senate vote.

Conservative Democrats who

By Rebecca Adams / March 10, 2001

strayed from the party felt trapped in a week of tough choices. Corporate America was putting intense pressure on Democrats to pass President Bush's tax cuts and kill the ergonomics policy that President Bill Clinton issued in November. Business interest groups made it clear that rejection on both counts would carry political consequences.

Senate Minority Leader Tom Daschle, D-S.D., acknowledged March 6 that he was struggling to fight the growing clout of business groups that were willing to invest much of their political capital in the issue. He blamed the fractures in Democratic unity on "the pressure that groups across the country are bringing to bear on many of my colleagues."

Centrists said they weighed the risks of rejecting their party's base supporters against the need to protect themselves from attacks by business groups.

"It was an emotional vote, no matter which way you voted," said John B. Breaux, D-La., who sided with Republicans.

The Republican victory showed Democratic leaders that with control of Congress, the White House can mobilize quickly when the stakes are high. "President Bush doesn't mess around," said Rep. Jack Quinn, R-N.Y., who backed labor. "When he's ready to go, he goes."

Using an Untested Tool

Republicans used an untested legislative tool known as the Congressional Review Act (CRA), which allows lawmakers to erase major rules by a simple majority in each chamber. The 1996 law (PL 104-121) limits debate and forbids amendments, leaving opponents little room to maneuver. *(CRA, p. 163)*

Democrats protested the use of the CRA as an "atom bomb" because it bans the administration from writing a substitute regulation that is "substantially the same form." Any new rules, if issued, would likely be stalled in litigation for years.

"We may be saying for the final time that we cannot address ergonomics in the workplace," Daschle said.

In the first week of February, many lawmakers considered the battle over the ergonomics regulations history. The CRA was an unfamiliar device that barely registered with them. Few seemed to know that business lobbyists had already begun convening meetings to target lawmakers who might be susceptible to industry pleas.

At one such closed-door meeting held Feb. 6 at the headquarters of the National Association of Manufacturers (NAM), nearly 100 out-of-town business executives and Washington lobbyists talked for hours about how to overturn the regulation, according to participants.

Against the Grain

These lawmakers voted against the majority of their party on the resolution (S J Res 6) to overturn ergonomics standards issued by the Clinton administration. No Senate Republicans opposed the motion.

SENATE Democrats FOR: (6)		HOUSE Democrats FOR: (16)		HOUSE Republicans AGAINST: (13)	
Baucus	Landrieu	Boyd	Carson *(Okla.)*	Boehlert	Ferguson
Breaux	Lincoln	Clement	Clyburn	Gilman	Grucci
Hollings	Miller	Cramer	Dooley	Horn	King
		Hall *(Texas)*	John	LoBiondo	McHugh
		McIntyre	Sisisky	Petri	Quinn
		Skelton	Spratt	Saxton	Smith *(N.J.)*
		Stenholm	Tanner	Weldon *(Pa.)*	
		Taylor *(Miss.)*	Turner		

They also were briefed by aides of Nickles and Michael B. Enzi, R-Wyo., chairman of the Senate Health, Education, Labor and Pensions subcommittee that oversees policy for the Occupational Safety and Health Administration (OSHA). Nickles and Enzi were the eventual cosponsors of the CRA resolution.

As the executives discussed which lawmakers they needed to win, they considered the dangers that Democratic senators might face in bucking their leadership and labor interests.

"I talked to Mary Landrieu," one executive said, according to participants. "But she was worried: 'What if labor comes after me?' "

Landrieu, of Louisiana, was one of six senators who ultimately voted with Republicans to rescind the rules. Like Landrieu, many of the Democratic defectors in both chambers were from conservative Southern states with strong business interests they did not want to cross.

After the vote, Landrieu acknowledged that she was concerned about labor's reaction, but said she hoped "the people representing labor in my state trust me to put the state's best interest first."

"It was a tough vote," she added.

Pent-Up Tensions

Business groups won the issue largely because they were more organized, united and aggressive than labor interests.

Part of business groups' ire stemmed from the confrontational way the regulations were issued. Last year, with budget negotiations stalled over ergonomics language in the fiscal 2001 Labor-HHS-Education spending bill, the White House abandoned efforts to compromise and issued the controversial regulations.

The rules, which took effect Jan. 16 and would have been enforced beginning Oct. 14, would have required employers to educate workers about ways to prevent injuries from repetitive motions such as typing, sorting or lifting heavy loads. If a worker reported an injury, employers would have had to reconfigure the workplace to prevent recurrences. Workers who reported injuries lasting seven days or longer would have been eligible for compensation of up to 90 percent of their salary for as long as 90 days if they had been unable to work.

Business interest groups, which had been fighting the developing rules for years, were livid.

But Nickles had a plan. He realized that the business community was unified to an almost unprecedented degree on the need to overturn the ergonomics rules. And as the co-author of the CRA, Nickles believed that Republicans had an effective way to kill the Clinton rules.

At the time, labor groups thought they had won. The rules were final —

"Labor thought they had us. Little did they know what was about to hit them."

— An aide to Sen. Don Nickles, R-Okla., who orchestrated the vote for the Republicans.

---

which meant that if the incoming president wanted to change them, he would have to call for a public debate and solicit new comments.

Labor officials figured that the political and legal fallout from such a high-profile debate would chill the new GOP administration's interest in scaling back the rules. They dismissed the use of the review act as a remote possibility, saying they thought they had enough votes to stop it.

"Labor thought they had us," said a Nickles aide. "Little did they know what was about to hit them."

A Campaign of Calls

Determined to kill the regulations, Washington business groups rallied their members to lobby senators in their home states.

A coalition of business groups known as the National Council on Ergonomics solicited contributions, organized telephone marathons and unleashed e-mail campaigns. As part of the alliance's efforts, the National Federation of Independent Business (NFIB), the U.S. Chamber of Commerce and NAM dispatched business owners to knock on lawmakers' doors during the Presidents Day recess.

Democrats who switched sides said the pressure was intense.

"No contest," said Sen. Max Baucus, D-Mont. "The lobbying was 20-1 against the reg."

To Sen. Zell Miller, D-Ga., it must have seemed that he was courted by every interest group in Washington.

Among his visitors were officials from the American Insurance Association, the American Soft Drink Association, the Food Marketing Association and the Georgia Chamber of Commerce, as well as officials from the U.S. Chamber, NAM and NFIB.

On the labor side, he heard from the AFL-CIO, the American Postal Workers Union and the United Auto Workers of America.

On Feb. 27, NAM flew in nearly 500 executives to coax lawmakers to rescind the regulation.

Two businessmen — brothers Leighton and Bill Lee — were among the local business owners who traveled to plead at least half a dozen lawmakers for relief.

"This regulation could really hurt our business," said Bill Lee, a manufacturer from Connecticut whose products are used in airplanes and medical equipment. "We care about our workers and do everything we can to protect them. But this rule just goes too far."

Many of the lawmakers who met with Lee and his brother — especially freshmen Republicans such as Rep. Rob Simmons of Connecticut — were sympathetic before the meetings and enthusiastic afterward.

After a week of lobbying, Nickles invited about 50 executives to his office to finalize an endgame strategy. He counted enough Democratic supporters to ensure success if he used the CRA.

Nickles knew he had the support of House GOP leaders and the administration — President Bush agreed to back efforts to rescind the ergonomics rules at a Feb. 27 White House meeting.

So, with little warning, on March 2 Nickles and Enzi requested a vote on March 6, giving Democrats and their labor allies only four days, including the weekend, to mobilize.

By then, Democratic leaders had heard that a CRA resolution might be looming. But they had only just started to develop a strategy to counter the push from business that had been in full swing for weeks.

As labor lobbyists realized their predicament, they scrambled to step up their efforts. AFL-CIO President John Sweeney, Teamsters General President James P. Hoffa and other high-ranking labor officials began personally calling lawmakers such as Sen. Ernest F. Hollings, D-S.C., who eventually sided with business.

By March 6 — the day of the Senate

With Ergonomics Standards Overturned, Will GOP Target Other Clinton Rules?

The successful use of the 1996 Congressional Review Act (PL 104-121) to quash controversial ergonomics rules may tempt House and Senate Republican leaders to apply the same strategy to other Clinton administration regulations they find objectionable.

"It's only the beginning," House Majority Whip Tom DeLay, R-Texas, said March 8. "Both the House and Senate are looking for [more] opportunities.

But GOP leaders acknowledge they probably lack the votes to overturn other rules. Unlike the ergonomics regulation, others either deal with topics that never have been put to a vote or concern popular issues such as environmental protection, which many lawmakers hesitate to oppose.

Acting on the ergonomics rules was "something we needed to do on a timely basis," said Speaker J. Dennis Hastert. The Illinois Republican said the regulations overreached and would have been too expensive to implement, but added he is not yet considering similar moves with other rules.

However, Senate Assistant Majority Leader Don Nickles, R-Okla. — who led the drive to overturn the ergonomics regulations — refused to rule out further action on other rules if enough support can be found before time runs out for votes under the review act.

"The Clinton administration went on a binge in their last months where they couldn't get things done legislatively," Nickles said. "We'll just measure the intensity of opposition among members in both parties and see if there's some other things where obviously the Clinton administration went too far."

Republicans might take aim at a regulation that bars companies from receiving government contracts if they have violated labor, environmental or consumer laws.

And many GOP lawmakers from Western states would like to overturn the ban on logging and road development in about 58 million acres of roadless areas of national forests — a move favored by mining, logging and other resource industries. However, the ban is viewed as a regional issue and has not been as heavily lobbied by business groups.

"Making the case for environmental issues is harder . . . than making the case for withdrawing the ergonomics rules," said Sen. Larry E. Craig, R-Idaho. "Ergonomics already was debated on the Senate floor [last year] and a good number [of senators] view roadless areas as something that doesn't affect their states."

Another tempting target would appear to be controversial medical privacy rules that have aroused the ire of health care trade groups. However, the Department of Health and Human Services has already called for new comments on the standards, and many health care lobbyists believe such a move is sufficient, saying they do not want to kill the rules, just make them more business-friendly. (*Medical privacy, p. 90*)

The fact that the Bush administration has other ways to adjust or kill regulations may eliminate the need to use the Congressional Review Act (CRA) again. A number of regulations could face renewed rule-making or be challenged in court.

An Unused Law

Until the ergonomics vote, the review act had never been used to overturn a regulation. But the swiftness with which Republicans used the 1996 law to dispatch the ergonomics rules left some GOP leaders positively giddy.

"If I were king, I'd use the CRA every day," said Rep. Charlie Norwood, R-Ga.

That is just what Democrats fear.

"If the Republicans are successful today, you will see this applied over and over and over again," said Senate Minority Leader Tom Daschle, D-S.D., before the vote. "They're just going to get started."

Scores of Clinton administration regulations were delayed Jan. 20 by White House Chief of Staff Andrew H. Card Jr. so federal agencies could actively review them and determine which were candidates for revision.

Some of the rules would:
- Phase out the use of snowmobiles in national parks.
- Set energy efficiency standards for clothes washers and air conditioners.
- Strengthen restrictions on development near wetlands.
- Reduce water pollution and waste from large farms.
- Scrutinize arsenic levels in drinking water.
- Mandate a review process for genetically modified crops.

Other stalled rules include those that would:
- Add protections for Medicaid patients in managed-care plans.
- Reduce the exposure of mine workers to diesel particulate matter.
- Set standards for lead-based paint in housing.
- Require health care employers to use newer needle devices to protect workers from blood-borne pathogens.
- Upgrade vehicle fuel systems.

Many lobbyists believe the CRA will probably be reserved for "the grossest abuses of power," as U.S. Chamber of Commerce lobbyist Randel Johnson calls the ergonomics rule.

"I know other people think differently," Johnson said March 8. "But this was a tough battle. . . . And the fact that this was a tough vote for some members makes it even tougher next time."

— *Adriel Bettelheim and Rebecca Adams*

vote — scores of labor supporters, wearing bright yellow and red "Hands off Ergo" lapel stickers, were scurrying around the Capitol in packs.

But the campaign came too late.

"This was rushed through before anyone knew what was happening. I think that was intentional," said Bill Samuel, a top lobbyist for the AFL-CIO. "And they spared no expense in promoting their position."

A top Democratic aide said March 7 that he was still shell-shocked. "We just started meeting the week before the vote," he said.

Time for Debate

Supporters of the regulation voiced outrage that the process had moved so quickly, with little time for debate.

"There is no question that the business community brought enormous pressure to bear very quickly on this issue and gave working families little opportunity to defend themselves," Edward M. Kennedy of Massachusetts, ranking Democrat on the Senate Health, Education, Labor and Pensions Committee, told reporters March 6.

Kennedy and other Democrats argued that lawmakers did not have enough time to digest a long-awaited Institute of Medicine report, released in January, which estimated that repetitive motion injuries could cost $50 billion annually.

The report found that work-related repetitive motions cause injuries to employees, but also said the degree of impairment could vary widely from one worker to another.

Both sides cited the report in floor arguments but with different conclusions.

Business owners complained that the rules were complicated and vague, would not protect workers and could send some companies spiralling into bankruptcy. Labor groups countered that protections were long overdue for workers who in some cases would suffer for years.

Estimates of how much it would cost to implement the rules varied widely. OSHA pegged the cost at $4.5 billion annually, but business groups said it would total more than $100 billion.

"As a result of these injuries, these workers lose wages, they lose hours of work, they lose the ability to provide for their family," George Miller, D-Calif., ranking Democrat on the House

Lobbyists Lionize Nickles

Business groups praised Nickles' role in killing the ergonomics rules.

The day after the Senate voted to rescind the Clinton administration's ergonomics rules, lobbyists were still filling the reception room outside the chamber to congratulate Assistant Majority Leader Don Nickles, R-Okla., and to be photographed at his side.

While the House was preparing to vote, business lobbyists ignored the action on the other side of the Capitol and lingered to speak with Nickles, who orchestrated the Republicans' strategy to swiftly repeal the regulations. As the Republicans' chief whip, Nickles' job was to keep all GOP senators on his side and he did so through a coordinated lobbying effort with business groups. One of their main targets was Arlen Specter, R-Pa., who was persuaded to reverse his position on the issue.

Business lobbyists were jubilant at Nickles' performance. "He's a star in the Senate and he will continue to be a star," said Randel Johnson, vice president of labor and employee benefits for the U.S. Chamber of Commerce. Talk like that may renew speculation that Nickles, who will have to step down as deputy majority leader in 2002 because of term limits, will challenge Trent Lott, R-Miss., for the post of majority leader if the GOP retains control of the Senate. But Nickles has told friends he would rather be a committee chairman.

Nickles not only sponsored the resolution (S J Res 6) used to erase the ergonomics rules, he created the procedural method used to kill them. In 1996, Nickles joined with Harry Reid, D-Nev., to write the Congressional Review Act, which was tucked into a regulatory overhaul measure enacted as part of a bill raising the debt limit (PL 104-121).

Reid has since said the review act was inappropriately applied in the case of overturning the ergonomics rules (he voted against the repeal), but Nickles takes a great deal of pride in his role in writing the law.

Nickles has taken a less-is-more approach toward regulation since he entered Congress 21 years ago. He has gained plaudits in recent years from the health care industry for his role in the patients' bill-of-rights debate.

For the past two years, Nickles has led the fight to block Democratic attempts to pass legislation that would expand the right of patients to sue their insurers. Nickles has managed to unify most Senate Republicans behind arguments that Democratic efforts, led by Edward M. Kennedy of Massachusetts, would drive up health care costs and increase the number of uninsured patients in America beyond the current total of 43 million.

"He was already way up there, in terms of attention, by virtue of health care," Johnson said March 8. "[Killing the ergonomics regulations] just adds to that."

Nickles' legislative skills have won him grudging respect from the opposition. "Senator Kennedy certainly respects him as a tough adversary," said Jim Manley, Kennedy's spokesman. "They've had some tough debates on the Senate floor, [and] we've always found him to be a skilled debater."

— *Rebecca Adams*

Business and labor lobbyists surround Specter, center, after a March 6 hearing. Specter had indicated he would vote to keep the rules in effect, but ended up voting against them.

Education and the Workforce Committee, said on the floor March 7. "But one of the things we know is that most of these injuries are preventable. The workplace can be adjusted."

Republicans questioned why a worker who injured himself off the job should be compensated if his work tasks exaggerate an injury.

"This ergonomics standard is very broad and presumes that every muscle strain and pain is caused by work instead of gardening on the weekend or playing football with friends," said Cass Ballenger, R-N.C., a member of the House Education and the Workforce Committee. "How could business possibly be expected to control these costs?"

'A Gift to the Unions'
Nickles criticized the regulation as "probably the most expensive, intrusive regulation ever promulgated, certainly by the Department of Labor, maybe by any department in history." He called it a "gift to the unions," and pressed all Senate Republicans to support the resolution — including Arlen Specter of Pennsylvania, who had said for weeks that he saw no reason to delay the Clinton rules and who had consistently voted in the past to move them forward.

But on the day of the vote, Specter called an emergency hearing of the La-

bor-HHS-Education Appropriations Subcommittee, which he chairs. After hearing from representatives of labor, business and OSHA, Specter declared that he could no longer "see how Congress can come to grips with this."

Some Democrats who voted with their leaders to uphold the regulations said they would have preferred to have the Labor Department revise the standards by re-opening them for additional comment, an option the Bush administration could use to change scores of Clinton administration regulations.

Health and Human Services Secretary Tommy G. Thompson did just that recently when he called for new comments on Clinton's medical privacy standards. *(Medical privacy rules, p. 90)*

Some Democrats and moderate Republicans who voted to rescind the regulations pointed to a March 6 letter by Labor Secretary Elaine L. Chao in which she told committee chairmen that she would restore worker safety protections through "a comprehensive approach to ergonomics, which may include new rulemaking."

Both Breaux and Landrieu said they would offer an ergonomics amendment to the pending bankruptcy bill (S 420, HR 333) that would require the Department of Labor to issue another set of rules within a short time, perhaps two years.

Breaux said his amendment would

address the three top concerns of business regarding repetitive-motion injuries. It would require the Labor Department to create a process to certify businesses that are in compliance with the new rules and would require that ergonomics rules be applied only to "reported" work-related injuries.

It also would ensure that state workers' compensation laws are not undermined. Many such laws are less generous than the Clinton rules would have been to injured workers.

The fiscally conservative "Blue Dog" Democrats in the House are considering similar bills. But labor officials warn that they are not counting on Congress to nudge Bush to create worker-safety regulations. They consider the rescission of the ergonomics standard the clearest signal yet that the Bush administration is seeking a war with labor.

Lobbyists next expect the White House to move administratively to revise a so-called "blacklisting" regulation that would block companies from winning government contracts if they had violated labor, environmental, tax or antitrust laws.

Labor Provoked
Bush provoked labor three weeks earlier by signing four executive orders that unions opposed. Those orders:

• Require federal contractors to tell workers that they can receive rebates on the portion of union dues used for political activities.

• Eliminate job protections for federal contract workers whose companies go out of business or lose contracts.

• Dissolve the National Partnership Council, which Clinton used to try to improve relations between unions and federal agencies.

• Revoke Clinton's policy encouraging federal contractors to pay union wages.

Sen. Patty Murray D-Wash., chairman of the Democratic Senatorial Campaign Committee, warned that if the GOP is spoiling for more fights with labor, it will get them.

"It's amazing that [Republicans] want to take labor on in this way," she said. "They're really in store for a battle, and they've really set the other side on fire." ◆